THIRTEEN STORIES

by

John Isaac Jones

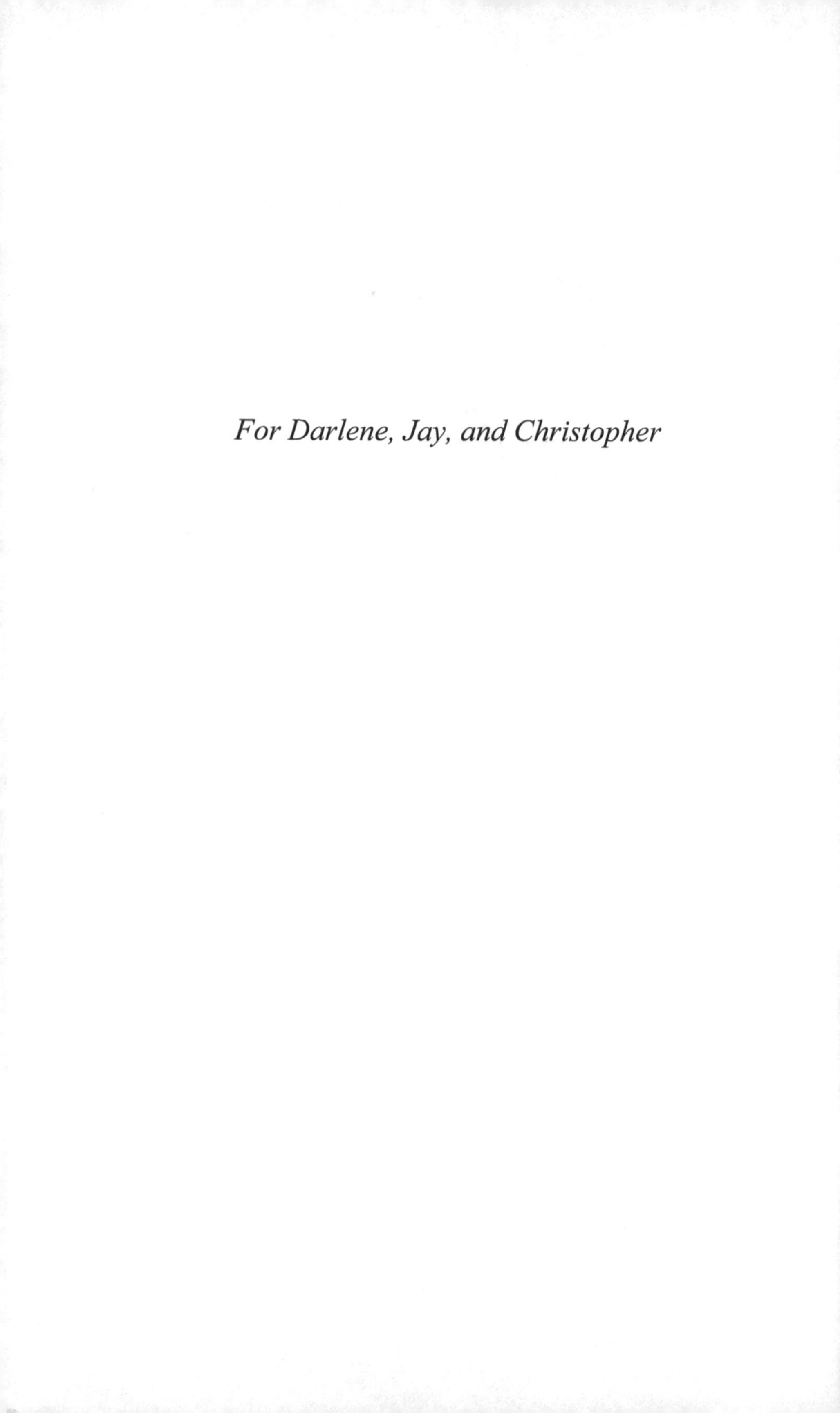

For Darlene, Jay, and Christopher

FOREWORD

Great day in the mornin'! It appears you are preparing to read the work of a very gifted author. I place John Isaac Jones right there on the top shelf of southern authors, alongside Lewis Grizzard and Rick Bragg.

The day I came across John I. (his preferred title) and his work *Alabama Stories* could be compared to an exceptional day of fly rod fishing for bluegill on West Neck Creek. I was so impressed with the stories, the author's gift of creativity, and down-home style that I purchased a paperback copy for a longtime friend who enjoys this genre. He loved it as much as I did!

John I. possesses that unique flair to share his stories on paper just as smoothly as if he and the reader were relaxing on a summer day, sipping lemonade in the shade of an old oak. For an author, that skill is priceless, and for the reader, fascinating.

Another treasure contained in John I.'s many works is that he uses well-placed descriptions like an artist uses colors. He also strokes our emotions to generate laughter, surprise, anger, love, and tears. Readers from the baby-boomer generation will find themselves recalling many occasions, feelings, and events in their own lives. Those fortunate readers born later may remember hearing similar actions and stories shared by parents or grandparents. In other words, John I.'s stories are an ideal fit for all ages because they speak to the universal human heart.

I trust you will enjoy these thirteen creations that span a wide array of settings, plots, characters, and unforgettable conclusions. And, within each story, you will find all of the aforementioned literary skills of John Isaac Jones. In today's topsy-turvy world, you will discover solace and a refreshing boost to your spirit while bonding with the many characters and their stories. Your time spent down south in the 1940's – 1980's will renew your faith in humanity because there are real people like John I.'s characters living among us.

I'll move along now so you can dive into *Thirteen Stories* by John I. Jones. I was honored to be asked to read this compilation of fascinating stories while in manuscript form. I can honestly say it was a real pleasure, for many reasons.

Thank you for your time. I also hope that after you complete this enjoyable book, you will take a few minutes and post a review where you purchased *Thirteen Stories*.

"Keep smilin'...and readin'."

Lee Carey, author

Lee Carey is the author of eleven novels and two compilations of short stories. His most recent work is a Georgia Family Saga, titled 'Fishin' in My Family Closet'. His website is LeeCarey-author.com. Lee and John I. are fellow authors and close friends.

TABLE OF CONTENTS

GOING HOME

Archie was ready to die. At least he thought he was. The sentence had been formally read, he had had his last meal, and the prison chaplain had asked God to have mercy on his soul. Now, as he sat quietly in his cell, the hour was upon him. In the distance, he could hear the doors of the outer cells opening and closing. The warden and his entourage were coming to take him to the electric chair. The sound of rattling keys and the opening and closing of steel doors grew nearer and louder, then he heard the door to the death row cellblock open and a chorus of footsteps tromped across the concrete floor.

With military precision, the entourage stopped in front of Archie's cell. There was the warden, two assistants, the chaplain, the executioner, and the prison physician. The warden faced Archie.

"Archibald William Johnson?" he asked.

"That's me," Archie replied.

With business-like certainty, the warden unfolded an official-looking document. Then, he put on his glasses and began reading.

"The State of Georgia has decreed that you be executed in the electric chair at Valdosta State Prison at midnight on April 23, 1961, which is today. The hour is now approximately 11:35 p.m. Some preparation time will be needed to carry out the court's order. You must come with us so we may carry out the wishes of the state."

Seconds later, the two assistants entered the cell, placed handcuffs on Archie's wrists, and escorted him out. Then the seven men, with Archie in front, started walking out of the death row cellblock.

"Good-bye, Archie," said Charley Fancher, another death row inmate whose cell was directly across from Archie's.

Archie nodded at his old friend.

"May God have mercy on you," said Moses Washington, an older black man, who had been Archie's best friend during his years on death row.

"Bye, Moses," Archie said.

"In about fifteen minutes, you gonna be in hell," said Ray-Ray Hollingsworth, whom Archie had once fought over a piece of cornbread in the prison mess hall.

Archie glanced ominously at Ray-Ray, then acted like he hadn't heard the words.

The entourage stopped in front of the door to the death row cellblock. The warden unlocked the door, waited for the others to pass, then relocked it. Now the seven men were starting the long walk from death row to the execution chamber.

As the entourage passed through the steel and concrete corridor, Archie tried to appear as brave as possible. At age forty-seven, he was a thin, smallish man—maybe five feet, eight inches—with sad eyes and thinning hair. He had two missing teeth and a slight stubble of beard. Jutting over the collar of his prison uniform, on the right side of his neck, was the top of a cross, a chain-gang tattoo he had acquired as a teenager in the state reformatory. Archie had not been a model citizen. He had been in and out of scrapes with the law for as long as he could remember. At the moment, he had been in state prison for eleven years—eight on death row after he was convicted of murder during the robbery of a convenience store near Albany. Archie and his accomplice had taken just over $1100 in the robbery and were making their getaway when a customer, an off-duty cop, came out of the store and started firing. As the robbers' car backed up, then swung around and headed for the street, Archie, who was on the passenger side, took dead aim and dropped the cop with a single shot to the chest. Then they sped away.

After almost a year, Archie was captured in Tennessee, then returned to Georgia. In the first trial, there was a hung jury because the state's chief witness, the clerk, couldn't remember important details of the robbery. In the second trial, however, a new prosecutor was brought in with a new witness and won a murder conviction. The judge said he had no choice but to sentence Archie to death. There had been too many prior felony convictions and Archie wasn't showing sufficient remorse. Over the next ten years, Archie's state-appointed attorneys appealed his conviction all the way to the state supreme court, where it was upheld. With that decision, Archie and his attorneys knew it was only a matter of time before the execution would be held.

Two days before the scheduled execution, Archie had spoken with his lead attorney, who said he had found incriminating evidence against the state's new witness and had presented it to the court and the governor. The lawyer said he couldn't make any promises, but there was "a very good chance" that the governor would commute the sentence and grant him a new trial. It was Archie's only hope.

The group had reached the execution chamber. Once the warden unlocked the door, Archie was led inside and the attendants uncuffed his hands, seated him in the wooden chair, and began strapping him in. Strong leather straps were tightened securely around his ankles, his arms, and his chest. The silver dome was lowered and fitted over his head. Finally, satisfied that everything was ready, the attendants stepped away from the prisoner.

The warden stood in a small alcove in the execution chamber, some ten feet from the electric chair. Behind him was a clock and a telephone. He looked at the clock. It read 11:58. There was a long deathly silence, then, at just after 11:59, the warden looked toward the executioner, who was standing behind the electric chair, his hand on the switch. As the seconds ticked away, the warden started to raise his hand. The executioner put his hand on the switch. Suddenly, the phone rang.

The warden answered the phone.

"Governor?" the warden asked.

All eyes and ears inside the execution chamber turned to the warden.

"Yes," the warden said. "We're about to conduct the execution even as we speak...."

For several moments, the warden listened.

"Yes, sir," he said. "I understand...."

The warden continued listening and said "Yes, sir" another six or seven times. Finally, everyone in the execution chamber could see the conversation was about to an end.

"Yes, governor," he said finally. "I will see that your instructions are carried out."

The warden hung up the phone.

"Unstrap the prisoner," he said. "The prisoner has been given a reprieve. The governor says the chief witness against him has recanted his testimony and the judge has granted a new trial."

The warden turned to face Archie.

"You're a free man," he said. "You're going home."

Archie was stunned at the news. It was a miracle. He had given up all hope and now the long and tireless efforts of his attorneys had finally brought some positive results. Archie couldn't believe he was a free man. And he was going home.

Suddenly, Archie found himself on a bus bound for his hometown of Plum Tree, Georgia. It felt so good to be out. To breathe fresh air, to see green grass and bright sunshine, and be able to swing his arms without fear of hitting an iron bar or a wall. He was anxious to get to Plum Tree. He couldn't wait to see Main Street and how it had changed over the past eleven years. He wanted to go to the Mexican Chili Parlor and see his sister Mable. He wanted to see his old friends at the pool hall. Then he planned to see Big Betty down at the Morris Hotel. He hadn't been with a woman in a long time.

Most of all, he wanted to go back to the old family farm and see his mother. She had a spare bedroom and he could sleep all he wanted. She had canned vegetables from the garden and a cow that gave a gallon of fresh milk a day. Oh, how he longed to be in her comforting presence, to see the peacefulness in her eyes, to sit at her table and eat some of her fried peach pies.

Once the bus arrived, Archie, suitcase in hand, wasted no time walking the two blocks to Main Street. There, at the corner of Main and Chestnut, he stopped and looked for the Mexican Chili Parlor. It was gone. There was a hardware store where the restaurant had once stood. He stepped back to the curb and surveyed the entire street. Yes, this was the place, but there was no more Mexican Chili Parlor. Well, so much for my sister, he thought as he continued walking down Main Street. The old five and dime store where Archie had shoplifted marbles and candy and toy cars was still there. There was Snellgrove's Drug Store, the old Post Office, and Tom Anderson's Office Supply. At the corner of Main and Fourth Street, he turned right and headed for the Smokehouse Pool Hall.

The moment Archie entered the door, Grady Sizemore yelled, "Archie!"

Suddenly, all the pool players stop playing pool and many stepped forward to greet their old friend.

"When did you get out?" Grady asked.

"I beat a murder rap," Archie said. "I'm a free man."

"Well, congratulations," he said. "Jaybird's in the back room playing blackjack. He'd love to see you."

Over the next fifteen minutes, Archie reacquainted himself with his old friends. There was Harry Pickett who Archie had worked with at the Plum Tree Sanitation Department. There was Rusty Walden for whom he had fenced a truckload of stolen men's shirts down in Florida. Archie was so happy to see Floyd Abernathy, his old friend from high school who had been paralyzed in an auto crash while running from the police after a supermarket heist. There were other old friends—"Big Willie" Wilson, Charlie Dupree, and Tommy Hammock—all of whom he had known since childhood.

Suddenly, the room to the back room opened and Jaybird Watson emerged. Jaybird couldn't stop laughing when he saw Archie.

"A free man?" he said over and over. "A free man? I can't believe it. You know there's something I been wanting to talk to you about..."

With that statement, Jaybird invited Archie to go to the back room so they could talk privately. Several minutes later, once they were seated, Jaybird began.

"There's a service station in Defuniak Springs, Florida run by an old man," he said. "He sells gas and diesel fuel to truckers. He sells thousands and thousands of gallons of diesel every day and he always has lots of cash on hand. My friend says he sometimes has $10,000 to $15000 at a time...."

Archie could see where the conversation was going.

"Whoa! Whoa!" he said. "If you're angling for me to do a job with you, I'm not interested. I'm going straight."

"Don't be stupid," Jaybird said. "It's just an old man. We could hit him in the head and be gone before anybody knew what happened. There could easily be five or six grand apiece in it."

"No," Archie said firmly. "I'm going straight."

Jaybird shook his head with approval.

"You want to have a nip with me?" he said. "I got a fresh pint of Miller's Hollow moonshine in the trunk of my car."

"No," Archie said again. "I quit drinking. I don't mess with that stuff no more."

"Just for old time's sake?" Jaybird asked.

Archie shook his head. He could see that all Jaybird wanted to do was get him in trouble again. Moments later, he said good-bye to his former partner in crime, grabbed his suitcase, and stepped back out on the street. Once outside again, he peered down Fourth Street where, some two blocks away, he saw a sign that read Morris Hotel. Some ten minutes later, he was standing in front of the sign.

He went inside to the desk.

"Who would you like to see?" the clerk asked.

"Big Betty," Archie said.

The clerk seemed surprised.

"Big Betty?" he said. "We have several girls that are much younger than her."

"No, I want to see Big Betty," Archie said firmly.

"Okay," the clerk said. "That's six dollars for the room and twenty-five dollars for Big Betty."

Archie plunked thirty-one dollars cash on the counter and the clerk handed him the key.

"That's room 241," the clerk said.

The moment Archie opened the door, Big Betty stared at him as if she had seen a ghost.

"Archie," she said. "What happened? I thought you were a goner! I read in the papers they were sending you to the chair. How'd you get out?"

After several minutes of explaining about his reprieve, Big Betty was ready to get down to business.

"Okay," she said. "Get those clothes off. I'm going to make a new man out of you."

Archie loved being with Big Betty, even though she was in her late forties now. She had gained some weight in recent years, and the wrinkles around her lips were deeper now, but she was a woman who truly knew her business. She had great hands and she knew how to use them. Also, she took pride in her work. "I know how to satisfy a man," she had once told him. "Any man..."

As promised, Archie was a new man when he walked out of the Morris Hotel. Back out on the street again, he hailed a taxi.

"I'm going to the Chalfant farm," he told the driver.

Outside of town, he glanced out the cab window at Plum Tree High School where he had attended classes off and on for almost eleven years. There, many years ago on the front lawn, he had fought Harold Bowling over an ice cream cone until the principal had separated them. The old sycamore tree—much larger now—stood in the corner of the playground where he had played softball and horseshoes and tag with his classmates. There was the high hill made up of Georgia red clay overlooking the playground where Archie and his friends would slide down the hill on cardboard boxes after a rain. Moments later, he saw the windmill on the old Chalfant farm and he knew he was nearing his destination. The cab stopped, Archie got out and paid the driver.

As the cab pulled away, Archie instinctively peered across a pasture through a thicket of pines and sweet gums at the old family farmhouse some one hundred yards away. This was where he had grown up. This was the world of his childhood. Then, suitcase in hand, he started walking down the dirt road from the highway to the farmhouse. As he walked, he realized he had forgotten how much he loved South Georgia in late April. Birds were singing, dogwoods were in bloom, yellow honeysuckle hung in heavy pods along the fences and hedgerows, and the entire countryside was rife with vibrant greens and yellows.

Suddenly, he stopped. There, to his left, overgrown with weeds and blocked by a fallen tree, was what remained of the old path to the river. It was down this path he walked hand-in-hand with Maynelle Thompson many, many times. He was seventeen, she was sixteen, and he vividly remembered the Sunday afternoon they walked down that very path to the river, went skinny-dipping, made love, and professed their eternal devotion to one another. Eight months later, however, after Archie was sent to the state reformatory for stealing a car, she visited him and told him she was going to marry Hollis Whisenant. Hollis had a steady job at the mobile home manufacturing plant, she said, and he wanted to make something out of himself. It was nothing personal, Maynelle explained, but she wanted a man with a future.

Now Archie was walking past the waving, amber fields of broom sage where he and his cousins had played cowboys and Indians and caught lightning bugs. As he rounded a bend in the road, he glanced toward the vegetable garden. There was his mother tilling the soil with a hoe. She was hilling pole beans.

"Mama!" Archie called.

The old woman slowly raised her body, pushed her glasses up on her nose, and turned to the direction of the sound. A huge smile burst across her face.

"Archie!" she yelled. "Is that you?"

"It's me, mama!" Archie yelled back, and then he watched as his mother came running between the rows of okra and tomatoes and sweet corn as fast as her heavy frame would allow. It was so good to be home. So good to find some peace and comfort and security for a change.

Finally, she had reached him and mother and son clasped one another with all their might. As he looked into his mother's face, huge tears were rolling down his cheeks. Somehow, some way, in his hearts of hearts, he knew he would never look into his mother's eyes again.

Finally, Archie released the embrace and wiped away the tears.

"Come on," his mother said. "Let's go to the house. I just made some fresh peach pies."

Those were the exact words Archie wanted to hear.

Moments later, he was seated at his mother's table. First, she served him a glass of cold cow's milk. Then she turned and started to the stove. With absolute pure lust, he watched as she took down the warm, cloth-wrapped peach pies from of the oven. Moments later, she delivered two of them on to the plate in front of him. Archie, not wasting any time, quickly sliced up the two half-moon fruit pies and dabbed them with huge chunks of fresh cow's butter. He watched the butter melt, slowly and surely, into the flaky pieces of pie, waiting for each dwindling chunk of butter to ooze into the innermost crevices of the crust and filling so that, at just the right moment, he could luxuriate in that perfect bite. Seconds later, that moment arrived. Archie took a bite and closed his eyes. He felt the savory warmth of the melting butter and fresh peach course across his taste buds. Oh great God, he thought, this has to be the most wonderful taste in all the world. Archie felt like he had died and gone to heaven.

Just as he was feeling the full rush of the warm, buttered peach pie, his entire body suddenly convulsed like a clenched fist as 120,000 volts of electricity surged through his every vessel, organ, tissue, muscle, and sinew. His chest thrust violently forward; his arms and legs twisted desperately against the leather straps. Then, a blinding streak of hot light flashed fatally across his consciousness. Everything was dark and silent.

With a nod of his head, the warden signaled for the prison physician to do his duty.

The medical officer, who was wearing a stethoscope, stepped forward and examined Archie for respiration, pulse, and heartbeat.

Moments later, having finished his exam, he turned to the warden.

"The prisoner is dead," he said.

****The End****

BOONE

1

For as long as I can remember, my mother was a practicing registered nurse. Throughout my childhood, when I was near my mother, I was constantly surrounded by hypodermic syringes, penicillin tablets, skin ointments, potions for the eyes, mercurochrome swabs, adhesive tape, antiseptics, bandages, cotton balls, and a whole host of other nursing-related articles too numerous to mention.

Although she was licensed to work in a hospital, a doctor's office, or a nursing home, my mother specialized in at-home, private care for the terminally ill. Caring for people who were awaiting their final, inevitable end held a special fascination for my mother. She felt it was somehow her personal destiny to be with the dying in their final days. She was very proud of those cases in which she had helped care for, counsel, and prepare patients to meet their deaths as calmly and as resignedly as possible.

In the late spring of 1949, when I was eight years old, my mother undertook the care of an invalid woman named Miss Mary McDaniel, a gray-haired, bedridden woman in her late 60s who had become paralyzed after a stroke several years earlier. Initially, her husband Boone had hired a neighbor woman named Crick to come live in the home and care for his wife. For several years, Crick ran the household, cooked and cleaned, and took care of Miss Mary's medical needs as best she could. In the winter of 1948, however, Miss Mary had a second stroke, and the doctor told her husband that she needed full-time, professional nursing care.

Boone asked Miss Mary's physician, a Dr. James Fordham, if he knew of a good private duty nurse he would recommend. Dr. Fordham said, as a matter of fact he did and explained that my mother had just finished a case with an elderly man near Attalla who had died after a terrible bout with pancreatic cancer. Dr. Fordham explained how my mother had provided expert care to the dying man and made his final meeting with his maker as comfortable and peaceful as possible. The doctor recommended my mother highly.

Three days later, my mother, my father, and I drove the 45 miles from our home near Hamilton to the backwoods farming country of Thompson's Bend, Alabama, so that my mother could be interviewed as a possible private duty nurse for Miss Mary McDaniel.

When my mother sat down for the interview, Boone and Mary began asking questions about her background. After only ten minutes, they discovered that my grandmother, Gladys Georgia McKinney, and Miss Mary were long-lost third cousins. That made my mother and Miss Mary fourth cousins. In fact, my grandmother, who had grown up with Miss Mary in Thompson's Bend some 40 years earlier, had been a bridesmaid at Boone and Mary's wedding in 1912. That clinched it. A family acquaintance was all the reference that Boone and Mary needed. My mother was hired on the spot.

In mid-May of 1949, I was near the end of the second grade in grammar school. One Friday afternoon when I got in from school, my mother called me into the bedroom where she was packing a suitcase. Once I was seated on the bed, my mother explained that she was going to live with the McDaniels. She said that Hilda, a neighbor woman who did our housekeeping, would be helping me get ready for school each day. She reminded me that, as usual, I was responsible for helping my father with the chores, doing my homework, and making sure that my ears were clean each morning before I went to school. She said I would come to live with her at the McDaniel farm when school was out for the summer.

***

So three weeks later, I was sent off to the deep backwoods of North Alabama to live with my mother on the McDaniel farm. For the trip, Hilda had packed up everything my mother had instructed: toys, clothes, toiletries, books, and all the personal items and other gear I would need for my great adventure. Once I was packed, Hilda pecked me on the cheek, reminded me to put on clean underwear every day, and warned me to "watch out for rattlesnakes in them woods." My father and I climbed into our black 1947 Oldsmobile and he delivered me to the McDaniel farm.

The farm was a shadowy, foreboding underworld where real time had ceased to exist many, many years before. Standing darkly within a grove of giant oak trees, the McDaniel farmhouse was a weathered, unpainted, clapboard structure with a tin roof and six gables, a single lightning rod at each gable. Originally constructed in the late 1880s, the farmhouse was built in the time-honored shotgun design with a hallway down the middle and rooms branching off to either side. Over the years, however, new rooms—a pantry, a storage room, and an enlarged kitchen—had been added, and the original shotgun design had been lost.

The interior of the farmhouse was an eerie place. All the rooms had a musty, decaying smell like old clothes that had hung in the closet too long. Most of the furniture had been ordered out of a Sears and Roebuck catalog from the early 1900s. All of the nightstands and bedside tables had knobbed legs and inlaid mirrors like something out of an English late, late movie. All the bedrooms had fireplaces and the mantle over each featured a hand-carved etching of winged, angelic-faced cherubs playfully holding a burning torch. According to the style standards of 1910, the home was considered elegant. Since there was no electricity in the home, all the fires—whether in the cook stove or the fireplaces—were wood-fed. At night, the only sources of light were kerosene lamps.

My bedroom was a musty-smelling front room with tall Victorian windows and a well-used, stone fireplace with faded, sepia photos of Boone and Mary's ancestors on the mantle. The mattress on my bed was filled with pine straw and when you laid on it or turned over in your sleep, there was a sharp, snapping sound of dried pine needles being crushed. The pillows were made with real down-home goose feathers and sometimes a large, stiff one would punch through the pillowcase and stab you in the neck when you changed positions in your sleep.

Later that summer, I would catch lightning bugs outside and then release them within the musty bedroom so that I could marvel at the warm, translucent flashes of yellow light in the darkness. One night, I chased an errant lightning bug into the closet. Following the insect's brilliant glow to a stack of clothing, I found a huge box full of pint and quart fruit jars hidden underneath. I knew that canned fruit and vegetables were kept in the pantry near the kitchen, so I wondered why the fruit jars had been hidden in the closet. Curious, I retrieved a flashlight and inspected further. The fruit jars were crammed full of cash in rolled-up wads. There were huge double handfuls of five, ten, and twenty-dollar notes crammed into the fruit jars. There had to be thousands and thousands of dollars hidden in the closet.

Frightened at my discovery, I closed the box and returned the clothes on top of it. The next morning I told my mother what I had found. She admonished me to never go near the closet again and to not breathe a word of what I had discovered. She said Boone didn't trust banks after what happened in 1929. I promised to do as she had ordered.

One morning, my mother sat me down in my bedroom with an album of old family photos. Boone had a brother who fought for Admiral Dewey when the Americans routed the Spanish at Manila Bay during the Spanish-American War. Included in the album were 50 to 60 old sepia photos of American soldiers and sailors posing triumphantly in front of the gallows where they had hanged thousands of Spanish soldiers. In photo after photo, I gazed in awe at the dead soldiers hanging lifelessly from the gallows as the Americans—weapons held victoriously aloft—posed like mighty hunters, infinitely proud of their kills. I remember my young mind thinking how horrible war and death must be.

Miss Mary's room was located directly across the hallway from my room. Her bed, a cast-iron, turn-of-the-century model, faced the fireplace where Boone always kept a fire going. When Boone was in the room, he sat in a rocking chair facing the fireplace while his dog Nero lazed on the warm hearth at his feet. Beside Miss Mary's bed was a window that looked out on the front porch and the dirt road that passed in front of the house. Many days, in her bedridden loneliness, Miss Mary would look out the window and up the road to see an occasional car or wagon passing.

***

During the first few weeks of my stay, I spent all my time near my mother. To occupy myself, she would give me chores and I would gather eggs, bring in wood for the cook stove, or feed the dogs. The house woman, Crick, was a muscular, raw-boned country woman in her late 30s who had never been married and never stopped working. Uneducated and unattractive, Crick was deeply religious and had no understanding of personal hygiene. On hot days, her body odor would be so foul it would pervade the whole house. If I had to go into the kitchen and Crick was cooking over the stove, I would rush right past her as quickly as possible because the heat from the cook stove intensified her body odor to a truly overwhelming degree. On several occasions my mother threatened to buy deodorant and force Crick to use it, but somehow she could never bring herself to actually do it.

When I wasn't doing chores I would play under the oak trees in the front yard with my toys. I had a set of little plastic circus characters I would arrange in the top of a shoe box. There were three horsemen, several clowns, some ballerinas, a high-wire act with plastic acrobats, and a mustachioed magician in a black cape. I would pretend I was the master of a three-ring circus, and in my child's mind, I could set them performing at a moment's notice.

Boone McDaniel was a small, hunch-backed man in his late 70s who had a drawn face and a constant stubble of beard. He always dipped Bruton snuff and never wore anything but bib overalls, brogans, and a long-sleeved khaki shirt buttoned at the top. Boone was the epitome of the backwoods Alabama farmer whose entire life had been spent near the earth, farm animals, and crops.

The thing I remember most about Boone was his hat. He had a black felt hat that he had been wearing probably 10–15 years, and maybe even longer. The hat was so old that the felt at the front of the crown where he grasped it actually had holes worn in it. When Boone took his hat off to eat or sit by the fire, there was a bald, shiny spot right on the very top of his head.

At first, Boone wouldn't have anything to do with me. Either he didn't know what to make of me or he could see no reason to befriend me. After all, I was 8 years old and he was 78. Boone had never had any children of his own and I wasn't sure if he was capable of relating to anyone as young as me.

In the mornings when he went to the fields he would see me playing with my circus toys and make some brief, off-handed comment. Then, together with his dog Nero, he would trudge off to the cotton fields. At lunch, he would return to the farmhouse and go directly into Miss Mary's room. There he would stoke the fire and talk to Miss Mary about the crops and business and share his day with her. Once he had eaten, Boone would check the fire again, ask Miss Mary about her health, and then return to the fields.

2

After I'd been there for about three weeks, however, something caused Boone to change his mind. For some reason he decided he wanted to get to know me. I don't believe it was due to loneliness because Boone McDaniel was too hard a man to allow himself such a vulnerable trait. I think I was more of a curiosity than anything else. The old man probably wanted a closer look at this young, modern boy from the nearby town.

So, one morning as I was playing under the oak trees, Boone came out of the house. As usual, his dog Nero was waiting at the back porch steps and when Boone's foot hit the ground, Nero fell into lockstep behind his Lord and Master. As he rounded the corner of the house, he saw me playing. At first, Boone said nothing, walked past me, and started toward the fields as usual. On that particular morning, however, after he had taken several steps toward the fields, he suddenly stopped and turned to me.

"Hey, little turd-knocker," he said tentatively in a low, uncertain tone.

I looked up from my circus toys.

"Yes, sir," I answered.

"You wanna go to the fields with me today?"

"I have to ask my mother," I replied.

"It's okay," he said. "Come on."

If Boone approved, I knew it would be okay with my mother so I joined him and his dog Nero that day for the first of our many walks during the summer of 1949.

For hours on end, Boone, who walked with a labored, begrudging limp, would lead me and the dog down the cotton rows that were sometimes a full quarter-mile long. We must have been a strange sight: this wizened, hunched-over creature, his aging dog Nero, and me, a slight, skinny kid, walking through a green sea of knee-high cotton plants that seemed to stretch forever and ever to the horizon.

We would walk for what seemed like endless miles,

gathering the sandy soil on our shoes. Intermittently, Boone would stop and inspect the cotton plants. Then he would mutter something to the dog about the state of the crop—not enough rain, too much fertilizer, seeds planted too deep, or whatever. Then, after his pronouncement, we would start walking again. Further on, Boone would stop to talk to one of the Negro hired hands who was plowing. Boone would ask the hired hand if he thought the ground was too wet or too dry or too something. The black man would offer a reply and Boone would bend down over the plow and take some of the fresh earth from one of the blades. He would rub it between his fingers, and then he would tell the hired hand to adjust the blade angle on the plow or pull the mules a little closer to the furrow. Finally, having delivered his input as farm owner, Boone would start limping back down the cotton rows again, and the dog and I would follow.

At the end of the fields, Boone, Nero, and I would arrive at the river and have a seat under a tree within the sound of the raging water. Boone warned me to never go near the river at that point. There were water moccasins "bigger'n yo' arm down there," he'd say, referring to the heavy undergrowth along the riverbank. He recalled that during the spring plowing of 1931, a Negro hired hand had stopped at the end of the cotton rows and gone down to the river to get a drink. Boone said the man had been bitten seven times. The luckless plowman had made his way back up the river bank to the plow and the mules but had collapsed and died before he could go any further.

***

I had a crazy uncle named Milford who liked to brag that he was a big-time farmer. Uncle Milford had 10 acres with 5 in cultivation, 2 mules, a small tractor, a milk cow, several calves, and about 30 chickens. Boone, on the other hand, was a real farmer with over 600 acres and almost 400 in cultivation. Boone had 9 mules, 5 hired hands, 83 head of cattle including 13 bulls and 17 cows nursing calves, 53 head of hogs including 9 brood sows, and literally hundreds of chickens. On my Uncle Milford's farm, I would go with my cousin Albert to gather eggs, and if we found 20, it was a big deal. At Boone's, it was nothing for me to gather 200 eggs in one afternoon. Boone also had five horses, not counting a prize palomino he hired out as a stud, three wagons, one of which had rubber tires, and four riding saddles. Boone never owned a car or a tractor. He said they were too expensive and he "just didn't believe in 'em." If Boone McDaniel needed transportation, he would either walk or hitch up a two-horse wagon.

Some of my happiest hours that summer were spent riding a cowboy rig that Boone had built for me with an old saddle. Boone had seen me cutting Tom Mix and Lash LaRue posters from the back of cereal boxes and he knew I was caught up in the cowboy craze that swept the late '40s. So Boone strapped an old saddle across a piece of lumber under the tool shed and tied it down so I could play like I was riding a horse. When I wasn't in the fields with Boone I would spend endless hours bouncing in the saddle pretending I was a host of glorious cowboy heroes: The Lone Ranger, Roy Rogers, Gene Autry, Tim Holt, Lash LaRue, and Kid Colt.

Boone knew my name was Billy, but he always called me "little turd-knocker." I guess the only way a 78 year old could see an 8 year old like me was as a miniature human being whose only purpose in life was to leave behind little pods of excrement like a horse-drawn spreader rhythmically leaves fertilizer in the furrow during planting time. In agricultural parlance, these fertilizing machines were called knockers because they made a thick clunking sound as the mule pulled them down the furrow. On the other hand, Boone's life was so closely intertwined with the lives of animals that he may have seen human beings, me included, in the same light in which he saw his cows, pigs, chickens, and horses: creatures whose only visible legacy to the earth was the daily digestive waste they left in their paths.

***

After he got to know me, Boone would give me money to

buy candy from the peddler. Since Boone didn't have a car and never went to the grocery, he bought all of his household goods from the local peddler. The peddler, a fat, jolly, red-faced man named Howard, drove a converted school bus around the countryside and either sold or bartered his store-bought goods to the farmers for their produce.

"Now I'm going to give you a 25-cent piece so you can go see the peddler and buy some sweetnin'," Boone would say, taking a time-worn change purse from the bib of his overalls and withdrawing a quarter.

So, with the quarter in hand, I would race down the cotton rows to meet the peddler. When I would arrive, Crick would always be there counting eggs that would be swapped for goods. She would count a dozen eggs and the peddler would make a pencil mark on a small pad. Finally, after she had counted 20 or 30 dozen, the peddler would tell her how much credit she had for the eggs. Then he'd turn to me.

"How much money you got today?" he'd ask.

I'd hold up the quarter.

"Well, start picking," he'd say.

Twenty-five cents was a lot of money when you're eight years old. And it was 1949. First I would get red jawbreakers and some Tootsie Rolls. Then I'd choose two or three of those little banana-flavored candies shaped like cricket bats, some peppermint sticks, a cherry-flavored all-day sucker, and some licorice. I'd round out my treasure trove with some bubble gum, a handful of Kit-Kat chewies, some chocolate kisses, and three or four grape-flavored sour balls. Finally, the peddler would tell me I had 25 cents worth, and I'd stop picking.

With my pants pockets bulging with candy, I would race back across the cotton field. Breathlessly, I would rush up and Boone would be standing alone, gazing across the cotton rows and talking to his dog Nero. He'd turn to me, and I'd show him the pocketful of candy.

"That's lots of sweetnin' you got there," he'd say.

"Wanna piece?" I would ask.

He'd shake his head.

"No sweets for me," he'd say. "Not after my accident." His intonation emphasized the word "accident" and when he said that he would reach down and rub his crooked right leg. I didn't figure the candy would go too well with his dipping snuff anyway, so I didn't press the issue.

Other than Miss Mary, the only creature Boone had any true affection for was his dog Nero. Nero was an aging black-and-white-spotted feist that was Boone's alter ego and constant companion. Boone said he couldn't remember for sure, but Nero was either 13 or 14 years old.

Nero was one of eight pups that had been born in a hay shed behind the barn, Boone said. When the pups were only a few days old, the hay shed caught fire during a lightning storm and the frantic mother dog started carrying the pups out of the burning shed. She succeeded in bringing out one pup. When she returned for the others, the fire had spread so rapidly that she and the other puppies were trapped and perished in the smoke and flames. Boone said he named the surviving puppy Nero because the emperor Nero had played the fiddle while Rome burned.

There were three other dogs on the farm, but Nero was top dog, and all the others knew it. Another dog, a chow-collie mix named George, would sometimes join us on our walks, but he always had to defer to Nero. If Nero approved, George could accompany us to the fields. If Nero didn't approve, and somehow Boone could tell when Nero disapproved, George couldn't come along. If George tried to go with us when Nero was in a bad mood, Nero would growl and chase him away. If George persisted, Boone would curse the dog and chase it back to the farmhouse.

Sometimes during our walks, Boone would ask me what I thought about God and the Bible. Boone said that preachers claimed if you were a good person on Earth, you would go to heaven where harps played, angels sang, the streets were paved with gold, and you would eat honey and drink milk all day.

"Do you believe that?" he'd ask me earnestly.

"That's what the Bible says," I would reply, recalling my teachings from the Baptist Church Sunday School my mother and I had attended in the town.

Boone would look at me and say nothing, and then we

would start walking across the cotton fields again. After we had walked a little ways, he would stop to inspect the cotton plants.

"I don't see much use for preachers," he would say absently, looking closely at a wilted cotton boll. "'Bout all they're good for is to marry you and to bury you."

***

If any of the other farmers in Thompson's Bend had a problem breeding a horse, a cow, or a hog, they would consult Boone who was the known expert in such matters. Early one morning, Boone and I walked across the mountain to another farmer's house where a calf that was being born had somehow turned inside the cow. The farmer had grabbed the calf and tried to pull the calf out, but the cow, in terrible pain, collapsed. When Boone arrived, the cow was on the ground near death, and the calf was half-in and half-out.

Like some sort of mysterious birthing wizard, Boone gently pushed the calf back inside the cow. Then, while the farmer held the cow's head, Boone put his whole arm inside the cow and repositioned the calf in the birth canal. Once positioned properly, Boone gently pulled the newborn calf out of the cow as smoothly and surely as if the birth had been perfectly natural.

The mastery Boone showed when he hired out his prize stud, a giant palomino stallion, to service a mare always held a certain fascination for my eight-year-old eyes.

When a farmer would bring a mare to be bred, Boone would inspect her first. Sometimes Boone wouldn't bring out the stud if he felt the mare hadn't been in heat long enough, and the farmer would plead and argue with Boone to go ahead and put the stud on her.

"It won't take," Boone would say. "She's got to have more heat before it will take. Let nature work on her a few more days, and then bring her back."

They would usually take Boone's advice.

One farmer, a stocky, red-faced Irishman named James Mullins had brought a dappled filly across the river on the ferry and talked Boone into putting the stallion on her before, in Boone's judgement, she had been in heat long enough.

"I'll put him to her," Boone said finally, "but you have to pay for the service. And if it don't take and you have to bring her back, then I'm charging you again."

"Okay. Okay." the Irishman agreed reluctantly, wanting to breed his mare and get back across the river as soon as possible.

Boone put the stallion on the mare and the stud did his thing. Sure enough, the mare wasn't impregnated, and three weeks later the Irishman was back to have the stud put on her again. The Irishman paid Boone the stud fee a second time and never questioned Boone's judgement again.

***

The only relief for the cold, brazen hardness that lived inside Boone McDaniel was Miss Mary. Everything he did, he did for Miss Mary, and the only time he ever seemed to be truly happy was when he was with her in her room with a good fire going and his dog Nero lazing on the hearth. During those times, he felt secure and at peace with himself and the world around him.

My grandmother said it had always been that way and the day he finally married Miss Mary in the spring of 1912, Boone was the happiest man in North Alabama. For more than two years, Boone had courted Mary, trying to get her to marry him, my grandmother said. Mary, a beautiful young woman, told Boone she liked him and wanted to marry him, but she couldn't leave her father to live alone.

When she was five, Miss Mary's mother died of fever and left her and her younger brother Benjamin to be raised by their father. Then, after Benjamin was killed in a hunting accident in 1910, all the family that Mary had left was her father.

As fate would have it, my grandmother said, Mary's father fell ill with the flu the following winter and had to close the hardware store he operated at Moody's Chapel. While he was sick, he raved on and on about how he was losing business by being closed. After several days he started improving, and although weak and pale, he left the sickbed and reopened the hardware store despite Miss Mary's protests. Three nights later he closed his business again and came home with severe chills and a high fever. He died in Mary's arms the following morning.

When Boone heard about the death, he rushed to Mary's side to comfort her and help clean up the family business. Then, two days after her father's funeral, Boone proposed again that she marry him. This time Mary accepted. After the marriage, Boone bought a small farm on the north side of the Tallapoosa River and planted cotton and corn and started breeding animals. Miss Mary wanted to help with the farm work, but Boone wouldn't have it. He said he didn't want her "out there tussling in the fields with the hired hands." He wanted her to stay at home, cook for him, keep house, and mother his children.

But Miss Mary would never become a mother, my grandmother said, because Boone's accident occurred three months into the marriage. Boone decided he wanted to build a herd of riding horses to sell to the local farmers, so he bought a stud, an aging Appaloosa stallion, to start the herd. During the first spring the old stud performed well and successfully impregnated all four of Boone's mares. Then, Boone decided to hire out the stud to service the mares of nearby farmers. That's when the problems started. For some reason, the old stud lost his ability to penetrate. In one of the breeding sessions, in which the stud failed again and again to penetrate the mare, Boone became frustrated and tried to force the male inside the female. The old stud, apparently angered at the interference, kicked Boone in the testicles. The blow slammed Boone against the side of a hayrack and knocked him unconscious.

Boone was immobilized for over seven months, my grandmother said. At first, the doctors said he would never walk again. When the horse had kicked him, the powerful blow had not only ruptured Boone's testicles, it had also cracked several small bones at the base of his spine. This meant there was nerve damage and possible paralysis. When Boone finally decided he was well enough to get out of bed and walk, he simply fell on the floor. His right leg was permanently paralyzed and crooked at the knee. The doctor said Boone would have to learn to walk with the crooked leg.

Miss Mary sent off to Sears and Roebuck and bought Boone an apparatus that would help him learn to walk again. For several weeks, he hobbled around the house on the device until he regained enough strength in the good leg to take some halting steps. Finally, Boone learned to walk again, but he had to hunch his back over to do it.

Once Boone was mobile again, the doctor said he was lucky to regain his ability to walk but explained it would be asking too much to expect to regain his ability to produce children. As a result, Boone and Mary spent the rest of their lives childless. At one point, Mary had talked about adopting a child, my grandmother said. They had even hired a lawyer and talked to the state adoption people in Birmingham, but nothing ever came of it. Finally, they decided to spend their lives together without children. This singular piece of happenstance bound Boone to Miss Mary in the most incredible way imaginable, my grandmother said. As a result, the depth of the love and devotion he had for Miss Mary was frightening, she said.

3

One hot morning in late August, I was with Boone in the cotton fields when I heard my mother calling from somewhere in the distance. I scanned the cotton rows until I located the sound of her voice. More than 500 yards away, I could see my mother waving. I ran down the cotton rows as fast as I could and finally, breathlessly, I was within earshot of my mother.

"Tell Boone that Mary is getting worse and he should come right in," she said.

I raced back down the cotton rows and told Boone. He turned immediately and started trudging back down the cotton rows as fast as his awkward walk would allow.

When Boone went into Mary's room, the old woman was gasping for breath. Miss Mary had always looked pale and weak, but that morning she was white as a sheet. The long gray hair that normally flowed over the shoulders of her nightgown seemed to be dull and lifeless. Her breath was coming in great heaves and gasps.

My mother gave her a shot and she began breathing more regularly. My mother told Boone her heartbeat was erratic, but she seemed to be stabilizing. Around mid-afternoon, Dr. Fordham arrived. After taking her vital signs, he removed a vial of medicine from his satchel.

"Give her a shot of this now," the doctor said, handing my mother the vial. "Take her heartbeat and respiration hourly. If she goes into convulsions, give her another shot," the doctor said.

Throughout that night, Miss Mary slept peacefully while my mother and Boone waited at her bedside. In the early morning hours, my mother went to a small anteroom to sleep for a few hours, giving Boone strict instructions to call her if Miss Mary's condition changed.

All that night, Boone stayed in Miss Mary's room, dozing in the rocking chair and keeping the fire going. Intermittently, he would awaken and check on Miss Mary and then go back to the rocking chair to doze again.

The next morning about daybreak, Boone awakened my mother. The old woman was gasping for breath again. My mother took her pulse.

"Her heartbeat is down to 38 times a minute," my mother said, turning to Boone. "We'd better get the doctor."

Boone nodded his approval. My mother called Crick and told her to go across the woods to the Chalfant's place.

"She's going to die!" Crick screamed frantically. "Oh, I know Miss Mary's going to die. Oh, Miss Mary, we love you so! God, please don't take Miss Mary."

"Stay calm," my mother ordered firmly. "Go over to the Chalfant's place. Get them to take you to Moody's chapel and call the doctor."

"Oh, Lord Jesus, in all your mercy, please don't take Miss Mary away from us," the farm woman wailed. "Oh, please, dear Jesus… "

My mother got up, took Crick by the shoulders, and shook her. "Keep quiet!" my mother said authoritatively. "Go call the doctor!" she said again. Crick, sobbing like a child, left the room.

After Crick left, Boone sat on the side of the bed and held his wife's hand. My mother gave her a shot and the old woman took several deep breaths. Suddenly she opened her eyes. Boone was elated.

"Mary! Mary!" Boone said, excitedly. His tone was almost pleading.

Miss Mary had a soft, peaceful smile on her face. She looked at Boone then turned to the window.

"Look!" Miss Mary said, sitting up in bed and pointing out the window. "Look out the window!"

Boone looked at my mother curiously. My mother held her hand and patted her shoulder.

"Mary! Mary!" my mother said. "It's me, Virginia."

The old woman couldn't see or hear anything my mother was saying. Her eyes were fixed on the window.

"Boone!" Miss Mary said. "Look! Look out the window!"

The old man bolted upright and looked out the window. Not seeing anything, he turned back to her.

"Mary, what is it?" he asked anxiously

"I see my daddy comin' down the road," Miss Mary said calmly, pointing out the window. "Look! Look! Don't you see him?"

Boone looked out the window then he looked back at my mother. They exchanged knowing glances.

"It's him! It's him!" the old woman said with certainty. "I tell you, it's my daddy. I can see him coming."

Boone looked at my mother again.

My mother didn't answer.

"It's my daddy and he's coming to get me," Miss Mary said again, still staring out the window and peering up the road.

Boone, shaking his head slowly and sadly, said nothing. Stone-faced and still holding his wife's hand, he looked at my mother as she placed the stethoscope against Miss Mary's breast.

"He's here now," Miss Mary said with wild-eyed excitement. "And he's going to take me with him."

Boone looked at my mother expectantly, almost fearfully. Then, without another word, the old woman fell back on the pillow, her frail head collapsing softly in a nest of long, gray hair. For a brief instant, her upper body jerked forward. Then she seemed to relax and a peaceful look dawned across her face.

"She's dead," Boone said knowingly, watching as my mother pressed the stethoscope against the old woman's chest. My mother listened for a moment and then sadly removed the stethoscope and nodded in agreement.

"She lost her mind before she died," Boone said.

My mother, folding up the stethoscope, looked at Boone and said nothing.

Crick, who had returned from the Chalfant farm, suddenly rushed frantically into the room. For a moment, she stared at the old woman's corpse. Then, in a sudden flash of hysteria, she broke down sobbing and rushed to the side of the bed.

"Oh, Miss Mary!" she said, getting down on her knees. "May God bless you and keep you. May you go straight through the pearly gates and be happy forever and ever with Jesus. Oh, Miss Mary, we loved you so much."

Boone, irritation in his eyes, looked at Crick on her knees, sobbing and praying at his dead wife's bedside.

"Get out of here with that!" Boone said sharply, ordering the woman out of the room as if he were dismissing an errant dog. Crick, sobbing uncontrollably, left the room like an obedient child.

My mother pulled the sheet over Miss Mary's body. For a moment, Boone—not a flicker of emotion on his face—looked at the sheet draped over his dead wife. Then Boone told my mother he and Nero were going for a walk. I knew he didn't want me to go with him.

Three hours later, Dr. Fordham arrived and pronounced Miss Mary officially dead. My mother filled out the death report and Dr. Fordham signed it as her official death record.

After the doctor left, I went out to the tool shed to play cowboy on the old saddle Boone had set up. As I bounced up and down in the saddle, the wood piece the saddle was tied to made a loud, clunking sound. First, I played like Roy Rogers on Trigger, then The Lone Ranger on Silver, and finally Gene Autry on Champion. For some 20–30 minutes, I bounced up and down in the saddle, the clunking of the wood piece drowning out all other sounds. Finally, I grew weary of the play-horse. As I took my foot out of the stirrup to dismount, I suddenly heard a strange sound. I stopped and listened. It was a low, mournful, whining sound like a forlorn animal crying for its mate. It was coming from somewhere beyond the barn.

I went to investigate. As I passed through the barn hallway, I checked all the stalls. Then I followed the sound through the barn hallway to the corn crib. There, in front of the corn crib, I saw Nero sitting alone. I could hear the sound coming from inside the corn crib.

I left Nero undisturbed and went around to the back of the corn crib where the mud chinks had dried and fallen out of the cracks between the logs. I shaded my eyes and peered inside. There, through the cracks, I could see Boone sobbing like a little child. The old man was sitting among the ears of unhusked corn. He would make a low, wailing sound like an old bitch dog having pups, and then he would beat his clenched fists into the ears of corn.

It crossed my mind to go in and tell Boone he shouldn't be so sad. Somehow, my better judgement told me not to. Finally, I tiptoed away from the corn crib and went back to the house feeling very sad for Boone.

Later that afternoon, the funeral home people came and took Miss Mary's body away. Boone thanked my mother for her help with Mary, but asked her to stay on until the day after the funeral to help Crick around the house. Boone said she knew about things like that and he would pay her well.

My mother supervised the funeral arrangements, and the following day, my mother and I, Boone, and my grandmother attended Miss Mary's funeral at the Pilgrim's Rest Baptist Church. Just about everybody in Thompson's Bend was there. My mother said she saw cousins she didn't even know she had. My grandmother wept like a little child when the gravediggers threw the clods of fresh earth in on Miss Mary's casket. It was all very sad.

4

I'll say one thing for Boone McDaniel: he had an unswerving certainty to his actions. Unlike many men, Boone McDaniel knew exactly what he wanted in this world and he put that desire into action without the slightest hesitation. After Miss Mary was buried on a Saturday afternoon, Boone came home that night, fed the cattle, the hogs and the chickens, and went for a walk in the fields with Nero. Around sundown, he returned to the house, had supper, and then went straight to bed.

Early the next morning, a Sunday morning, before anybody else got up, Boone put on clean overalls, a clean khaki shirt, and went down behind the barn. On his way out of the house, he reached in the back porch pantry and got the 12 gauge shotgun he used to scare the crows out of the vegetable garden. Outside, at the back porch steps, Nero was waiting as usual. As if Nero knew exactly what was about to happen, he fell in stride behind Boone and they went down behind the barn together.

Boone killed the dog first. A point-blank blast from the 12 gauge shotgun decapitated Nero. Boone then reloaded the shotgun and pulled off his right shoe. He sat down on the ground, leaned his back against the side of the barn, held the gun against his left breast, and pulled the trigger with the big toe of his right foot.

Apparently Boone had intended for the shotgun blast to go directly into his heart. Unfortunately, he had used the big toe on his right leg, the bad one, to pull the trigger. The shotgun barrel had somehow slipped downward when it discharged, and the charge had passed just under Boone's heart, shattered his upper ribs, ripped a huge hole in the bottom portion of his left lung, and left his small intestines a mess of ragged, bleeding flesh.

My mother was the first to be awakened by the shot. Instinctively, she jumped out of bed, awakened Crick, and together they rushed down behind the barn. There they found the dead dog and Boone lying against the side of the barn with a gaping gunshot wound in his left side. Blood was gushing out of the wound, down the side of his overalls, and onto the ground.

"Oh, God! Oh, God!" Crick said hysterically, her face white with terror. "I'll go get the doctor."

"No!" my mother said calmly. "Help me get him in the house first."

My mother removed the shotgun and ordered Crick to go back to the house and bring some sheets. Upon Crick's return, my mother worked quickly to pack a sheet into Boone's wound and, using two others to fashion a makeshift stretcher, she and Crick managed to get Boone into the house as I held the doors.

Once inside the house, my mother and Crick managed to carry him into the front bedroom. Then, on my mother's orders, Crick raced off to get the doctor again and my mother began wrapping Boone's wounds to contain the bleeding. Even as I watched my mother tell Crick to rush across the pasture to the Chalfant's home again, I didn't really believe she felt the doctor could do any good. She just wanted to get the hysterical Crick out of the way. She did ask me to stay in the room with her after Crick left.

Boone, bleeding profusely, lay in the same bed Miss Mary had died in. My mother had propped his back up with pillows. He was losing blood rapidly. His breath came in enormous, labored heaves, and each time I could see his left lung inflating and deflating like a toy balloon. The wadded-up sheet my mother had packed inside the wound was already saturated with blood, and the dark red liquid of life was trickling down on the bed frame and onto the floor.

Suddenly, Boone opened his eyes and looked straight past my mother out the window.

"Oh, God," Boone said, staring out the bedside window. "Oh, great God Almighty!"

"What is it, Boone?" my mother asked anxiously, glancing out the window herself.

"It's Mary!" Boone said, as if he couldn't believe his eyes. "Oh, Jesus, I can see her! I can see her! I can see her plain as day! She's comin' up the road," he said. "And she's comin' to get me!"

I saw my mother visibly shiver when Boone said that. Her eyes bulged in a way like I had never seen before.

Suddenly, Boone started shaking as if he was trying to get out of the bed. It was as if he was ready to go to the fields or the barn or somewhere. My mother, still holding one hand on the bloody, wadded-up sheet in his side, put her other hand on his shoulder and tried to hold Boone on the bed.

"Boone! Boone!" My mother said desperately. "You've got to stay in bed."

A massive stream of red, hot blood from the soaked sheet continued trickling down on the floor. Inside Boone's open chest, I could see his left lung inflate then slowly deflate as he sucked in the last giant gasps of precious, life-giving air.

My mother, her eyes still bulging, holding one hand on the wadded sheet in Boone's side and another on his shoulder, looked frantically at me, not knowing, probably even wondering, if I was taking all this in the proper vein.

Then suddenly, Boone's face turned a white ashen color. As he stared out the window, Boone was calm as a cucumber and grinning like I'd never seen him grin before.

"I'll be glad to see you again, Miss Mary," he said, still smiling and peering out the window. "Oh, Lord God Almighty! I'll be so happy to see you again."

For a brief moment, Boone, still smiling big as day, turned from the window and stared straight into my mother's face. A cold deathly glaze formed over his eyes. Then his hand fell, and his crooked body slumped back softly against the pillows. Boone McDaniel was dead.

****The End****

FOR LOVE OF DANIEL

Jack and Frances

North Alabama, 1955

Jack Griffin woke up. He rubbed his right eye, his good one, then rolled over and glanced at the clock. It was 6:35, Monday morning. He had to be at work at eight. Through the window, he could see a gray, overcast sky and hear light rain clinking on the window panes. Jack sat up in bed, stretched his arms, and threw his feet on the floor. Moments later, he was dressed and in the kitchen. Quickly, he cleared the previous night's dishes and food scraps off the table, then wiped it clean with a damp cloth. Then he grabbed an oak water bucket sitting beside the sink and headed to the well. Every morning, once he was awake and dressed, the first thing he did was go to the well.

Outside, the rain was a light drizzle as he strode across the yard. He dropped the metal bucket into the well, then jiggled the rope until the bucket fell on its side and started to fill. Once filled, he hefted the metal bucket up and poured the water into the wooden container. Back inside, he placed the full water bucket beside the sink and began preparing two bologna and mayonnaise sandwiches. Once finished, he placed the sandwiches, along with two apples and a store-bought sweet cake, into a small black lunch pail. Then he dipped cold beef stew out of a pot into a bowl, grabbed two cold biscuits, and sat down to eat. Suddenly, remembering there was no milk, he got up.

Moments later, he was strolling across Highway 17 to the home of Miss Frances Hathaway, his neighbor who lived across the street.

"Morning, Miss Hathaway."

"Morning, Jack," she said, opening the door. "Don't look! Let me get my wig."

Jack stood in the doorway and politely looked away as she went to the corner of the living room, then, standing in front of a mirror, hastily pulled a black wig over her head. Satisfied she was presentable, she turned back at Jack.

"You know I can't face the world without my wig."

"Can I get some fresh milk?"

"I don't have a full gallon. I got maybe half a gallon."

"That will be fine."

Jack watched as she went to the refrigerator in the kitchen and returned moments later with a container of fresh milk.

"Thank you, Miss Hathaway!" he said, taking the container.

He pressed fifty cents into her hand and turned to go.

"Will you look at the light in my pantry?" Frances said. "I can't get it to come on. I've changed the bulb."

"Can it wait until this afternoon? I got to be at work in an hour."

"That will be fine."

Moments later, jug of milk in hand, Jack was walking back across the highway to his home. As he walked, Jack struck the portrait of a small man, maybe five foot, six inches tall, with a thick, round torso, a sun-burned face, and slight traces of gray around the edges of his black hair.

Back at home, he wolfed down the cold beef stew, then shaved and dressed for work in his daily uniform of overalls with rolled-up bottoms, a denim shirt, and black high-top work shoes. His eye patch always went on last. Any time he was working or in public, Jack wore a shop worker's cap. He believed his eye patch was not as prominent when he was wearing the cap. Finally, lunch pail in hand, he went to the back porch and retrieved his bicycle.

Moments later, he was riding across the front yard on the bicycle. As he set upon Highway 17, he saw Frances, wearing a ridiculous-looking black wig, putting out tomato plants.

When she saw Jack, she stood up.

"You want to have supper tonight after you finish the light?"

"Yeah. I'll make sure I'm hungry."

Frances smiled and waved.

For nine years now, Jack had been living across the highway from Frances and, during that time, they had forged a mutually beneficial relationship. Jack, a master mechanic, would fix her car and do odd jobs around the house. The previous year, when a tornado had sent her chicken house tumbling across the pasture, Jack had torn it apart and rebuilt it on the original spot. She offered him $10 for his work, but he said $5 would fine if she would make up the rest in canned peaches and green beans. If Jack needed sewing done or had questions about cooking, he would always go to Frances.

***

Twenty minutes later, Jack was pedaling the three miles to his job at the Cotton States Tire reclamation plant in Hokes Bluff. Although Jack was a master mechanic, he didn't own a car because he was unable to pass the vision test for a license. As he pedaled the bicycle, his thoughts wandered back to his childhood.

Jack had never had a family. Born in a home for unwed mothers in Tuscaloosa, he was put up for adoption only days after his birth. During gestation, Jack's left eye, for whatever reason, didn't develop and, when he was born, his left eye socket was a dark, sunken hole with a tiny, withered eye inside that looked straight up. The iris was filled with a milky-colored liquid and he had no sight in the eye. At age six, Jack was sent to the state orphanage at Montgomery, where he grew up. Intelligent and well-behaved, Jack was a good student and, despite his handicap, he excelled at shop classes and showed a talent for mechanics.

Now, at age 43, Jack had carved out a reasonably normal life for himself.

He worked full-time at the tire reclamation company. Hour after hour, he would use a front-end loader to transport old tires from the company warehouse to an incinerator some fifty yards away. It was a dirty, thankless job, but the supervisor left Jack alone and it paid eighty cents an hour, which was a good salary. Jack had no social life. He never went out to eat or to movies or visit friends other than Miss Hathaway, so, once his simple needs were met, he was able to save a large part of his salary.

Once Jack arrived at the plant, he punched in, fired up the front-end loader, and began work. It was an uneventful day. He hauled thirty-three loads of old tires from the warehouse to the incinerator. Just before lunch, the office secretary brought him a piece of cake. She said the owner was celebrating his birthday and he wanted his employees to enjoy it with him. Jack wolfed down the chocolate cake with relish. That afternoon, he punched out at 5:20, then rode his bicycle back down Highway 17 to his home.

***

Back at home, he changed clothes, had a glass of milk, then went across the street to Frances' house. She greeted him, then together they went to the pantry and Jack inspected the light. After removing two screws, he could see the wire to one terminal had burned through and would have to be shortened, then reattached. Jack set about fixing the light. As Jack worked, Frances watched.

Frances Hathaway was one of those unfortunate women who was doomed to remain forever unmarried. First, she was very tall, every inch of six foot four inches and, when she stood beside most men, she towered over them so much there was no semblance of the two being "a couple." Further, she had a long, horse-like face with a huge, prominent nose. Then there was her hair. When she was in her early twenties, the hair on top of her head began to fall out. Not on the sides, only on top. Once the condition set in, she was almost bald-headed by the time she was twenty-five. For a while, she combed her hair so that the hair on the sides would cover the top, but that looked worse than ever. Finally, she settled for wigs, but it seemed that every hairpiece she bought looked more artificial than the last. Now, at fifty-one, she had retired from a department store over in Hamilton with a small pension and, with a garden, chickens, and a cow, she lived quite comfortably.

Once the defective wire was reattached, Jack replaced the housing, then pulled the switch. The light illuminated the pantry.

Frances smiled.

"Thanks," she said, handing him one dollar.

"Can I get a dozen eggs instead?"

"Sure!"

Ten minutes later, they were seated at the table eating meat loaf, green beans, and mashed potatoes.

"How's the beans?" Frances asked. "Did I get enough salt?"

"Beans are perfect."

They ate quietly for several minutes.

"Do you ever miss not having a family?" Frances said.

"Oh, yeah. Many times," Jack said thoughtfully. "Especially when I was young. When I was three or four, I remember the parents coming to the orphanage every year to see the kids who were up for adoption. They would stop and look at me, see my eye, then quickly move on. Kids on either side of me would get adopted, but nobody wanted me because of my eye."

Jack stopped and dipped more mashed potatoes.

"Didn't that bother you?"

"Of course. I knew the parents wanted a child with two good eyes, but there was nothing I could do. After a few years, I just quit hoping."

They ate quietly.

"I know the feeling," Frances said finally. "When I was a teenager, I dreamed of finding a nice boy and getting married and having a family. All around me, my friends were dating and having weddings and kids, but there was nobody for me. After I turned twenty, I kept thinking I would surely be married by the time I was twenty-five. Then when I was in my late twenties, I thought for sure I would be married by the time I was thirty, but it never happened."

"We have to go on in this world," Jack said finally,

helping himself to more meatloaf. "That's all we can do."

"Yeah, maybe you're right. Ready for peach cobbler?"

"Sure."

Moments later, Jack was digging into a bowl of peach cobbler.

Frances watched as he ate.

"They're having all-day singing and dinner on the ground next Sunday at church. You want to go with me and Mildred?"

Frances and her older sister Mildred attended services every Sunday at Old Harmony Baptist.

"No. I think I'll stay home. I've got some things to do."

She peered at him for a long moment.

"Don't you like me?"

"Yes, Miss Hathaway. I like you. Fact is, you're my best friend. I depend on you just like you depend on me, but we shouldn't go spoiling things by getting too serious."

Her head dropped. She looked away without answering.

Visitor

The following morning, Jack was awakened by the roar of high winds and huge sheets of rain pelting the walls and windows of the small clapboard structure. He sat up in bed, threw his feet over the side, and went to the window. To the north, he could see intermittent flashes of lightning followed by bursts of thunder, which rattled the window panes. *It's going to be a miserable ride to work today*, he thought. Quickly, he dressed, went to the kitchen, and took the water bucket to go to the well.

When he opened the front door, he stopped. Huge rivulets of rain were dripping from the roof amid a steady downpour. For a long moment, he waited in the doorway for the rain to slacken, then suddenly, out of the corner of his eye, he noticed a clump of clothing and a suitcase on the porch. Instantly, he was taken aback. He moved closer. Now he could make out the figure of a young woman wearing a flowery head rag and dressed in a heavy men's overcoat. She was asleep. Her back was turned to him. For a long moment, he peered at her without making a move. Then, water bucket in hand, he cautiously moved closer.

"Hello!!" Jack said. "Hello!! Hello!!"

The clump of clothes didn't move.

"Hello!!" Jack said again, louder this time.

The clump of clothes moved slightly and the woman, still half-asleep, turned her face to Jack and opened her eyes. Jack wasn't wearing his eye patch.

"Ooh!" she said, upon seeing Jack.

"Why are you sleeping on my porch?"

The woman sat up and rubbed her eyes. When she sat upright, Jack could see her belly was swollen with child.

"I'm sorry," she said. "I didn't have anywhere to go. My husband and I got into an argument and he pushed me out of the car. This was the nearest house I could find in the rain.

I'm sorry. I don't want to be any trouble."

Jack peered at her.

"Your husband left you out in the rain? And you're carrying his child?"

She nodded.

"I don't want to be a problem. I'll just leave."

She slowly started to stand up but, with her heavy belly, Jack could see it was a chore.

"No! No! You don't have to leave. Maybe I can help you. Where is your family?"

She looked at him as if he had said a dirty word.

"Family? What family?"

"You don't have any family?"

"No."

"And your husband? Where is he now?"

"God only knows."

"You don't have anywhere to go? You don't have anyone to help you?"

The woman shook her head.

Jack studied the woman for a moment. Suddenly, the wind shifted and rain began to blow on the porch.

"Well, you can't stay out here. Let's go inside. Let me see if I can help you."

He reached down and offered his hand. She hesitated.

"What happened to your eye?"

"I was born that way."

She grimaced slightly, then took Jack's hand and he pulled her to her feet. Uncertainly, she stood upright and Jack put his arm under hers for support.

"Come on!" he said, taking her suitcase. "Let's go inside."

***

Moments later, the woman was seated on a small couch. Now that she was out of the heavy overcoat and head cloth, Jack could see that she was in her late thirties, petite and pretty with blonde hair, blue eyes, and long legs. Jack made coffee while they chatted.

"What kind of man would leave his pregnant wife out in the rain?"

"You don't know Carl. He goes crazy when he gets mad."

Jack sat a cup of hot coffee on the table in front of her.

She looked at it, then tasted it.

"Do you have a little sugar?"

Jack brought her a small bowl of sugar. He watched as the woman measured a small amount in a teaspoon, dumped it into the cup, then stirred it.

"We left Birmingham last night and were going to Nashville so he could do another show. We stopped in Trussville for a hamburger and got into an argument. He found out I had been with another man and that's when he put me out of the car. He said this child wasn't his."

Jack studied her.

"I don't want to be no trouble," she continued. "If I didn't have this baby, I wouldn't have stopped."

"I can't put you out like this. Not with you being pregnant and all."

Jack inhaled and pondered her dilemma.

"I've got to go to work right now," he said finally. "But you can stay here today. I'll be back this afternoon and we'll figure this out. There's some beef stew and cornbread and fresh milk in the refrigerator. If you want to rest, you can use my bed over there. I don't have time to change the sheets, but I'll get them out and you can do that."

"That's very kind of you. I promise I won't be too much trouble. All I want to do is have this baby and get back on the road."

Over the next twenty minutes, Jack washed, shaved, and put on fresh clothing and his eye patch. Finally, lunch pail in hand, he started out the door.

"Now make yourself at home. I would feel awful if something bad happened to you."

"You go ahead. I'll be just fine. I'll be here when you get in this afternoon."

"By the way," Jack said. "What's your name?"

"My real name is Wanda Sue Smith, but my stage

name is Suzanne."

"Stage name?"

"Yes. Suzanne Glamore. I'm an entertainer."

Jack had never known an entertainer before.

"Which do you want me to call you?"

"Suzanne!"

"Okay, Suzanne, my name is Jack. I'll see you this afternoon."

***

Ten minutes later, Jack was pedaling the four miles to the tire reclamation plant. The rain had stopped, but the dirt shoulders of the asphalt road were wet and muddy and Jack had to pedal harder to maintain speed. He felt a certain excitement at the prospect of having a woman in his house. Other than Frances, she was the only woman who had ever been inside. Part of him worried that the woman might have the baby while he was at work. Another part of him worried she might steal something and be gone by the time he returned.

That day, Jack loaded only twenty-eight loads of tires into the incinerator. Usually, he would load more than that, but the intermittent rain and mud had slowed down his productivity. Finally, he punched out at 5:22 that afternoon. During the ride back to his home, he wondered what he would find when he arrived.

When Jack opened the door, the woman was at the sink.

"I changed the sheets on the bed and cleaned up your kitchen a little."

"You didn't have to do all of that."

"I wanted to do something.... You helping me and all."

"When are you supposed to have your baby?"

"Next few days."

"I better go over and get my friend Miss Hathaway. She's a midwife and knows about these things. You stay right here."

"I ain't going nowhere."

***

Fifteen minutes later, Jack reappeared with Frances.

"This is Miss Frances Hathaway."

Suzanne gave her a suspicious smile.

"How many babies you delivered?"

"One hundred four."

Suzanne peered at her.

"I guess you'll do. I don't have much choice."

"When's your due date?"

"Doctor in Birmingham said April 21."

"That's three days away."

Frances studied the woman for a long moment, then turned to Jack.

"I'm going to have to examine her. That way, we can get some idea of what to expect. It would be best if you wait outside while I do this."

"I understand," Jack said. "Just tell me what you need."

Over the next thirty minutes, Jack waited outside while Frances examined the woman. Finally, she came out.

"She's going to have this baby in the next couple days. You going to let her stay here?"

"What else can I do? She hasn't got any family or anywhere to go. Aren't there homes for cases like this?"

"There's the home for unwed mothers in Birmingham, but that's more than eighty miles. We can't move her; she's going to have this baby any day."

Jack peered at her thoughtfully.

"Then we don't have much choice."

Frances nodded.

"Well, we better prepare. Can you let her have the full bed?"

"I can do that. I'll clean out the other room and make myself a palette in there."

***

That night, Frances cooked a meal of fried chicken, black-eyed peas, and boiled potatoes.

"My! My!" Suzanne said as they ate. "I hadn't had any home-cooked food in so long, I'd forgotten what it tastes like. All I ever eat is fast food."

"You're going to have to put lots of nourishment in your body," Frances said. "The baby needs it more than you."

They ate quietly for several minutes.

"What are your plans after having the baby?" Frances said.

"Where I'm going, I'm not going to have time for a baby."

"Where are you going?" Frances said.

"I'm going out to Hollywood to be a movie star. I'm going to have my name in lights and everybody in the whole world is going to know who I am."

Frances cast a furtive glance at Jack.

"What are you going to do with the baby?" Frances asked.

"I don't know. I can't take it with me. I guess I'll put it up for adoption."

A long silence as they ate.

Finally, Suzanne spoke.

"Do y'all want this child? It would be a good thing for the both of you, considering neither one of you has a family."

Jack looked at Frances.

"Do y'all want this child?"

"What about the papers?" Jack asked. "You can't just leave the baby here without any legal documents."

"Why not?" Suzanne continued. "Who would ever know what happened but us? This is not Atlanta. Out here in the country, the authorities don't check on those things like they do in the big cities."

Another long silence as they ate.

"Who is the father?" Frances asked.

Suzanne hesitated.

"I'm not sure. It might be Bill's. Then again, the father could be a man I met who was on his way to Texas. We spent a couple nights together in Birmingham."

"I thought you were married," Jack said.

"No, not really," Suzanne continued. "Me and Carl

told everybody we were married for appearances' sake, but we never were. Chances are, if the truth be told, it's Carl's baby."

"He doesn't want the baby?"

She laughed.

"Carl has got even less need for a baby than I do."

A long silence.

"Well, you're going to have the baby first," Frances said finally. "We really can't decide anything until you have the baby."

***

Over the next two days, the mother-to-be stayed at Jack's house and slept in his bed. Both days, while Jack worked, Frances would come in and cook and clean and prepare for the birth. She had brought some old loose-fitting clothes for Suzanne to wear and counselled her to rest, stay quiet, and drink plenty of milk. Also, she had gone into town and stocked up on cloth diapers, baby oil, and powder.

"I've got a little opium the doctor gave me," she said. "When you start to dilate, I'll give you some. It will make the birth a lot easier."

***

On the afternoon of the second day, Jack was dog-tired when he pedaled the bicycle into the front yard. Frances was sitting on the front porch.

"How's she doing?" Jack asked.

"She's asleep right now. She's going to have that baby tonight."

"Is everything ready?"

"I've done all I know to do."

"Then we'll have to wait."

Daniel

That night, Jack was suddenly awakened from a sound sleep by loud screams. At first, he trembled at the sound.

"Push!! Push!" he could hear Frances saying in the other room. "Push! Push with all your might!"

Then there was another loud scream and still another.

Suddenly, the screaming stopped, then there was the sound of a baby crying. The sound sent cold shivers up Jack's spine. Moments later, he was out of bed and in the living room. There he found Frances sitting on the couch rocking a newborn infant in a blanket.

"It's a little boy. And he's a fine one."

For a brief moment, Jack pulled back the edge of the blanket and peered at the sleeping child. Curiously, he used his index finger to feel the soft skin on the baby's arm. At his touch, the child opened its eyes, yawned, and looked straight into Jack's eyes. Still holding Jack's eye, the infant's tiny hand reached out and grasped Jack's finger. Jack started to pull the finger away, but the child clung tenaciously to the finger, so Jack ceased trying to pull it away. The infant continued clutching the finger, then moments later, dozed off to sleep again and released the finger.

Jack smiled happily.

Then he turned back to Frances.

"How's the mother?"

"She's still asleep. She's going to need to rest for a day or two."

Jack didn't reply.

Frances peered at him.

"If she leaves this baby, do you think me and you could take care of it?"

Jack shook his head.

"I'm not sure. It would mean a big change in our lives. Both of our lives."

"Together we could do it. If we organized and planned."

"What about the papers?" Jack asked.

"What about the papers? If we go into town and tell them what happened, they might take the baby away. If we don't say anything, who is going to ask?"

Frances peered at the infant.

"It would be nice to have a child in my life. Wouldn't you like to have a child?"

Jack studied her for a long moment.

"Yes," he said finally.

***

The next morning, Jack was up early. When he went into the living room, Frances was asleep on the couch. As quickly and as quietly as possible, Jack prepared a lunch, washed, shaved, and left for work.

When Suzanne awoke around noon, Frances was waiting with a bowl of chicken soup.

"How you feeling?"

"I'm weak," Suzanne said, sipping the soup. "I need a little time to get my strength back, then I'm going to be gone."

"You've got to stay for a while to nurse this baby."

"How long will that be?"

"Couple or three weeks at least."

"I can't be here that long."

Suzanne finished the soup and handed the bowl back.

"You got a set of bathroom scales?"

"I think I got some in the garage," Frances replied. "I'll have to check."

***

Over the next two days, Frances spent more time at Jack's house than she did her own. In the mornings, before Jack left for work, she would appear and start cooking, cleaning, and washing. One moment, she was counselling Suzanne about giving herself time to recover, then she was changing diapers, supervising nursing, and attending to the baby while Suzanne slept. She had bought an alarm clock so Suzanne could nurse the baby every four hours and a set of bathroom scales.

The moment Suzanne saw the scales, she had to try them.

"My Lord!" she said. "I weigh 123 pounds. I'm going to have to lose some weight before I can go back on the chorus line."

On the third day after the birth, Suzanne said she couldn't stay in bed any longer. Once she was up, she had breakfast, popped open her suitcase, and spread out an array of clothes, shoes, movie star magazines, and an assortment of lipstick, makeup, and fingernail polish. Frances watched curiously as Suzanne applied makeup and lipstick. Once Suzanne was finished, she squeezed herself into a pair of tight blue jeans, slipped on some tennis shoes, and announced she was going for a walk.

"I need to exercise. I got to get back to a size 6."

She was gone for almost an hour.

"My goodness, this is the backwoods around here. What do y'all do for fun?"

"What do you mean?"

"Don't you ever party or go to the movies or just hang out with your friends at the local diner?"

Frances smiled.

"There's too much work to do. We don't have time."

Suzanne shook her head.

"I couldn't live like this. I would go crazy with boredom."

***

Over the next few days, Suzanne occupied herself with walking, doing her nails, and reading the Sears and Roebuck catalog while Frances attended to the baby. At night, Frances would cook and counselled Suzanne she needed to eat.

One night, when Jack arrived home, Frances had another home-cooked meal waiting. Once they sat down to eat,

Suzanne turned to Frances.

"You do a good job being a mama. Much better than me. What are y'all going to call him?"

"We can name him?" Frances said.

"Sure! This baby belongs to y'all as far as I'm concerned."

Frances glanced at Jack, then back to Suzanne.

"Are you truly and honestly going to leave this baby with us?"

"Yes. I'm serious as a heart attack. Don't you believe me?"

Frances looked to Jack. He was helping himself to more mashed potatoes.

A long silence.

"So I'll ask you again. What are y'all going to call him?"

"We'll name him Daniel," Frances said finally. "After the man in the Bible God saved from the lion's den."

"You going to call him Daniel Griffin?"

"We'll call him Daniel Jackson Griffin," Jack said.

"That's a nice name," Suzanne replied.

Once the meal was finished, Frances put away the food, washed dishes, and counselled Suzanne she needed to wake up just around midnight to nurse the baby. Once Frances had gone home for the night, Suzanne and Jack sat on the front porch in the darkness and sipped iced tea. From the nearby river, they could hear a chorus of bullfrogs.

A long silence.

"Frogs are louder than usual tonight," Jack said finally. "I think it's because of the full moon."

Suzanne laughed.

"A full moon will make frogs croak louder?"

"That's right."

"I never heard that," she said, still chuckling. "Y'all people in these hills are just full of wisdom."

They were quiet again. The bullfrogs croaked away. Finally, Jack spoke.

"Can I ask you a question?"

"Sure."

"You think a woman like you could ever be interested in a man like me?"

Suzanne peered curiously at him in the darkness.

"Are you sweet on me?"

"Maybe…. a little. I was just wondering."

"I could never fall for a man like you. We're too different. Way, way too different."

"With this eye patch, I'm not much to look at, but I'm a hard worker, I'm honest, and I try to be a good person."

Suzanne laughed.

"You ever been married, Jack?"

"No."

"Have you ever been with a woman?"

"Yeah. A few times."

Suzanne inhaled, then turned back to him.

"Where I'm going, you would never fit in. Out in Hollywood, you've got to be perfect. What's more, you're too old."

"I'm not all that old. I'm forty-three, six years older than you."

"If I was in Hollywood and people saw me with you, they would say 'what's that beautiful woman doing with that one-eyed man?'"

"When I wear my patch, it don't look all that bad."

"It's pretty bad. You would never pass in Hollywood."

A long silence as Jack sipped his iced tea.

"And you ain't got nothing," Suzanne continued. "I'll bet you don't even own this house."

"No, I don't. I rent, but I work and I keep the rent paid."

Another long silence.

"Don't feel bad, Jack. Men fall in love with me all the time. All I got to do is snap my fingers and men come crawling."

Jack studied her.

"But I appreciate the offer. You and Frances have been really nice to me and I am thankful."

Suddenly, they heard the baby crying.

Suzanne got up.

"I got to go in now and nurse the baby."

***

The following afternoon, when Jack came home from work, Suzanne was alone with the baby. When he walked in, he saw a huge poster of a chorus line on the wall. The caption read "Naughty Girls!" and featured a line of scantily-dressed, lace-stockinged women kicking their heels in the air.

When Jack saw it, he stopped.

"I hope you don't mind me putting up my poster."

"That's fine."

"See the fourth girl from the left?" Suzanne said, getting up to indicate. "That's me! Don't you think I'm beautiful?"

Jack looked at the poster.

"Oh yes. Very pretty."

"The one on the end, the brunette, that's Doris. She's my best friend."

"Very pretty."

Jack turned to go to the bedroom.

"I'm going to change clothes."

"When's the amazon coming over?"

Jack peered at her for a long moment.

"She'll be here. She said she was going to cook tonight."

***

Two hours later, the three of them sat down to a vegetable dinner.

"Is beans and potatoes and cornbread all y'all ever eat around here? Don't you ever have filet mignon or potatoes au gratin?"

"This is not the Ritz," Frances said. "We're poor folks."

Suzanne shook her head in frustration.

"My Lord, I could never live back in these sticks. Y'all are out here in the middle of nowhere. No stores, no theaters.

No restaurants. I couldn't spend my nights listening to the frogs."

"Sometimes we listen to the radio," Jack said.

Suzanne laughed.

"Well, whoop de-do! You ain't even got a television. Y'all know there's a big wide world out there. Right?"

"We're just simple country folks," Jack said.

Suzanne laughed again.

"And an outhouse. I hadn't used an outhouse since I was a little girl visiting my grandmother down in Macon. Oh, Lord, I'll never forget the smell. This kind of living is for country folks. I'm a city girl myself."

Jack looked at Frances.

They ate quietly.

"Jack, can you do me favor?" Suzanne said. "Can you move your patch a little to the left? I can still see inside that blank eye of yours."

Jack looked at Frances.

She nodded slightly.

Instantly, Jack got up from the table and went to the mirror and adjusted the patch.

"Is that better?" he asked, returning to the table.

"A little better," Suzanne replied. "I can still see part of the inside, but I guess it will be okay now."

Jack looked at Frances. She didn't answer.

***

That night, after Suzanne and the baby were asleep, Jack and Frances sat on the front porch in the darkness listening to the frogs.

"I'm going to the church singing with Mildred on Sunday. Do you think you and Suzanne and the baby will be okay for a couple of hours?"

"We'll be fine. Have you told Mildred about the baby?"

"No. I'm going to wait."

"How long? You know when she finds out, she's going to have something to say. Your sister goes by the book."

"I know. I'm going to wait until the time is right."

Exodus

A week passed. All that time, Suzanne was becoming more and more restless. In the mornings, decked out in blue jeans and tennis shoes, she would walk the two miles to the Burma Shave sign on Highway 17, then back to Jack's house. Every day, after returning from her walk, Suzanne would quiz Frances about her appearance.

"How do I look? Can you tell I've lost weight?"

"You're thinner than you were."

"Do I look like the woman in the poster?"

Frances glanced at the poster, then back at Suzanne.

"Pretty close."

You're not lying, are you?" Suzanne said. "Just to be agreeable?"

"Why would I lie about it?"

***

One morning, Frances came early to check on the child, then, satisfied everything was okay, she returned to her house. That afternoon, she heard the baby crying. Instantly, she went back across the highway.

When Frances entered the house, the baby was still wailing and Suzanne was on the floor doing sit-ups.

"Don't you hear that baby?" Frances asked.

"Yeah, I hear it, but I don't know what to do. I don't know nothing about babies."

Frances went to the child.

Moments later, the baby was quiet again.

"What's was wrong?" Suzanne asked.

"A diaper pin was sticking it."

"I would never know to check for something like that."

Frances studied her for a moment.

"Don't you have any feelings for this baby?"

"Yeah. I have feelings for it. I wouldn't want to see anything happen to it, but I can't honestly say I love it. I don't need it. I've got too many other things in my life."

Frances studied her for a moment.

"How did you grow up?" she asked. "What kind of parents did you have?"

"My parents were divorced when I was three and I was raised by my father and my stepmother. My daddy owned a hotel on Atlanta's east side and he ran women. My daddy abused me and treated me like the women he ran. To my daddy, all women were split-tails. Me included. That's why I ran away from home when I was fifteen."

"Sounds like you didn't have much of a childhood. Is that why you're so cold-hearted?"

Suzanne stopped at the word.

"Cold-hearted? Is that what I am?"

She peered thoughtfully at Frances.

"Yeah. I guess you could say I'm cold-hearted. That's how you become when you're raised like I was. You get hard or you don't survive. That's one thing I learned from my daddy. He used to say: 'If you don't take care of number one, nobody else will.' He said that's the only way to make it in this world. Yeah. I'm cold-hearted because I have had to survive."

Frances didn't reply.

"And that's what's going to make me a star out in Hollywood. I'm going to do whatever I have to do to make it. They say that all a pretty girl has to do is give it up and those producers will make a big star out of you."

"You've already given it up a few times."

"Yeah," Suzanne replied. "I guess you could say that. I like to enjoy myself. I am a natural woman."

Frances studied her for a long moment.

"You're a Jezebel."

Instantly, livid anger flashed across Suzanne's face

"A Jezebel? You calling me a whore? That's easy for you to say! Look at me! I can get a man. You can't!!"

Instantly, she was in Frances' face.

"Did you hear what I said? I'm not like you. My hole

is not dry. I can get a man!"

Itching for a fight, she grabbed Frances' arm.

"Are you listening to me?"

Instantly, Frances slapped her hand away.

"I heard what you said."

Suzanne, fire in her eyes, wasn't finished.

"You think because I'm staying here with y'all, you can call me names and insult me? I know what you holier-than-thou Christian types are all about. You go judging people with your Bible stories. Hypocrites! That's what you are! All of you are just a bunch of hypocrites. Do you hear me?"

When Frances didn't respond right away, Suzanne grew even angrier.

"Do you hear me?" she shouted. "Hypocrites! That's all you are!"

Frances, calmer now, backed away.

"I'm sorry. I shouldn't have said it."

"That's right. You shouldn't have said it. Your mouth is bigger than your brain. You got any more questions?"

Frances peered at her.

"Yeah. Why are you so mean to Jack?"

"You mean about his eye patch and all?"

"Yes. He's very sensitive about it."

"I wasn't being mean. I was just telling the truth."

"Some things are better left unsaid."

"Not for me. The truth never hurt nobody."

***

At the end of that week, Suzanne was fit to be tied.

"I can't stay here any longer," she said over dinner one night. "I've got to get back on the chorus line. I want to know if y'all will help me."

"What do you need?" Jack said.

"First, I need to make some phone calls."

"I have a phone," Frances said. "You can use it to make whatever calls you want."

"They're long-distance. To Nashville and Birmingham. And I don't have any money."

"That's okay," Frances said. "I'll be glad to help you."

They ate quietly.

"And I need a couple new dresses. I saw some nice ones in the Sears and Roebuck catalog."

"Pick out the ones you want and I'll pay for them," Jack said.

"Thanks! Y'all been really nice to me."

The following morning, Suzanne showed Jack and Frances the dresses she wanted. Frances called in the order so the dresses would arrive faster.

***

Over the next few days, Suzanne prepared for her exodus. Every morning, she would put on jeans and tennis shoes and walk the two miles from Jack's house along the highway to the Burma Shave sign and back. At night, over the objections of Frances, she ate little or nothing and spent the days reading movie star magazines, chatting with Frances, and primping.

On Friday of that week, over dinner with Jack and Frances, she announced she was back to a size 6.

"When my new dresses get here, I'll be gone."

The two dresses arrived in the mail the following Thursday. Since Jack didn't have a full-length mirror, Suzanne went to Frances' house to try them on. She was happy with the fit and, after trying on several pairs of shoes, she found some she felt matched the dresses.

That afternoon, she made long-distance calls to Nashville and Birmingham on Frances' phone.

Frances sat in the living room and listened.

"It's the first farm on the left after the Burma Shave sign. There will be a red barn on the left side of the road with a 'See Rock City' sign. You can't miss it."

A pause.

"10:30 tomorrow? Okay. I'll be waiting."

***

Over dinner that night, she announced to Jack and Frances that she was leaving the following morning.

"We're going to need some information for the birth certificate," Jack said.

"What kind of information?"

"What's your real name?" Jack asked.

"My real name is Wanda Sue Smith from Decatur, Ga. I was born Sept. 9, 1918. If anybody wants to be sure of my identity, I've got a heart-shaped tattoo on my right arm."

She pulled up her sleeve to show them the tattoo.

"That tattoo is what police call an 'identifying characteristic.' I guess you could say it's mine. What else do you want to know?"

"Who should we put down as the father?" Jack asked.

"Yourself. I don't know who the real father is."

Jack and Frances looked ominously at one another.

"Anything else? Suzanne asked.

"Will we ever hear from you again?"

"Probably not."

***

The next morning, Jack was up early and went to work. At 10:30, Frances, the baby, and Suzanne, decked out in one of her new dresses, were waiting on the front porch at Frances' home, when a new Ford sedan pulled into the yard.

"Well, I guess this is good-bye," Suzanne said, picking up her suitcase. "I want to thank you and Jack for helping me."

"We were happy to do it."

Suzanne took a letter out of her purse.

"Give this to Jack."

Frances took the letter.

Suzanne turned to the baby.

"Oh, little Daniel. I wish you well in this world. These people will love you and take care of you because your mama sure can't. Especially at this time in my life. So I'm leaving you with these people, knowing that you will be safe and in good hands."

Then she kissed the baby on the forehead and gave Frances an awkward hug.

"Please take care of Daniel."

Moments later, she went down the steps and got into the waiting car. As the vehicle pulled out on the highway, Suzanne waved good-bye one last time.

"If you want to write, send me a letter addressed to Suzanne Glamore, Hollywood California. I'll get it."

Then she waved again. Frances watched as the sedan sped off down the highway.

***

That night, Jack read Suzanne's letter.

Dear Jack:

Thanks for all the things you and Frances did for me. I don't know how I would have made it without y'all. I wanted to tell you that I took $200 out of your stash in the shed. I knew you had money hidden out there when you went to get the money for the COD for the dresses. I know you won't miss it. That will buy me a bus ticket to Los Angeles and living expenses for a while. By then, I'll be a big star and I'll pay you back. As for the baby, he belongs to you and that amazon woman that lives across the street. I don't have time to go before a judge and declare myself the mother of that baby and sign a bunch of papers. I know y'all will love that child and take care of him. I wish y'all the best. Thanks for everything.

Suzanne.

Jack folded the letter thoughtfully then went to the bedroom and placed it inside an old shoe box where he kept important papers. Then he went outside to the tool shed in the back yard. Inside, he reached down a fruit jar where he kept cash. Last time he had checked, there was just over $200 inside. It was empty. Instantly, he went to the corner of the shed and pulled a heavy canvas cloth from atop an old planting plow. Then he reached inside and withdrew another fruit jar. He opened it and counted the money.

There was $723 inside. All of the money was still there. Quickly, he replaced the lid and returned the jar to its hiding place, then left the shed and started across the highway to Frances' house.

Mildred

Ten minutes later, Jack was across the highway at Frances' house. When he walked in, Daniel was asleep.

"Sit down," she said. "We need to talk."

Jack took a seat on the sofa.

"It would be best if Daniel lives with me. I can't be running across the highway at midnight to feed him or change his diaper. I've got indoor plumbing and more room, so he can spread out as he grows."

"That's fine."

"Also, we're going to need a few things. A cradle, a stroller, and a high chair. Also, we're going to have to get a goat."

"A goat?"

"Yes. This baby has got to have fresh milk every day at least for a few more weeks. Remember, his mother is not here anymore."

"I'll see what I can do. Is that everything?"

"For now."

Frances studied him for a moment.

"Jack, do you think we can raise this child?"

"I don't see why not. We'll have to be organized and work together, but I believe we can do it."

She smiled.

"Yes. I believe we can too."

"Now you're the expert in these things," he continued. "Just tell me what I need to do and I'll do it."

"Thanks, Jack. Thanks so much!!"

***

The following morning, a Saturday, Jack, Frances, and the baby loaded up in Frances' car and went into Hokes Bluff to the second-hand store.

"Frances!" Mrs. Henderson, the store proprietor, said upon seeing the infant. "Is this your new baby?"

"Oh, no, he's not my child. This is a nephew of mine. I'll be keeping him for a while."

"That's nice," Mrs. Henderson said. "Babies always brighten up a household."

Over the next thirty minutes, they found a cradle for two dollars and a high chair with a broken leg. Once Jack had inspected it, he said he could fix it and Frances offered one dollar. The woman accepted.

When Frances asked about strollers, the proprietor said they didn't have any in stock at the moment. After Jack spotted an old used stroller with two wheels missing, he asked about it.

"Oh, that old thing," the woman said. "That's from the thirties. It's still got the white ceramic handles. You wouldn't want that."

Frances looked at Jack.

"I can fix it," he said.

"I'll give you a dollar," Frances said.

"Sold!"

Before they left, Frances also bought two baby blankets, an electric bottle warmer, and some used baby clothes.

Once the goods were loaded, they were driving back home.

"Now that's the story we're going to tell," Frances said. "If anybody wants to know how we got this baby, we're going to tell them he's my nephew and we're going to be keeping him for a while."

"What if people ask where your sister lives or her name?"

"You don't have to provide too many details. Just say it's my nephew and leave it at that. Can you remember that?"

"I'll remember."

That afternoon, Jack rode his bicycle over to a farm near Hamilton and bought a goat. Since Jack had no way to transport the animal, he paid the farmer to deliver it to Frances' farm.

***

By the end of the first week, Jack and Frances had laid the groundwork for their great adventure. Before leaving for work every day, Jack would stop at Frances' house and check on her and Daniel. If she needed grocery items, Jack would make a list and pick them up on his way home. Once he arrived home, he went directly to Frances' house and provided her some "relief," as she called it. Frances taught Jack how to milk the goat and strain and boil the milk before it was fed to the baby. Very quickly, he became quite expert at warming baby bottles, changing diapers, and burping the infant.

Over the next few weeks, again and again, Frances found herself consulting *Miss Busby's Original Guide to Midwifery*, her long-time personal Bible on the subject. She had delivered over a hundred children, but she had never faced the task of raising one. As a result, she had to bone up on all of the dos and don'ts of infant care. The child had to have a rigid feeding schedule; his bottle had to be warmed to just the right temperature; the child's sleeping environment had to be just so; the list was endless. Also, Frances, an avid newspaper and magazine reader, found herself constantly clipping and saving articles on infant care.

On Saturday mornings, which they dubbed "diaper day," Jack would get up early and build a fire around the old wash pot in Frances' backyard. Once the diapers were boiled and clean, Jack would fish them out, place them in a wicker basket, then hold the basket while Frances strung the wet diapers along a clothesline. After he had repaired the leg on the high chair, Jack bought the materials and made a cradle. He painted it light baby blue and, in darker blue on either side, he stenciled the word "Daniel." At his work, Jack found an old toy wagon in a storage shed, which had wheels that perfectly matched those on the stroller. He asked if he could have it. Once the supervisor approved, Jack took the wagon home and placed all four wheels on the old baby stroller. Frances was delighted.

By the end of the first month, Jack and Frances were

on a firm schedule. Jack continued to work and Frances divided up her time between Daniel and her farm duties. Jack already had his own garden well underway, but Frances, due to the additional time she was spending with the baby, asked Jack to help with hers. She asked him to string pole beans and make tomato beds. Also, there was a leak in the barn roof and she asked that he repair it. He was happy to oblige.

***

By late May, Jack and Frances had had Daniel for a month. Daniel was a good baby. If he was crying, she could rest assured something was wrong. His diaper needed changing, he was hungry, a safety pin was sticking him. He was not the kind of child who cried for no reason. After the first month, he began to sleep through the night without crying. And he was a very active child. Sometimes, early in the morning, he would awaken early and Frances would hear him jabbering to himself. She would get up and go to the crib and, upon seeing her, Daniel would kick and make noise until Frances picked him up.

One afternoon when Jack came in from work, Frances announced it was time to tell Mildred.

"We're becoming very attached to this child. We need to have some idea of where we stand."

"What if she wants to take the child away?"

Frances took a deep breath.

"I'm going to try to convince her not to. We can't hide it from her forever. She's my sister."

"I guess you're right."

***

The next morning, a Saturday, a late model sedan pulled up in the front yard at Frances' farmhouse and a middle-aged, smartly-dressed woman got out. Mildred Gibson was tall for a woman, almost six feet, but she didn't strike the amazon appearance of her younger sister. Dressed in a gray business suit, she was in her late fifties and had been widowed for several years. She had married young and had three children, two of which now had families of their own. Her youngest child, Andy, had been killed in an auto accident as a teenager. For over twenty years now, she had been the director of children's welfare services in Tallapoosa County. As a public servant, she was a member of the Tallapoosa County's auxiliary police force. She had arrest powers and she knew how to shoot a gun.

"Oh, baby sister!" Mildred said upon getting out of the car. "How you been doing?"

Frances leaned her towering frame down to hug her older sister.

"I'm doing fine."

Mildred turned to Jack.

"Hi, Jack!!"

"Morning, Mildred."

"So what is this surprise you want to show me?" Mildred said.

"Come on in," Frances replied.

Inside, Frances led Mildred to the second bedroom.

Instantly, Mildred was taken aback upon she saw the sleeping baby.

"My God!" she said. "A baby? Where did you get a baby?"

Frances explained what happened.

"What are you going to do with it?"

"Me and Jack are going to raise it."

"Baby sister, are you out of your mind? You can't keep this child!"

"Why not? You know I've always wanted a child."

"Yeah, but not like this. This is not the way you do it."

The two sisters studied one another for a moment, then Mildred turned back to the cradle.

"He's a beautiful little boy."

"If it's at all possible," Frances said, "I'm going to keep this child. Jack wants him too."

"In the eyes of the law, you don't have a legal claim. Since the child was abandoned, he should be put into an orphanage."

"He'll never get the kind of love in an orphanage he'll get from me and Jack. What do I have to do to get a legal claim? Can I adopt him?"

"You could, but that's a long process. You would have to get approval from the proper authorities and have legal papers drawn. Also, since you're a single woman, it might be impossible."

"What if the mother is nowhere to be found?"

Mildred shook her head in indecision.

"You would still have to go through the legal process."

Mildred stopped. She still couldn't believe it.

"Are you two really serious about this?"

Frances was unflinching.

"We're dead serious."

Mildred turned to Jack.

"And you're going to help her raise this child?"

"Yes. I've always wanted a child to care for. Neither one of us have ever had a family."

Mildred took a deep breath, looked from one to the other, then back at the child. She shook her head.

"This is just too strange. Too crazy. What do you want me to do?"

"I want you to tell us what we have to do to keep this child," Frances said.

"I've told you," Mildred said. "Sooner or later, you'll have to prove you have a legal right."

Mildred looked from Jack to Frances.

"You know it's my job to report cases like this."

"I know that," Frances said. "Suppose we went ahead and raised the child and you never said anything? Couldn't you make an exception? For me?"

"Oh, my God, I know how much you've always wanted a child."

Mildred looked from one to the other.

"I could lose my job if I don't report it."

"I know," Frances said. "You couldn't do it for me?"

Mildred shook her head indecisively.

"I guess I could just look the other way. I could pretend I didn't know anything about this child."

"Who's going to know?" Frances said.

"But if somebody else brings attention to it, I've got to enforce the law."

"Oh, Mildred!" Frances said. "It would mean so much to me and Jack."

"I'll protect you as long as I can," Mildred said. "But if a third party brings it to my attention, I'll have to file a case."

"Thanks!" Frances said. "I knew I could depend on you."

"Thanks!" Jack said.

"As far as I'm concerned, I don't know anything about this child. We'll let it ride and we'll see what happens. But I wouldn't be advertising the fact that you have him. The more people who know about him, the more people who can start asking questions."

"I know," Frances said. "We'll keep it quiet."

Mildred was still peering into the crib.

"He's such a beautiful child."

Raising Daniel

So with renewed confidence they could escape with raising Daniel as their own, Jack and Frances continued their great adventure.

One spring morning, three days after Daniel celebrated his first birthday, Frances was washing dishes at the sink and Daniel was playing in a nearby playpen Jack had made. The child was making baby talk and banging a plastic toy hammer on the sides of the playpen.

Frances turned to him and smiled.

"Hey, baby," she said.

Daniel looked up and smiled.

"Mama! Mama!" he suddenly blurted out. Then he banged the plastic hammer on the sides of the playpen. "Mama! Mama!"

Frances stopped. Her eyes filled with tears. She never dreamed she would ever hear those words directed to her.

She went to the playpen, picked up the child, and clutched it to her breast.

"Mama! Mama!" the child said again and again. "Mama! Mama!"

***

One night after dinner at Frances' house, Jack was sitting on the front porch sipping iced tea and listening to the frogs.

"Jack!" Frances called.

Immediately, Jack went inside and found Frances and Daniel on the living room floor. The child was playing with several magazines scattered about the floor.

"Watch this!" Frances said.

She gathered several magazines nearest the child and placed them several feet away. Instantly, Daniel's face screwed up with annoyance. Then, he stood up, took several halting steps to the magazines, and sat down again.

Jack burst out in joyful laughter.

Then Frances, giggling with delight, again moved the magazines away from the child. Again, he stood up, took several steps to the magazines, then plopped to the floor on his bottom again.

"He's walking," Jack said.

Frances shook her head with pure amazement and joy.

***

As he grew older, Jack and Frances could see that Daniel was going to grow up to be an alert, curious child. With deep blue eyes and a headful of blonde curly hair, he was highly intelligent and interested in anything and everything.

"I want to keep this child busy," Frances said. "Idle hands are the devil's workshop."

With Daniel, Frances now had a way of sharing her knowledge and education with a small child. That had always been a dream of hers. So only days after his second birthday, she ordered children's books, a small blackboard, and educational games out of the Sears and Roebuck catalog. She taught him the ABC song, his numbers, and how to spell simple words. Day after day, she worked with him. She taught him to color, draw, and finger-paint. One of his favorite activities was singing children's songs. Once Daniel had heard a song a few times, he quickly memorized it and, at night, long after he was supposed to be asleep, Frances would hear him in his room singing "Mary had a Little Lamb" and "Old McDonald had a Farm."

Frances, an expert seamstress, had an old pedal-powered sewing machine and she made Daniel's shirts out of flour sacks. Each time she bought flour at the grocery, she would check the pattern to be sure she had a different one. Then, back at home, she would measure and snip and sew together the shirts.

***

When he turned three, Frances began to give him chores. First, she taught him to bring the chickens into the henhouse for the night. In the afternoons, when Daniel saw Frances take the milk bucket from the side cupboard, he knew she was going to milk the cow, and instantly, in his black baseball cap, white shirt, and blue denim overalls, he would fall in lockstep behind her.

Before she started milking, she would send him into the nearby field with a small container of crushed corn. Once the chickens heard the child's tapping on the side of the metal container, they would instantly stop whatever they were doing and come running. The child would scatter a tiny bit of the corn on the ground, then head back to the chicken enclosure behind the barn. Instantly, the chickens would gobble down what feed was on the ground, then run after the child. Once all of the birds were inside the enclosure, Daniel would dump the remainder of the corn into a feed trough. Finally, as the farm fowl ate, Daniel would gather the eggs then lock the door behind him for the night.

"Look, Mama!" he would say proudly, displaying the eggs. "Look at all the eggs I found."

"My! My!" Frances would say. "You're such a big boy! We'll have plenty of eggs for breakfast."

***

For his fourth birthday, Frances put together a birthday party with cake, ice cream, and presents. In attendance were Jack, Frances, and Mildred, and the excited child couldn't wait to open his presents. Jack had bought a wind-up bulldozer and some toy dump trucks. Frances had bought clothes while Mildred had bought several children's books and a toy bubble maker. After the party, Frances and Mildred sat on the front porch and watched Daniel as he played in the front yard. He would dip the plastic hoop into the slippery liquid, then blow bubbles in the air. After marveling for a few seconds, he would run after them and, at just the right moment, gleefully pop them with his finger. At one point, as Mildred watched, she made a startling observation.

"I'll swear, Daniel is the spitting image of Andy," she said, referring to her late son.

Frances nodded.

"He does look a lot like Andy."

"It's scary," Mildred continued. "When I see him running across the yard, it's almost like Andy has come back to earth."

Frances peered at her sister.

Mildred's face was white as a sheet.

"Oh, God! Oh my God!" she said.

"What's wrong?"

"Look at him!"

"What is it?" France asked again.

"Look at the way he runs! The way he holds his head! It's Andy! I tell you, it's him! Andy has been sent back to me! God has sent Andy back to me!"

Suddenly, Mildred burst into tears of joy. For a moment, she sobbed uncontrollably as Frances watched helplessly. Frances had not seen her sister cry since she was a small child.

Moments later, Daniel, finished playing with the bubble maker, bounded onto the porch.

"Come give your Aunt Mildred a hug!" Mildred said.

Dutifully, the child went to her and hugged her.

"Thanks for the bubble maker. I love you, Aunt Mildred."

"I love you too, baby."

Daniel pulled back and looked at her.

"Why have you been crying?"

"I don't know," she said, wiping her eyes.

"Don't cry, Aunt Mildred," he said, patting her shoulder. "It's okay. Don't cry! Everything is going to be all right."

Mildred looked at Frances, pure joy in her face, then turned back at Daniel.

"My! My! You're such a fine boy!"

***

Over the next year, Daniel became Jack's shadow. Everything Jack did, Daniel thought he had to do it. While building a new floor for the back porch, Daniel watched closely as Jack put a piece of lumber on a saw horse, then cut it to the desired length with a handsaw. Once the piece had been cut, Daniel wanted to try it himself. Although Daniel's hand was much too small for the saw's handle, Jack placed the tiny hand inside it, wrapped his own hand around the child's, and went through the motions of cutting the new piece. Once cut, Daniel, his face swelling with pride, looked to Jack for approval.

"Good job!!" Jack said.

Jack was always making toys for Daniel. He would spend endless hours carving little wood figures of men and animals for Daniel to play with. In the backyard at Frances' house, Jack built a spinning jenny. Hour after hour, he and Daniel, whose short legs could barely touch the ground, would spin round and round on the contraption, all the while Daniel squealing with pure joy. Sunday afternoons would always find Jack and Daniel in the backyard at Frances' house playing ball or catching lightning bugs or flying a kite. If Jack wasn't at work, Daniel was at his side.

***

One spring day, Jack took Daniel fishing for the first time at the river behind his house. Together, they dug bait. Jack spaded up huge shovelfuls of dirt behind the shed and Daniel, unafraid of the rapidly wiggling creatures, got down on his knees, gathered the earthworms, and placed them in a tin can. Then Jack rigged up cane poles. Once they arrived at the fishing hole, Jack showed Daniel how to put the worm on the hook and adjust the float. When Daniel caught his first fish, he squealed with pure delight. That day, they caught eleven hand-sized bream.

Upon arriving home, Daniel presented the fresh fish to Frances.

"Look, Mama!"

"Oh, my!!" she said. "Did you catch these?"

"Yep," he said proudly. "Will you cook them for supper?"

"I sure will."

***

Every Christmas, Daniel couldn't wait to receive presents from his "Aunt Mildred." She always bought expensive presents, gifts that Jack and Frances couldn't afford and, when her car pulled into the yard on his fifth Christmas, Daniel went bounding down the porch steps to meet her.

"Aunt Mildred! What did you get me?"

Once inside, he quickly began opening gifts. The first one he opened was a toy football. The moment he pulled the inflatable football out of its box, his first reaction was "We don't have any way to blow it up."

"You haven't opened all of your presents," Mildred said.

Daniel looked at her and smiled. The additional presents included a needle and a tire pump for inflating the football.

"My Aunt Mildred thinks of everything," Daniel said.

"Your Aunt Mildred is very thorough," Jack said.

"She likes to see things get done," Frances said. "And done right."

Twenty minutes later, the football was inflated and Jack and Daniel were in the front yard tossing it back and forth. In later years, it would prove to be a gift that would change Daniel's life.

When Mildred left that day, Daniel went to her and gave her a hug.

"Thanks for the football," he said. "I love you, Aunt Mildred."

"I love you too, baby."

The Accident

At the age of five, fishing in the river on Saturdays had become a ritual for Jack and Daniel. When Jack arrived home from work on Fridays, Daniel announced he wanted to go fishing the following morning. One Saturday morning in the early fall of 1960, Jack and Daniel were preparing to go fishing. While Jack rigged the lines, Daniel went behind the shed to dig bait. The container he was using for bait was a small tin can with the jagged edge of its lid still attached. Once the can was filled with earthworms, Daniel went running back around the side of the shed, carrying the bait in the tin can. As he rounded the corner, he slipped and fell and the tin lid of the can cut a nasty gash across his right cheek. Instantly, when Jack saw the blood flowing, he picked up the child and rushed to Frances.

"We're going to have to take him to the doctor."

Once Frances had stopped the flow of blood with a towel, the three started to Dr. Morgan's office in Hokes Bluff. Both Jack and Frances had known Dr. Morgan for years. He had been the attending physician on several of the births Frances had overseen as a midwife.

"What are we going to tell the doctor about Daniel?" Jack asked as they rode in Frances' car to the doctor's office.

"I'm going to tell him what we've been telling everyone else. Daniel is my nephew. I'll go in with Daniel. I'll talk to Dr. Morgan."

Once Frances signed in, Dr. Morgan, a late-fiftyish balding man wearing thick glasses, examined the child.

"A bad cut," he said. "He's going to need some stitches."

Moments later, he was sewing up the cut.

"Frances, I didn't know you had a child."

Frances froze at the question. She could feel her hands start to tremble.

"It's my younger sister's child," she said nervously. "I've been keeping him."

"You got a sister other than Mildred?" he asked. "I thought she was your only sister."

"Oh, no!" Frances lied, trying to stay calm. "I have a younger sister in Wetumpka."

"I never knew that," he said. "How long you had this boy?"

"A few years now," she replied.

Frances moved to change the subject.

"Dr. Morgan, do you think he could get an infection from this?"

"I'll give you some penicillin," Dr. Morgan replied. "That will take care of it."

Long silence.

"Your sister in Wetumpka," Dr. Morgan said. "What's her name?"

Frances could feel her throat tightening with the new question.

"Gladys," she lied again, wanting desperately to change the subject. "Is your son still down at the university?"

"Oh yes," he replied. "He's doing quite well in his studies. Made the dean's list again last semester. I'm expecting great things from him when he graduates."

Frances was relieved that he didn't return to the original subject.

"I'm sure he'll make a fine doctor," Frances said. "Just like this father."

Moments later, he was finished

"Okay," Dr. Morgan said. "Looks like he's all fixed again. Bring him back in two weeks and I'll remove the stitches."

Frances, relieved that the conversation was over, quickly left the office.

***

One day, when he was five, Daniel was sitting in Jack's lap when he noticed the eye patch for the first time. For a long moment, Daniel stared at the patch, then reached out and pulled it back so he could see inside Jack's deformed eye. Jack didn't move to stop him.

Daniel didn't react when he saw the deformed eye. For a long moment, he peered at it curiously. After a moment, he returned the patch to its original position, then he opened and closed the flap several times.

"I want to do it," Daniel said.

Jack removed the eye patch, shortened the string, and placed the patch over Daniel's eye. He ran to a mirror.

He laughed out loud when he saw himself.

"I look like my daddy," he said with a squeal of joy.

Moments later, he returned the patch to Jack.

Once Jack had replaced the eye patch, Daniel hugged him.

"I love you, Daddy," he said.

School

In the early spring of 1961, it was time for Daniel to go to school. On the first day of enrollment, Frances took her pride and joy to Hokes Bluff Elementary School to enroll him in the first grade. At the school, she met the principal and, on the enrollment forms, she listed Jack as the child's father and herself as mother. Later, she met Daniel's first grade teacher and introduced Daniel. Frances explained she had done some home teaching and the child already knew his ABCs, how to count, and do simple math. The teacher said she felt the child would be a good student and she looked forward to having him in her class.

When Frances prepared to leave, the school principal explained that before the child was officially enrolled, he had to go to the county health department to get his vaccinations. Frances promised to take care of it. That afternoon, Frances and Daniel went into town and bought school books, new clothes, and school supplies to prepare him for his first year at school.

***

The following week, she took Daniel to the health department to get his vaccinations. After she filled out the forms, the clerk examined them.

"The county health department doesn't have a birth certificate for your child. Can you provide one for our records?"

Suddenly, fear filled Frances' heart. This was the moment she had been dreading.

"I don't have one."

"Was the child born in Tallapoosa county?"

"No, he was born in Wetumpka County," Frances lied.

"We have to have a valid birth certificate before we can give a student a vaccination. It's a state law."

"Let me see what I can do."

When she returned home, the first thing she did was call Mildred.

"I was afraid of something like this," Mildred said. "Let's talk to the lawyer. We've got to know exactly where the law stands on this."

***

Attorney Cecil Grambling was a stocky, middle-aged man with a balding head, sagging jowls, and a constant scowl on his face. When Mildred, Jack, and Frances took a seat in his office two days later, he came straight to the point.

"How did y'all get possession of this child?"

Jack explained the episode with Suzanne.

"You haven't broken any laws," he said. "You can file a delayed birth certificate. It requires the date and place of birth, names of both parents, the child's name, and the signature of the person attending the birth."

"That's all?" Mildred said. "We don't have to swear to anything?"

"No," the attorney continued. "Just fill out the form. Then you'll have to sign an affidavit stating that all of the information is true and correct. I wouldn't lie, although people do it all the time. Now, I should warn you that when the birth certificate reaches the state health department in Montgomery, they may have some questions."

"We can deal with that," Mildred said.

That afternoon, Mildred, Frances, and Jack went to the county health department and filed a delayed birth certificate. The mother was listed as Wanda Sue Smith and the father as "unknown." Afterward, both Jack and Frances signed the affidavit. Once they had an official birth certificate, Frances showed it to the clerk at the county health department and Daniel received his vaccinations.

***

Two weeks later, while Jack was at work, a sheriff's car appeared at Frances' house. A deputy got out and Frances met him at the door.

"I have a court summons," he said. "Sign here."

After signing, Frances opened the document and read it.

"You are being summoned to appear at the Tallapoosa Courthouse at 9 a.m. on October 3, 1961 for a custody hearing regarding the case of Daniel Jackson Griffin vs. The State of Alabama."

Moments later, Frances was calling Mildred.

***

The following day, they were back in Cecil Grambling's office.

"The state wants to know why the child hasn't been in the orphanage in Montgomery for the past six years," the attorney said. "They're going to try to take the child."

"Why would the orphanage be so anxious to take custody?" Mildred asked.

"They want the $2,100 the state pays every year for the care of a new child. It all comes down to money. You're going to have to appear and answer charges as to why you have this child."

"Can they take Daniel away from Jack and Frances?" Mildred asked.

"They can if we don't put up a good case. In such cases, the first thing the court has to do is try to locate the child's mother. If they can locate her, they will determine whether she is fit to take custody. If they can't locate her, they'll have to find an alternative. Do you know anything about the mother's whereabouts?"

"No," France said. "Last time we saw her, she said she was going to California to be a movie star."

"California is a big state. Did she mention a city? Names of friends or relatives?"

"No," Frances replied. "She said to send a letter to Hollywood, California in her name and she would get it."

“We’ll need to hire a private investigator to try to find her. That will take a while and it’s expensive.”

“How much is expensive?” Frances said.

“Around $250.”

Frances inhaled.

“Whew!”

She looked to Jack.

“Can you help with that?”

“It will wipe out my savings, but I can do it.”

“What about your fee?” Mildred asked.

“I’ll need $500 to handle the case.”

The two sisters looked at one another.

“We can handle that,” Mildred said.

Custody hearing

The Tallapoosa County Courthouse was a four-story, white-washed stucco building that took up an entire block on Broad Street between Eight and Ninth Avenues in Hamilton. When Circuit Judge Tom Murphy took his seat on the bench on the morning of Nov. 3, 1961, Jack, Frances, and Mildred were seated with their attorney at one of the counsel tables. On the opposite side of the aisle was Will Patterson, a tall, early-thirties man wearing glasses and smoking a pipe, representing the state. Once Judge Murphy rapped the gavel, the courtroom grew quiet.

"We're here today to decide the custody case of Daniel Jackson Griffin," the judge began. "Mr. Patterson, state your case."

"Your honor, first of all, I want to say I'm not sure what happened here. This child's birth record either fell through the cracks in the system or someone tried to deliberately hide it. Personally, I suspect the latter."

"What do you mean!" the judge asked.

"First, a birth certificate was not filed until six years after the birth. This child has been hidden from state purview for six years."

The judge shook his head.

"I can't see that any laws were broken. A delayed birth certificate has been filed. There is nothing unusual in that."

"This child should have been handed over to the state orphanage the day he was born."

"You're beating a dead horse," the judge said. "A birth certificate has been filed. What are your other objections?"

The attorney stopped, shuffled through some papers, then turned to face the judge again.

"Your honor, I have to tell the court that this child's care-givers, Jack Griffin and Frances Hathaway, not only have no legal right to this child, but they can't provide the same opportunities that are available at the state's orphanage."

"What are you saying?" the judge said.

"This couple is unfit to raise this child. This man lives alone in a rude shack outside of town. For transportation, he rides a bicycle. Furthermore, he works at a lowly job at a tire reclamation plant. The woman is fifty-seven years old, far too old to raise a young child. Also, she is a poor pensioner who ekes out a living from her small farm..."

The judge interrupted.

"That's not unusual. Most everybody I know around here just ekes out a living," he said with a grin. "Sometimes I think that's all I do... just eke out a living."

A ripple of laughter from the audience.

"Please continue," the judge said.

"This child should be in an environment where he can be around boys his own age. This child should be able to broaden his social horizons so he will have friends for the future. The services the orphanage offers are much broader and richer than what he currently has."

He stopped and shuffled through some papers. For a long moment, he read a document, then turned back to the judge.

"Lastly, Jack Griffin and Frances Hathaway live in separate homes and are not married. That's not a proper environment for a small child."

"Hold it!" the judge said, turning to Jack and Frances' attorney.

"Mr. Grambling," he said. "Is that correct? Your clients aren't married?"

"That's correct, your honor."

For a moment, the judge peered at Jack and Frances, made a note on a legal pad, then returned to the state's attorney.

"Please continue."

"Finally, I want to impress upon the court that, as the state sees it, this child needs a structured, socially viable environment so he can grow up to be a stable, productive citizen. He doesn't have that at the moment. The orphanage will offer that."

Attorney Grambling rose to his feet.

"Your honor, for the past six years, Daniel Griffin has had a happy, healthy home environment with Jack Griffin and Frances Hathaway. He has developed a strong sense of self; he has a healthy social attitude and is an excellent student. While the circumstances through which this couple obtained the child are unusual, it does not diminish the fact that they have been loving, caring parents. I call Jack Griffin to the stand."

Moments later, Jack appeared in front of the bailiff and was sworn in.

"Name and occupation," Attorney Grambling said.

"Jack Griffin. Loader operator at Cotton States Tires."

"Mr. Griffin, tell the court how you and your partner gained possession of this child."

Jack proceeded to tell the court how Suzanne had had the baby and left it with him and Frances. Once he was finished, the judge turned to him.

"Why didn't you reach out to the authorities once the baby was born?" the judge asked.

"Because Frances and I wanted a baby to care for. We had both been single all of our lives and wanted to have a family."

The judge continued.

"So when this wayward woman, this Wanda Sue Smith, drops an unwanted baby in your laps, you decided to keep it?"

"Yes, sir."

Satisfied, the judge turned back to Attorney Grambling.

"Proceed," he said.

"Now, Mr. Griffin. Tell the court about the life you and Miss Hathaway have had with this child over the past six years."

"Oh, we've been very happy. We do things together, he has chores to do on the farm, we go fishing a lot, and we build things. He has brought a lot of happiness into our lives."

"And the child refers to you and Frances as Daddy and Mother."

"Yes, sir."

"What about your finances? With your work at the

reclamation plant and Frances' pension, do you have enough to make ends meet?"

"Yes. And some left over."

Attorney Grambling turned, looked across the aisle.

"Your witness."

Attorney Patterson rose to address the court.

"Your honor, I'm saying to you, this case smells to high heaven. This couple, the circumstances under which they obtained the child as well as his current living environment are very unusual. I'm saying to you that you should rule that this child be sent to the state orphanage in Montgomery."

Judge Murphy looked askance at the attorney.

"Let me decide how to rule in this case," he said. "After all, I am the judge."

Attorney Patterson looked away.

Judge Murphy turned to the other attorney.

"Mr. Grambling, call your next witness."

Moments later, a tall, early thirties, dark-haired woman was sworn in.

"Name and occupation, please."

"Rebecca Medlin. Teacher at Hokes Bluff Elementary."

"You have been Daniel Griffin's first grade teacher for the past few months?"

"Yes."

"During that time, have you noticed any problems with this child? Emotional? Social problems? Any maladjustments?"

"No. Daniel is a very well-adjusted child. He plays and gets along well with the other children. He pays attention, minds the rules, and is an excellent student."

"He could read and write before he started school?" Attorney Grambling said.

"Yes."

"Did he tell you how he learned to read and write before going to school?"

"Yes. He said his mother taught him."

Attorney Grambling turned to the judge.

"Your honor, as you can see, Jack and Frances have

tried to nurture this child in every way possible."

Then he returned to the witness.

"And when Daniel comes to school each day, his clothes are clean, he has all of the supplies he needs?"

"In every way."

"Does he ever say anything negative about his parents or give you any hint that he doesn't have a happy life at home?"

"No. None whatsoever."

"Thank you!" the attorney said. "You may be excused. I now call Frances Hathaway to the stand."

Moments later, Frances was sworn in.

"The state has said that your partner Jack Griffin only has a bicycle for transportation. Is that correct?"

"Yes."

"Is that a problem with caring for the child?"

"No."

"Please explain."

"I have a car. A good one. If one of us or Daniel needs anything, I always have transportation."

"And you can take Daniel wherever he needs to go."

"Yes."

Attorney Grambling looked across the aisle.

"Any questions?"

"No."

"You may step down," the attorney said. "I now call Mildred Gibson to the stand."

Once she was sworn in, Mildred took a seat.

"Name and occupation."

"Mildred Gibson, director of Tallapoosa County Children's services."

"In your official capacity, have you had occasion to know Daniel Jackson Griffin?"

"Yes."

"Are you aware of any problems with this child? Emotionally? Socially? Health-wise?"

"No. In fact, Daniel is one of the most loving, well-behaved children I have ever seen."

"You are the sister of Frances Hathaway?"

"That's correct."

"Has your opinion of this child been colored by your relationship with Miss Hathaway?"

"No. Not in the least."

"You may be excused," the attorney said.

Mildred started to step down.

"Hold it!" the judge said. "I have some questions."

Mildred sat down again.

"You've been in charge of children's welfare services in Tallapoosa county for some twenty years now. In all that time, I have heard of very few cases where a birth went unreported. How did it happen that in this unreported case, the plaintiff happened to be your sister?"

"When I first became aware of the child, my sister said the child had been adopted."

"Did you ask her to show you the papers?"

"No. I felt she was telling the truth. She's my sister."

The judge peered at her for a long moment. He appeared satisfied.

"Okay," he said. Step down. Proceed, Mr. Grambling."

"We now call Hoyt Stephens to the stand."

An early forties, medium height man with a limp was sworn in.

"Name and occupation."

"Hoyt Stephens. Private investigator."

"Mr. Stephens, you have been searching for Wanda Sue Smith, the biological mother of this child, for over a month now?"

"That is correct."

"Where have you searched?"

"Los Angeles, the state of California, Nashville, Tennessee, and Birmingham. According to the information we have, those were the last places she was known to be."

"Did you locate her?"

"No."

"And you feel you have done an exhaustive search?"

"Yes. We have searched police, public, and utility records in each of those locations."

"You may be excused," Attorney Grambling said.

The private investigator stepped down.

"That's all, your honor," Grambling said. "In summation, I want to say it would be a terrible injustice to remove this child from the custody of Jack Griffin and Frances Hathaway. They love this child and have been caring surrogate parents to him for the past six years. As you can see from the testimony, he is a happy, healthy six-year-old. To deny this child his current environment would be unfair and unjust to both the child and his surrogate parents. That's all."

Judge Murphy turned to the other counsel.

"Mr. Patterson?"

The other attorney rose to address the court.

"Your honor," he began. "this child should never have been with these two people in the first place. Neither of them can offer this child a decent home. This child should be in the state orphanage in Montgomery, where he can be around boys his own age. What do these two have to offer?"

Attorney Grambling quickly rose to his feet.

"Their love, your honor. That's what they have to offer. The same love they have been offering this child for the past six years."

"Are you finished?" the judge asked.

"That's all," Attorney Grambling said.

The judge looked to the other attorney.

"Anything else, Mr. Patterson?"

"No, your honor."

Judge Murphy took a deep breath, then peered across the courtroom.

"In cases like this, the court would rather have one or both of the child's natural parents to take custody. Since the mother can't be located and the father is unknown, we've got to find alternatives. The state wants to place this child in the orphanage in Montgomery. While orphanages have certain advantages, I feel in this case it might be traumatic to suddenly move this child out of a loving home into a totally new environment. From the testimony, it appears that the defendants have been good parents to this child and will continue to do so. The only question I have is this: why aren't these two married? Here they are raising a child together, but they are not bound by the bonds of holy matrimony?"

Attorney Grambling spoke up.

"My clients have been close friends for over ten years."

Judge Murphy continued.

"I'm aware of that, but it just doesn't look good to grant custody to two people who are not married. Marriage binds up a family into a total unit."

Attorney Grambling hesitated before he answered.

"Your honor, are you saying custody would be granted if my clients were married?"

"That's correct," the judge replied. "The child needs both a legal mother and a father."

"Your honor, would the court permit a short recess?"

"Granted!" the judge said, rapping his gavel. "Court is recessed for thirty minutes."

Five minutes later, Jack, Frances, Mildred, and their attorney were in a courthouse conference room.

"You heard the judge's words," Grambling said. "If you two will get married, he will grant custody."

Frances answered first.

"If that's what it takes to keep Daniel, I'll do it."

Jack inhaled. For a long moment, he looked away, then turned back to the attorney.

"Can Frances and I talk privately for a moment?"

"Sure."

Jack and Frances moved out of earshot.

"There is something I wanted to tell you," he said in a low whisper.

"What's that?"

"I might not be able to do all the things you would expect out of a husband."

Frances looked at him.

"What do you mean? You have always done everything I asked of you."

"I mean… some things in the bedroom."

"There are no problems we can't solve if we work on them together."

Jack studied her for a moment.

"Do you really mean that?"

"Of course I mean it."

He didn't answer right away.

"This is our only chance," she said.

"Okay," he said finally. "If we can get Daniel and call him our child, I'll do it."

Twenty minutes later, all parties were back in court.

"Your honor, my clients have decided to be married," Attorney Grambling said.

"Good!" the judge replied. "That's a wise decision for the child's sake. Once you have provided me with a marriage certificate, I will grant custody to you."

***

The following morning, Jack, looking starkly out of character in a gray suit, and Frances, all six foot four of her decked out in a white velvet dress, were married in a simple ceremony at the Justice of the Peace's office in Hamilton. When the JP announced that the groom could kiss the bride, Jack stood on tiptoes and Frances leaned her towering frame way down to touch the lips of her new husband.

"Now you can start calling me Frances," she said.

Jack laughed.

"Yes, Frances. Whatever you say."

An hour later, an official copy of the marriage certificate was delivered to Judge Murphy. Two days later, Jack, Frances, and Mildred were back at the court clerk's office to sign the custody papers. Two weeks later, a county deputy appeared at Frances' house and delivered the official documents.

Over the next few weeks, Jack and Frances' lives underwent a set of wholesale changes. First, he gave up his house and moved all of his belongings into Frances' home. There wasn't room for all of his furniture, so they sold what they could, then stored the remainder in Frances' barn. Next came a period of adjustment as they worked out the details of bathroom time, getting Jack's personal belongings situated, and learning to live together. After several weeks of trial and error, they worked it out. It was for Daniel.

Jack's Transformation

So Jack and Frances entered into a new phase in their lives with Daniel. In school, thanks to Frances' early tutoring, Daniel was an excellent student and, since he was a strong, sturdy child, he was very athletic. In the fall of 1962, after he enrolled in the second grade, Daniel announced that he wanted to sign up for the Pee-Wee football program. So, the following afternoon, when classes were dismissed, Frances met Daniel at school and, together, they met Coach Dan Watkins and his wife Elena.

"Now you know the mothers of players are expected to volunteer at the games," Elena said. "They sell drinks, hot dogs, programs, and such to fans. Will you be available to volunteer?"

"Oh yes," Frances replied. "I'll help any way I can."

"Also, you should become a member of the Parent-Teacher Association. The money for the boys' uniforms and equipment come out of the proceeds of PTA cake sales, raffles, and yard sales."

"I would like that."

So, just like that, Frances became a "football mom." Thereafter, on Friday afternoons, she was responsible for picking up Daniel at school after practice. Usually, she would arrive early and watch as Daniel and the other boys scrimmaged on the field. Once practice was over, she would talk to the coach.

"Daniel is a fine running back," Coach Watkins said one afternoon. "He's got speed, strength, and quick moves. He's going to be one of our best players."

Two days later, when Frances told Mildred about Daniel's new undertaking, she was quick to join in.

"I want to go to the games and see him play."

"We'll go together," Frances said.

***

Three weeks later, when the day of the first game of the season rolled around, Frances and Daniel couldn't wait.

"Daddy, my first game is Saturday. Are you going?"

"I don't think so."

"You've got to go, Daddy. I want you to see me play."

Jack looked at Frances.

Maybe later," Jack said.

"You've spent so much time playing football with me that you have to go see me in a real game."

Daniel turned to Frances.

"Mama! Can you get Daddy to go to my football game?"

"If he doesn't want to go, there is nothing I can do."

"Please!" the child begged.

"Maybe later," Jack said.

***

Three hours later, when Daniel, Frances, and Mildred returned home from the game, Daniel bounded into the house. He was beside himself with excitement.

"Daddy!" he yelled "We won! We won!! I scored the winning touchdown."

"I'm so proud of you," Jack said.

"You've got to go to the next game and see me play. Will you go?"

"Maybe."

Daniel looked at Frances then dropped his head and went to his room.

"It would mean so much to Daniel if you would go to his games. He wants you to see him play."

"I really would like to…"

"What is it? What's stopping you?"

Jack peered at her for a long moment.

"You know the way kids are…"

"What do you mean?"

"Kids stare at my eye patch like I'm some kind of freak. They don't say anything, but I know what they're thinking."

Frances studied him for a moment.

"Jack! You're much more concerned about that eye patch than other people. People see it, but they accept it and go on. You're making far too much of it."

"I just don't feel comfortable."

"You've got to start going places with me and Daniel. We're a family now and we have to act like a family. You got dressed up for our wedding. I thought you looked very handsome."

Jack shook his head.

"I'm asking you to do this for Daniel."

"I know. That makes it even harder."

"At least give it a try."

Jack shook his head and looked away.

"Look! I'm going to make you a new eye patch. It will cover all of your eye socket."

"You don't have to do that."

"But I want to. It's for us. And Daniel."

Jack inhaled resignedly.

"And I want you to grow a mustache," she continued. "A thick, bushy one. With your dark hair, the mustache will make the eye patch less noticeable. Will you grow a mustache?"

"If it makes you happy…"

***

The following week, Frances went to a fabric shop in Hamilton and bought a small swath of heavy black cloth. After making a model, which covered Jack's entire eye, she sewed together several pieces then ironed and starched it to give it body. By then, Jack had the makings of a small mustache and it was time for him to try the new patch.

When he came in from work the following afternoon, Frances had the new patch ready. Jack took the new patch, examined it, then hung it over his eye and looked in the mirror.

For a long moment, he didn't answer.

"What do you think?" Frances asked.

"You were right. The mustache makes the eye patch less noticeable."

For several moments, from various angles, he examined himself.

"It's better. Much better."

Frances inspected the mustache.

"Let me trim your mustache a little. It needs to be more even at the ends."

Jack sat perfectly still while Frances did the trimming.

"Now. How's that?"

Jack returned to the mirror.

"Better. Much better."

"Now will you go to Daniel's next game with me and Mildred?"

"Yeah, I'll go."

***

At the game the following Saturday morning, Frances introduced Jack to the coach and then took her post at the refreshment stand. Once the game was underway, Jack and Mildred seated themselves in the stands. At first, Jack was quiet and standoffish, but once he saw Daniel and the team take the field, his interest quickened. Near the end of the first quarter, when Daniel took the ball on the nine-yard line and started around the left end for the goal line, Jack jumped to his feet, threw his fist in the air, and start cheering.

"Run, Daniel!" he yelled. "Run! Run!"

Seconds later, when Daniel crossed the goal line for a touchdown, Jack let out a loud whoop of pure joy and hugged Mildred.

"That's my boy!"

Once the game ended, the Hokes Bluff team had won again.

On the way home, they stopped at a local burger joint. Jack and Frances waited in the car, while Daniel and Mildred went inside to place their orders.

"Now that wasn't so bad, was it?"

"No. I had fun. Nobody stared at my patch."

"Will you go to church with us on Sunday?"

"I'll give it a try."

***

The following Sunday would be a day Jack would always remember. Frances dressed him up in the gray suit he had worn at their wedding. She bought new shoes, underwear, and a blue tie. Once he was ready, she inspected him.

"You look very handsome, but you need some deodorant."

"Deodorant?"

"Yes. You can't go to church smelling like that."

Jack grimaced.

"I feel like a pig being led to slaughter."

"Now this is for me and Daniel."

Seconds later, Frances appeared with her deodorant and Jack used it.

When Jack arrived at church, he was reserved at first, but after he was welcomed by the minister and greeted warmly by several parishioners, he started to feel comfortable. That day, he sat in the pews alongside Daniel, Frances, and Mildred, and sang songs and listened to the sermon. He seemed right at home. When services were over, the minister was at the church steps to say good-bye.

"Jack, I hope you will come again."

"I'll be back."

***

The following week, Frances, Daniel, and Jack went into town to pay bills. As they were walking up the street to the water department, Daniel stopped in front of a motorcycle shop.

"Daddy," he said. "Why don't you get a motorcycle? You wouldn't have to work as hard getting around."

"I don't think I could pass the vision test for a license."

"You could ask."

Later that afternoon, Jack called the Department of Motor Vehicles.

"A vision test is not required," the clerk said.

The following Saturday morning, Frances, Jack, and Daniel went into town and Jack bought a motorcycle. Once Jack paid for it, he fired it up, and he and Daniel rode it home. Daniel was ecstatic. Thereafter, he was always dreaming up reasons for him and Jack to take a ride. They would go to the store, run errands for Frances, and just go joy riding.

Only a week after Jack got the motorcycle, he stopped wearing overalls, denim shirts, and heavy work shoes. He began dressing in blue jeans with a silvery belt buckle and wearing motorcycle boots.

When Frances saw him for the first time, she asked what he was doing.

"I'm changing my look," he said.

Frances smiled happily and looked at Daniel. He returned the smile.

During football season, nothing made Daniel prouder than to arrive at practice on the motorcycle. When they would come roaring into the parking lot, the other boys would gather around to see the motorcycle.

"Rev 'er up, Jack!" the boys would urge. "Get 'er some gas!"

Jack would rev the engine into a mighty roar as the delighted youngsters would watch and applaud. Daniel was the envy of all the other boys.

***

During this period, Mildred continued to be an integral part of Daniel's life. Alongside Frances, she worked PTA events, was a regular at church with them on Sunday, and attended all of Daniel's football games. Jack and Mildred would sit together in the stands while Frances worked the refreshment counter.

At one game, Jack and Mildred rose to their feet when Daniel took the ball deep in Hokes Bluff territory and went racing down the sidelines.

"Run, Daniel!" Jack shouted. "Run!"

Mildred, caught up in the enthusiasm, joined in.

"Run, Andy!" she shouted. "Run!"

Jack looked at her.

"Andy?"

Mildred caught herself.

"I meant Daniel. They look so much alike."

***

Over the next four years, Jack and Frances' life began to blossom in ways they could never have imagined before they adopted Daniel. As a result of having the child, they suddenly became a part of the community and they found it extremely gratifying. For the first time, their lives were full. Frances was busy with her PTA duties; she was supervising cake sales, selling raffle tickets, cooking potluck meals for charity events, helping at yard sales, and attending meetings. During football season, she stayed busy with Daniel, volunteering her services at his games. Finally, church had become a "family activity" and every Sunday, she, Daniel, Jack, and Mildred were in attendance.

The biggest transformation was with Jack. During Daniel's second football season, Coach Watkins named Jack the "equipment coordinator." This meant, after each game, Jack was responsible for gathering helmets, shoulder pads, and other equipment, and seeing they were accounted for and safely stored for the next game. After his initial foray into church-going, he later became a parishioner and, when Daniel and Jack were baptized together, Jack became an official member.

During the 1965 football season, the Hokes Bluff team played in the state championship. For the event, Jack, Frances, Daniel, and Mildred went in her car to Birmingham and stayed overnight in a hotel. Frances and Mildred got a room together. Jack and Daniel got their own room. It was the first time Jack had ever stayed in a hotel.

In the game, the opposing team, the Butler Knights

from Montgomery, were ahead at the half 14-7. At the end of the third quarter, Hokes Bluff recovered a fumble and scored a touchdown to even the score at 14-14. In the closing seconds, Hokes Bluff intercepted a pass and, after only two plays, Daniel ran a touchdown for the Hokes Bluff win.

The following morning, the victory photo appeared on the front page of the local newspaper. In the photo, along with the championship trophy, Coach Watkins, Daniel, and the other team members, there was Jack, eye patch perfectly in place, beaming at the camera.

Several days after the game, Mildred commented to Frances.

"I've never seen you so happy!!"

"My life is full," she said. "I've got a family. Someone to be with me and share my life. It has made me come alive."

"And I can't believe how much Jack has changed," Mildred continued. "He gets out, he goes places, he's not afraid to meet people anymore. He's a totally new person."

Frances peered at her.

"It's a miracle. An absolute miracle."

Suzanne's Return

In late May of 1966, Daniel, at age 11, finished the sixth grade at Hokes Bluff Elementary. In the ceremony, the principal presented Daniel with a diploma and a small trophy for his performance on the Pee-Wee football team. Back at home, Frances threw a party. She baked a cake, prepared home-made ice cream, and hung festive garlands about the house. In attendance were some of Daniel's football friends, several classmates, and, of course, his Aunt Mildred. Once the party was over and the guests were gone, Frances was cleaning up the kitchen and Daniel was playing on the tire swing in the front yard, when a strange car appeared. It was a shiny black sedan with out-of-state plates and seemed starkly out of the place within the rough farm surroundings.

"Mama!" Daniel called. "Somebody is here."

Frances wiped her hands on her apron and went to the front door.

At the screen door, she stopped and peered outside. The driver's side door opened and a middle-aged man, dressed in a suit and looking very business-like, got out. Then he went to the passenger side and opened the door. Moments later, a smallish woman, late forties and looking very expensive, stepped out. Instantly, she surveyed the premises as if she had been there before. First, she looked across the road at Jack's old house, then she started across the yard to the door. Frances, seeing the woman's approach, stepped out on the porch.

"Hello!" she said. "Can I help you?"

The woman didn't answer at first.

"Do you remember me?"

Frances peered closer.

"No."

"I'm Suzanne."

Now Frances recognized the woman.

"You're the woman that was here eleven years ago?"

"That's right."

"What do you want here?"

"I've come for my child."

"There is nothing here that belongs to you."

She looked at Daniel.

"That's my child. He belongs to me."

The man stepped forward.

"Miss Hathaway, my name is James Alverson. I'm Mrs. Rothstein's attorney. We have come here to get the child."

"I don't know what you're talking about," Frances said. "Y'all get out of my yard."

Suddenly, the screen door opened and Jack stepped out on the porch with a shotgun.

"Leave here!" Jack said. "Now!"

The two hesitated for a moment, then Jack stepped forward and pointed the shotgun.

"Get away from me and my family!" he shouted. "This is private property and you're trespassing."

"Mr. Griffin," the man said. "Please be reasonable."

Jack, livid anger in his eyes, started down the steps. Once he was on the ground, he cocked the shotgun and pointed it.

"Wait! Wait!" Alverson said. "We don't want any trouble. We're leaving!"

Hurriedly, the attorney took Suzanne's arm and led her around the car to the passenger side. He opened the door.

"I'm going to get that child," Suzanne said. "He belongs to me."

"Get the hell out of here!" Jack said.

"You can either let me have him and I'll take him through the courts," Suzanne said.

"You're going to have to take him," Frances said.

"Go! Go!" Jack shouted.

Quickly, the two got into the car. The engine started. As it pulled away, the woman put her head out the window.

"I'll be back."

Daniel, Jack, and Frances watched as the car pulled

away. Once the car was out of sight, Daniel turned to Frances.

"Mama! Who was that woman?"

"I don't know," she said.

"What did she mean when she said I belonged to her?"

"I don't know."

"Tell me," Daniel said. "I want to know."

"Some crazy woman. Don't worry about. Go ahead and play."

Frances looked to Jack for an answer.

"Go ahead and play, son," Jack said. "We'll talk about it later."

Daniel looked curiously from one to the other, then returned to his play.

***

That night, after Daniel was in bed, Jack and Frances sat on the front porch in the darkness. As always, the frogs were singing to the night.

"The cat's out of the bag," Frances said. "What are we going to tell Daniel?"

"If she takes us to court, we're going to have to tell him the truth. Let's see how far she goes."

***

The following Monday afternoon, while Jack and Frances were in the garden picking pole beans, a county sheriff's car pulled into the yard. Sheriff Sam Gilbreath got out. They went to meet him.

"Morning, sheriff," Jack said.

"Morning, Jack. I got some court papers to serve you."

"What's it all about?"

"Looks like a woman is suing you for custody of that child."

He handed the summons to Jack.

"Sign here!" the sheriff said.

Jack signed and the sheriff drove away.

They examined the document.

"Let's talk to Mildred," Frances said.

***

The following morning, Jack, Frances, and Mildred were back in Cecil Grambling's office.

"As the child's biological mother, I have to tell you she can probably get custody."

"She's not going to take that child," Mildred said. "He means too much to us."

"We've got our work cut out for us," the attorney said. "It's going to be a tough fight."

That night, they discussed it with Daniel.

"Is this woman going to take me away from you and Daddy?"

"No!" Mildred said. "Not if we can help it. We love you with all of our hearts and we're not going to lose you."

"How can she take me away? Y'all are my mother and father and my aunt."

"There is something we have to tell you," Frances said.

Over the next twenty minutes, they explained to Daniel the circumstances of his birth. Once they had finished, the child studied them for a long moment.

"So y'all are not really my mother and father?"

"That's right," Jack said.

"But I don't want to live with somebody else. Somebody I don't know. Somebody I've never learned to love. I'm happy with y'all. I love y'all."

"And we love you and want to keep you," Jack said. "But there is a chance we may not be able to. We'll have to see what happens in court."

Suddenly, Daniel burst into tears. Then he quickly got up, went to his room, and slammed the door.

The Hearing

Three weeks later, on June 22, 1966, Circuit Judge Tom Murphy called the custody hearing to order in the same courtroom where the first case had been heard five years earlier. At one counsel table sat Jack, Frances, Mildred, and their attorney. Across the aisle sat Suzanne, decked out in an expensive designer dress and shoes, and her attorney. The first witness was Frances.

"Isn't it true," Attorney Grambling said, "that eleven years ago, Mrs. Rothstein left the child with you and your husband with the agreement the child was yours to keep?"

"Yes, sir."

"And, at the time, she appeared to have no love for the child. No affection? No sense of caring? No maternal attitude? She just wanted to be free of the baby?"

"Yes."

"Please tell the court her exact words."

"She said she was going to Hollywood to become a movie star and she didn't have time to take care of a child."

"Didn't have time for a child…" Attorney Grambling said, repeating and turning to the judge. "Now I ask you, your honor… does that sound like the kind of woman who is fit to raise a child?"

Attorney Alverson rose to his feet.

"Objection, your honor," he said. "That happened eleven years ago. My client is not the same person today she was eleven years ago. She is an older, wiser woman now."

"Sustained."

Grambling took a deep breath then turned back to Frances.

"During the last eleven years, you and your husband have loved and cared for this child. You have given him food, clothing, and shelter, attended to his personal needs, and sent him to school. Is that correct?"

"Yes, sir."

Grambling turned to the other attorney.

"Your witness."

"No questions," Alverson said. "I now call Mrs. Suzanne Rothstein."

Seconds later, Suzanne was sworn in.

"Name and occupation?"

"Suzanne Rothstein, Hollywood film producer."

"Mrs. Rothstein," Attorney Alverson said. "Please explain to the court why you feel you now have a right to legal custody of this child."

For a moment, Suzanne looked around the courtroom, then began speaking.

"I made a mistake eleven years ago, your honor. A terrible mistake. At the time I left my child, I was just a young, naïve woman who didn't know what I wanted in this world. I had my head set on dreams of Hollywood stardom. I had stars in my eyes and I couldn't see anything else."

Grambling interrupted.

"Your honor, Mrs. Rothstein was thirty-seven years old when she abandoned this child. That's not what I would consider young and naïve."

"Objection, your honor," Alverson shot back. "Counsel is not a witness here."

"Sustained."

Alverson continued.

"Now, Mrs. Rothstein, please tell the court how your situation has changed."

"Now I'm married to a successful Hollywood producer. We have a beautiful house in Beverly Hills, we go to parties at the homes of famous actors and directors, and we have vacation homes in Hawaii and Florida."

The judge studied her.

"In short, you're quite a bit wealthier now than you were when you abandoned the child."

"Yes," Suzanne said.

Attorney Grambling rose to his feet.

"Your honor," he said. "Mrs. Rothstein can offer this

child things that money can buy, but she can't offer him the love of a caring mother and father."

"How would you know what she can offer?" Alverson shot back.

"Because I've personally watched my clients care for this child for the past six years. They have been good, loving parents."

"Objection, your honor," Alverson said. "Please remind counsel that he is not a witness in this case."

"Sustained!" the judge said. "Mrs. Rothstein, let me ask you a question. During all those years you were building a career in Hollywood, did you have any concern for the welfare of the child? Didn't you wonder about him? If he was being fed and sheltered? If he was even alive?"

"Yes," she said. "Many, many nights I have lain awake wondering about Daniel. All the time, I was hoping and praying he was healthy and happy."

Grambling was quick to respond.

"Your honor, she says she spent many wakeful nights wondering about the welfare of this child. During all those nights she was worrying, she never bothered to call and check on the child. She never bothered to write a letter or send money for the child's welfare."

Alverson rose to respond.

"Your honor, Mrs. Rothstein is a senior vice president at Monogram Studios in Hollywood. She is a very busy woman."

"If she was as concerned as she claims," Grambling continued. "She could have communicated with the child. At least a phone call. A letter."

"Your honor, as I explained, Mrs. Rothstein is a very busy woman."

Judge Murphy returned to the witness.

"So what makes you think you can be a good mother to this child at this late stage?"

"First of all, I'm the child's natural mother. He is my flesh and blood and I love him. Next, as an older, wiser person, I'm at the age I can be a good mother. Most of all, I want to be a good mother and share my life with him."

"How can you say you love this child when you haven't seen him for the past eleven years?" the judge asked.

Suzanne was quick to respond.

"Because I'm his natural mother. I want him to know me as his natural mother. That's the only reason I need."

Judge Murphy turned to Attorney Grambling.

"Do your clients question the fact that this woman is, in fact, the biological mother of the child?"

"No, your honor," Grambling replied. "My clients readily admit that this was the woman who had the child, then abandoned it to my clients' care eleven years ago."

"All right," Judge Murphy said.

"Your witness," Grambling said.

"No questions."

"Summations?" the judge said.

Attorney Grambling stepped in front of the bench.

"Your honor, I want to say to the court that it would be a gross injustice to remove this child from the care of my clients. Over the past eleven years, this child has grown to love them as if they were his natural father and mother. To put the child into the care of a new care-giver who the child has never known and never loved would be highly unfair to both the child and my clients."

"Mr. Alverson?"

Mrs. Rothstein's attorney stepped in front of the bench.

"Your honor, there is no question that my client is the natural mother of this child. All parties agree to that. I must impress upon you that the laws of the state of Alabama make it very clear that if a natural parent is available and of sound mind, the custody of a child should go to that parent. The law cannot be circumvented."

"I know what the law says," Judge Murphy replied. "Is that all?"

"That's all, your honor," Attorney Alverson replied.

"Very well," the judge said.

The judge's eyes swept across the courtroom. He looked at the clock.

"I'm going to adjourn for lunch. At 1 p.m., I will return with my ruling. Court dismissed until then."

Ten minutes later, spectators and courtroom combatants had spilled out into the courthouse corridor. Jack, Frances, and Mildred were talking among themselves when Suzanne and her attorney stepped out. The moment Frances saw Suzanne, she went directly to her.

"You low-life slut!! Do you have any idea what you're going to do to this child?"

Suzanne quickly turned to face her.

"What does it matter to you?" she said. "That child belongs to me. I'm his real mother. Not you."

"I've watched this child grow up for the past eleven years," Frances said. "I know this child has been happy and healthy all that time."

"You don't know crap!" Suzanne said with a laugh. "You're just one more redneck stuck back in these God-forsaken hills. I'm going to get Daniel and you can't stop me. I don't want my son growing up eating beans and cornbread for the rest of his life."

Instantly, Mildred, who had been listening, stepped up.

"You're not getting that child!"

Suzanne was quick to respond.

"Who's going to stop me? Some dime store social worker like you? I wipe my feet on people like you every day. You're just as big a redneck as these two… The amazon and Mr. One-eye."

Suzanne turned to go. Mildred stepped forward, grabbed Suzanne's arm, and pulled her face close to her own.

"You heard what I said."

"Get your God-damn hands off me!" Suzanne screamed, angrily slapping Mildred's hand away. "Who do you think you're talking to? I buy and sell rednecks like you every day."

Quickly, Suzanne turned, and she and her attorney started down the corridor.

"You're not taking that child!" Mildred said.

Instantly, fire in her eyes, Suzanne turned on her.

"You freaking redneck! I'll kick your butt nine ways from Sunday!"

Suddenly, she rushed forward and swung her hand at

Mildred's face. Instantly, Mildred backed away.

Suzanne's attorney rushed forward.

"No! No! Mrs. Rothstein!" he said, grasping Suzanne's arm to keep her away from Mildred. "This woman is a member of law enforcement."

"I don't care who she is," Suzanne said. "No redneck tells me what to do."

"Come on!" the attorney said.

For a moment, Suzanne peered angrily at Mildred, then, as her attorney pulled her arm, she reluctantly turned and started down the corridor.

"I'll see you in hell before I let you take that child," Frances shouted.

Suzanne didn't look back.

"That bitch!! That low-life slut!!" Mildred said under her breath as she watched Suzanne disappear down the courthouse corridor.

***

Promptly at 1 p.m., Judge Murphy returned to the bench and the courtroom combatants returned to their places at the counsel tables.

"I remember this case from six years ago," he began. "At the time I made my ruling, I explained that I was granting custody to Jack and Frances Griffin only because the child's natural mother couldn't be found. Now that has changed.

"I commend the defendants for their efforts to care for this child over the past eleven years. If there were more people who would undertake the care of abandoned children like these two, there wouldn't be nearly as many lonely children in orphanages and state welfare programs.

"On the other hand, the law is the law and I must abide by it. The law states that, in such cases, if either of the biological parents are available to care for the child, custody must be granted to that parent. I know this may seem harsh and unfair to the defendants and the child, but the law is the law. With that in mind, I hereby grant custody of the child, Daniel Jackson Griffin, to Mrs. Suzanne Rothstein."

A hush fell across the courtroom.

At the words, Frances collapsed in sobs. Quickly, Mildred and Jack moved to console her. A big smile broke across Suzanne's face and she hugged her attorney.

Judge Murphy continued:

"Mr. Grambling, when and where can your clients turn over the child to Mrs. Rothstein?"

"Some time will be necessary to gather the child's belongings and get him ready," the attorney said.

"How much time?"

The attorney turned to Frances.

"How much time will you need to get the child ready?"

"Two days," she replied. "Can they come to my house to get him?"

The attorney turned back to the judge.

"Two days, your honor," the attorney replied. "Can Mrs. Rothstein come to the Griffin home to take custody?"

"Actually, we prefer a neutral location," Attorney Alverson replied.

Quickly, Suzanne tapped her attorney's shoulder and whispered in his ear.

The attorney turned back to the judge.

"That's fine, your honor," he said. "My client is agreeable that the hand-over of the child can take place at the Griffin home."

"Very well," Judge Murphy said. "Hand-over of the child will take place on June 24 at 10 a.m. at the Griffin home on Highway 17. That's two days away."

***

That afternoon, when Daniel came in from school, Jack, Frances, and Mildred sat down with him in the living room.

"We have bad news," Mildred began.

"What is it?"

"We were at court today and the judge said you're going to have to go with that woman."

Daniel looked from one to the other.

"They're going to take me away from y'all?"

Frances nodded

"It's a court order," Mildred said. "There's nothing we can do."

The words had not fully registered with the child.

"Why am I going away? I don't even know this woman."

"We know that," Frances said. "But there is nothing we can do."

Suddenly, Daniel burst into tears and ran into Frances' arms.

"Please, Mama," he pleaded, grasping her tightly. "Don't let them do this to me!"

"I'm sorry," Frances said. "We love you and want you to stay with us, but there's nothing we can do. We've got to follow the law. The day after tomorrow, she will come here to get you. You'll have to be ready."

"Where is she taking me?"

"I don't know," Frances said. "Now I want you to straighten up and be brave about this. We've got to follow the law."

"Oh, Mama," he said, burying his face in Frances' bosom. "I love you so much."

***

The following night, the night before the hand-over, Jack, Frances, and Mildred were sitting on the front porch at Frances' house. They talked in the darkness while a chorus of frogs croaked loudly down at the river. They were having a conversation they could never have imagined a year earlier.

"It's going to kill me to see her take Daniel," Frances said.

"Me too," Jack said. "When Daniel goes away, our lives will go away."

"We've got to stop her," Mildred said. "One of us is going to have to kill her."

For several moments, they sat quietly in the darkness. The only sound was the bullfrogs.

"Let me kill her," Jack said finally. "Tomorrow I'll hide behind the woodpile and, when she and her lawyer pull up in their big car, I'll drop her. I've got punkin' balls for my shotgun. She will die instantly. With her out of the way, Daniel will be able to stay with y'all. Y'all can take care of him until he's grown."

Mildred looked at him.

"Then you'll spend the rest of your life in prison and Daniel won't have a father. That child is going to need a mother and a father over the next ten years."

They were quiet again. Down at the river, the frogs continued their chorus.

"Maybe I could hit her with my car," Frances said. "I could make it look like an accident."

"There's no time for that," Mildred said. "Things like that take time to plan and pull off. They'll be here in the morning."

They were quiet again. The only sound was the croaking frogs.

"Then it would be you that goes to prison rather than Jack. Then Daniel wouldn't have a mother. Remember, we're doing this for Daniel."

They were quiet again.

"So what do we do?" Frances said.

"I don't know," Mildred said. "We have to follow the law."

Frances peered at her.

"You always say that, but this time, the law has let us down. So I ask you again, what do we do?"

They were quiet again. The frogs grew louder.

"I'll do it," Mildred said finally. "I'll take care of it."

"What are you going to do?" Frances said.

"I don't know, but I'll see that it's taken care of."

They were quiet again. The bullfrogs were croaking away.

Suddenly, Mildred burst into tears. Jack and Frances peered at one another. In the darkness, they could see Mildred wiping her eyes.

"What's wrong?" Frances asked.

"There's something I have to tell y'all," Mildred said. "When I was at the doctor's last week, he said I have a cancer in my stomach. He said it was inoperable and I didn't have long to live."

"Oh, no!" Frances said. "How long?"

"Six, maybe seven months."

"Oh, God! What did I do to deserve all of this grief?"

"We've all got our crosses to bear in this world. I've borne mine long enough."

"What are you going to do about Suzanne?" Jack asked.

"I'm going to see that she is put away. I'm going to see that she is put away for good."

Down by the river, the bullfrogs were suddenly silent.

The Hand-over

The following morning, promptly at 10 a.m., two county sheriff's cars and the big black sedan pulled up in the front yard at Frances' house. Suzanne, in a white cashmere dress, and her attorney got out and waited at the sedan. Moments later, Sheriff Gilbreath was walking across the yard to the front door steps. The front door was open.

He called.

"Jack? Frances?"

Jack appeared at the door.

"Is the child ready?"

"He's ready," Jack said. "We're coming right out."

Moments later, Frances, Mildred, and Daniel stepped out on the front porch. Daniel, looking very teary-eyed, was neatly dressed and had a suitcase. Jack, Frances, Mildred, and Daniel strode down the steps to meet the waiting sheriff.

Once they were on the ground, Frances handed the suitcase to the sheriff, then she turned back to Daniel for a final good-bye.

"Oh, Mama," Daniel said, crying softly. "I love you."

"I love you too," Frances said, kissing him on the forehead. "Now be brave. Take the sheriff's hand and go with him."

Daniel turned and took the sheriff's hand. Then together, they began walking toward Suzanne, who was waiting at the black sedan. Once they reached her, the sheriff gave her Daniel's hand. In the other hand, she took the suitcase. For a moment, she peered down at the child, then seeing his tears, she took a handkerchief from her purse and knelt in front of him.

"Let me dry your tears. I'm your mother now. Everything is going to be just fine."

Daniel, his eyes red from crying, looked hatefully at

Mrs. Rothstein, then waited as she wiped away his tears. Once finished, she took his hand again and, together, they started walking toward the black sedan. After several steps, Daniel suddenly turned and looked back at Frances. Upon seeing her, he jerked his hand free of Mrs. Rothstein's and started running back across the yard to Frances.

"Mama! Mama!" he screamed.

Suzanne turned.

"Come back here! You belong to me now!"

Instantly, Suzanne started running across the yard in pursuit of the child. At the very instant Daniel reached Frances and ran into her arms, Mrs. Rothstein was only a few steps behind him.

Suddenly, a pistol shot rang out.

Blam!!

At the sound of the shot, the front of Mrs. Rothstein's white cashmere dress turned a crimson red as her life's blood flooded into the innermost threads of the fabric. For an instant, her face took on a look of shocked surprise, then her eyes rolled back into her head and she fell face first at the feet of Frances, Daniel, Jack, and Mildred. Instantly, a pool of warm blood began to form under her prostrate form and seep into the dirt and gravels of the driveway.

"Mildred!" Sheriff Gilbreath shouted, moving toward her. "Drop that gun!"

The .45 revolver Mildred was holding fell to the ground.

The sheriff stepped forward and picked it up.

"What are you doing taking the law into your own hands?" he said. "You're supposed to let the law dispense justice."

Mildred peered at him.

"Sometimes the law doesn't dispense justice."

The sheriff drew a deep breath.

"Yeah. Maybe you're right."

Then he motioned to a deputy to take her into custody.

"You're under arrest for murder," the deputy said.

Once the deputy placed handcuffs on Mildred's wrists, he turned back to the sheriff.

"What about her?" he said, indicating Suzanne. "Want me to call an ambulance?"

"Ambulance won't do her any good. Call the coroner."

For a moment, Sheriff Gilbreath turned and took a step to get a closer view of Suzanne's body.

"Right through the heart. Those .45 slugs really make a mess."

Satisfied, he turned to address Frances.

"Frances, you and Jack go ahead and keep that boy until I can talk to the judge. I should know something official by tomorrow."

***

Two days later, Judge Murphy granted permanent custody to Jack and Frances. In the ruling, he said, now that the child's birth mother was deceased, it was only right that Daniel should continue to live with his long-term caregivers. So, over the next ten years, Jack and Frances finished raising Daniel and, over those years, he made them very proud. At Hokes Bluff High, he was an excellent student and football star and, upon graduation, won a football scholarship to the University of Alabama, where he studied law. After graduation, he married his high school sweetheart and set up a practice near Gadsden. Years later, he would be elected a state senator and finally a circuit judge. Over those same years, Jack and Frances lived happily to be a ripe old age.

***

Mildred didn't live long enough to stand trial. At her arraignment, the judge set the trial date for Jan 3, 1967. After spending less than a week in the county jail, her condition worsened and she was transferred to a hospital in Birmingham, where she was due to begin radiation treatments. The night before the treatments were set to begin, Daniel, Frances, and Jack visited her.

"This is probably good-bye," Mildred said. "I'm not sure how many of these treatments my body can take, but it's my only choice. I love y'all. Over these past few years, y'all are the only family I've had."

After several days of radiation treatments, Mildred appeared to show some improvement, but, only days after the seeming improvements, she slipped into a coma and died peacefully in her sleep on December 28, 1966. She was buried at the Old Harmony Baptist Church, the country church on Highway 17 where they had worshipped together.

The following spring, Jack and Frances had a headstone erected at her grave. Frances said she had requested something simple and memorable. Once erected, the headstone read:

Mildred Dianne Gibson

1899-1966

Thanks for Daniel!!

The End

LONELY MAGNOLIA

1

Within the world's computing community, Dr. Carl Wingate was known as a genius. A native of South Georgia, he had grown up on a thousand-acre cotton farm near Valdosta and, in 1975, at age fifteen, he had built his first computer from components he had ordered out of a magazine. Once the teenager had assembled the components—two floppy drives, a crude motherboard, and a primitive keyboard and mouse—he used a television as a makeshift monitor and started to write software. In less than a year, he had written two pieces of crude word-processing software and, by today's standards, a very primitive database program. Six months later, he sent a letter to the company that manufactured the components and explained he had written a new operating system for the computer, which was not only more efficient, but faster than the current one. Two months later, the company said they wanted to buy his new operating system and sent him a check for twenty-five hundred dollars.

After graduating high school, young Carl enrolled at the Georgia Data Processing Institute in Atlanta to study computing. From the very first day, he took the university by storm. In the college computer labs, he began research to determine optimal combinations for matching central processing unit speeds and addressable memory. During his third year, he wrote a white paper on the subject, Wingate's Theory I, which was hailed around the world as a major breakthrough in computing technology. The following year, his theories were expanded in another white paper, Wingate's Theory II, and, shortly afterward, its precepts were adopted by hardware manufacturers throughout the industry.

Upon graduation, he founded Wingate Solutions, a hardware manufacturing firm near Atlanta, which became a major player in the computing industry in only two years. After the third year, however, Dr. Wingate felt he should change direction. While he loved hardware, he felt software was a vaster, more extensive endeavor than its counterpart. Hardware was cold and inanimate, he felt, whereas software, like language literacy, was an infinite world to be explored in all of its various multi-faceted ramifications. Essentially, he saw the study of computer software as an extension of human action. Anything human beings could do with their hands or their minds could be done with software, he felt.

So the following year, he retooled Wingate Solutions to become a software manufacturing firm. In only a few months, hundreds of programs, word processing, spreadsheets, databases, and operating systems—the main program that controls all other applications—were pouring out of the company. Over the next ten years, Wingate Solutions became the premier software manufacturer in the world and, in 1992, the company's brochure bragged "there is no computer on earth that doesn't have a Wingate program on its hard drive."

Over the succeeding years, Dr. Wingate's honors and accolades were the stuff of legend. Twice, the World Digital Council (WDC) awarded him the "World's Top Computer Scientist" award. Four separate times, he was the keynote speaker at the WDC's annual banquet in Vienna. His white papers were collected and archived at WDC's world headquarters in Vienna and early models of the crude computers he had built were placed in computer museums in New York, Brussels, Sydney, and Tokyo. In 2009, he was awarded an honorary doctorate by the Georgia Data Processing Institute. Finally, in 2014, WGS presented Dr. Wingate its lifetime achievement award for "contributions to the digital world which far exceeded that of his peers." By late 2015, everybody who was anybody in the computing industry knew who Dr. Carl Wingate was and held him in the highest regard.

***

Now, in 2016, Dr. Wingate was a multimillionaire, a world-renowned celebrity and, at age 56, ready to retire. He told friends he wanted to steal away to his beach home in Daytona Beach, Florida and enjoy his golden years at the beach, tending his roses and doing the occasional consulting job. First, however, he wanted to find himself a new wife. Unfortunately, his first wife, Marjorie, mother of his daughter Becky, had died in the fall of 2010 of breast cancer. Her sickness had been a long, drawn-out affair, and from the day she was diagnosed, it was three more years before she passed. It had been a very trying experience for Dr. Wingate, but he now felt he was ready for a new mate.

At first, his efforts to meet a new wife focused on dating family acquaintances and friends. Colleagues would invite him to dinner with sisters, secretaries, and professional associates, hoping to strike a spark. His daughter Becky had arranged dates between her father and fellow teachers at the high school where she worked, as well as members of the local Women's Club where she was a member, but, out of all those, Dr. Wingate was unable to find anyone who struck his fancy. At one point, he asked the hygienist at his dental office to go out with him and she accepted. On the date, however, he was bored silly. All she wanted to talk about were crowns, porcelain veneers, and artificial implants.

Finally, during a WDC conference in Brussels, Dr. Lars Hansen, president of Omega Digital Forum in Stockholm, told Dr. Wingate he should try online dating. Noting that the previous year he had found a wonderful wife for his own life, he told Dr. Wingate the advantages of online dating far exceeded the trial and error tactics of conventional dating. Online dating was not only more efficient, but a suitor could explore a much larger field of candidates in a much shorter time. Best of all, he noted, "Women come to you. You don't have to go to them." After all, Dr. Hansen explained, for one of the world's most renowned computer scientists, online dating should be a natural.

Dr. Wingate was very excited. As a younger man, before online dating was going full speed ahead in the mid-nineties, he and his team at Wingate Solutions had written numerous programs for dating websites. Basically, these involved gathering generic information about a candidate, entering it into a database, then cross-referencing this information with other candidates to find a match. The entire exercise had been fun and Dr. Wingate's company had made millions from the software.

So, in early 2016, Dr. Wingate decided to take the plunge into online dating. In his online searches, he quickly discovered there were websites that offered women of virtually every imaginable race, nationality, or ethnicity he could imagine. Names of the websites included Asian Cupid, Latin Love, Chocolate Romance, Sexy Seniors, Russian Romance, and the list went on and on. Dr. Wingate, being the native Southerner he was, knew he wanted a southern woman. Thus, he refined his search to dating sites that featured primarily women in the southern United States. Finally, after numerous searches, he decided on a site called Southern Singles, based in Miami, which claimed to have "the largest database of beautiful southern women in the USA." As he scrolled through the listings of candidates featured on the introductory pages, he saw page after page of beautiful middle-aged southern women.

Satisfied this was the avenue he wanted to pursue, Dr. Wingate pulled out his credit card, paid the sixty-nine-dollar six-month fee, signing on for the site's platinum plan. Once he was officially a member, he set about creating a profile. He dubbed his profile "Computer Pro," then began to answer the multitude of required questions. There were questions about age, profession, likes and dislikes, marital status, hobbies, children, pets, and similar such inquiries a prospective mate could be interested in knowing. There were miscellaneous questions such as favorite color, pet's name, and zodiac sign. He listed his hobbies as reading, growing roses and tomatoes, and repairing personal computers. Finally, after his profile was created, he uploaded a photo to the site. It was a picture made five years earlier at a computer conference in Nashville in which he was a bit tipsy, but he felt no one would actually notice or care.

Finally, he came down to the nub of the project, describing his ideal woman. From the first, he had had a clear idea as to the look and personality traits he was seeking in a potential spouse. First, he jotted down notes, then thoughtfully wrote them out. Finally, satisfied he had sufficiently described the woman of his dreams, he copied and pasted the text into his profile's "ideal woman" field. It read: "I am a professional computer consultant seeking a southern woman, aged 40-50, who is intelligent, thin, has a sense of humor, and loves to cook southern food. No smokers please. An interest in gardening is a definite plus." As he reread the statement, he pursed his lips in satisfaction. Finally, feeling he had sufficiently cast his bread upon the waters, he decided to wait. That afternoon, he was going deep-sea fishing with friends and, that night, he had dinner plans with his daughter and her husband at a restaurant in Daytona Beach, so he decided to leave his search for a new mate until the following day.

***

The following morning, as soon as Dr. Wingate was out of bed and had coffee, he sat down and fired up his computer. Immediately, he went to the Southern Singles website to check his email. There were nine replies. Of the nine, he knew immediately there were several in whom he had no interest. One woman, profile name Motorcycle Mama, aged 48 from Mississippi, said she was seeking a "fun-loving man who liked to go camping on motorcycles." The note she left read, "What kind of Harley do you own?" Immediately, Dr. Wingate deleted Motorcycle Mama from his list.

There were several others he dismissed quickly. There was Cute Realtor, a forty-six-year-old recently widowed real estate broker, Me and My Guitar, a forty-eight-year-old aspiring folk singer, and Daffy Daphne, a forty-two-year-old dark-haired woman with a sinister look who said she believed she was Imogene Coca in another life. Finally, after more than an hour, Dr. Wingate had trimmed the list down to four candidates that he deemed suitable.

They were Classy Lady, a retired businesswoman, who

said she was seeking a wealthy man to travel the world with her. Next came Miss Fitness, a yoga instructor and health enthusiast who said she liked to eat raw eggs and run two miles every morning before breakfast. Dr. Wingate laughed. Next on the list was Ready to Start Over, a forty-seven-year-old woman with a pretty face and sad eyes from South Carolina who said she had been recently windowed. Finally, the last candidate was Lonely Magnolia, a forty-two-year-old secretary from Savannah, Georgia who said she was divorced and looking for new friends.

Dr. Wingate immediately deleted Miss Fitness. There was no way he was going to get up and run two miles every morning before breakfast. Then he turned his attention to Ready to Start Over. As he scrolled through her "more photos," section, he started to feel a certain uneasiness. In two of the photos, she seemed downright depressed. Somehow, as he peered into the sadness in her eyes, he could sense an indescribably deep loneliness and despair. He deleted her from the list. Next, he left an email with Classy Lady asking her about places she had traveled, what books she liked to read, favorite movies, and her childhood. Then he reread Lonely Magnolia's profile.

"Friends first!! I am an honest, good-hearted woman seeking an honest, good-hearted man," the profile stated. "I am a simple person who likes home life, cooking, reading, watching television, and flower gardening."

The tone seemed vague and evasive, so he clicked on the "more photos" button for a better look. There he found several more photos. There was one in a bathing suit, which, for a forty-two-year-old woman, was not bad. There was another in formal wear and still another in which, wearing a broad-brimmed white hat and gloves, she was down on her knees planting a bed of zinnias.

As he scrolled through "more photos," one in particular caught his eye. It was a photo of her standing among the branches of a young, newly flowered magnolia tree. Once he enlarged the shot to full screen, he could now see her facial features up close. She had deep blue eyes, thin lips, and a very faint, come hither smile. He couldn't put his finger on it, but her smile was almost a pout. It was an expression somewhere between disappointment and quiet joy. Somehow, as he peered at her smiling face, perfectly framed by the soft pink magnolia blossoms, he was taken in by the quaint charm of the image. Nice, he thought. Very nice. I'm going to have to dig deeper.

Moments later, he was typing an instant message to Lonely Magnolia, explaining he had read her profile, liked it, and wanted to chat. First, however, he asked that she read his profile to determine if she had an interest in him. Finally, satisfied he was making headway in his pursuit of a new woman for his life, he shut down the computer. That afternoon, he went to the beach alone. That night, he had dinner with his daughter.

When he returned home later that night, he had an email from Classy Lady and Lonely Magnolia. Instantly, he opened Lonely Magnolia's email.

"Good evening!! I am happy that you have shown an interest in me. Upon reading your profile, you seem like a very intelligent, interesting man. This afternoon, I am going to a Daughters of the Confederacy meeting and tonight, I plan on playing bridge with some friends. Tomorrow night, however, I'll be on the Southern Singles website around 7 and, if you are available, I would be happy to chat with you. Looking forward to meeting you. Thanks for the interest! Lonely Magnolia."

Dr. Wingate smiled. There was an innate warmth and cordiality to the message. He liked her easy felicity with words. That was a mark of intelligence. He would make it a point to be online tomorrow night at seven. Moments later, he deleted the email from Classy Lady without having read it. He had no further interest.

***

Shortly before seven the following night, Dr. Wingate logged in to his Southern Singles account. Moments later, he opened a chat window with Lonely Magnolia. It was 6:58.

Computer Pro: Good evening!

Lonely Magnolia: Good evening! How are you?

Computer Pro: Fine. And you?

Lonely Magnolia: I'm fine. I'm pleased to meet you here. You say you're 56.

Computer Pro: Yes.

Lonely Magnolia: Is that your true age?

Computer Pro: Yes. Is that too old?

Lonely Magnolia: No. Age is just a number to me. I judge people by what's in their heart, not by their age. Lots of men on this website lie about their age. And you live in Florida?

Computer Pro: Yes. Near Daytona Beach.

Lonely Magnolia: That's nice. I've never spent any time in Daytona, but I've passed through there a few times. It seemed like a lovely place. I've heard the beaches are very nice.

Computer Pro: Oh, yes. Some of the most beautiful white sand beaches in the world.

Long pause.

Lonely Magnolia: I'd like to make one thing clear from the start. I want us to be friends first. Friends before we talk on the telephone or meet. I really don't want to jump into anything.

Computer Pro: That's ok. I understand.

Lonely Magnolia: If the relationship grows and we decide to meet face-to-face, then I'll give you my phone number and we'll see how it goes.

Computer Pro: That's fine. How long do you want to give it?

Lonely Magnolia: Three months. That's plenty of time to see if we are a good match or not.

Computer Pro: I'll agree to that.

Long pause.

Computer Pro: Do you have a camera? If you had a camera, we could see one another as we chat.

Lonely Magnolia: No. I don't have a camera. Even if I had one, I wouldn't know how to connect it up. All that stuff is so complicated. And expensive. I can't afford it.

Long pause.

Dr. Wingate didn't want to ruffle any feathers.

Computer Pro: Yes. I understand.

Lonely Magnolia: So you're a computer expert? You have your own company?

Computer Pro: Yes. I'm the owner and founder of Wingate Solutions…

Over the next hour, they chatted. Her real name was Sadie Collins. She was a secretary at an insurance company in Savannah and had grown up on a farm just outside Waycross. Divorced for two years, she had no children and was looking to be married again. From the information she had provided, he gathered she led a quiet suburban life in the old district of Savannah; working, tending her flowers, reading, and playing bridge with friends. As he reviewed their initial conversation, he felt she was a little standoffish, but that was to be expected. Like her, he didn't want to rush into a relationship. Actually, he would have been very skittish if she had thrown herself at him. He was afraid of women who were too aggressive. All in all, he was happy with the start. When he shut down his computer that night, he made a note on his personal calendar. It read "March 3 – Met Sadie!"

In many ways, Dr. Wingate had not had a lot of experience with women. As a child, he had not been close to his mother. With a husband and five children to care for, his mother was always busy working on the farm. During his teenage years, he did have a close relationship with his older sister Alma for a while, but, after she married at age sixteen, it ended abruptly. When he finished college, he had met Marjorie on a double date. After only four months, he proposed, and they were married two weeks later. During those days, the primary focus of his life was computers and women and family matters took a backseat to his professional life. If truth be told, he had rushed into marriage with his wife Marjorie, but after Becky was born, he knew there was no turning back. Until now, he had never had the time or taken the time to develop a close relationship with a woman. Now he had the time.

2

Dr. Wingate didn't want to appear overly anxious to speak with Sadie again, so he waited a day. Two nights later, when he logged in and opened a chat window, he didn't have to wait long.

Lonely Magnolia: Carl? How are you?

Computer Pro: Fine. And you?

Lonely Magnolia: Feel good tonight! What did you do today?

Computer Pro: This morning, I attended to my tomatoes. They're doing so well. You know, here in Florida, if you put anything in the ground, it will grow. This afternoon, I went to the beach and read one of my colleague's white papers on super algorithms.

Lonely Magnolia: Super what?

Computer Pro: Algorithms. Algorithms are a set of self-contained actions which must be performed to achieve certain tasks in computer programming. Algorithms perform calculation for data processing and automated reasoning tasks. It's all very complicated.

Long pause.

Lonely Magnolia: Whew! All of that is way over my head. Let me ask you a question. Why would a man as complicated as you be attracted to a simple woman like me? I mean, I'm not really simple, I've been to college and I traveled the world when I was married, but I'm not nearly as educated or intelligent as you. I don't have anywhere near the kind of intelligence you have.

Computer Pro: To be perfectly honest, I'm at a point in my life where I need simplicity. I have fought the world for financial and professional success long enough. I'm ready to take it easy for a while and do simple, uncomplicated things.

Long pause.

Lonely Magnolia: That's a good answer. A very good

answer.

Over the next hour, they chatted about their childhoods growing up on a farm. She recalled how her mother would send her to the garden to cut "a mess of okra" and how the little "whiskers" on the okra would sting her fingers. He explained that every September when it was time to pick corn, the little "whiskers" on the corn shucks would cause him to itch and he would be scratching his arms for days after picking corn. They discussed milking cows, planting watermelons, and hauling hay.

Lonely Magnolia: My life on the farm was so long ago that now it's like a dream. I wouldn't trade anything in this world for having grown up on a farm, but now that it's ended, I wouldn't go back. Too much hard work.

Computer Pro: Yes. My feeling exactly.

Lonely Magnolia: What kind of food do you like?

Computer Pro: As southern as you can get. Fried chicken, green beans, mashed potatoes and gravy with biscuits. What's the old saying? You can take the boy out of the country, but you can't take the country out of the boy.

Long pause.

Computer Pro: Do you like to cook?

Lonely Magnolia: I'm an excellent cook. I learned to cook from my mother. I make a great pot of hopping John with sweet cornbread. Years ago, my mother taught me how to overcook the black-eyed peas so the pods break apart and the hopping John is soupy. I like to eat it with fresh scallions and Texas hot sauce.

Dr. Wingate could feel his mouth watering.

Computer Pro: My God!! I think I love you!

Lonely Magnolia: LOL! When we start dating, I'll have you over one night for a batch.

Suddenly, Dr. Wingate's mind flashed on a scene in which he was seated at a beautifully appointed southern table with Sadie seated across from him. He was unfolding his napkin, preparing to dig into an old-fashioned southern meal of hopping John and sweet cornbread. In his mind's eye, he slowly stirred the soupy concoction with a spoon, then delicately selected the correct combination of black-eyed peas and bits of bacon and onions to create the perfect bite. Then, as he began chewing, he followed the initial spoonful with a bite of sweet cornbread. For a long moment, he savored the delicate flavor as the taste sensations rolled across his palate. He felt like he had gone to heaven.

Computer Pro: My! My! You are such a talented person. I'm surprised some man hasn't snapped you up as a wife before now.

Lonely Magnolia: I'm in no hurry to get married again. I've had some offers, but like I told you, I want to take it slow and easy before I jump into marriage again.

***

Over the next two weeks, they shared numerous chat sessions and talked about anything and everything under the sun. Quickly, Dr. Wingate discovered Sadie was a very intelligent woman with a wide variety of interests. In late March, he was in Boston for a three-day conference with other computer scientists at the Massachusetts Institute of Technology. As the speaker yammered on and about the recent mechanization of computer programming and how one size fits all programming was destroying creativity within the digital community, Dr. Wingate thoughts turned to Sadie. He didn't want to be here, he told himself. He wanted to be back in Palm Harbor, sipping a glass of sweet iced tea with extra lemon and chatting with Sadie. That night, before he boarded the plane for Daytona Beach, he checked his mobile. He had a new message from Sadie.

***

When he logged in the following morning, he went straight to her message.

Lonely Magnolia: I hoped you would be online tonight so we could talk. I know you said you would be gone, but I miss our little chat sessions. I guess you're off with your friends discussing algorithms and subroutines or some other such complicated things. I will try again in the morning.

The moment he opened a chat window, she was waiting.

Computer Pro: Good evening!

Lonely Magnolia: Hi!

Computer Pro: I missed you!

Lonely Magnolia: I missed you too!

Computer Pro: How are you today?

Lonely Magnolia: Actually, a little tired. I was up reading late last night reading poetry. I read "Song of the Chattahoochee" again. First time since high school. Brought back so many memories.

Computer Pro: Oh, yes. It's a great poem. "Out of the hills of Habersham, down the valleys of Hall, I hurry amain to reach the plain, run the rapid and leap the fall…"

Lonely Magnolia: "…Split at the rock and together again, accept my bed, or narrow or wide, and flee from folly on every side, with a lover's pain to attain the plain, far from the hills of Habersham, far from the valleys of Hall."

Computer Pro: Very good!!

Lonely Magnolia: LOL!! My mother first read that to me when I was ten or twelve. I never forgot it.

Long pause.

Lonely Magnolia: What plans do you have today?

Computer Pro: This morning, I've got to finish writing some code for a database program. This afternoon, I'll either read or go to the beach.

Lonely Magnolia: Do you ever get lonely?

Computer Pro: Sometimes. Usually, if I have my work to do, I don't think about being lonely. It's the time when I don't have anything to do that I start to feel lonely.

Long pause.

Computer Pro: When my wife was alive, she filled up my life during the times I didn't have work to do. It's nice to have someone to do that.

Lonely Magnolia: Yes. I know the feeling. I too miss not having someone else in my life.

Long pause.

Lonely Magnolia: My! My! You're so easy to talk to. Somehow, I feel like I've known you all my life.

Computer Pro: Yes. I feel the same way.

After the chat session that night, Dr. Wingate felt he was onto something good with Sadie. This one is a keeper, he thought. She was so open and honest. Her self-honesty; that was what he liked best. Here was a woman who could recognize and tell the truth about herself. A rare trait, Dr. Wingate thought. He liked that. And very intelligent. This is the one, he thought. This is the woman I've been looking for. This is the woman I will make into the love of my life.

***

Over the next two months, Dr. Wingate and Sadie chatted every day. Over that period, their chat sessions were a whirlwind of shared life experiences, old memories, personal observations, and slices of life. Here are the highlights:

April 4

Lonely Magnolia: Had an argument with my boss today. At times, he is so unreasonable.

Computer Pro: What happened?

Lonely Magnolia: He threw a fit because I put the wrong date on a letter to the main office. He said small mistakes like that reflect badly on our local office.

Computer Pro: There's probably some truth to that. He didn't threaten you with your job, did he?

Lonely Magnolia: Oh, no! Nothing like that! He was just very cold toward me the rest of the day.

Computer Pro: Then I wouldn't worry about it. He's probably already forgotten about it!

Long pause.

Lonely Magnolia: Yeah. You're probably right. He does have a short memory about those things. Thanks for trying to make me feel better. You have a way of calming me down.

Computer Pro: That's ok. That's what friends are for.

***

April 11

Computer Pro: Attended to my tomatoes this morning but spent most of the day thinking about you.

Lonely Magnolia: Yes. I have spent a lot of time thinking about you lately.

Computer Pro: When can we meet?

Lonely Magnolia: I thought we had already talked about this. Remember, we agreed to give ourselves some time to learn one another.

Computer Pro: You're right! I promised to be patient. I will live up to my promise.

Long pause.

Lonely Magnolia: Well, I've got to go in now."

Computer Pro: Oh really, couldn't you stay just a little longer? What was the story you were going tell me about your brother?

Lonely Magnolia: It will have to wait until tomorrow. I need to get into bed.

Computer Pro: Ok! Good night!!

When he closed the chat window that night, he was afraid he had said something wrong.

***

April 20

Computer Pro: Beautiful sunset this afternoon. The rays of the evening sun paint the bottoms of the clouds an orange-reddish color. Know what I mean?

Lonely Magnolia: You're a poet.

Computer Pro: Thanks.

Lonely Magnolia: Yes. I know exactly what you mean. There are few things on this earth more beautiful than a sunset. Were you at the beach today?

Computer Pro: Oh yes. Big surf today. So much water, there were no boats in the inlet except Coast Guard patrol boats. Lots of dead jellyfish.

Long pause.

Computer Pro: I hope someday we can walk along the beach here together.

Lonely Magnolia: So do I.

***

During the month of May, Dr. Wingate could feel his heart being drawn ever closer to Sadie.

May 4

Lonely Magnolia: It's early May. My zinnias and petunias are coming up beautifully. They grow well with these warm days we've had lately.

Computer Pro: Like our relationship?

Lonely Magnolia: Yes. You could say that. Our friendship has grown quite nicely over the past two months. We've become very good friends. I always look forward to my chat sessions with you.

Computer Pro: When can I meet you?

Lonely Magnolia: Remember our original agreement? Three months before we meet. We have not reached that milestone yet. You did agree to that.

Computer Pro: Yes. I'm aware of that. I guess I'm getting a little anxious. I have developed quite a yen for you over the past two months.

Lonely Magnolia: I feel the same way about you. I look forward to our chat sessions, but I feel it is best if we wait a while longer. Remember, you did agree to three months.

Computer Pro: Yes, I did. We'll have it your way.

Lonely Magnolia: Thanks for your understanding…

***

May 14

Computer Pro: Oh, Sadie, I think about you every hour of every day. You are in my heart and mind.

Lonely Magnolia: Yes, Carl. I feel the same way. Our hearts have grown closer and closer over the past two months and you have become such an important part of my life.

***

Two nights later, over dinner with his daughter Becky, he told her about Sadie.

"I think I'm in love," he said.

"Oh, Daddy," she replied. "I'm so happy for you. You're the kind of person who needs someone in his life. Are you going up to Savannah?" she asked.

"Not yet," he said. "She wants to wait a while. She says she wants us to be good friends first. I'll probably go next month."

"That's a sound approach," she said. "She wants to be sure it's right before she commits to anything. I can see the sense of that."

"I just wish it was sooner rather than later."

"Just be patient," the daughter said. "She seems like a very nice person and when the time is right, you and she can get together. Have you talked marriage?" she asked.

"Not yet, but I think we will very soon. She says she wants to get married again."

***

May 22

Computer Pro: Hurricane warnings out today.

Lonely Magnolia: If I lived in Florida, I would be scared to death of hurricanes. I remember when I was growing up in Waycross and the tornadoes would come. We would hide in the tornado shelter and wait until it passed. I would be so upset and frightened. That's how I feel tonight. Can you talk to me long enough to calm me down?"

Computer Pro: Absolutely.

Long pause.

Lonely Magnolia: Today while gardening, I raked my hand through some loose soil and scooped up an earthworm that was at least eight inches long. It was so long I thought was a snake and I slung it out of my hand. When I did, Green started barking and barking.

Long pause.

Computer Pro: Green? You have a dog?

Lonely Magnolia: Oh, yes. I've had him several years.

Computer Pro: And his name is Green.

Lonely Magnolia: Yes. Don't you think that's a nice name?

Computer Pro: I've never heard of a dog named Green.

Lonely Magnolia: My father had a hound named Blue.

Long pause.

Dr. Wingate didn't want to ruffle any feathers, so he continued with the original discussion.

Computer Pro: When I was growing up, my cousin and I would fiddle earthworms out of the ground and use them for fish bait.

Lonely Magnolia: How would you fiddle them?

Computer Pro: Bend over a small bush, then rub a stick across the trunk real fast. This vibrates the ground around the roots and irritates the earthworms and they crawl out of the ground.

Lone Magnolia: That's a new one on me!

Long pause.

For some reason, Dr. Wingate wanted to discuss the dog further.

Computer Pro: Is Green a good dog?

Lonely Magnolia: Oh yes, he runs and sits and rolls over and does all of things that most dogs do. He's very intelligent.

Computer Pro: Can he talk?

Long pause.

Lonely Magnolia: What? Of course he can't talk. He's a dog. You know, sometimes you say the craziest things.

Computer Pro: Sorry. I was just trying to be funny. I didn't mean to go astray.

Long pause.

Computer Pro: Get it? Astray? Dog? LOL!

Long pause.

Lonely Magnolia: Well, I guess it's time for me to go in.

Long pause.

Computer Pro: I didn't offend you, did I?

Lonely Magnolia: Oh, no. It's getting late. I really need to get to bed. I have to be in the office at 9 tomorrow.

Computer Pro: Ok. Good night.

When he shut down his Southern Singles account that night, he wondered why anyone would name their dog Green.

***

The next night, when he opened a chat window on Southern Singles, she was waiting.

Lonely Magnolia: Carl? Are you there?

Computer Pro: Yes. I'm here.

Lonely Magnolia: Good evening, darling. I hope you are well. We are having a huge rainstorm here in Savannah tonight. The wind is whipping around like there is no tomorrow and the rain is pouring down. I wish you were here with me. I wouldn't feel so lonely.

Computer Pro: I long for the day when I can be by your side.

Lonely Magnolia: That day will come. It won't be much longer.

Computer Pro: I miss you every day and every night. You are constantly in my thoughts.

Lonely Magnolia: Yes. And you're constantly in mine.

***

In late May, the three-month waiting period was drawing to a close.

Computer Pro: The three-month period will be over in two more days.

Lonely Magnolia: Yes. I know. You have been very patient. Thanks!!

Computer Pro: Are you still happy with our relationship?

Lonely Magnolia: Yes. Very much so. In fact, I think I've fallen in love with you.

Long pause. He hadn't expected that response, but he was happy when he heard it.

Computer Pro: Yes. I feel the same way. Then can we meet?

Lonely Magnolia: Yes. Can you come to Savannah?

Computer Pro: I sure can. When?

Lonely Magnolia: Are you free tomorrow night?

Computer Pro: Sure am.

Lonely Magnolia: I know how much you like southern food. I know just the place.

Computer Pro: Where?

Lonely Magnolia: A little place called Southern Dining Emporium. It's just a few doors down from my house. They make the best chicken and dumplings.

Computer Pro: Sounds great! Let's do it!!

Lonely Magnolia: Ok. Go to online maps and search for Southern Dining Emporium. It's at 1420 Peachtree Lane in Savannah.

Long pause as Dr. Wingate launched his maps application and started to search.

Lonely Magnolia: Did you find it?

Computer Pro: Hang on! I'm searching.

Long pause.

Computer Pro: Still searching… Got it! Yeah. Looks like a nice little place. They're open until 10 tomorrow night. What time?

Lonely Magnolia: How does 7 sound?

Computer Pro: Perfect! How will I recognize you?

Lonely Magnolia: I'll be wearing a light blue dress and white shoes.

Computer: I can't wait to meet you.

Lonely Magnolia: Neither can I.

Computer Pro: I love you!

Lonely Magnolia: I love you too!

3

The following morning, Dr. Wingate was cruising up I-95 from Daytona Beach to Savannah. It was about a three-hour drive. As he cruised up I-95, he was happy and excited that he was about to meet the love of his life. His plans called for them to have a few dates, then he would invite her to his Florida home for a weekend.

Just after 5:30 that afternoon, his GPS instructed him to turn off I-95 into the historic district of Savannah. After a series of twists and turns, he found Peachtree Lane and a moment later, the Southern Dining Emporium. The façade matched the photo he had seen online. Parking spaces were full near the front, so he drove to the next block, parked his car, and walked back to the restaurant. The time was 6:48. He was early. That was okay. He didn't mind waiting. He wanted to be sure to be there when she arrived.

For some fifteen minutes, he watched as a greeter welcomed couples and families went into the restaurant. At 7:05, he saw as a woman that looked like Sadie arrived at the restaurant entrance. She was a medium-height blonde wearing a light blue dress and looking around expectedly. That's Sadie, he told himself. Quickly, Dr. Wingate rushed forward.

"Sadie!" he called.

The woman turned, glanced at him with an annoyed expression, then turned and took the hand of another man and started walking into the restaurant. Miffed, he continued to wait.

Over the next fifteen minutes, he waited patiently. Couples and families continued to stream in and out of the restaurant. He had taken a position near the entrance so he could get a close look at all incoming patrons. She said she lived near the restaurant, so apparently, she intended to walk. As he watched the door, he also kept an eye on the sidewalk in both directions in front of the restaurant. At 7:30, when there was still no

Sadie, he became worried. Something had happened. Or she had fallen ill or had an accident. At 7:40, he was getting desperate and asked the greeter if he had seen a short blonde in a blue dress and white shoes. The greeter shook his head in ignorance. Finally, at 8 p.m., Dr. Wingate decided she was a no-show and returned to his car.

***

Hurt and disappointed, Dr. Wingate drove back to Daytona Beach that night. When he arrived back home and logged into his Southern Singles account, he opened a chat window for Sadie. Instantly, he got a warning message of "Profile unknown!" Then he searched the site for Lonely Magnolia and got the same message: "Profile unknown!" Dr. Wingate shook his head in frustration. Somehow, she had disappeared. Moments later, he began searching online databases for a Sadie Collins in Savannah. He searched phone, real estate, and telephone records. There was a Sarah Collins listed, but her age was twenty-three. He knew that wasn't his Sadie. Finally, after he had searched until noon and, all the while, found no trace of Sadie, Dr. Wingate was baffled at his dilemma. He was determined to get to the bottom of it.

After lunch, he decided to try a different tack. He called the Southern Singles website and explained he was trying to get information about one of their subscribers, but his inquiry was met with a curt "we can provide no information about our members." After he hung up, he wondered what his next move would be. Finally, he launched a search into Sunshine Internet Services, the parent company that owned Southern Singles, and obtained a legal address for the corporation. Then, he called his attorney and told him what had happened. After explaining the story, Dr. Wingate instructed his attorney Mark Fletcher that, if Southern Singles could not provide information with which he could locate Sadie, he wanted to sue for alienation of affection.

***

Two weeks later, the attorney called Dr. Wingate and explained that a meeting had been set up between himself, Dr. Wingate, and one Robert Wall, CEO of Sunshine Internet Services. He explained that the meeting was set for two days later at the corporation's offices in Miami. The attorney said the company CEO had assured him he would provide all available information about Lonely Magnolia. Dr. Wingate promised he would be sure to be present.

***

The offices for Sunshine Internet Services were located in a high-rise in the harbor district of Miami. Robert Wall was an early thirtyish boy of a man with a quiet smile and a shock of red hair and a long, flowing beard. After pleasantries, the three were seated in the CEO's office and ready to get down to business.

"I'm not sure if you remember me," Wall began. "But I was a member of the programing team that performed coding on some of your early dating site software."

Dr. Wingate peered at the younger man. He didn't recognize him.

"I don't remember you," he said. "What can you tell me about Sadie?"

The younger man cleared his throat.

"I'm afraid I have to tell you, Dr. Wingate," he said, "there is no such person as Sadie Collins."

Dr. Wingate peered at him incredulously.

"What do you mean there is no Sadie Collins?"

"Sadie Collins, profile name Lonely Magnolia, is a virtual woman created for Southern Singles. When our website first launched in 2004, we didn't have enough real candidates to meet the demand for all of the various types of women our subscribers were seeking. For instance, some of our subscribers were seeking women in categories for which no real women were available. As a result, your programmers wrote software to create a host of virtual women. Lonely Magnolia, aka Sadie Collins, was one of those."

"I don't believe you," Dr. Wingate said. "You're a liar.

Sadie is just as alive and breathing as you and me."

The young CEO shook his head sadly.

"As you should know, artificial intelligence is so well-developed these days that virtual people quite often seem more real than actual people."

"You're out of your mind," Dr. Wingate said. "That woman is just as alive as me or you."

"Again, I have to tell you it was your company's software that created Sadie," he said. "Do you remember the names of the personality types that were created for the templates?"

"No, refresh my memory," Dr. Wingate said.

"Think back!" the young CEO said. "Remember the names of the templates? Needy Widow. Lonely Fat Girl, Queen Bee, Southern Belle… Now which template do you think Sadie Collins was born out of? Do you remember in version 3.6, you suggested that any self-respecting southern belle should be able to quote Song of the Chattahoochee for her prospective lover? Remember your memo to integrate the poem into the artificial intelligence portion of the software?"

Dr. Wingate was flabbergasted. He looked at his attorney for some assurance. There was none.

The young CEO continued.

"And the three months she made you wait. Remember the software was designed to tease, then lead on a lover for exactly three months because three months was the average subscription term for site members?"

Dr. Wingate peered angrily at the younger man. His first instinct was to slap him, but he controlled himself. Yes, he remembered the memos about the Southern Belle template and the Song of the Chattahoochee integration. Most of all, he remembered the glitch in the original software, which was never corrected in later versions. The glitch involved two databases: one for favorite color, which was left empty, and the other for pet's name, which had been switched. In the program, the only choices for pets' names were colors like red, yellow, and blue. He remembered that Sadie hadn't chosen a favorite color. Now he knew why her dog was named "Green."

"So Sadie Collins was nothing more than a fiction created

by a computer program?" asked the attorney

"I'm afraid so," Wall said.

"In that case," the attorney replied, "you are guilty of false and misleading advertising. When you place a profile on a dating site, subscribers should have every confidence that the person they are communicating with is real and alive."

"Talk to Dr. Wingate about that," the young CEO replied. "He created the software that created Lonely Magnolia."

"I've heard enough," Dr. Wingate said, turning to his attorney. "Come on; let's go!"

Instantly, they arose from their chairs.

"What's wrong?" the young CEO said. "Can't you handle the truth? You're the great computer genius, Dr. Carl Wingate. Don't you recognize your own software?"

Dr. Wingate and his attorney had reached the door.

"Wait!" the young CEO called after them. "Don't I get an apology? You threaten to sue me, then come to my office, waste my time, and don't even offer an apology?"

Dr. Wingate and his attorney were gone.

***

Three days later, a story appeared in a Miami newspaper with the glaring headline "Computer Genius Falls in Love with Virtual Woman." The story's source, Florida Internet Services CEO Robert Wall, stated, "Of all the people who should have known that this woman was a fiction, it should have been Dr. Wingate. After all, he created the software that created her."

Over the next month, the story took the world by storm. It was published in newspapers throughout the world. Eventually, the story reached members of the World Digital Council in Brussels. Shortly afterward, articles and editorials about Dr. Wingate and his lapse in judgment began appearing in print and online computer magazines. One online magazine reported the story with the headline "Poor Dr. Wingate!" A cartoon in the World Digital Council's monthly magazine portrayed a photo of Dr. Wingate sitting at his personal computer holding out his arms to a middle-aged woman on the screen. The caption read "My darling, will you marry me?" Another online magazine carried a headline that read "Dr. Wingate's Fatal Love." The great computer genius had become the laughing stock of his profession.

***

Meanwhile, back at his Florida home, Dr. Wingate couldn't believe what had befallen him. He now hated himself. He had been had in the worst possible way. Here was the great genius who had laid the foundations for the digital age. He had done for digitization what Newton had done for mathematics, what Galileo had done for astronomy. Now look at him! He had been taken to the cleaners like some ten-year-old child would be taken by Gypsies at a county fair.

As a man of science, Dr. Wingate had committed the unpardonable sin. As a scientist, he had ignored the basic precepts that scientific discipline demanded. He had allowed his heart to take control over his reason. He had taken appearance for reality. He had allowed falsity to take precedence over truth. He had closed his eyes at a time when they should have been wide open. It was the most grievous error a dedicated scientist could make and it had a devastating effect on him.

4

Over the next few months, something terrible happened to Dr. Wingate. He shut himself up away from the outside world in his Florida home and, save for the occasional visit from his daughter Becky, he only ventured out to buy food and pay bills. He became a total recluse for almost five months. The only social communication he had with the outside world was through email. Some friends said he started to drink, which was totally out of character for Dr. Wingate. Until now, he had been an absolute teetotaler.

Then one day, he appeared on his front porch, carrying a suitcase.

Upon seeing him, Mrs. Harris, his next-door neighbor, who was tending to her roses, inquired.

"Dr. Wingate," she asked, "are you going on a trip?"

"I'm going to Savannah to see Sadie," he said.

"You've been talking about her for some time now," she said. "You and she must be deeply in love."

"Oh, yes," Dr. Wingate replied. "We are very much in love."

"Good for you!" she said. "I'm very happy for both of you!"

Moments later, he waved good-bye and Mrs. Harris watched as the car sped off down the street.

***

Two days later, Dr. Wingate was arrested in Savannah. With a handful of withered flowers, he had been going door-to-door in the neighborhood near the Southern Dining Emporium, looking for Sadie.

Several residents told him he had the wrong house, but after he returned to the home of a policeman for the second time, the officer questioned him. After only a brief inquiry, the officer suspected something was amiss and asked Dr. Wingate to go downtown with him.

At police headquarters, his daughter was called and he was released to her custody. Upon leaving the police station, the officer in charge told Becky her father needed a psychiatric evaluation.

***

Upon their return to Florida, Becky checked her father into the psychiatric hospital at Daytona Beach. After two days of tests and evaluation, the hospital said their prognosis was that Dr. Wingate should remain there. Two days after the evaluation, Dr. Phillip Halloran, chief psychiatrist at the hospital, asked the daughter to visit.

As requested, Becky appeared for the visit at the appointed time and met Dr. Halloran. Moments later, they were strolling down the antiseptic hospital corridors, then stopped at the door to an observation room. This was a room equipped with a one-way window through which doctors could observe a patient without their knowledge. Dr. Halloran pushed a button and a curtain drew back to reveal Dr. Wingate. The walls of the room had been padded and Dr. Wingate was constrained in the hospital bed. His arms, legs, and head were free, but his torso was in constraints.

"Observe," Dr. Halloran said.

Becky Wingate peered at her father.

"Sadie!!" her father was saying to an imaginary person. "You look so funny in that hat. I remember when I was a child, my Aunt Henrietta had a hat like that. She loved to wear it to church for all of the other women to see it."

Then he burst into delirious laughter.

"What's happened to him?" the daughter asked.

"He refuses to release the feelings of ecstasy he felt during online conversations with this Sadie," Dr. Halloran said. "To perpetuate these feelings of ecstasy, he has created his own culture, his own world, which only he understands."

The daughter peered at him.

"His own world?" she asked.

"Observe," he said, nodding toward Dr. Wingate.

Dr. Wingate was smiling.

"Sadie!" he said. "Now listen to the joke. You've got to listen to the joke. I listened to yours and you have to listen to mine. What did the baby banana say to the mother banana?"

He waited.

"You don't know?" he said.

He waited again, then blurted out, "I don't peel good."

Then he again burst into uproarious laughter.

For a moment, he was quiet. Seconds later, he picked up a newspaper, glanced at it, then threw it aside.

"Sadie," he said, "do you like the flowers? And the chocolates? I'm sorry they didn't have the light caramel. I know how you love the light caramel. The man said they had the light caramels on back order, but they wouldn't be in until next week."

In the observation booth, Dr. Halloran continued, "He refuses to leave the love bubble he has created. He fears the world that exists outside of his love for this Sadie and he will do anything and everything within his power to remain safely within this bubble of security and peace he has created for himself."

"Is there no hope?" the daughter asked.

The psychologist shook his head sadly.

"Just keep him drugged and in constraints so he doesn't hurt himself."

***

In Greek mythology, there is the famous story of Pygmalion, the sculptor who fell in love with a beautiful statue he had sculpted. Like Pygmalion, Dr. Wingate had fallen in love with his own creation. Unfortunately, as in the Greek myth where the Goddess Aphrodite changed the statue Pygmalion had created into a real woman whom he then married, there was no such divine intervention for Dr. Wingate. He knew his Sadie was gone forever. As a result, rather than live with the heart-breaking torment of being without the person he loved, Dr. Wingate had gone to her.

***

The following October, a category 4 hurricane swept through downtown Miami and knocked out power in most of the high-rise buildings in the Harbor District. Among the businesses that were blacked out was Florida Internet Services, parent company of Southern Singles. After electricity in the building had been out over ten hours, CEO Bob Wall, whose servers were down all that time, was losing thousands of dollars. As a result, he personally went with the maintenance crew to the building's electric switching station to insure that power was restored ASAP. Unbeknown to the young CEO, as he stepped inside the switching station, one corner of the room was filled with water from a leak, which had spilled into one of the transformers and he was standing in part of the puddle. When the superintendent threw the main switch, Bob Wall's body was instantly reduced from flesh and bone to charred rubble as thirty million volts of electricity shot through his every vein, muscle, bone, and sinew. It was a horribly excruciating death at the young age of thirty-three. Some observers claimed his untimely death was karmic payback for what he had done to Dr. Wingate.

****The End****

ANNIE

Billy and Roy were just two mischievous boys—probably meaner than most eleven-year-olds—but still just bored country kids looking for some adventure and excitement. Having grown up together in the small farming community near Hamilton, the two youngsters were more like brothers than first cousins. Their grandparents, John and Gladys McKinney, had migrated to that part of north Alabama in 1922 and homesteaded two forty-acre plots of land from the U.S. government. Over the years, the McKinneys had built a house and a barn, cleared and farmed the land, and raised two daughters. As their offspring grew up and married off, the McKinneys gave their newly wedded offspring plots of land on the homestead to build homes and raise their own families.

So when Billy's and Roy's mothers were married, they settled on the McKinney family homestead in houses that were within a stone's throw of one another. As a result, Billy and Roy had been playing together since the day they were born. After their grandfather died in 1949, the boys' grandmother requested that their parents arrange for one or both of the boys to come spend nights with her because she hated being alone at night. The parents approved, and the two boys were delighted.

At home, Billy and Roy were well-behaved eleven-year-olds because their fathers were strict disciplinarians and expected them to toe the line. But once they were away from their parents at their grandmother's house, they loved to engage in every form of mischief imaginable. They knew their grandmother would let their boyishness run free and wild, and she would engage them in forbidden conversations.

Although the two eleven-year-olds found many forms of entertainment during those nights at their grandmother's house, their favorite pastime was spying on the residents of their grandmother's rental houses.

Mrs. McKinney had three rental houses on her property. The best one was a two-bedroom white frame home across the road from the grandmother's house that rented for $35 a month. She called it her Good House. The boys' grandmother kept the house in good repair and the tenants were mostly factory workers who were reasonably well-to-do, drove a nice car, and had enough personal pride to keep the premises clean and presentable. Billy and Roy seldom spied on the residents of The Good House because they had to cross the road to get to it and the only place they could spy was in a muddy field some thirty yards from the house itself. Also, it was the number one source of rental income for their grandmother and they didn't want to disturb that.

Their grandmother's second rental home was a concrete block house located just down the road from her home, and she always referred to it as The Block House. This structure was quite downscale from The Good House and, for many years, a family named Shaw—a man, his wife, and their three daughters—had occupied that dwelling. The Block House was usually rented by tradesmen types—cabinet-builders, plumbers, brick layers, and such who worked steadily and could afford to pay the $25-a-month rent. Roy especially loved to sneak around and spy on the Shaws at night because he had a crush on Mary Alice, the oldest girl in the Shaw family.

When Billy and Roy spied on the Shaws, which was quite often, they would hide in the tall grass just beyond the wild plum bushes near the Shaws' back porch. In the summertime, the boys knew the Shaws would have visitors, and after dinner, the men and the boys would sit on the front porch and talk, and the women and the girls would sit on the back porch and drink iced tea and gossip.

When the women were drinking iced tea, Billy and Roy knew they would come out to the plum bushes to pee every thirty or forty minutes. The two eleven-year-olds would duck down low in the high grass and wait. Then, they would watch and listen in the darkness as the women would squat and urinate, still laughing, talking, and giggling amongst themselves.

One night, Billy and Roy were hiding and listening to the women peeing in the plum bushes when Roy, knowing that his beloved Mary Alice was among the group, became overcome with excitement and started giggling. Roy couldn't contain himself, and the women, not dreaming there was a soul within ten miles, screamed in fright. Quickly, they jumped up, jerked up their panties, and scampered out of the grove of wild plum bushes in chaos. Billy and Roy, frightened that the men would come to investigate, raced back across the field to their grandmother's house. Billy, leader of the two, had warned his cousin again and again that he shouldn't become so excited while they were "spying" because it "blows our cover," he said, using a term he heard in a radio spy show.

Their grandmother's third rental house was a small, ramshackle structure under two big oak trees that stood on the opposite side of a cornfield behind her house. That home, which their grandmother called The Little House, was more of a shack than anything else. There were three rooms: a living room and bedroom in front, and a full-length single room in the back that served as a combination kitchen-dining room. The Little House was always in very poor repair and the people who rented it were invariably people who lived on the economic edge. If someone came along and offered to pay their grandmother anything at all to rent The Little House, Mrs. McKinney would strike a deal.

Thus, over the years, there had been a succession of strangely colorful ne'er-do-wells who had rented The Little House and Billy and Roy had "spied" on every one of them. There was an older couple, the Turleys, who smelled of axle grease and always had several old, abandoned cars littering the front yard. The husband claimed to be a part-time mechanic, part-time electrician, part-time sawmill worker—part-time this and part-time that—but he never went to a job. His wife, a huge, bespectacled woman with bad breath and a hairy wart on the end of her nose, made tacky plastic roses in the kitchen all day and sold them to churches. Some mornings, when Billy and Roy were at their grandmother's house, they would hear a shotgun blast from across the cornfield at The Little House and their grandmother would explain that Mr. Turley was killing wild birds for the couple's breakfast.

At one point, a one-legged traveling salesman, his insane wife, and their skinny, undernourished son had lived in The Little House. Some afternoons, Billy and Roy would hear loud, hysterical screams coming from across the cornfield, and they would race through the cornstalks and peek over at The Little House. In the front yard, they would see a young, very unattractive woman shouting to the sky and throwing herself on the ground, screaming, "Take me, Lord! Oh, God, please take me into your loving arms, sweet Jesus!" All the while, her little, undernourished son would stand on the ramshackle porch crying hysterically as he watched his mother scream and plead and flail her body against the ground.

Once, during the Christmas holidays, Billy and Roy gave the undernourished little boy a piece of coconut their grandmother had carved from a freshly broken coconut shell. Billy and Roy wanted to play a trick on the little boy so, before they gave it to him, they both peed on it.

The hungry little boy eagerly took the piece of coconut, inspected it, smelled it, and then bit off a piece and began chewing. He chewed for over a minute, saying nothing.

"How does it taste?" Billy asked the child with an air of expectancy.

"Okay," the little boy said seriously, chewing the crunchy, fresh coconut fruit.

"Does it taste good?" Billy asked again.

"It's okay," the hungry child reiterated, taking another bite. "A little salty, but—okay."

Billy and Roy looked at each other, giggled, and then darted off into the bushes and laughed themselves silly at their mischievousness.

Over the years, the list of tenants in The Little House who had provided entertainment for Billy and Roy during the nights they spent with their grandmother had grown quite large. Although there had been a long list of memorable adventures, far and away the tenant who had provided more entertainment than all the others was Annie Atkinson.

The first time Billy and Roy saw Annie was late one

afternoon in January of 1952 when she walked into the yard at their grandmother's home and asked to speak to "the woman of the house." Annie, looking very stern and severe, was wearing a black, high-collar Victorian dress with ankle-high, button-up shoes and was carrying a black umbrella with ruffles around the edge. A mass of long, black hair had been swung up majestically on top of her head, and she walked with a definitive air of dignity, grace, and pride. In many ways, she looked starkly out of place in the little north Alabama farm community.

When the boys' grandmother came to the door, she invited the woman inside. Annie explained that she wanted to rent the little house down under the oak trees. She told the boys' grandmother that she would pay the rent each month as soon as she got a check from her husband. If he didn't mail the check, she said, he would bring the money during one of his periodic visits.

As she negotiated with their grandmother, Annie glanced into the front bedroom and saw Billy and Roy. Although the two boys appeared to be reading Lash LaRue comic books, they were actually eavesdropping on every word of the negotiations. They had seen Annie from the moment she had walked into the yard, and as she talked with their grandmother, they hoped with all their hearts that their grandmother would rent The Little House to this strange woman.

"When does your husband send the check?" the grandmother asked.

"Second or third of the month," Annie replied, pushing her wire-rimmed glasses up on her nose proudly.

"Then I'll expect the rent no later than the third day of the month," the grandmother explained.

"Soon as I get the check," the woman said, "I'll bring it to you."

Both women grew quiet and the boys' grandmother studied Annie.

Oh, please say yes, Grandma, the boys begged in their hearts as they listened. *Please, please, please say yes.*

"Okay," their grandmother said finally. "I'll let you have

it for ten dollars a month, but you'll have to clean the windows and watch for the old black cat."

"Black cat?" Annie asked.

"There's an old black cat with the mange that comes to The Little House from time to time. If you feed it, it'll start coming over to my house."

"I won't feed it," Annie promised.

The grandmother seemed to be satisfied.

"And you have to watch for rats," she added. "I'll give you some strychnine, and if they get real bad, you'll have to put it out."

"I'll take care of that too," Annie promised.

"Okay," the grandmother said. "I take you at your word."

Mrs. McKinney shook hands with Annie. The deal was done. Then, proud and haughty as ever, Annie pulled a ten-dollar bill out of an ageing, frilly black purse and handed it to the boys' grandmother. Annie said that was the first month's rent and announced that she would be moving into The Little House the following Saturday. As she got up to leave, she glanced into the front bedroom again and saw Billy and Roy with their heads seemingly buried in two Lash Larue comic books. As the door slammed behind her, Roy and Billy darted to the window and watched as Annie strode back across the yard and out to the dirt road with her severe Victorian look and her ruffled umbrella.

The following Saturday morning, as promised, an old pickup truck loaded with Annie's belongings pulled into the front yard of The Little House. From the cornfield, Billy and Roy watched as the Negro man driving the truck helped Annie unload five suitcases, an old steamer trunk, a wooden table and chairs, a weathered sofa, a cook stove, a single bed, and a wind-up Victrola. As they watched, Billy and Roy agreed they should give Annie time to get settled in before they started spying on her.

Over the next few weeks, Annie and Mrs. McKinney became quite close friends. Annie would come to visit their grandmother at night and the two women would play a card game called High, Low, Jack, and Game. During those sessions, Billy and Roy would sit in the corner and watch the games and listen to the women talk.

At first, Billy and Roy kept their distance from Annie. Annie was different from any woman the boys had ever seen. She was dressed in clothes that made her look like something out of the old *Liberty* magazines they had seen in their grandmother's closet. Annie had a way of tilting her head and peering at the two boys through her thick glasses in a manner that made them shiver. The stare she gave them would bore a hole in stone, and when she affected the look through the thick glasses, the lenses would magnify her eyes into huge gleaming lights that made her look like some glassy-eyed demon from hell. When she turned that look on Billy and Roy, they would look away and quickly jump up and run outside to play.

As a result of the visits, the boys' grandmother became something of an expert on Annie. Mrs. McKinney told the boys that Annie had been a stage actress in North Carolina in her younger days and she had appeared in plays all over the South. Annie had grown up in a wealthy family near Atlanta and had had great expectations as a young girl. After her father died, however, the family discovered that her father was deeply in debt, and when she left the family in 1931, she was destitute. As a result, she took odd jobs wherever she could. The boys' grandmother warned them that, while Annie appeared innocent enough in her old-fashioned clothes, there was a deadly side to her that would come out if provoked. She told the boys that Annie carried an ice pick in her frilly purse and she would stab them if they bothered her. This was all Billy and Roy needed to delve further into Annie's private life.

That night, the boys went to spy on Annie for the first time. After they had crossed the cornfield, they ducked down inside the broom sage patch at the edge of the field, and then, staying low, made their way to within thirty feet of Annie's house. Then they raised their heads to peek over the broom sage. The curtains were open and the light was on.

"I can see Annie," Billy said authoritatively, peering at the window.

"What's she doing?" Roy asked.

"She's at the cook stove," Billy said. "Come on."

Billy motioned for Roy to follow him.

In an instant, the two darted out of the high broom sage and dashed across the yard to a huge oak tree that was less than fifteen feet from the house. They waited for a moment.

Billy peered around the side of the oak tree at the house. He motioned to Roy again and, in a flash, the two boys were under the floor. While the corners of the house were built on stone foundations, the rear of the house was much higher off the ground than the front. This meant there was a crawlspace three to four feet high under the floor on the house's back side. Underneath, there was a big crack in the wood flooring under the dining room and a small crack in the floor under the kitchen area. For years, these two vantage points had been Billy and Roy's favorite places for spying.

In the darkness under the house, Billy peered through the small crack in the kitchen floor. As he peered through the crack into the house, he could see Annie standing at the cook stove.

"My God!" Billy whispered.

He could see Annie was naked as she minded a pot on the stove, her small breasts sagging and deposits of cellulite hanging high on both thighs.

"My God!" Billy whispered excitedly again.

"What is it?" Roy whispered eagerly.

"She's naked, butt-ass naked."

"Let me see," Roy said urgently.

"What a minute!" Billy said impatiently.

"No, I want to see," Roy said. "Let me see."

Billy motioned to his cousin to remain calm. Above him, Annie, stirring the contents of a pan with one hand, was fondling her breasts with the other. She had the look of a woman who was in dire need of a man.

"Jesus!" Billy said, his eyes big as saucers.

"Let me see!" Roy said impatiently. "Let me see!"

Billy moved away and his cousin put his eye up to the crack in the floor. As he watched, Roy started snickering as he stared at the naked woman. Then, unable to control himself, he doubled over with excited laughter.

"Shhhhhh!" Billy said urgently, putting his finger to his lips.

"Ha! Ha! Ha!" Roy giggled. Now he was laughing so hard, he couldn't control himself.

Suddenly, the two boys heard a loud thumping on the wooden floor above them. Roy muffled his laughter and both boys grew deathly quiet.

"Billy! Roy!" Annie called from above.

Both boys were deathly quiet.

"Billy! Roy!" she called again. "Are you boys down there?"

From above, Annie stomped the floor again.

"Billy! Roy!" the boys heard Annie demanding loudly. "I know you two are down there."

The boys were quiet.

"You two better get out from here!" she screamed. There was a pause. They could hear Annie, very agitated, trying to catch her breath.

"If you don't get out from here, I'll tell Mrs. McKinney and she'll whip your butts. You hear me!" the woman shouted.

The two eleven-year-olds looked at each other. Instantly, Billy motioned to Roy to flee. Stealthily, the two scooted out from under the house, raced back across the cornfield, and were on their grandmother's back porch in minutes.

"Have you boys been sneaking around Annie's house?" the grandmother asked the boys two days later.

"Oh, no!" Billy lied. "We haven't been anywhere near The Little House."

"Roy?" the grandmother, looking very stern, asked the other grandson.

"Oh, that's right, Grandma," Roy lied. "We haven't been near The Little House."

"Now don't you boys lie to me," the grandmother said sternly. "Annie said she saw you and Billy running through the broom sage patch two nights ago."

"Oh, it wasn't us," the boys said in unison.

"Okay," the grandmother said finally, seemingly satisfied. "Maybe it was a dog or something she saw. Annie's eyes aren't real good."

Several days later, the two boys were fishing in the creek behind their grandmother's house. After they had baited their hooks and set out the poles, they were walking along the edge of the cornfield when they glanced over at The Little House.

"Look," Billy said, pointing. "There's a man at Annie's house."

The boys could see Annie sitting on the front porch. Across from her sat a small, sallow-faced, bespectacled man wearing brogans, overalls, and a blue denim shirt buttoned at the top.

"Who is that?" Billy asked.

"Let's go ask Grandma," Roy said.

Back at the grandmother's house, the two boys found her peeling apples when they burst into the kitchen.

"There's a man over at Annie's house," Billy reported breathlessly.

"That's Journey," the grandmother said calmly, looking up from her apple peeling. "He's her husband."

Billy looked at Roy with a knowing smile.

"Well, he's sort of a husband," she said on second thought, "but not really a husband."

The grandmother explained that Annie and Journey had been married for seven years, but he only came to visit from time to time. Journey was an "okra man," the grandmother said, who provided fresh okra to the local grocery stores over in Calhoun County. Once Journey had rented a plot of land from a farmer, he would pay to have the land plowed, fertilized, and planted in okra. After the crop grew to maturity, Journey would hire workers to pick the okra and deliver it to the grocery stores.

"Annie doesn't see much of Journey between March and October because he's with the okra crop," the grandmother continued. "She hates being alone. That's why she comes over to visit with me."

The grandmother grew quiet as she peeled an apple. The boys were waiting for their grandmother to finish.

"Grandma," Billy asked curiously, "what did you mean when you said he's not a real husband?"

The grandmother looked up from her apple-peeling.

"Journey's a 'sexual," she said.

"A what?" the two boys asked together.

"A 'sexual. A queer. He likes men."

Billy and Roy looked at each other.

The grandmother stopped her narrative briefly as she cut a core from a large apple. The boys were listening.

The grandmother explained that Annie had told her that, although she and Journey had been married seven years, they had never had male-female sexual relations. She said Journey had never had sex with a woman because he had to have a man's "juices" to stay alive.

The grandmother explained, "When Annie and Journey were living in Calhoun County, Annie said Journey had an okra patch right behind the big army base there. On weekends, the whores would come in from the nearby town and the soldiers would take them out in the pine thickets near the okra patch at night.

"After the soldiers were finished," the grandmother continued, "they would hang the congers on the pine trees. Annie said Journey would slip out of the house early on Monday mornings and go over and gather the congers off the pine limbs."

The grandmother stopped again.

"What are congers?" the boys asked.

The grandmother tossed a long apple peel into the pan, and then she looked up at the boys, seemingly irritated.

"It's what a man uses when he—" the grandmother suddenly stopped herself. "There are some things you boys don't need to know at your age."

The grandmother returned to the apples.

"What are congers?" Billy asked again.

"I told you," the grandmother broke herself off again. "There are some things—now y'all get on out of here and go play."

The two eleven-year-olds looked at one another, not understanding the subjects their grandmother was describing.

"Now you boys get on out of here," she ordered again. "I've got to finish these apples."

Later that afternoon, while they were fishing back at the creek, they devised a plan.

"Let's go spy on Annie and her husband tonight," Billy

suggested.

"We can't!" Roy said. "We promised Grandma."

Billy looked at his cousin mischievously.

"We might see Annie naked again," Billy pressed.

Roy chuckled at the thought.

"Yeah," he agreed, giggling gleefully.

"But we've got to be careful," Billy counseled. "Grandma will have a fit if she finds out."

That night, very carefully and very stealthily, the two boys went about their appointed mission at The Little House. As the sun went down, they were waiting in the cornfield, and by the time deep darkness fell, they had moved into the broom sage patch.

"The coast is clear," Billy said, peering over the broom sage.

The two darted out of the broom sage to the oak tree and scooted into the crawlspace under the backside of The Little House. Through the big crack in the dining room floor, Billy could see one leg of Journey's overalls as he sat at the table.

"They're eatin'," Billy whispered in the darkness. "Spaghetti and meatballs. I can smell 'em."

The two boys waited. Some ten minutes later, they heard Annie clearing the table and then washing the dishes. Finally, things were quiet. They listened.

"Now stop that!" Journey said abruptly. "I don't like that."

"Journey, I need you," Annie said urgently. "I need your seeds."

"You know I don't like to do it with a woman," he said. The boys could hear the irritation in his voice.

"You're my husband," Annie pressed. "Just do it to me until I get a child. I'm forty-four years old, and I'm not barren."

"I told you no," the man replied. "We've talked about this a hundred times. When we got married, we had an agreement."

"I know," Annie answered. "But I'm so alone. I'd love to have a child."

"When we got married," the man continued, "you said all

you wanted was companionship."

"But I never see you," Annie countered. "You're always gone. If I had a child, I'd have someone to be with me."

The man didn't answer.

"The child could be ours," Annie started again. "It would belong to just the two of us."

"Now what would I do with a child?" the man asked defensively. "A child would just be in my way. I don't have time for a child."

"You wouldn't have to do anything," Annie said. "I'd take care of it. I just want someone to love, somebody that I can hold on to."

There was another long pause.

The man didn't answer.

"Please don't leave me again," Annie pleaded.

"I have to go back and take care of the crop," the man said. "I've got thirty acres of okra. I can't just plant it and leave it."

Another long pause.

"You're going back to Chester, aren't you."

The man didn't answer.

"I knew it," Annie said bitterly. "I hate that man. Oh, I hate him so."

Above them, the two boys could hear Annie weeping softly. Somehow, the two boys had never even dreamed that such a strange woman could shed tears. They waited, hoping to hear more. Some ten minutes later, they heard Annie's feet moving across the floor.

"She's going to bed," Billy whispered, peeking through the big crack. "And he's still at the table."

Under the floor, the two boys could hear Annie crying softly in the bedroom. Fearful they might be discovered, the boys quickly and quietly scrambled out from under the floor of The Little House and raced back across the cornfield.

The following week was the last week in February and the March rent was due. On the third day of March, Mrs. McKinney went to Annie's house to inquire.

"I'm sorry," Annie said, "but Journey hasn't sent me the check yet."

"When do you expect to get it?" the grandmother asked.

"He said if he wasn't back in two weeks, he'd mail it. I'm sure I'll be getting it soon," she said.

The grandmother studied the woman.

"You agreed to pay the rent by the third," the grandmother pressed.

"I know," Annie said apologetically, "but I won't have it until Journey gives it to me."

"Okay," the grandmother said finally. "But once your husband comes back, I'll be expecting my money."

"You'll get it, Mrs. McKinney," Annie promised.

The following week, just before dark, Billy and Roy were back at The Little House to get the latest on Annie. Once they were in the broom sage patch, they peered over at The Little House.

"Look!" Billy said. "It's the old black cat."

On the front porch, the two boys could see the old black cat their grandmother had warned Annie about. It was licking its paws as if it had finished a meal.

"Grandma's gonna be mad about that," Billy said. "Grandma hates that old black cat."

Then he turned to his cousin.

"Come on!" he said.

Moments later, the two boys were in the crawlspace at the small crack under the kitchen floor where they had seen Annie and her nakedness. Billy peered through the small crack into the kitchen area but could see only the bottom of the cook stove and the kitchen ceiling. The house was quiet. The two boys listened.

"Journey," they heard Annie say, "do you want some more canned ham? It's very tasty."

The two boys bolted upright when they heard Annie call her husband's name.

"Journey?" Billy whispered, looking at his cousin.

The two boys could hear Annie walking across the floor to the living room.

"Journey, darling," Annie said. "Let's hear some Guy Lombardo."

The two boys could hear the clicking sound of the old

Victrola being wound up. There was a moment of silence, and then they could hear the scratchy sounds of the song "Canadian Sunset" wafting through the house.

For several minutes, there was only the sound of the Victrola playing. Finally, the song stopped.

"I've always loved Guy Lombardo," Annie said. "His music is so calm and soothing."

"Who is she talking to?" Billy whispered.

Roy shook his head and shrugged.

Again, Billy stuck his eye up to the crack in the floor. Still, all that he could see was the bottom of the cook stove and the ceiling. Then he motioned to Roy that he was going to the big crack under the dining room.

Once he was in the new position, he was instantly startled by what he saw. Frantically, he motioned for Roy. Roy scooted to the other end of the house.

"It's Journey," Billy whispered. "He's there."

Roy peered through the crack in the floor. Above him, he could see the leg of a man dressed in overalls and brogans seated at the table.

"It *is* Journey," Roy said, turning to Billy.

Billy peered through the crack again.

"Yep, that's him," Billy noted conclusively.

In an instant, the two boys jumped up from their hiding place and started back across the cornfield. Billy stopped.

"Should we tell Grandma about the black cat?" he asked.

"If we do, she'll know we been back at Annie's house for sure," Roy concluded.

"Yeah," Billy said resignedly. "And she'll have a fit."

Two days later, Mrs. McKinney and her two grandsons made the long walk from her house to the mailbox out at the main road. After she had retrieved her mail, she saw Annie at her own mailbox. She waved.

"Annie!" the grandmother called.

"Hello, Mrs. McKinney," Annie answered.

"I'm still waiting on this month's rent."

"I told you," Annie said apologetically. "I'll give it to you as soon as Journey gets back."

"When did you say that will be?"

"About ten days from now," Annie said.

There was a pause.

"I believe that's the week of the twenty-third."

"I think that's right," Annie said.

Satisfied, the grandmother, mail in hand and the two grandsons in tow, started walking back to her house.

"Journey's still over there," Billy offered innocently.

"How do you know?" the grandmother asked, turning to her grandson suspiciously.

"Me and Roy saw him going in the house," Billy lied.

"That's not Journey," their grandmother said.

"But it is, Grandma," the boys insisted. "We saw him."

"It can't be!" she said. "He's over in Calhoun County."

"No, it's him," Roy confirmed. "We saw him."

The grandmother stopped. Her frustration showed in her face.

"Will you boys just stop this foolishness," the grandmother said, eyeing them sternly. "Is there no end to your tricks?"

Billy looked at Roy and shrugged, saying nothing. Quietly, the two boys walked with their grandmother back down the dirt road to her house.

The 23rd day of March, 1952, fell on a Sunday. When the boys' grandmother awoke that morning, she checked her calendar and noted that this was the day Annie had promised to have the rent. After Annie hadn't appeared at her house by late afternoon, the boys' grandmother asked them to go over to check on her. She said she would go herself, but she had a terrible case of rheumatism in her left leg and shoulder and could hardly move. She told the boys to tell Annie this was the day she had promised the rent.

The two boys made their regular trek through the cornfield to the broom sage patch and peered over at The Little House.

"Look!" Billy said, pointing.

Roy raised his head.

Annie, who was walking across the front yard to the road, was dressed up in the same severe Victorian outfit she was wearing when she had rented The Little House. She had her frilly purse and she was going somewhere.

"Let's tell her what Grandma said," Roy offered.

"No, wait!" Billy said thoughtfully. "Let's wait until she's gone and then see who that man is."

The two boys waited in the broom sage until Annie was out of sight; moments later, they were in the crawlspace under the house.

Breathlessly, the two boys stopped and listened.

"I don't hear anything," Billy said. "Come on!"

Expertly, they moved through the crawlspace to the other end of the house to the big crack. Then Billy peered up into the dining area. As before, all he could see was the leg of a man's overalls at the kitchen table.

"I say it's Journey," Billy said decisively. "And he hasn't moved."

"What are we gonna do?" Roy asked.

"Come on!" Billy said.

The boys scooted out from under the house. Outside, they stopped to listen again. Everything was quiet. Billy tiptoed to the kitchen window, but the curtain was drawn except for a small crack. Through the small crack, Billy could see the back of a man's head who was seated at the table. He turned to Roy.

"It IS Journey," he said, indicating for his cousin to take a peek.

Roy peered through the crack in the curtain.

"Why's he sitting at the table that way?" Roy asked.

"Let's find out," Billy said.

The two boys bounded around the side of The Little House to the front porch. For a moment, before stepping on the front porch, they stopped and listened. There were no sounds. Then, very quietly and cautiously, the two boys tiptoed across the porch to the front door. Billy stopped and listened. Hearing nothing, he gently nudged the door. It swung open.

"Yikes!" Billy said suddenly, responding to a powerful stench that emanated from inside the house.

Through the open door, the two boys could see all the furniture—the old sofa, the Victrola, a stack of old 78 rpm records as well as the weathered steamer trunk—they had seen

Annie and the black man unloading some two months earlier. Then, like expert cat-burglars, the two boys tiptoed into the living room. Everything was quiet. The stench their noses had sensed on the front porch was almost unbearable now. Instinctively, they stopped to gather themselves before looking in the dining room. Both boys knew that something horrendous was awaiting them. But they also knew that nothing could stop them.

Billy, the leader of the two, looked in first. For a moment, he stood transfixed, frozen stiff by what he was seeing. Then Roy, standing at his cousin's side, peered wide-eyed, also transfixed by the sight. Suddenly, the two eleven-year-olds—unable to contain themselves any longer—screamed in uncontrollable fright and ran out of the house.

"Grandma! Grandma! Grandma!" they screamed at the top of their lungs as they raced through the broom sage patch and across the cornfield. "Grandma! Grandma! Grandma!"

The grandmother, who was still nursing her rheumatoid leg and shoulder, heard the boys' screams long before they reached the cornfield. In fact, she was standing on the back porch waiting when they bounded into the back yard.

"Great God!" she shouted, holding her rheumatoid shoulder. "What's wrong with you kids?"

The two eleven-year-olds, their faces lily-white with fear, were gasping for breath.

"What's wrong? Tell me what's wrong!" the grandmother demanded again.

"Journey's there!" Billy said, panting for dear life and pointing toward The Little House. "Journey's there!"

"Now just calm down and talk to me," she said, somewhat calmer herself.

"Journey's at Annie's house," Billy said breathlessly, "and the black cat's eating him!"

"What? The black cat's eating him?" the grandmother blurted out disbelievingly. "Is this another one of you boys' tricks?"

"No, Grandma. It's true," Roy said, still trying to catch his breath. "I mean, the truth. I swear—Journey's been there all the time."

Now thoroughly agitated, the grandmother—who had forgotten her rheumatoid shoulder and leg—demanded that they calm down and talk sense to her. The boys, who had never been so frightened or breathed so hard in their whole lives, told their grandmother what they had seen. The grandmother listened patiently and waited until the boys had finished.

"This better not be one of your tricks," she warned Billy, still not believing the story.

"It's not," Billy said urgently. "I swear it's not."

The grandmother ordered the two to follow her to The Little House.

When she opened the door, the same powerful stench swept over her and she took off her apron and put it to her nose. Then, showing no sign of fear, she walked straight into the dining room.

For a moment, she gasped at the scene before her. The old black cat, with its back legs on the table and front paws resting on Journey's chest, was nibbling at his lower lip. The grandmother wasted no time taking charge.

"Shoo! Shoo! Get out of here!" she ordered, swinging her hand angrily at the cat.

The hungry animal, seeing the threatening woman, turned from its meal, jumped off the table, and darted out the door.

"My Lord!" she gasped in disgust, now seeing the full scene.

Putting the apron closer to her mouth and nose, she moved nearer. The boys, white with fear, their eyes big as saucers, and holding their noses against the stench, watched as their grandmother inspected the corpse.

Journey's face was bloated and red and the skin around his throat had a stretched, shiny look like the skin of a dog that had been killed on the highway and had been rotting for several days. The black cat had eaten most of the soft tissue around the man's nose and his lips and the grandmother and her two grandsons could see little nibbles the cat had taken out of his cheeks and eyelids. Dressed in Liberty blue overalls and a blue denim shirt buttoned at the top, Journey was sitting perfectly upright in the dining chair. Although his glasses were slightly askew, he was seated as if he were ready to eat. On closer inspection, the grandmother and the two boys could see that Journey had been tied into that exact seated position with several pairs of women's long, wool stockings.

The grandmother, still holding the apron to her nose, examined Journey's eyes and shook her head sadly.

"Looks like Journey got more of that strychnine than the rats did," the grandmother said. "I guess Annie just didn't want to be left alone anymore."

For another long moment, she examined the scene, then suddenly turned to her grandsons.

"You boys come on!" she ordered. "This smell is gonna kill me dead."

The grandmother, still holding her nose, turned and strode out of The Little House with Billy and Roy, still frightened out of their wits, right on her heels.

When they returned home, the grandmother told the boys to go across the road and tell Mr. Shaw to come bring his car because she had to go to town. By the time Billy and Roy returned with Mr. Shaw, their grandmother was ready. She had washed up, put on her best black dress, and was wearing her light-blue pillbox hat. She got into Mr. Shaw's car and ordered the two boys to stay put until she got back.

An hour later, the grandmother returned, except this time she was riding in a sheriff's car and they drove straight to The Little House. The grandmother, holding a knit handkerchief to her nose, escorted the three deputies inside the house and showed them Journey's rotting carcass. Thirty minutes later, a red ambulance arrived, and they carried Journey out of The Little House in a clear plastic bag.

When Annie came home later that afternoon, the sheriff's car was there waiting for her. Annie went right up to the house as if she had somehow been expecting it. As she walked across the yard, the deputies got out of the car and approached her. She seemed a little surprised, but she didn't put up any fight when the deputies told her she was under arrest for murder.

Naturally, Billy and Roy were there to witness the proceedings. They watched from the edge of the broom sage patch as the deputies put chrome-plated handcuffs on Annie's wrists. As the deputies led Annie around the side of the sheriff's car, she looked up and saw Billy and Roy watching. Instinctively, she somehow knew the two boys were the forces behind her downfall.

Annie snarled at them.

"Vermin, you are!" she shouted at them angrily. "Do you hear me? Vermin! Pestilence!"

She shook her handcuffed fists at the two boys in livid anger.

Then one of the deputies pushed Annie's head down and she got into the back seat of the sheriff's car. The deputy slammed the door. As the sheriff's car pulled away from The Little House and out on the highway, Billy and Roy watched sadly.

As with "sexual" and "congers," the two boys didn't know what the words "vermin" and "pestilence" meant. So, as the sheriff's car faded into the distance, Billy and Roy stood at the edge of the broom sage patch and sadly waved goodbye to Annie for the last time. Of all the renters in their grandmother's Little House, Annie had provided the most fun and entertainment. Billy and Roy would miss her terribly. They were just two eleven-year-old boys—meaner than most probably—but still just two bored country kids looking for some adventure and excitement.

****The End****

THE AGREEMENT

Chapter 1

Alma Dawson woke up. Slowly, she sat up in bed, rubbed her eyes to clear away the haze of sleep, and looked at the clock. It was 7:30. She had to be at work by nine. This was Friday. She had to order two new bolts of cotton fabric for City Hall and clear out the stockroom for the new fall line. Also, her daughter Darlene would be coming home from college this afternoon. It would be a busy day. Hurriedly, she got up, slipped into a bathrobe, and went to the kitchen. Once coffee was made, she took a cup and seated herself in front of the television. She flipped through the channels and stopped on a morning talk show.

"The key to a successful marriage," the host was saying, "is communication and respect. Respect begins with knowing your own space and respecting the space of your partner."

"Partner," she said to herself as she got into the shower ten minutes later. It was such an alien word to her. The word felt empty and meaningless on her lips, since her husband had been killed in a construction accident three years earlier. Now, three years later in 1961, she was reconciled to spending the rest of her life alone and had not given a thought to another man. The thought of being intimate with a man and cultivating a loving relationship at this point was like a long-lost dream. At forty-eight, she was well beyond childbearing age and, although well preserved, slight traces of crow's feet had started to creep in around her eyes and mouth. *What in the world could a man possibly want with me now?* She wondered if love would ever find her again.

Once she was showered and dressed, she started out the door, then suddenly remembered the half-bushel of peaches on the back porch. Quickly, she went back through the house, grabbed the peaches, and placed them on the kitchen sink. *That will be my project for tomorrow*, she thought.

By 8:30, she was strolling down Oak Street to her work at Hobson's Fabric Shop on the square in her little town. Aliceville, Georgia was a small country hamlet of some two thousand people and had experienced little or no change over the past thirty years. Located just off I-75 between Macon and Valdosta, the tiny community supported the surrounding cotton farmers, the local agricultural college, and the occasional tourist that wandered by for emergency gas or food. As she strolled past the white picket fences under the spreading arms of the giant white oaks, she remembered how much she loved late August in South Georgia. The sweltering days of mid-August were gone and the cool nights that promised autumn was just around the corner had started to creep in.

At the corner of Oak and Main Streets, Alma saw Helen Winslow bent over in her flower garden.

"Morning, Helen," Alma said. "Those red petunias are so pretty."

Helen, a tall woman in her seventies with long, totally gray hair, stood upright.

"Thanks," she replied. "They could use some more rain. It's been so dry this summer. You doing okay?"

"I'm fine," Alma said. "Off to work."

"How's Tom doing?" she asked, referring to Alma's boss.

"Oh, he's fine," she replied. "As long as business is good, Tom is fine."

Helen laughed.

"Have a good day," Helen told her.

"You too," Alma replied and continued walking.

Once she reached the fabric shop, she stopped and rapped on the glass in the front door. Moments later, the owner, Tom Hobson, a medium built, balding man in his early fifties, opened the door.

"Morning, Alma," he said.

"Morning, Mr. Hobson," she replied.

Once she was inside, he locked the door behind her. The shop didn't open until nine.

"We need to sort out the button rack," he said. "Large buttons are mixed in with small ones and black and colored buttons are thrown in with the white ones. Customers can never seem to put buttons back where they find them."

"I'll take care of it," she replied.

"Also, I have a doctor's appointment at 12:30," he said, "so you may have to work through your lunch hour."

"That makes us even," she replied. "I have to meet Darlene at the bus station at 4:30."

"Fair enough," he replied.

That afternoon, she left the shop at the appointed time and walked across the town square to the bus station behind the county courthouse. Once the bus from Atlanta arrived, she stood outside the door and waited. Her heart leaped with joy when her twenty-one-year-old daughter, Darlene, appeared.

"Baby, I'm so glad to see you," she said, hugging her daughter.

Darlene pecked her mother on the cheek and swung a heavy book bag off her shoulder.

"Mom, I've got two suitcases and a dress carrier," she said. "I'll need your help."

Once the luggage was gathered, mother and daughter started walking the three blocks to the family home.

***

That night for dinner, Alma had prepared meatloaf, mashed potatoes, green beans, and hot biscuits. They ate quietly.

"All of your classes going okay?" the mother asked.

"They're fine, Mom," the daughter replied.

There was an awkward pause. Alma sensed Darlene was preoccupied about something.

"What about your job in the library?" Alma asked.

"It's okay, Mom," she said. "It's a distraction from my studies, but it's okay."

Alma peered at Darlene.

"Is something bothering you?"

The daughter stopped eating and looked straight into her

mother's eyes.

"What are we going to do about the money?" she asked bluntly.

Alma inhaled.

"I was afraid you were going to say that."

"Mama, we can't just sweep this under the rug," Darlene replied. "I've got to finish my senior year. New classes start on September fourteenth. I've got to be signed up and have my tuition paid by September sixth."

Alma didn't reply.

"Mama!" Darlene said impatiently. "Talk to me about this."

"Baby, I know! I know!" the mother shot back. "I know how important it is. I'm just not sure how I'll do it yet, but I promise I'll come up with something."

Darlene could see she had upset her mother.

"Oh, Mom, I'm sorry," the daughter said. "I don't mean to pressure you about this, but we have to do something."

"I know! I know!" the mother replied.

"Thanks, Mom," Darlene responded.

They continued eating.

"If you do the work study program this last year, how much will the remaining total be?"

"About fourteen hundred dollars," Darlene said.

"Oh, my Lord, baby," Alma said, shaking her head. "I don't know where I can get that kind of money."

"Mama, it's my future," the daughter replied. "My calculus teacher says I'm one of the best students he has ever had. I have to graduate."

Alma continued eating.

"I told you my senior year would be the most expensive."

"There's no money left in the trust?"

"Mama, that money was all gone six months ago. That's why I've been cooking in my room. I can't afford to eat at the cafeteria anymore."

"Baby, I'm sorry," the mother replied, turning to take a pencil and pad from the table behind her. "What is the exact amount?"

"The exact total is $1422."

Alma scribbled the number on a pad and shook her head doubtfully.

"Let me see what I can do."

Darlene got up from the table.

"Mom, I'm sorry," she said. "I've got to study for an organic chemistry quiz on Monday."

"But you haven't finished your meal," the mother said.

"I'm not really all that hungry," Darlene replied. "I had a sandwich on the bus. I have to go study."

Alma finished eating and started cleaning up the kitchen.

That night, before she went to bed, she went to her daughter's room to say goodnight. Darlene announced that she was spending Saturday with her friend Linda Powell and would be studying late Saturday night. Alma asked her daughter to attend church with her on Sunday. Darlene agreed.

***

Friendship Baptist Church was the community church in Aliceville. Located one block off the town square, it was a squat white structure with a small belfry and a seemingly endless cemetery surrounding it. Inside, Alma and Darlene, dressed in their Sunday best, were singing the lyrics to "I'm bound for the Promised Land."

"On Jordan's stormy banks I stand and cast a wishful eye, to Canaan's fair and happy land where my procession lies," they sang. "I am bound for the promised land, I am bound for the promised land. Oh, who will come and go with me? I am bound for the promised land."

Once the song was finished, the pastor, Rev. Willard Mize, took to the pulpit to begin the sermon.

"Today's sermon will be taken from the Book of Revelation," he said solemnly. He opened a well-worn Bible and started reading.

An hour later, as always, Alma was waiting at the church's front door to congratulate the pastor on the day's sermon.

"I enjoyed the sermon today," she said. "You always seem to find new meanings in Revelation."

"Thank you!" the reverend replied, shaking Alma's hand and glancing over at the daughter.

"Darlene! How are you?" he asked. "What's happening up in the big city?"

"Oh, I'm studying hard every day," Darlene replied with a polite smile.

"That's great," the reverend added. "I'm happy for you and wish you every success."

He turned back to Alma.

"Can I speak with you privately just a moment?"

"Sure," Alma replied.

"When you clean the church next time, please check that old broom closet in the adult Sunday school room. There is something in there that smells."

"Yes, reverend," she replied. "I'll take care of it."

The reverend moved on to speak with other members of the congregation and Alma and Darlene started to go. As they did, someone called Alma's name.

She turned.

It was her brother Carl, a stocky, sunburned, fiftyish man who was putting his children into the family car. Once everyone was safely inside, he slammed the door and walked over.

"Sister Alma," he said, hugging her.

Then he turned to the daughter.

"My! My!" he said proudly. "Aren't you a pretty thing? I'll bet all those boys in Atlanta are chasing you every which way."

Darlene smiled.

"Don't have a lot of time for boys," Darlene replied. "I spend all of my time with my nose in a book."

"I'm sure that's what it takes to make good grades," he continued. "Good to see y'all. I've got to get back to the family."

***

Back at home that afternoon, Alma gathered Darlene's freshly washed clothes, folded them, and helped her pack for the return trip. Once packed, Alma had her daughter try on two new dresses she was making. The shoulders and the hemline on one were a perfect fit. The second dress, the blue flowery one, was a little large in the shoulders and would need some adjustments.

At 4:15, Alma and Darlene were waiting at the station when the bus pulled in. They watched as the driver loaded her luggage into the undercarriage, then Darlene, ticket in hand, prepared to board.

Alma took her daughter in her arms and looked at her face-to-face.

"I want to say one thing before I let you go," she said. "I'll get the money. I'm not sure how, but I'll get it. You can count on it."

"Thanks, Mom," the daughter replied. "I know you will. I love you. Bye."

Alma watched as her daughter boarded the bus and took a window seat. Finally, all of the passengers were loaded and Alma waved good-bye as the bus, in a haze of diesel smoke, pulled out of the station.

Once Alma was back at home, she went straight to the big chest of drawers in her bedroom and opened the secret compartment. She pulled out an old shoebox, then, while sitting on the bed, started to rifle through the contents. There were old mortgage papers, a warranty deed, her late husband's pocket watch, her mother's wedding ring, an insurance policy, and about seventy dollars in cash. She removed the insurance policy from its sheath. The value of the policy was five hundred dollars. She read the fine print closely, trying to determine the cash value, but the information was vague. She studied the watch and her mother's wedding ring. There wasn't much value to the watch, she thought, and she could only part with her mother's wedding ring in an absolutely dire emergency. Finally, she set the insurance policy aside, returned the other items to the shoebox, and returned it to its hiding place. As she prepared for bed, she realized she didn't have a lot of financial resources. She received fifty-five dollars a week salary plus ten per cent commission on fabrics she sold at Hobson's; she had thirty dollars a month coming in for her church cleaning, and she made another twenty dollars a month on outside sewing jobs. The total came to around three hundred dollars a month and, by the time she made the mortgage payment of ninety-five dollars a month, she had to watch every last penny to make ends meet. Maybe she could borrow money on the equity in her home.

***

At lunch on Monday, she went to the Farmers and Merchants Bank down the street from work and got the application for a loan. That night, she meticulously filled out the form requesting to borrow twelve hundred dollars. The following day at lunch, she returned to the bank. The bank's mortgage representative was a blondish, baby-faced man in his late twenties.

"I don't think we can help you," he said after reviewing the application. "The equity in your home is not quite eight hundred dollars and, with our current policy, the most we could lend would be about four hundred dollars. That's on the high side."

"I need more than that," Alma replied. "Who else can I talk to?"

"You can talk to Mr. Tipton," he replied. "He's the president, but I'm afraid he will tell you the same thing."

Alma had known Bill Tipton from a distance for more than twenty years. She remembered he was a teller when she was in high school. After she was married, he had negotiated the original mortgage for her and her husband. Over the years, Alma had been good friends with his late wife Bonnie Faye and frequently worked with her on church projects.

Moments later, Alma was in his office.

"Good morning, Alma," Bill said as she entered his office. She took a seat, handed him her application, and explained her dilemma. He glanced through the application, checked a small notebook, then turned back to her.

"Alma, I wish I could help you," he said. "But in your situation and with your income, we can't loan you more than about four hundred dollars."

"I've been doing business with this bank for over twenty years," she replied. "Doesn't that count for anything?"

"Yes," he said apologetically. "And we appreciate your business, but the way times are now, four hundred dollars is the best we can do. I'm sorry."

***

Back at home, she returned to the chest of drawers, withdrew the shoebox, and removed the insurance policy.

At the bank the following day, the president welcomed her into his office a second time.

"Alma, I'd love to help you, but we don't make loans on insurance policies," he said finally. "The best way to get money from a life insurance policy is to get it directly from the company. Call the company and see what the cash value is."

That afternoon, when she spoke to the insurance company, the clerk said the policy had no cash value at present. The full five-hundred-dollar value on the policy could not be redeemed until she was fifty-five. Alma angrily slammed down the phone.

When she showed up at the bank the following day, the president was amused at her tenacity.

"There's just no stopping you," he said with a smile. "What do you have this time?"

She untied the handkerchief and showed him the wedding ring.

"That's a nice ring," he said, examining it. "This must have a lot of sentimental value."

"It does," she said. "But this is an emergency."

He slowly shook his head, then handed the ring back to her.

"Alma, I'm sorry to have to say no for a third time, but banks don't lend money on wedding rings," he said. "That's the domain of pawn shops."

She took a deep breath.

"Can you loan me anything on it?"

He shook his head sadly.

"I had to try," she said. "Thanks for your time."

She got up and turned to go.

"Alma," he called.

She turned.

"Please sit back down," he said with a welcoming gesture.

She took her seat again.

"I admire you for your interest in your daughter's education. It's only natural that a loving mother wants the very best for her daughter."

He hesitated to continue.

"Yes?" she nudged.

"I've known you a long time and, to be honest, I've been a secret admirer…"

"A secret admirer?" she asked.

"Yes, a secret admirer," he replied. "You know, I find you to be a very attractive woman."

"What does that have to do with loaning me money to pay for my daughter's education?"

"Well…" He started to say something, then stopped.

He was silent for a moment.

"Go ahead," she prodded.

"Perhaps, we could… work out something," he said finally.

"What do you mean…'work out something'?"

He got up from his desk and peered out the window at the street for several moments.

"You know, the county flushes that fire hydrant every Tuesday," he said offhandedly. "What an incredible waste of water…"

"What is your point, Mr. Tipton?"

He turned back to her.

"As you know, I'm getting up in years. I'll be sixty in November. My wife passed three years ago and I sometimes find myself feeling lonely…"

He stopped.

"I still don't follow you."

"You're a very attractive woman," he replied. "Of course, I've been aware of that since you started coming into the bank many years ago…"

She stared at him, refusing to believe where he was going with the conversation.

"Perhaps we could arrange for some private meetings between us in exchange for your daughter's tuition…"

Suddenly, livid anger shot through her.

"Mr. Tipton!" she said angrily, getting up from the chair. "What do you think I am? Some harlot? I'm a Christian woman. I could never do anything like that."

"Alma," he said apologetically. "I didn't mean to offend you. I can see that you intend to get your daughter through her last year of college no matter what it takes. On the other hand, you don't have the financial resources to accomplish that. I thought we could…help one another."

She had heard enough.

"I can't believe you would say something like that," she said. "I'm a respectable woman. Do you understand? Not some harlot who sells her body! Thank you and good day!!"

With that, she grabbed her purse, jerked open the office door, and stormed out of the bank.

Back at home, she collapsed on the bed and started crying. She never dreamed the pursuit of her daughter's college education would take such a sordid turn. *How could he dare to propose something like that?* she thought. What would her friends and neighbors think? Not to mention her daughter and her brother. Her head was spinning with doubts and fears and unresolved expectations. Finally, tired, weary, and frustrated, she fell asleep and slept throughout the night.

At work the next day, she called her daughter and asked her if she had checked with the college financial offices for any available state or federal programs to help college students. Darlene said she had done so numerous times. Back at home that night, Alma did the addition again. Perhaps she had made a mistake, but, after doing the math for the umpteenth time, she got the same result. Even with the four-hundred-dollar loan from the bank, she was going to be seven hundred dollars short. The numbers spoke for themselves. She had a week to come up with the money. It didn't look good.

***

On Saturday, the truck from the farmer's market delivered

two bushels of purple peas, one bushel of green beans, and two pecks of cucumbers to her door. Immediately after the delivery, she started shelling the peas and snapping the green beans for canning. Saturday afternoon, she spent cleaning the church and found a dead mouse in the old broom closet the pastor had mentioned. On Sunday, she attended Sunday school and worship services and the pastor complimented her on her cleaning. That afternoon, she started peeling the cucumbers to make dill pickles. As she drifted off to sleep that night, she thought perhaps she should reconsider the bank president's offer.

On Monday morning on her lunch break, she went to the bank. Once she arrived, she peeked inside his office and saw Bill was with a customer. For a moment, she started to sign the register, then lost her nerve and walked back to Walden's Drug for lunch. On Tuesday, she returned to the bank and went inside.

"Please sign the register," the secretary said. "Mr. Tipton has two customers ahead of you."

She signed the register and took a seat. While waiting, she could see Bill Tipton in his office talking to a farmer, gesturing and arguing about something. Moments later, the farmer left and another person went in. Finally, after waiting some ten minutes, she got up and left.

That afternoon, as she was leaving work, Mr. Hobson pulled her aside.

"Alma," he asked. "Are you okay?"

"I'm fine," she replied. "Why do you ask?"

"Lately, you seem distracted," he said. "It's like your mind is not on your job. Mrs. Carter said you gave her four yards of the blue cotton material she is using to make curtains when she only needed three."

"It was a mistake," Alma replied.

He looked at her and inhaled.

"I guess anybody can make a mistake."

On Wednesday, she screwed her courage to the sticking place and marched inside the bank unafraid. No one was waiting. She glimpsed into the president's office. He was alone. *This is it,* she thought. *No more indecision*. She quickly signed the register and the secretary said, “Go right in.”

“Good afternoon, Alma,” he began. “How are you today?”

“Fine, thank you,” she said, taking a seat.

“How can I help you?”

She looked at him nervously, trying to find an entry point.

“Yes, go ahead,” he said impatiently.

“Can we close the door?” she asked.

“Sure,” he replied. He stood, walked around his desk, closed the door, and reseated himself.

Alma cleared her throat.

“Mr. Tipton, I have been thinking about the offer you mentioned when I was in your office last week…”

“You have reconsidered?”

She nodded.

“If I agreed to something like that, how would it work?”

“What exactly are you asking?” he said.

“You do remember the proposal you made to me last week?”

“Yes!” he said. “It still stands.”

“If I agreed to accept, how would it work? How would the meetings take place? Where and when would they occur?”

He studied her for a moment.

“What would you feel comfortable with?” he asked.

“What would YOU feel comfortable with?” she replied.

“Would you like to meet at a motel?”

“Oh, no,” she replied quickly. “I don’t have a car. That would be out of the question.”

He looked thoughtfully at her.

“Could we meet at your house?”

“It would have to be on weekends,” she said. “I work during the week and, if my daughter is visiting over the weekend, we would have to reschedule.”

“I understand,” he said thoughtfully.

“How often would we meet?” she asked.

“Three times a month?”

“What about two times a month?”

He got up and stared out the window at the street for several moments. Finally, he turned.

“I could work with that.”

He looked at her.

"Will you try to make the experience as enjoyable as possible?" he asked.

"I am not a woman who takes my duties lightly," she replied.

He laughed.

"It could be a pleasant experience for both of us," he offered.

She changed the subject.

"You will take all of the necessary birth control measures during our meetings?"

"Of course," he said.

She was silent.

"When would the agreement end?" he asked.

"When my daughter graduates…"

He cleared his throat.

"When is that?"

"Next May."

He looked at her, took a deep breath, and walked to the window.

"When shall we have the first meeting?" he asked with his back to her.

"Are we in agreement that the contract ends upon my daughter's graduation?"

"Yes," he said, turning back to her. "We are in agreement."

"My daughter starts her new classes on September fourteenth. Would the Saturday night of September twentieth be acceptable?"

"Yes," he replied.

For a long moment, neither said anything.

"The money for my daughter's tuition is due on September sixth."

He pursed his lips thoughtfully and looked at the calendar on his desk.

"Have the college send the bill for your daughter's expenses to the bank to my attention," he said solemnly, marking the calendar. "If anyone questions my actions, I will say the money is a personal loan."

They stared at one another for a long moment in silence.

"Is there anything else you want to ask?" he asked finally.

"Knowledge of the agreement will remain strictly between us?"

"Absolutely," he said.

Another long silence.

"So we have an agreement?" he asked.

"Yes, we have an agreement," she replied.

Chapter 2

That night, she couldn't sleep. She kept trying to imagine what it would be like to have illicit sex with Bill Tipton. Tall, with graying hair and well preserved for his age, he was not a particularly handsome man, but he was not unattractive either. Always well dressed and clean-shaven, he had a quiet, no-nonsense manner. There was a little paunch in the waist, but he would be pleasant, she told herself, trying to find as much good in the situation as possible. She knew she didn't have to worry about violence or ill feelings from him. As she retraced her thoughts, she still wasn't sure she could do it. In her heart, she needed more convincing. Even if she didn't approve of what she was about to do, she was going to have to make the best of it. It was something she had to do. It was her duty.

Throughout the week of September 20, her thoughts turned again and again to the first meeting. On the evening of the 19th, he called and asked if he could arrive at eight p.m. She said that would be fine and she spent the evening cleaning the house. By seven p.m. the following evening, she had taken a shower, washed her hair, and perfumed her body. As she prepared herself, she was strangely reminded of her wedding night and the first time she had sex with her late husband. It seemed so ironic. Promptly at eight p.m., she saw his Chrysler sedan pull up to the curb. As she saw the headlights shut off, she waited nervously for the doorbell to ring. When she opened the door, he was wearing a business suit and carried a white box under his arm.

"This is for you," he said, handing her the box.

Once inside, she led him into the bedroom.

"The bathroom is over there," she said, pointing. "There is a new bar of soap and a fresh towel."

Once he went into the bathroom, she opened the package.

It was an expensive piece of white, lacey lingerie. It had been purchased in Atlanta at Whitman's department store. As she stared at the label, she could hear him taking a shower. Hurriedly, she slipped on the nightie, turned off the light, and crawled into bed.

***

The following morning, she got up early, had coffee, and sat at the sewing machine for almost an hour resizing the shoulders on the blue flowery dress she was making for her daughter. A master seamstress, she quickly cut out the new shoulder pieces, unstitched and removed the old ones, then expertly sewed in the new pieces. Once finished, she held it up for visual inspection. It was perfect.

Two hours later, as she walked to church services, she wondered how many of her fellow parishioners had noticed the Chrysler sedan parked in front of her house on Saturday night. The sermon was taken from the Book of Job and the pastor kept asking the congregation if they had examined their own lives and determined if they would have had the patience of Job.

On Monday morning, Mr. Hobson said a national sewing machine company was opening a new store down on I-75 and would be providing some stiff competition. He said she needed to push for as many new sales as possible. At lunch that day, she ran into Helen. They had bacon, lettuce, and tomato sandwiches and chitchatted about gardening, recipes, and their families.

Two weeks later, during the second meeting, she felt far more comfortable. The ice had been broken. She had some idea of what to expect. After he left that night, she drifted off to sleep and, for some unknown reason, dreamed of princes and white horses and maidens in distress being saved by gallant knights in shining armor.

***

Over the next two months, her life became a fixed routine.

The cycle of work, meetings with Bill, church cleaning, church services, and side sewing jobs made her life very predictable. She loved staying busy.

The second week in November, she was walking to work when Helen called her over.

"Want to have lunch at Walden's today?" she asked. "I want to talk to you."

"Sure," Alma said. "I'll be there around 12:30."

At lunch, Helen said her daughter Doris had just gotten a new job at the new Tri-State Sewing Center.

"She knows a lot about sewing," Helen said, "but she's not a master like you. Would you mind giving her some tips?"

"Sure," Alma replied.

That Saturday, Alma met with Doris at Walden's. After a brief conversation, she took Doris to her home, sat down at the sewing machine, and gave her some sewing lessons. She explained the advantages and disadvantages of different stitches for different parts of a garment. She explained that, in most cases, a single seam was sufficient for the inside of a sleeve whereas shoulders always required a double seam. When Alma finished, Doris was very impressed.

"Oh, Alma," she said, "why don't you come to work at Tri-State? They would love to have you. With your knowledge, you could not only teach sewing classes, but you could sell sewing machines and fabric. You know, they pay twenty-five dollars for every person you get to sign up for a sewing class. And they have four full rooms of fabric. You could make three or four times what you are making now."

Alma looked at her interestedly.

"I could use the money," she said, "that's for sure, but I don't have a car. How would I get to work?"

"You could ride with me," Doris said quickly. "If you will help me learn sewing at your level, I would be honored for you to ride to work with me."

"Sounds good," Alma said. "I'm not sure what I'm going to tell Mr. Hobson."

"Tell him whatever," Doris said firmly. "You deserve much better than what you have."

"Do you really think so?" Alma asked.

"On Friday afternoon, I will meet you at Walden's," Doris replied. "I will take you down to Tri-State and you can talk to the manager."

After Doris left, Alma thought perhaps she was right. She certainly had a much broader knowledge of sewing than she was being paid for. On the other hand, she felt comfortable selling fabric, but had never sold sewing machines or taught classes. *It can't be that difficult,* she told herself. As she closed the sewing machine, she felt a rising tide in her life. She didn't know where it was coming from, but in her heart and mind, she sensed she was suddenly casting off the shackles of the old and embracing the freedom of the new. She wasn't quite sure why.

On Friday afternoon, as planned, Alma went with Doris to Tri-State to meet the manager. Abigail Abercrombie was an unsmiling, bespectacled woman in her early fifties.

"You have great experience," she surmised at the end of the interview. "You are doing stitches on the new machines that it takes some students months to learn."

"Thank you," Alma said.

"When do you want to start work?"

"I'll have to work out a notice with Mr. Hobson," she said. "He has been very good to me."

"I understand," the manager replied.

***

During the meeting with Bill on Saturday night, Darlene called and told her mother she wanted her to come to Atlanta to meet her new beau, Mark Freeman.

"Oh, baby," Alma said. "I'd love to, but I can't afford to come to Atlanta."

When she hung up the phone, Bill asked, "Your daughter wants you to come to Atlanta?"

Alma nodded.

"I'm going up for the big game between Georgia Central and the Engineers on Thanksgiving," he said. "Do you want to go?"

She stared at him.

"I couldn't afford to pay for a room," she said.

"I would take care of it," he replied.

She studied him.

"We'd have to sleep in separate rooms," she said. "For my daughter's sake."

"I understand," he replied.

"Sure you don't mind?" she asked.

"No, not at all," he replied.

***

On Monday morning, she told Mr. Hobson she had been offered a job at Tri-State.

"Oh, Alma," he said almost apologetically, "I'll miss you. You've been such a good employee, but I know you'll be fine. Tri-State is one of the biggest sewing machine manufacturers in the USA. I'm sure you'll do well."

She spent the following Friday night packing for the trip to Atlanta. As she packed a suitcase, she recalled that she hadn't been to Atlanta in fourteen years. She wondered what Darlene would think when she appeared with a strange man.

On Saturday, they arrived in Atlanta just before noon. Bill got two rooms at the Atlanta Suites hotel and they started for the stadium. Outside the stadium, Darlene happily hugged her mother and Alma introduced Bill.

"Where's Mark?" Alma asked.

"Mom, I'm sorry," Darlene said. "He had to go back home this weekend. His father is very sick."

Once they bought tickets and started walking into the stadium, Bill stopped in front of a souvenir stand to examine some hats.

"These will help keep the sun off us," he said, trying on one. "We don't want to get sunburned."

After trying several, he decided on one and turned to Darlene and Alma.

"Do you want one of these?" he asked. "It will not only prove you are a true Engineer fan, but it will keep the sun off your face."

"Sure," Darlene replied.

Once Darlene and Alma were outfitted with hats, Bill bought three red Georgia Engineers pennants to wave during the game.

"Thanks, Bill!" Darlene replied. "Can I call you Mr. Bill?"

"Absolutely!" he replied.

After Bill excused himself for the men's room, Darlene turned to her mother.

"Is he our beau?" Darlene asked.

Alma didn't know how to answer.

"He's a good friend," she said.

"Are you and he staying in the same room?"

"No!"

Darlene studied her mother.

"How did you meet him?"

"I've known him a long time."

"He is such a generous man," Darlene said.

***

Although Alma knew nothing about football, she waved her pennant and cheered in unison with Bill and Darlene. Every time the Engineers would score, Bill and Darlene would look at each other and cheer. At the half, the score was 14-14. After Central went ahead with a field goal in the fourth quarter, it appeared Central was going to win. On a final drive late in the fourth quarter, the Engineer quarterback threw a make-or-break pass into the end zone and it was hauled in by the receiver. As he raced across the goal line with the winning score, Bill and Darlene cheered and hugged one another with pure joy.

At Thanksgiving dinner, Darlene and Bill dominated the conversation with discussions about politics, the economy, and her studies. Bill explained that he had attended Georgia Engineering "in his youth" and had been a rabid football fan ever since. After dinner, Darlene returned to her dorm room and Alma and Bill retired to their hotel rooms.

On the return trip to Aliceville the next day, Alma told him, "I think my daughter likes you."

The following week was her last week at Hobson's and the

days seemed to drag on interminably. Alma would be so glad when it was over. She couldn't wait to launch into her new job. On Thursday, in the late afternoon, her brother Carl appeared. He asked her to come outside to talk. She could see he was upset. He didn't hug her.

"People are talking about you, Alma," he started.

"What?"

"Hazel Wilson told Pauline Stoddard that you and Bill Tipton went up to Atlanta together for the big game last weekend."

"So?" she replied. "That's my business."

"When Pauline Stoddard knows something, the whole world knows. Now everybody in church is talking…"

She didn't answer.

"This is a small town," he said. "Gossip spreads like wildfire."

"They can think what they like," Alma said confidently. "I'm leading my own life for a change."

"Alma, it don't look good for you to be running around with a man at your age when you're not married to him."

"I'm a grown woman," she said defiantly.

"Alma," he said. "What's happening to you? These people have been your life all these years."

"Things are different now," she said.

He could see he was not gaining ground.

"You're my sister," he said. "How do you think it makes me feel to see you spending weekends with a man you're not married to?"

"I'm sorry if my actions hurt you," she said, her voice trailing off.

He looked at her disapprovingly.

"I've got to go," she said. "I've got work to do."

"Alma, please listen to me," her brother said.

"I've got to go," she said.

She turned and went back inside.

He brother shook his head disconsolately and watched helplessly as she walked away.

***

On Friday, she said good-bye to Mr. Hobson and thanked him for her employment. On Saturday, she spent the day canning squash and preparing for her new job. She had studied all of the new sewing machine literature the Tri-State manager provided. There were four new stitches she had not seen before. She promised herself she would practice those when she started work on Monday.

On Sunday, she went to church. As she started up the church steps, she noticed that the only person that came to greet her was Helen.

"Alma," Helen said. "Thanks for helping Doris. You have meant so much to her."

Alma acknowledged the compliment and waved to Emily Harrison, but her old friend pretended not to see her. Other members of the congregation hurried past her into the church.

After services, as always, she waited outside to speak with the pastor. Several times, she tried to approach the pastor, but he always seemed to be speaking with someone else. Finally, when all of the other church members were gone, he approached her.

"Good morning, Alma," he said. "May we speak privately for a moment?"

"Sure!"

"I wanted to ask you something," he said.

"Are you not happy with my cleaning?" she asked.

"No, that's not it."

He looked at her long and hard.

"Have you strayed away from the teachings of our Lord and Savior?"

She stared at him.

"Strayed? In what way?"

"In matters of adultery," he replied self-righteously.

"Why do you ask me that?"

"Members of the congregation are talking…"

"What are they saying?"

He inhaled.

"Talking about you and Bill Tipton."

She looked at him.

"That's my business and no one else's," she replied.

"As long as you come to this church, it's the business of the Lord."

She didn't answer.

"Reverend, I'm sorry; I have to go," she said. "Have a good day."

With that, she turned and started to walk away.

"Alma," he called after her.

She turned.

"Your services cleaning the church will no longer be needed," he said solemnly. "Hilda Wilson will be cleaning the church from now on."

Deeply stung, she stopped. She could feel livid anger building inside her.

"Do you understand?" he asked.

She glared at him. She tried desperately to remain calm, and then suddenly, involuntarily, rage took over.

"You can take your job and stick it where the sun don't shine!" she shouted. "Do YOU understand? Where the sun don't shine…"

The reverend looked her disbelievingly.

He glared at her, shook his head, and turned back to the church.

As he walked away, she couldn't believe she had said that to the reverend. Suddenly, from God knows where, she had a new sense of boldness and self-confidence she had never known before. She was no longer going to live in fear of what others thought of her. *I'm leading my own life for a change,* she said to herself. *No more shrinking, obedient violet.*

***

The following Monday, she started work at Tri-State. From the moment she entered the door, she threw herself headlong into her duties. There was so much to learn. In speaking to customers, she learned very quickly to identify those who had little sewing experience. These were the customers she pitched the classes to. She always looked for new housewives who had just set up housekeeping or older housewives who were looking for new sewing projects. She had learned the company's machines from top to bottom. She knew every stitch; she understood the different pattern formats from each manufacturer. By the end of the first week, she had sold three sewing machines, signed up nine new students for sewing classes, and sold 141 yards of fabric. When she got her check at the end of the week, she couldn't believe it. It was $314.22. That was more money than she made at Hobson's in a month.

On Monday, she went to Farmers and Merchants Bank and opened a savings account. It was the first time she had ever had one. Now that she had extra money, the repair projects that she had not been able to afford—the light over the stove, the hanging gutter on the porch, and the old dead tree in the back yard—would get completed. She must not squander her newfound wealth, she told herself. She knew her standard of living and she vowed to not veer far from it. Most of all, she wanted her daughter to have a good Christmas.

***

At Christmas, Darlene came home. Alma had a little tree with brightly colored lights she set up in the living room. She had cooked a small turkey and dressing with giblet gravy and made fruitcake and ambrosia salad. On Christmas morning, mother and daughter exchanged gifts. Darlene had purchased a newer, bigger purse "for all your money" and a gift certificate to buy a new kitchen blender. Darlene's eyes widened with interest when she opened her mother's main gift. It was a new leather jacket.

"Oh, Mom," she said happily. "This is beautiful."

"Try it on!" Alma said.

Darlene slipped on the jacket and her mother inspected the fit.

"It's perfect," she surmised expertly. "Sleeves, shoulders, and waist are perfect."

Darlene examined the label.

"Mom," the daughter said. "This is Italian leather. It is very expensive."

"I splurged a little on that," she said. "I'm making good money now."

On Sunday, Darlene asked why her mother wasn't going to church.

"They didn't approve of my relationship with Bill," she said.

Darlene looked at her.

"Let 'em go to hell," Darlene replied firmly. "They're just a bunch of hypocrites anyway."

Alma laughed at her daughter's resoluteness.

"Thanks for the support, baby!" she said and hugged her daughter.

***

By mid-April of 1962, Alma Dawson was very prosperous. For the week of April 16, she received a check for $432.18. For the first time in her entire life, she was financially independent. Once the agreement was completed, she would have no obligations to anyone. Her next goal was to buy a car. She already had a valid license.

That afternoon, on the drive back home, Doris told her she should talk to Roscoe Morgan in Albany about a new car.

"At least he's honest," Doris said. "Daddy used to buy cars from him and always seemed happy."

On Saturday, Doris and Alma went to Morgan Motors in Albany. Finally, after scouring the lot, she chose a light-blue 1960 Pontiac sedan. The salesman drew up the papers and handed her the keys.

Alma looked at the keys, then at Doris. She was giddy with excitement.

"Now watch that gas pedal," the salesman said. "You know that thing will be on eighty before you know it."

"Oh, I'm not a fast driver," she said.

She got into the car and started the engine. It was the first time she had driven a car in five years. Once she put the car in gear and pulled off the lot, she felt perfectly comfortable. When she arrived home, she parked it in the driveway, then started in. Reaching the porch, she stopped. She wanted to see how the car looked parked in front of her house. As she stepped out to the street and looked at the car and the house, she was very impressed with herself. *My, my,* she thought, *you've come a long way.*

***

The final meeting was on May 3, 1962. Bill had arrived early and she had not had time to clean the house to her specifications. While he was in the shower, she made up the bed and started tidying up the living room. Once he emerged from the shower, he took his hat and prepared to leave.

"Darlene graduates on Sunday," she said.

"You plan to attend?"

"Of course," she replied.

"Would you like for me to accompany you?"

"Sure, if you like…"

"We could go in my car."

"Would you mind?" she asked. "You know your way around Atlanta much better than I do. I will pay for the gas and my room."

"You don't have to do that," he said.

"I want to," she replied. "I have money now. Remember?"

He smiled.

***

On the morning of May 17, 1962, Bill and Alma arrived early at the Georgia College of Engineering stadium for graduation ceremonies. They listened quietly as the president spoke of the future of the graduates and their prospects for meeting the new modern world. Once the grandiose speech was finished, the president started handing out diplomas. When he called the name "Sharla Darlene Dawson," Alma cried tears of joy as she watched her daughter, dressed in a gray graduation gown and mortarboard, march across the podium to receive her diploma.

After the ceremony, they met Darlene as she stepped off the podium.

"Congratulations, baby," Alma said, hugging her daughter. "I'm so proud of you."

Next, she turned to Bill.

"Congratulations!" he said and hugged her.

Once he released her, he handed her an envelope.

She stared at it.

"Open it later," he said happily. "That's my gift. You'll be interviewing for jobs very soon and you know I will give you a good reference."

"Thanks, Mr. Bill," Darlene replied. "Thanks very much."

***

Both said little on the trip back to Aliceville. The moment of truth was upon them. After the sedan stopped in front of her home, Alma asked him to come in for coffee.

"As you know, the agreement is at an end," she started. "I have fulfilled my obligations."

He looked at her.

"Yes, you have," he said. "What do you plan to do now?"

"I want to go my own way," she said firmly. "My life has changed a lot over the past nine months and I want to pursue it on my own. I hope we can always remain friends."

"So do I," he said.

He studied her for a moment.

"Do you have feelings for me?" he asked finally.

"Yes," she said. "I've become very fond of you, but now that the agreement has ended, I want to go my own way."

"You know I've fallen in love with you," he said.

She stopped and peered inquisitively at him.

"What?" she asked in disbelief. "You've fallen in love with me?"

He nodded.

"People don't fall in love as a result of the situation you and I were in," she replied.

"I did," he said. "In my heart, I've been in love with you for many years. The agreement only deepened it."

"I'm sorry," she said. "I don't feel that way…"

He studied her silently.

"We had a business arrangement," she continued. "Love and affection were never part of it."

"I know," he said. "Can Darlene and I still be friends?"

"Sure," she said. "You know she thinks the world of you… I'll always owe you for that."

He was trying to gather his thoughts.

"You're breaking my heart," he said finally.

"I'm sorry," she replied. "That was never my intention."

He looked away and stared at the floor.

"We can still be friends," she replied.

"I wanted more than that," he said.

"I'm sorry," she said. "I just want to find my new life on my own."

"I respect your wishes," he said.

For a long moment, he stared at her, then got up to go.

"I'll miss you," he said.

Alma didn't reply.

She watched sadly as he strode across the room and closed the door behind him.

Chapter 3

This can't be love, she thought as she watched his sedan pull away from the curb. *People don't fall in love as a result of what happened between us*. This was a business arrangement, something she had to do for her daughter and, once finished, there was nothing remaining. Love is built on longtime friendships, personal chemistry, and an essential affection between two people. People fall in love after dating and learning one another. She certainly wasn't in love with him. She was fond of him and had infinite respect, but that basic feeling of deep friendship and endearment she had for her late husband was absent. She knew that for sure. She told herself she was smart enough to recognize the difference between what love was and what it was not.

Over the next two weeks, Alma settled into her new life. She was in the office by 7:30 each morning, organizing the sewing classes, ordering new fabrics, interviewing for sales jobs, and supervising three salespeople and two sewing instructors. She even had a plate glass window in the sewing classroom replaced after some kids had knocked it out with a baseball. On Saturdays, she had been getting her hair and nails done at Mildred's Beauty Shop in Albany. The faulty light over the kitchen table had been replaced, but a half-bushel of yellow squash she had planned to pare and can had rotted on the kitchen sink. *So be it,* she thought. She was a businesswoman now.

Although she was totally absorbed in her job, she felt a lingering emptiness inside. Something was missing. She wasn't sure where it was originating, but there was a gnawing loneliness inside that continued to crop up again and again. She refused to believe that the end of the agreement and the intimacy was the root cause of the emptiness. Maybe if she threw herself into her job long enough, the feeling would go away, she told herself.

During the last week in May, Darlene came home for the weekend. On Saturday morning, she announced that she and Mr. Bill were going to Albany to go shopping. There were some new skirts at Coleman's Department Store she wanted to look at.

"Morning, Alma," Bill said upon arrival. "You look very nice today with your new hairdo."

"Thanks!" she replied.

"Mom!" Darlene interjected. "We're leaving. We'll be back early afternoon."

They started to leave. Bill turned.

"Alma, you're welcome to go with us."

"Oh, I know," she replied. "I'm very busy today. Y'all go ahead and have a good time. Just take care of my daughter."

"I will," he replied.

***

Once she heard the door shut, the house was quiet again. Somehow, she felt uneasy that Darlene was with Bill rather than her on a Saturday when she was visiting. She wanted her daughter and Bill to stay friends, but she didn't want her daughter to neglect her for him. On Sunday afternoon, she helped Darlene pack her suitcase for the trip back to Atlanta. Darlene would be staying with her friend Diana while interviewing for jobs.

On Sunday, before putting her daughter on the bus, Alma asked, "Can I come up to Atlanta and visit you next weekend?"

"Visit me?"

"Yes," Alma replied. "I have a car now. Remember?"

"What would you do in Atlanta?"

"Well, I could visit my daughter and do some shopping in the big city…"

"That's fine," Darlene said. "You can meet Diana."

The following Saturday, Alma put on her new store-bought dress, got her hair and nails done, and made the two-hour drive to Atlanta. On arrival, Alma met Diana; they chitchatted and Diana left to go to work.

"What are you doing tonight?" Alma asked.

"I'm getting ready for my interview tomorrow," Darlene replied.

"I want you to do me a favor."

"Want me to take you shopping?"

Alma shook her head.

"I want you to go to a bar with me."

The daughter laughed out loud.

"A bar?"

"Yes," Alma said. "I've never gone into a bar as a single woman. When your father and I were dating, we would go a beer joint every now and then and I would act like I was drinking. I just want to see what it's like..."

Darlene looked at her mother and laughed.

"Mother, are you sure?" she said, staring at her mother in disbelief.

"Yes, I'm sure."

Darlene laughed again.

"You've been spreading your wings lately…"

"Don't you think I deserve it?"

"Yes, I do," Darlene replied. "Come on; I'll take you down to the Peachtree Pub."

Ten minutes later, mother and daughter were strolling down Peachtree Avenue in downtown Atlanta. In the east, dark, rain-heavy clouds were threatening. Finally, the two women stopped in front of a lounge.

"Go right in, ladies," the doorman greeted. "Ladies are free…"

Inside, the room was dimly lit and smelled of stale beer and smoke. A jukebox with brightly colored lights blared at the back of the room and several couples were dancing on a small dance floor. Alma and Darlene took a seat and a waitress appeared.

"I'll have a beer," Darlene said.

"Same here," Alma replied.

As the waitress turned back to the bar, Darlene looked at her mother and started laughing out loud.

"What's wrong?"

"This is so wild," Darlene said. "Me and my mother in a bar together."

Alma surveyed the men at the bar. There was an overweight man with a rough, dirty look watching a baseball game on the television behind the bar. Another younger man, wearing a tee shirt and glasses with long hair, was laughing and joking with the bartender. At the end of the bar sat an older man holding his head in his hands and occasionally tossing back a shot of whiskey. One of the women on the dance floor had tattoos all over both arms. Another woman who was dancing was so drunk she could hardly stand up. As she examined the scene, Alma suddenly had a feeling of disgust and loathing. The people, the place, the pungent smell of bathroom deodorizer, the alcohol, and the overall sordidness of the place was making her sick. She sensed these were lonely, desperate people who needed alcohol to help them escape their loneliness.

The waitress reappeared with their beers.

Alma took a small sip of beer. She had forgotten how much she hated the taste of alcohol in any form.

She looked at her daughter.

"Let's go!" Alma said. "Let's get out of here."

"Mama, we just got here," the daughter replied.

"I know," Alma said. "But I'm ready to go."

The daughter burst out laughing.

"Come on!" Alma said, getting up to go. "This place is making me sick."

Darlene paid the check and they left.

Outside, there was a pouring rain. For a moment, they stood outside the bar; thunder clapped and lightning flashed in the east.

"My car is right up here," Alma said. "We'll get soaked if we try to make it back to Diana's apartment."

Mother and daughter dashed out into the rain and ran the half-block to Alma's car. Alma quickly unlocked the door and they got inside. For a moment, they silently watched the pouring rain.

"Mama, what happened?" Darlene asked finally.

"It wasn't what I expected," she said.

Darlene laughed.

"Mama, let's be honest," the daughter said. "You wanted to go into a bar to see if you could still attract a man."

Mother looked at daughter.

"Mama, you're not twenty-five anymore…"

Alma didn't say anything. Then she looked into the car mirror and examined her face. The crow's feet around her eyes and mouth were deepening. Wrinkles were starting to show on her neck and lower chin.

"I'm sorry, Mama," Darlene said. "I didn't mean to be so blunt. I'm just trying to get you to be honest with yourself."

Alma inhaled resignedly.

"Did you break up with Mr. Bill?" Darlene asked.

"No, we're still friends."

"Why don't you like him?"

"Oh, he's very nice, but…"

"But what?" the daughter interrupted. "You could be doing a lot worse."

"Baby, he's twelve years older than me."

"You're not a spring chicken yourself."

Alma didn't reply.

"Mr. Bill is such a kind, loving man," the daughter continued. "You know you'd have to go a long way to find another one like him."

Alma didn't reply.

"He is stable, good-hearted, and he's got plenty of money."

"I don't mix money and love," the mother said firmly. "I could never care for a man simply because he had money."

"Mama, you're old fashioned," Darlene said. "Money has to be factored into a man-woman relationship. This is the sixties now. Would you rather be married to a poor man and live in a shack or a rich man and live in a mansion?"

"If you married a man purely for his money, you would be marrying him for the wrong reasons," Alma replied sharply. "You marry for love. You can't mix the two. Money is money and love is love."

The daughter shook her head disapprovingly.

"When I married your daddy," Alma continued, "we married because we loved one another, not because either of us had any money."

"Love and money are not oil and water," the daughter replied. "They work together, not against one another."

The mother studied her daughter and her words. There was a long silence as the rain peppered down on the car.

"I'm going back home," Alma said finally.

***

As she drove back to Aliceville, she knew her daughter was right. She could always depend on her daughter to make her be honest with herself.

On Monday, she was back at Tri-State. It was a very hectic day. She had two salespeople out sick and she worked the floor all day selling fabric and machines. She didn't have time for lunch and sent a clerk out to grab a sandwich. When she left work, she was exhausted and noticed Darlene had left two messages. She looked at the note. She didn't recognize the number.

The moment she walked in the door, the phone rang. It was Bill.

"Have you talked to Darlene?" he asked.

"No," she replied. "I've been at work all day."

"She had an emergency up in North Georgia and she called me."

"Is she okay?"

"Yes," he continued. "She and Mark were picnicking up in Union County when he had an accident. His car had to be towed and they were stuck in the wilds of North Georgia."

"What did they do?"

"They walked four miles to the nearest town and called me. I got them a rental car on my credit card."

"Thank God!" Alma said. "Thank you so much."

As she hung up the phone, she could feel the old emptiness start to creep in again. The sound of his voice brought a quiet warmth and comfort to her. Somehow, she missed the sense of companionship—even if illicit—she felt during the agreement.

She knew one thing for sure; Bill had not only lived up to his end of the agreement, he had brought quite a bit of extraneous goodness into the lives of both her and her daughter. No matter what she did with her life, she would always owe him for that.

The next day at work, she couldn't get her mind off of Bill. Late that afternoon, she called and invited him to dinner. He accepted.

***

That night, he sat quietly at the table, watching her cook.

"I'm confused," she said as she blended the mashed potatoes. "I'm not sure why, but I find myself wishing the agreement was in place again."

"You're missing the closeness," he replied.

She opened the oven to check the biscuits.

"What would it take to get you to marry me?" Bill asked. "You know that Darlene will be married someday and you will be totally alone."

Alma didn't answer at first. She was setting the table.

"I realize that the situation under which I fell in love with you is an odd one," he continued, "but it's still love to me."

Alma placed the mashed potatoes, green beans, meatloaf, and biscuits on the table.

"Do you have feelings for me?" he asked.

"Oh, yes," she said quickly. "Over the last three weeks, I have realized that I have more affection for you than I realized."

"So I will ask you again, what would it take to get you to marry me?"

"I want you to court me," she said. "During the courtship, there will be no sex. I want us to date the traditional way."

"Done!" he said quickly.

The following Saturday night, she dressed up in her new store-bought black dress and added some delicate touches of new perfume. When he appeared, he was smartly dressed in a sports shirt and dress pants and presented her with a bouquet of daisies. She unwrapped the daisies, placed them in a vase, and announced she was ready.

She had a wonderful evening. They went to Hartford's Steak House in Albany for dinner and dancing. On the way back, they stopped and walked hand-in-hand along the promenade on the Ocoee River. Finally, around 10:30, they returned to Aliceville.

"I had a great time tonight," she said. "I hope we can do it again."

He laughed.

"You're a funny woman," he said.

"No," she said. "I'm just hard-headed."

He kissed her and said goodnight.

That night, as she lay in bed, she started to see what was missing. Her life was in separate parts and the only thing that could bring all the pieces back together again was to admit her love for Bill. Love had been taken away from her once and now it was being offered again.

***

The following Saturday night, Bill brought a dozen red roses. They went to see an action movie in Albany, then had fried fish, corn on the cob, and hushpuppies at Claude's Catfish House in Tifton. After they returned to Aliceville, they talked in his car before she went in.

"There's a big exhibition between the Engineers and the Raiders next Saturday night in Atlanta," he said. "Want to go with me?"

"I'd love to," she said.

The following Friday night, he arrived promptly at 7:30. She already had a meal prepared. They ate and he watched television while she cleaned up the kitchen. At 9:30, he got up to say good-bye.

"Thanks for the meal," he said, reaching for his jacket.

Then he started for the door.

"One more thing," he said.

"Yes…?"

He reached in his pocket and pulled out a little fuzzy box.

She looked at it and opened the box.

It was a diamond ring.

"Oh, my God!" she said as she stared at its sparking brilliance.

Finally, she looked back at him.

"Will you marry me?"

She laughed.

"Give me some time to answer that…"

Disappointment flashed across his face.

"I don't know what else to do to win your love," he said resignedly.

He started for the door.

"Bill," she called.

He turned.

"Do you want to spend the night?"

"Is that what you want?"

She smiled.

"Yes," she said. "It will be like old times."

He laughed.

That night, as she crawled into bed, she told herself she would have sex with him because she had feelings of affection for him, not because it was her duty or because she had some financial obligation toward him. She would have sex with him for the regular reasons. As they put their bodies together again and again that night, Alma could feel the old emptiness inside herself slowly being filled. The need to be touched, the quiet satisfaction of a gentle kiss, the sudden, silly giggle at an off-handed comment, the feelings of a mutually confident closeness were what she had been missing.

The following morning, she packed a suitcase and, together, they headed to Atlanta. Before the game, she met Mark for the first time. A tall, quiet, brown-haired young man from Statesboro, he was very polite and effusive around Alma. After the game, the four had dinner at an Italian restaurant. When they returned to the hotel, Bill said his good-byes and went to the room. Mark said good-bye to Alma and went to his car while mother and daughter chatted in the lobby.

"I like Mark," Alma said. "He's very handsome and he is very ambitious."

"Thanks, Mom," she replied. "He makes me very happy."

Darlene studied her mother for a moment.

"Mom, will you tell me the truth?"

Alma nodded.

"Mom, I know Mr. Bill paid my tuition. Dorothy Hamilton said you were having an affair with him so he would pay my tuition. Is that true?"

"No," Alma replied. "Dorothy Hamilton doesn't know what she is talking about. I got a loan on the house to pay for your tuition."

The daughter smiled. That was what she wanted to hear.

"Are you and Mr. Bill together again?"

"Yes," Alma replied.

"Are you staying in his room?"

Alma nodded.

Darlene studied her mother.

"Are you in love with Mr. Bill?"

"Yes," Alma replied. "It has taken me a long time to realize it, but yes, I love Bill Tipton. We're going to be married late this month. I'll be a June bride and I want you to be there."

Darlene's eyes widened with pure joy.

"Oh, Mama," she said. "That makes me so happy."

The daughter, suddenly overcome with emotion, hugged her mother with all her might and started crying huge tears.

Alma held her daughter for a long moment. Finally, she broke the embrace and, using a handkerchief, wiped her daughter's tears. "Baby, I have to go to the room now."

"Bye," Darlene said.

She watched as her mother turned back to the hotel.

"Mom!" the daughter called.

Alma turned.

"I love you."

"I love you too, baby," Alma said with a wistful smile, then waved good-bye.

Moments later, as Alma walked through the hotel lobby and entered the elevator, she remembered the old saying "Follow love and it will flee; flee love and it will follow thee." The only thing she knew for sure about love was it was elusive. Over the past nine months, she had learned love is not easily defined or recognized. Although human beings have many clichéd sayings about the nature of love, none seem to quite capture the truth of its elusiveness. She had learned love works in mysterious ways and comes in different disguises and must be examined closely or it will be overlooked or dismissed. She had always known that love was a precious jewel, and once discovered, had to be nurtured and protected and treasured at all costs. She had been a good mother and now she wanted to be a good wife again. Love had found her a second time and she planned to hold on as long as she could with every last fiber of her being. She knew Bill would be her last and final love.

The End

THE SURROGATE

Our little town of Pecan Shadows, Georgia was a quiet farming community just off Interstate 75, some eighty miles south of Atlanta. Economically, it supported the needs of local cotton, peach, and pecan farmers, and the occasional tourists who ventured off the beaten path to buy gas or fast food. Most of the inhabitants were tight-knit third and fourth-generation families who never gave a second thought to living anywhere but Pecan Shadows. Our family, the Stokes, had first put down roots here in the 1880s when my grandfather Benjamin bought two forty-acre parcels outside of town and set up a cotton gin business.

Over the years, those early beginnings evolved into a local status quo in which members of the Stokes family were a mainstay in the town's daily and political life. By the late 1950s, a person with the last name Stokes not only ran but owned most of the town. I was the city's mayor and the county coroner; my brother Ned owned the hardware store and the auto dealership; my other brother Ross owned the local bank, and both my wife and Ned's wife Dee were teachers at the local high school. On any given day, it was very difficult to conduct business in Pecan Shadows without talking to a member of the Stokes family.

Although there were lots of people to love in the Stokes family, my favorite by far was my niece Becky, oldest daughter of my brother Ned. I guess you could say she was a natural choice for my affections since my wife and I never had children. From the day she was born, Becky was the apple of my eye. As a toddler with long blonde hair, big blue eyes, an angelic smile, and a pout that would coerce an adult to do anything on this earth to see her smile again, Becky was pretty as a picture in a magazine.

When she was four or five, Ned and I would take her to Wrenn's soda fountain on the square on Sunday afternoons.

"What kind of ice cream soda do you want, Becky?" I would ask.

"Panilla," she would say.

"You mean 'vanilla,'" I would offer.

"No, Uncle Carl, I want panilla," she would say. "Panilla is what I like and panilla is what I'm going to get."

She was darling.

As the years rolled on, the childhood sweetness slowly gave way to a colorful flourish of tomboy and, during that period, she liked to fish, hunt, and play touch football with the boys on Sunday afternoons. In junior high, she developed a fierce competitive spirit as a point guard on the girls' basketball team. Also, she gained a reputation as an unforgiving adversary who took no guff, whether man or woman. If you crossed her, you could rest assured there would be a payback. Once, when Juanita Phillips threw a milkshake on her during an argument at the drive-in, Becky patiently waited for the right time to exact her revenge. A month later, at a football game, Juanita was using a portable potty when Becky and two friends pushed the unit over on its side. The human waste and chemicals from the reservoir flooded the unit and, by the time Juanita could escape, she was a sopping mess of human waste and chemicals and stunk to high heaven. She never messed with Becky again!

By the time she entered high school in 1965, Becky had morphed into a strikingly beautiful young woman. An excellent student, she was popular with classmates who elected her homecoming queen during both her sophomore and junior years. While she dated quite often, she showed little interest in any one boy and vowed that she would not marry until she had her credentials to be a schoolteacher. Meanwhile, every eligible male in town yearned to become friends with her.

Then, only days after her seventeenth birthday, Becky's life took a new turn when a young man named Wilton Hosey came into town. Word was that Wilton came from somewhere up in Tennessee. Nobody knew exactly where, but local gossips claimed that after his parents were divorced, his mother was sent to prison and he came to Pecan Shadows to live with his grandmother. Everybody in town knew Mrs. Hosey. She was well liked and respected in the community and, with this in mind, Wilton, a strapping, capable kid with a tassel of brown hair and a wide grin, was accepted without malice or forethought.

At Pecan Shadows High, Becky and Wilton quickly became an item. They were seen together at football games, the drive-in, the swimming hole down at Parsons Creek, and, of course, on the square. At first, Ned kept his daughter's suitor at arm's length. Wilton would come to the family home to pick up Becky, but my brother showed him little more than casual interest. A cautious man, he wasn't going to jump too soon. Finally, however, after he saw Becky was dead serious, Ned started to warm up and hired Wilton for Saturdays and afternoons at the hardware store.

The high school prom that year sealed the deal. When Wilton and Becky appeared decked out in formal attire and were seen dancing across the floor at the high school auditorium, the whole town knew they were a match. The old women and the wives swooned, the town's fathers nodded their approval, and the general consensus was that Wilton and Becky were born to be together. It was a match made in heaven, as they say.

After high school graduation, a big summer wedding was planned at the local Baptist church. Dee was ecstatic that her daughter had found true love and, as most mothers do, she fussed endlessly about the bridal gown, the wedding cake, and the invitations. Ned, on the other hand, had some reservations. He mentioned to Dee that Wilton could not have come from very good stock if his mother was serving time in prison. Dee defended her future son-in-law with the comment that no child can help what his parents do. Ned begrudgingly accepted that. After all, she said, Becky was deeply in love with Wilton and that was what mattered most.

Once the newlyweds had set up housekeeping, Becky enrolled at the community college at Albany and Wilton continued to work in the family hardware store. Over the next few months, Ned said Wilton became restless in his new situation. At work, he started to come in late, tended to forget small details, and seemed to have a careless attitude. Ned took him aside and questioned him.

"I'm not sure I want to spend my life in a hardware store in a little town," Wilton said. "There's a big world out there."

"So what do you want to do?" Ned asked.

"I'm not sure," Wilton replied. "I want to look around."

Two weeks later, with Ned's approval, Wilton left the hardware store and went to work doing concrete construction over at Smith's Junction. Three weeks later, after an argument with his boss, he was unemployed again. Ned put him to work again at the hardware store, but only days later, Wilton left again and took a position as a sheet metal worker. Two months later, complaining that the work was "cutting up his hands," Wilton was unemployed again. From there, over the next year, Wilton was like a rudderless ship and had a string of menial jobs. He jerked sodas at Wrenn's Drugstore. Then there was two months of cutting pulp wood at Smith's Junction Next, he worked as a house painter, a plumber's assistant, and a clerk in the local photography shop. Finally, Ned sat down for a talk with him and asked if he would come back to the hardware store.

"If you'll come back and dedicate yourself," Ned said, "we'll talk about making you a partner in a year or two."

Wilton agreed to the proposal and settled in.

A year into the marriage, Dee asked Becky when she was going to be a grandmother. Becky explained that she and Wilton had been trying but, for some reason, she had not been able to conceive. Dee suggested it could be a medical problem.

"That's not it, Mom," Becky said. "I think it's because we just haven't been able to come together at the right time."

Dee accepted that, but the situation didn't change.

Eighteen months into the marriage, Dee suggested that she go to the fertility doctor over in Albany and have herself checked out. Becky reluctantly agreed, so she made the trip and submitted to a series of x-rays, physical examinations, and blood and serum tests. Two weeks later, the results came back.

"I can't have children," Becky told her mother. "The tests show that I was born with a closure in my womb that is preventing me from getting pregnant."

"Can they do surgery?" Dee asked.

"No," Becky said. "They said it would be too dangerous."

Mother and daughter cried together at the news. Ned, who desperately wanted a grandchild, suggested adoption, but, after consulting an expert, they learned it could take years and the cost was in the thousands for the lawyers. They were at a dead end.

Several months later, after a shopping trip to Albany, Dee called Becky and asked her to come over as soon as possible. When Becky arrived, her mother unfolded a copy of the *Albany Herald* and flipped through the pages.

"Read this ad!" she said.

Becky glanced down at the ad.

"Surrogate services for childless couples. We have helped thousands of women become mothers using healthy, professional surrogates. Parents who want children no longer have to be without a child to love. We can help!"

Becky looked up from the ad.

"A surrogate?" she asked. "How does it work?"

"We're going to talk to your Uncle Carl."

As a result of my medical training to be county coroner, everybody in the family saw me as the resident medical expert. Since Dee had been confiding the details of Becky's dilemma to my wife, I knew what the subject of the conversation was going to be before I arrived. I explained that the use of surrogates was quite common. After all, this was the late sixties. Many couples who could not have children employed surrogate mothers to bear a child, then, once the child was born, it was delivered to the employers, the fee was paid, and the arrangement was at an end. The parents had their child and the surrogate had her money for services rendered. It was strictly a business arrangement, I explained.

"How does the surrogate get pregnant?" Ned asked.

"Either through artificial insemination, which is very expensive, or through servicing sessions," I said.

"Servicing sessions?" my brother asked.

"Servicing sessions are scheduled meetings between the surrogate and the sperm donor in which they copulate naturally to conceive a child."

"You mean Wilton would actually have sex with the surrogate until she gets pregnant?"

"Yes," I replied. "These sessions are scheduled relative to the surrogate's menstrual cycle."

"Oh, Lord," Becky replied. "I'm not sure I could approve of that."

"It's according to how bad you want a child," I replied.

The conversation ended with that. Ned, Dee, and Becky said they wanted some time to consider it. If they decided to go through with it, they asked if I would help arrange it.

"Of course," I replied. "I'd do anything for Becky."

Two weeks later, I got a call from Ned. He said the three of them had discussed the matter with Wilton and all had agreed to proceed with the surrogate birth.

The surrogate was a woman named Trixie Underwood, a tall, thin woman with short dark hair in her late twenties. She had a proud, defiant bearing and, just by looking at her, you could see she was quite familiar with the seamier side of life. The most striking part of her appearance was the tattoo of a snake that coiled around her right arm from her wrist to her neck. I felt the snake tattoo was a bad sign, but I didn't say anything. She had been living with her mother at Smith's Junction and provided references stating she had been a surrogate mother for a couple in Atlanta two years earlier. She provided a notarized letter of recommendation and photos of the happy couple with their new offspring.

"My fee is ten thousand dollars," she said. "I expect half up front and the remainder upon delivery of the child."

That night, back in Pecan Shadows, I met with the family again.

"Ten thousand dollars is nothing for nine months' work," Ned said. "I don't mind paying that if it will get me a grandchild. How does she plan on getting pregnant?"

"Through servicing sessions," I replied. "These were used when she had the baby boy for the couple in Atlanta."

He turned to his daughter.

"Are you okay with that?"

Becky took a deep breath.

"I guess I don't have a choice," she replied.

"What about you, Wilton?"

"If that's what it takes for me and Becky to be parents, then I'm for it," he said.

My brother looked over to his wife.

She gave a slight nod.

"Let's sign the papers," Ned said.

Two days later, the surrogate, Becky, her parents, Wilton, and I met at the lawyer's office. Everything was drawn up legally, the surrogate received her initial payment, and all parties present signed the necessary papers. The agreement was that I would oversee and schedule the servicing sessions, which were to be held at her mother's home in Smith's Junction.

The day before the first session, Becky said she was very nervous about the whole thing and asked me to go with her to the first one. When we arrived at the surrogate's home, Becky had some words for her husband.

"Now go in there and do what you have to do," she said. "Then get right back out here to me."

"Becky," he replied, "there is no romance here. I'm doing this for you and me and nobody else."

I watched as he went into the home. For almost an hour, Becky fidgeted and tried to occupy herself. Finally, an hour later, Wilton emerged.

"Was everything all right?" Becky asked.

"Everything was fine," Wilton said.

The three of us rode back to Pecan Shadows in silence.

Over the next month, I scheduled four sessions. On the second visit, Becky asked me to accompany her again, but, for the third, she said she didn't want to go. She said she wanted Wilton to go alone.

"I love you and I trust you," she told Wilton, "so just go by yourself."

During the second month, I scheduled three sessions around the middle of the month. I determined she would be most fertile on the seventeenth, eighteenth, and nineteenth of August, so, for three days running, Wilton went to be with the surrogate on his own.

On the nineteenth, Wilton left the hardware store around

noon to go to Smith's Junction for the scheduled session. That afternoon, he didn't return. Around five, after Becky returned home from class, she called me, and I explained, as far as I knew, Wilton had gone for the session. By seven that evening, there was still no sign of Wilton. At home, Becky noticed that a suitcase and some of Wilton's clothes were missing. This raised the alarm with Becky.

"I know something terrible has happened," she said, explaining about the suitcase and the clothes. "I want you to go with me to Trixie's house to find out what's going on."

An hour later, Becky, Ned, and I were en route to Trixie's mother's house.

When we arrived, the mother met us at the door. I asked about the whereabouts of her daughter.

"Didn't she tell you?" the woman asked. "They went to California. They had all of their clothes packed and left at about sundown."

With those words, my heart rose into my mouth. Ned flew into a rage and Becky started sobbing.

"I'm going to hunt that son-of-a-bitch down and kill him," Ned vowed. "I mean, I'm going to shoot him down like a dog."

It crossed my mind to do the same thing, but I would have to find him before I could kill him. If he and the surrogate were in California, I had lots of searching to do.

Wilton and Trixie had made a clean getaway. Like thieves in the night, they had quietly and secretly done the deed under the trusting eyes of all those around them. There were no signs of premeditation. They had flown the coop with the family car and apparently were using her initial fee to finance the trip. It was a devastating blow for the entire family.

Obviously, Becky was the one who suffered the most. The first few weeks were the hardest. So she would not have to be alone in the house she shared with Wilton, she moved into the spare bedroom at her parents' home and shut herself away from the world. Her grades suffered, she stopped going to church, and every time I would see her, her eyes were red and puffy from crying. Dee said that day after day, when Becky returned from her classes, she would go straight to her room "to study," but after a while, she would hear Becky sobbing.

When she knocked on the door to comfort her, Becky always replied she was "all right." Before the evening meals, Ned would try to coax her out of her room to the dinner table, but she always begged off with, "I'm not hungry now. I'll eat later."

Although all of us knew she was hurt to the quick, Becky did her best to sustain a front of courage and independence.

Of course, as the news spread, everybody in our little town had an opinion.

"That boy never knew what he wanted," said Ila Jenkins. "He was all over the place more than anywhere else."

"It's a shame about poor Becky," said Wanda Lipscomb. "All she ever wanted was for him to love her."

"I knew he was a loafer," said Ross Morton. "Them kind is always here today and gone tomorrow."

"I never did trust that look in his eye," said Sally Lopes. "I saw that evil in his look from the very first."

Finally, two months after the incident, Becky summoned the courage to be seen in public again. Just for old times' sake, Ned and I started taking her on Sundays for a "panilla" ice cream soda. She started attending church with the family again. The redness around her eyes slowly disappeared, her grades improved, and I could see the old Becky I knew and loved so much coming back around.

A year after the incident, Becky graduated from community college and took an assistant's job at the local high school to complete requirements for her teaching degree. Ned bought her a new car, she moved back to the home she had shared with Wilton, and, from all appearances, she had survived the terrible betrayal with her mind and emotions intact. Despite all the appearances, in my heart, I knew she would never be the same. I thought the chapter was closed.

Then, five years later, as fate would have it, Wilton's grandmother died and he showed up in town again. Ned and I made sure we attended the funeral. We wanted to see this low-down dog and determine if we thought he was still worth killing. The nerve of this man was unbelievable. Once the grave was covered and the mourners began to leave, Wilton came over to us.

"Ned," he said, offering his hand. "How you been doing?"

Ned glared angrily at him.

"You're no friend of mine, you son-of-a-bitch," Ned said finally. "If you're smart, you'll get out of town before I blow you away."

Wilton didn't flinch.

"There's no reason for hard feelings," he said. "What I did five years ago is done and gone. Surely it's not the first time Becky's heart has been broken. My heart has been broken a thousand times."

Ned angrily grabbed his tie and jerked Wilton's face to his.

"If you're smart," he said, "you'll get out of town before sundown."

Wilton pushed him away.

"Who do you think you're talking to?" he said. "I ain't going nowhere. This is a free country and you can't make me do a damn thing."

Livid anger flashed across Ned's face and he started for Wilton. I grabbed my brother and held him back.

For a long moment, Ned glared angrily at him, then turned to me.

"Come on," he said, "before I do something that gets me sent to prison."

Word spread rapidly that Wilton was back in town. Everybody knew he was staying at his grandmother's home, but some townsfolk heard that, as soon as he finished settling the estate with the lawyer, he was leaving town again. Actually, it didn't happen that way. A week after Wilton showed up, a moving truck arrived in town, backed up to his grandmother's home, and unloaded its contents. Apparently, Wilton was going to be around longer than anyone suspected.

When Ned told Becky that Wilton was back in town, she fainted. After a whiff of ammonia, she came back around and started asking questions about her betrayer. She seemed almost happy that Wilton was back and said she wanted to see him.

The following week, Wilton went to the high school and met Becky. After the initial shock of seeing him again, Becky finally gained enough self-control to speak to him in a civil tone. Wilton told her he was sorry. He said he made a mistake and he still loved her. He said the surrogate was just an instant flirtation and Becky was the only woman he had ever loved. He pleaded again and again with her to take him back again. Finally, he asked her to have dinner with him that night. She said she would have to think about it.

That night, she came to her father's house to discuss the matter with Ned, Dee, and me.

"Hell, no!" Ned said the moment he saw where Becky was headed with the conversation. "I'll kill that son of a bitch before I let him in my family again."

"Now you shouldn't be too hasty in your judgments," Becky said. "Sometimes, you have to forgive and forget. After all, it's been five years."

"Forgive and forget?" Ned said. "After what he did to you? There are some things you can't forgive a man for and he has committed one of them."

"Daddy," she said finally, "Wilton is a good sort; he just can't make up his mind about what he wants in this world."

"I know he betrayed my daughter in the most vile, evil way you can imagine," he said. "From what I have seen, Wilton Hosey is not the road to your happiness."

"Daddy," she said, "you're always so cocksure about everything. Wilton apologized for what he did. He admitted making a mistake."

"You're going nowhere near that son of a bitch," he said. "If I catch him near my family again, I'm going to end up in prison."

Seeing she was getting nowhere, Becky put on the pouting look that always used to get her way.

"Daddy," she said, "will you do it for me?"

He stared at his daughter in sheer frustration.

"Oh, God!" he said finally. "Sometimes, you do things I will never understand."

"Please, Daddy?" she asked.

Ned took a deep breath and shook his head in indecision.

"Honey, if it's what you want, I'll go along with it," he said. "But don't ask me to put him on at the hardware store again because I'll say no."

Becky smiled at her victory.

"You realize," Ned added, "if it happened once, it could very easily happen again."

"I know! I know," Becky replied. "I survived it once. I think I can probably survive it again."

So Wilton and Becky started seeing each other again. Over the next few weeks, they were seen together shopping in town, attending church, and having ice cream on the town square. A month later, Wilton moved back into the house he and Becky had shared five years earlier. Becky continued her teaching career at the high school and Wilton started looking for employment. His elopement with the surrogate had left a bad taste in lots of people's mouths, but finally, Nathan Wilson, owner of the feed and seed store, needed a driver and hired Wilton for the job. Once Wilton was employed and living with Becky again, it was as if nothing had changed between them. They were still married, they still had the original home they started, and, apparently, they were a happy, loving couple again.

One night, Becky asked him about the surrogate.

"We got into a big fight over money," he said. "When I woke up the next morning, she had packed her clothes and was gone."

"You never heard from her again?"

"No," he replied. "It was good riddance, if you ask me. You're the only woman I ever really loved."

About six weeks after Wilton and Becky set up housekeeping again, Wilton got sick. One night, he awoke coughing up blood, running a high temperature, and complaining about severe pain in his stomach. The next day, he went to old Doc Bailey, who diagnosed his condition as stomach ulcers and put him on medication. Wilton was fine for a few days, then had another nighttime bout of coughing up blood and suffering from stomach pain. The day after that, old Doc Bailey prescribed more medicine for indigestion, doubling the dose.

For two days, Wilton was bed-ridden, then one night while Becky was at church, he apparently started to leave the house for some reason. Only partially dressed, he made it to the front porch and collapsed in the yard. When neighbors saw Wilton writhing in pain on the front lawn, they called an ambulance. As Wilton was loaded up, one neighbor said he was spitting up huge globs of a black, foul-smelling substance. The ambulance started to the hospital, but Wilton was dead on arrival. Instead of providing treatment in the emergency room, he was pronounced dead by the attending physician, and his body was covered with a sheet and delivered to the local morgue.

When I examined the body, I could see there was extensive swelling of the large intestine, hair loss, an enlarged liver, white lines around toenails and fingernails, and scattered splotches of discolored skin. From past experience, I knew immediately that death had been caused by acute poisoning with arsenic. On the death certificate, I scribbled the cause of death as "chronic ulcers." No one ever questioned my action. Becky and I had done our job. Justice had been served.

About a year after Wilton died, another stranger ventured into our little town. His name was John Tanner. A native of South Carolina, John came to Pecan Shadows to open a paint supply store and start a new life. His wife had died two years earlier and he had two small children, ages five and eight. In the course of enrolling his children in school, he met Becky and they started dating. After some four months, they were married and, over the ensuing years, Becky proved to be a good wife and good mother. After John's children were grown and married, both of them lived to be a ripe old age.

The End

PAULINE

It was two a.m. when Shirley Ann's car pulled into the front yard at Jenevieve's Colorado home. Once she was parked, a light illuminated at the front door and Jen, her short, stocky frame shrouded in a nightgown, appeared on the porch.

"I'm glad to see you made it," she said.

"It's been a long drive," Shirley Ann replied.

Moments later, Shirley Ann, tall and thin, with two bags in tow, was in the foyer of the home, hugging her long-time friend.

"It's good to see you," Jen said. "Go to the guest room and get a good night's sleep. I'll serve coffee at eight."

"Thanks," Shirley Ann replied. "By ten tomorrow, I want to be on the hiking trail at Henderson's Peak."

"We'll both be there," Jen replied.

"Good night," Shirley Ann said.

"Good night," Jen replied.

Some twenty minutes later, as Shirley Ann prepared for bed, her thoughts wandered back to her friendship with Jen. Beginning in high school in 1962, they had become fast friends in Palm Springs, California. Even after Shirley Ann married and divorced Jen's older brother Glenn, they remained close friends. Now, in 2005, they had been friends for more than 40 years. Although both owned homes in Palm Springs, Jen later purchased the Colorado home so she could be near her ailing mother, Pauline. After Jen moved, Shirley Ann made frequent weekend trips from Palm Springs to Colorado to visit and go hiking.

Finally finished in the bathroom, Shirley Ann crawled into bed and turned off the light. Although she was tired from the long drive, she lay wide awake, excited at the prospect of going hiking the following morning. *Tomorrow is going be a good day,* she told herself. *Jen and I will have lots of fun in the mountains*. Moments later, she was sound asleep.

***

The following morning, promptly at eight, Shirley Ann heard a rap at the door. She got out of bed, slipped on a nightgown, and went to the door. When she opened the door, Jen peered at her as if she had seen a ghost.

"What's wrong?" Shirley Ann asked.

Jen didn't answer.

"What's wrong?" Shirley Ann asked again. "Tell me what's wrong!"

"Pauline is dead," Jen said finally.

"What?" Shirley Ann replied. "When did you hear that?"

"Just now," Jen replied. "The assisted care facility said she died in her sleep early this morning. They took her body to the funeral home."

Shirley Ann's face grimaced in frustration.

"That's just dandy," she said. "I arrived last night to get some rest and relaxation and the old witch decides to suddenly die and disrupt my plans."

"Now, Shirley Ann," Jen replied. "Don't be talking like that. She was my mother. I know you and she had your problems, but please show some respect now that she has passed."

"I'm having nothing to do with her," Shirley Ann said. "I'm going to go hiking. As far as I'm concerned, she can burn in hell. She was the meanest, most downright awful mother-in-law a person could ever have."

"I wish you'd forgive her," Jen said. "She had her faults, but she was never as bad as you make her out to be."

"You don't want to know all of the reasons I have for hating her," Shirley Ann replied. "I could go on forever."

Jen, seeing she was making no headway, took a seat on the sofa. Then, slowly, her eyes filled with tears and she began to cry.

Shirley Ann inhaled, then took a seat beside Jen on the couch.

"Oh, Jen," she said finally, putting her arms around her friend. "I'm sorry. I know this has to be hard on you."

For a long moment, she held Jen in her arms.

"I'm sorry," Shirley Ann said again. "So tell me, what has to be done?"

Jen broke the embrace and dried her eyes.

"I've got to take the body to Palm Springs," Jen said. "Her insurance policy says she has to be cremated in Palm Springs."

"You have to take her?" Shirley Ann said. "You mean the policy doesn't cover her transportation to Palm Springs?"

Jen shook her head sadly.

"Well, good luck," Shirley Ann replied. "You're on your own with this one."

"Please go with me," Jen said. "It's three days. I'm not sure I can make a trip like that on my own. Especially with Mother in the car."

Shirley Ann smiled faintly.

"Are you afraid she'll come back to life and start raising hell with you?"

Jen shook her head in frustration.

"Please don't start," she said. "Will you at least go with me to the funeral home?"

"Oh, God!" Shirley Ann replied, shaking her head in frustration. "Just my luck! Just my rotten luck!"

She took a deep breath.

"Okay," she said finally. "Let's go. I guess that's the least I can do."

***

An hour later, Jen and Shirley Ann were at the Winkenhoffer Funeral Home talking to the director, a tall, impeccably dressed, unsmiling man.

"The body must be delivered to the Happy Home Crematorium in Palm Springs for vaporization within the next four days," he said. "That's when the policy expires."

"Vaporization?" Shirley Ann asked.

"Yes, that's the technical term we use for cremation."

"Vaporization?" Shirley Ann said again. "That sounds like

you push a button and she's instantly turned into ashes."

"Yes," he said. "That's basically what happens."

Shirley Ann peered at him curiously, a faint smile on her face.

"That's like burning in hell," Shirley Ann said.

"In a manner of speaking," the director replied.

"Can I watch?" Shirley Ann asked.

"Yes," the director replied. "Family members may witness the vaporization."

Shirley Ann looked at Jen.

"I might just go with you after all," she replied. "How long do you think it will take?"

"Three, four days, at most," Jen replied. "We could put Mama in the back of the station wagon and connect up the travel trailer to sleep in. That would slow us down some, but we should make it easily in four days."

"Okay," Shirley Ann replied. "But only if I can watch the... vaporization."

"We can both watch," Jen said.

"You'll need a permit to transport the body across state lines," the director said.

"Where do we get that?" Jen asked.

"I can issue one," the director replied. "You must have the permit in the event you are approached by law enforcement."

Jen turned to Shirley Ann. "So you'll do it?"

"Yeah," Shirley Ann replied. "This might be fun."

"Oh, thank you, Shirley Ann," Jen said, hugging her former sister-in-law. "Thank you so much. I knew I could count on you."

***

Late that afternoon, they had an oak coffin containing Pauline's body loaded into the back of Jen's station wagon. They had food for the trip, eight days' change of clothes for the trip there and back, and a small travel trailer hitched to the station wagon for sleeping. Jen slipped under the steering wheel of the station wagon and started the engine.

Two hours later, they were cruising westward across the

high plains desert of southeast Colorado.

"I've been having problems with the gas gauge on this thing," Jen said. "Sometimes it reads right and sometimes it doesn't."

"We don't want to be running out of gas."

"Yeah, I know," Jen said. "We'll fill up every time it gets to half-empty. We should be fine."

"I hope so," Shirley Ann said. "I'm feeling kind of creepy about this whole thing."

"Me too," Jen said. "I'll be glad when it's over."

***

As darkness fell that afternoon, they crossed the state line into northern New Mexico and, three hours later, the station wagon pulled off the main highway into a public rest area. Once parked, they checked the coffin, then went into the trailer to eat and prepare their bunks. Finally, they were ready for bed and said goodnight.

***

The following morning, after they had breakfast in the trailer, Jen headed the station wagon back out to the main highway. As she prepared to merge into traffic, an oncoming car suddenly started to veer off the main highway toward the shoulder.

"Look out!" Shirley Ann yelled.

Instantly, Jen jammed the brakes and the coffin slammed against the back of the front seat as the station wagon lurched to a sudden stop.

Jen looked at Shirley Ann, then turned to the coffin.

"Sorry, Mom!" she said.

Jen needed a moment to regain herself.

"We can't let that happen again," she said. "Let get the pillows from the trailer and put them in front and in back of the coffin. I want Mother to be as comfortable as possible."

Shirley Ann burst out laughing. "She's dead," Shirley Ann said.

"She's my mother," Jen replied.

Moments later, the station wagon was parked on the shoulder of the road. Jen retrieved the pillows and positioned them securely at the front and rear of the coffin to prevent another slide.

"I feel better now," Jen said, slipping back under the steering wheel.

"We wouldn't want anything to happen to poor Pauline," Shirley Ann said.

Jen looked at her and said nothing.

***

By noon, they were deep into the desert country of central New Mexico. Jen glanced at the gas gauge.

"This damn gas gauge," Jen said. "It makes no sense. I filled up an hour ago and now it says we only have a third of a tank."

"We better stop," Shirley Ann said.

"We'll stop up here on the Indian reservation."

Fifteen minutes later, the station wagon was parked at a service station on the Navapai reservation. Shirley Ann went inside to buy snacks while Jen pumped gas. As she filled the tank, an older Indian man came out of the station office and peered at the station wagon.

"Is something wrong?" Jen asked.

"Is that a human body you have in there?"

"Yes," Jen said. "It's my mother."

"Wait right here!" the man said.

"Is something wrong?" Jen asked.

"Wait right here!" he said again.

Moments later, one of the reservation's police officers appeared.

"Do you have a permit to transport this body over Indian lands?" he asked.

"Yes," Jen said.

Once she finished pumping gas, Jen fished through her purse and produced the permit.

"You realize it's against ancient tribal customs to carry a

corpse across the Navapai reservation," the officer said, examining the permit.

"The funeral home said that's all I would need," Jen said.

"Tribal elders won't allow it," the officer said. "They feel that outside human remains disturb the spirit of their ancestors in the happy hunting ground."

"So what am I supposed to do?" Jen asked.

"You can turn around and take a detour around Indian lands," the officer suggested.

"I can't do that," Jen replied. "I have to have the body in California two days from now."

"Sorry," the officer replied. "I can't let you continue."

"There's nothing I can do without turning back?"

The officer peered at her.

"You can allow the tribe to cleanse the evil spirits from the body."

"How do they do that?"

"By performing the cleansing dance."

"Oh, God!" she said. "How long will that take?"

"About two hours."

"Is that the only choice I have?"

"I'm afraid so."

Jen shook her head in frustration.

"Okay," she said. "Let's get on with it."

Shirley Ann, her arms loaded with soft drinks and snacks, appeared.

"What happening?" she asked.

"The tribe is going to do a dance to cleanse the evil spirits from Mother's body."

Shirley Ann burst out laughing.

"They've got their work cut out for them," she said.

"This is no time for sarcasm."

Jen turned to the reservation officer.

"What do I have to do?"

"Follow me," he said. "We've got to go to the sacred ceremonial ground."

An hour later, they arrived at a flat mesa in the foothills north of the reservation. There, two Indian men disconnected the trailer, removed the coffin, and carefully placed it atop a flat rock. While several others built a fire next to the coffin and donned ceremonial attire, Jen and Shirley Ann watched.

Twenty minutes later, some twenty to thirty Indians, dressed in ceremonial costumes, were dancing around the coffin and the fire to the beat of several native drums. Intermittently, the dancers waved giant shields made of eagle and hawk feathers to fan away evil spirits.

"Nobody will ever believe this," Shirley Ann said.

An hour later, the fire had died down and the drums stopped.

"Okay," the reservation officer said. "The chief is satisfied that the evil spirits are gone. You can go now."

Quickly, the Indian men returned the coffin to the station wagon and reconnected the trailer.

Jen turned to Shirley Ann. "Come on!" she said. "Let's get out of here."

***

Late that afternoon, the station wagon crossed the state line into Arizona.

Suddenly, Jen turned to Shirley Ann with a realization.

"Oh, my God!" she said. "We don't have the permit."

"What?" Shirley Ann asked.

"We were in such a hurry to get away from the Indians that we didn't remember to get the permit back."

"We can't turn back now," Shirley Ann said. "That's five hours."

"Yeah, I guess you're right," Jen said. "We'll lose ten hours if we turn back now. Maybe we'll be okay."

They rode silently for over an hour. Shirley Ann napped to kill time, then awoke and started reading a book. Still bored, she put down the book and turned on the radio. For some thirty minutes, they rode quietly with only the humming sound of the tires and country music in their ears.

Suddenly, Jen turned off the radio.

"Why did you do that?"

"I want to talk about Mother," Jen said.

"What's there to talk about?" Shirley Ann replied. "She's

gone."

"I think it's high time you forgave her," Jen said. "You can't carry that kind of hatred in your heart forever."

"Why not?" Shirley Ann replied. "Do you have any idea how many times I suffered silently as she made her catty remarks?"

"My mother was not an angel," Jen replied. "I know she had a mean streak a mile long, but she's gone now. She can't hurt you anymore. It's time for you to forgive and forget."

"No," Shirley Ann replied. "It's my turn now and I want to watch as she is fried to a crisp in that crematorium. That's why I made this trip."

Jen shook her head sadly.

They rode silently for several minutes.

"From the day Glenn and I were married until the day we were divorced," Shirley Ann continued, "she never missed a chance to accuse me of being a bad mother, a bad wife, and generally stupid and inept. I dreaded going to family functions because I knew she would be there to belittle me. To hear her tell it, I couldn't cook, I couldn't clean house, I couldn't even help my children with their homework. I'll always remember the time when Pam made a D in algebra and she raved on and on about how I should be helping her with her math. The truth was I had been tutoring Pam in algebra. Every night!"

Jen didn't respond. They rode quietly.

"Mother was the kind of person that was critical by nature," Jen said finally. "Lots of times, she would say things she didn't really mean."

"That doesn't mean her remarks didn't hurt," Shirley Ann replied. "Her sidelong comments about me hurt me to the quick. Especially when they were said in public."

"You never knew the way Mother grew up," Jen said. "There were six kids in her family and you had to be tough to survive. Mother wasn't all that mean; she just had to learn to be a survivor."

"She *was* mean!" Shirley Ann shot back. "Downright mean and cruel. She took delight in her cruelty. And the people she loved to hurt the most were the people who had never meant her any harm."

Jen didn't reply.

"Her kids were always little angels," Shirley Ann continued. "But all of her in-laws were low-down and rotten to the core. 'Shirley Ann can't cook,' she would say. 'The squash casserole has too much salt. The baked chicken wasn't cooked long enough. Doesn't Shirley Ann have a nicer dress than that? Why can't Shirley Ann keep a cleaner house?' Her abuse was like an unending record."

Jen didn't reply.

"No," Shirley Ann said finally. "I can't forgive her. I suffered too much for so many years to let it go. Even now, I try to push all those memories out of my mind because they hurt so much."

"She dead," Jen said, her voice raising. "She can't hurt you any more. Can't you show her some respect in death?"

"That's easy for you to say," Shirley Ann replied angrily. "You never had to take her abuse."

"She was my mother!" Jen shouted.

"She was a bitch!" Shirley Ann shouted back. "The most God-awful person I've ever known in my entire life."

"Shut up!" Jen shouted.

"No! You shut up!" Shirley Ann shot back angrily.

Suddenly, realizing what was happening, both women grew quiet for a moment.

"We're shouting at one another," Jen said finally.

"I know," Shirley Ann said.

They rode quietly. Finally, Shirley Ann spoke. "Are we finished talking about Pauline?"

"Yeah, we're finished."

"Can I listen to the radio again?" Shirley Ann asked.

"Yeah," Jen said. "Whatever..."

As they rode, Shirley Ann's thoughts wandered back to her mother-in-law. Even in death, Pauline was causing problems. Wherever she went, dead or alive, trouble and grief seemed to follow her. Maybe when the trip was finished and the body was cremated, she thought, all of the Pauline-caused problems in her life would be at an end. She would never have to worry about Pauline again.

***

Late that afternoon, the station wagon was halfway across Arizona and, after darkness fell, they stopped for the night at a travel resort. The following morning, they were up early, got everything packed, and decided to have breakfast at the resort restaurant. As they exited the eatery, Jen noticed two police officers, one with a dog, standing at the station wagon.

"Why is your dog barking at my car?" she asked.

"It's a cadaver dog," he replied. "Do you have human remains in that station wagon?"

"Yes," Jen said. "It's my mother. I'm taking her to California for cremation."

"Do you have a permit?"

"No," Jen said, explaining that the reservation officer had not returned it.

"Do you two have ID?"

Both produced their IDs and handed them to the officer.

The first officer examined the IDs, then turned to his colleague. "Stay with them," he said. "I'm going to call headquarters."

Ten minutes later, he returned.

"We're going to have to take you downtown for some questions."

"Why?" Jen asked. "We haven't broken any laws."

"Since you don't have a permit," he said, "we've got to check out your story. We've had nine corpses stolen in this county over the past three months."

"We haven't stolen a corpse," Jen said. "She's my mother. We had a permit and the officer at the Indian reservation didn't give it back."

"I don't have time to argue," the officer replied. "We're going downtown."

"Oh, that's just great!" Jen said.

"Either that or we can arrest you."

Jen gave a sigh of resignation.

"Let's go downtown."

Twenty minutes later, both were in a squad car en route to the local police headquarters. Behind them, another policeman was bringing the station wagon, the body, and the trailer. Finally, upon arrival, they were escorted into the interrogation room.

"Do you know William Bradford Graves?" the first officer asked.

"Never heard of him," Jen said.

"What about you?"

Shirley Ann shook her head.

The officers produced a mug shot of a middle-aged, unshaven man with tousled hair and a red swelling on the left side of his face.

"Do either of you know this man?"

They peered at the mug shot.

"Never seen him before," Jen said.

"Me neither," said Shirley Ann.

"You realize you could be prosecuted for lying to a police officer?"

"I have no reason to lie," Jen said. "I'm a law-abiding citizen. I'm telling the truth."

The first officer looked at the second, then turned back to the pair.

"What's the name of the funeral home in California?"

"Winkenhoffer," Jen said. "It's in Butte Springs. The director's name is Brian."

"I'll give them a call," the first officer said. "Make sure you two don't go anywhere."

Thirty minutes later, the officer returned.

"It's all cleared up," he said. "You're good to go."

"Thanks," Jen said. "Who is William Bradford Graves?"

The first officer looked at the second. "Should I tell them?"

"Yeah, go ahead," replied the second officer.

"He's the man we suspect is buying corpses."

"Why would he be buying corpses?"

The first officer looked at the second officer again, then back at Jen.

"Are you sure you want to know?"

"I wouldn't ask if I didn't want to know."

"He's a necrophile," the first officer said. "He buys corpses to make love to them."

Jen's jaw dropped.

"You mean he—?" Jen was too embarrassed to completely state her thoughts. "He does it with a corpse?"

The first officer slowly nodded his head.

Jen visibly shivered. "Can we go now?" she asked.

"You can go," the first officer said. "Sorry for the delay, but we've got our job to do."

Jen and Shirley Ann got up to leave.

"What part of California you going to?" asked the first officer.

"Palm Springs," Jen replied. "Coachella Valley."

"Be careful around the south side of that mountain," the officer said. "There's a lot of drug trafficking. We get some of it over here."

"Oh, we're not going anywhere near the mountain," Jen said. "We're staying straight on I-10 to Palm Springs."

"Okay," the officer said. "Have a good trip!"

***

An hour later, they were back in the station wagon, riding quietly as they cruised through western Arizona.

Finally, Jen spoke.

"Can we talk about Mother again?"

"Yes," Shirley Ann replied.

"Can't you find any good that Mother did in her life?" Jen asked.

"Nope," Shirley Ann replied. "Not a thing."

"She did lots of good things for the family," Jen said.

"Name one!"

"She paid for the last two years of Pam's college," Jen said. "That has to count for something."

"Bull!" Shirley Ann shot back. "Pam's education was paid with money Glenn borrowed from the bank."

"Oh, no," Jen replied. "That's the story Glenn told you. Mother borrowed money on her insurance policy and gave it to him."

"I don't believe that," Shirley Ann replied. "That's a total lie."

"It's true," Jen said. "The absolute truth."

"I don't believe it!" Shirley Ann said.

Jen, anger in her face, suddenly slammed on the brakes and pulled off on the side of the highway. Without speaking, she got out of the station wagon and went into the trailer. Moments later, she returned, a bound paper packet in hand. Inside the station wagon again, she untied the packet.

"These are Mother's insurance papers." Jen said, unfolding the papers.

For a moment, she scanned the document, then her eyes stopped.

"See right there," Jen said, indicating with her finger. "A withdrawal of $6600 in August of 1997. That's when Pam started her third year of college."

Shirley Ann looked up from the papers.

"I never knew that," she said.

"Now do you believe me?" Jen asked.

"Why would Glenn lie to me about it?"

"Because you and he were getting a divorce at the time and he wanted you to think he had more expenses than he really had," Jen said. "You know what a schemer he was."

"That bastard!" Shirley Ann said.

They rode quietly.

"I'm sorry, Jen," Shirley Ann said finally. "I never knew that."

"Well, you know it now," Jen said. "My mother did some good things in this world."

"Well, maybe she did do two or three decent things in her life."

"No, Jen said. "Your hatred is so deep you can't find them. She was a good mother. You wouldn't believe how she struggled to get us kids raised. Nothing meant more to her than her family. She was a good grandmother. I remember how proud she was of Pam when she graduated high school. She didn't finish high school herself and Pam made her so proud. And you can't blame her for being stingy. She came up hard and she learned to pinch every penny to survive."

Shirley Ann fell silent.

"Now," Jen said. "Will you please try to show more respect and appreciation for my dead mother?"

Shirley Ann didn't reply.

As they rode, Shirley Ann pondered Jen's words. Maybe Jen was right. Pauline had done some good things in her life. She had been devoted to her children. She had worked hard to support them. She had been a loving grandmother and, although she was beyond stingy, she had managed to do some good things for her grandchildren. The revelation that Pauline had paid for the last two years of her daughter's college came as a shock. Her ex-husband, for whatever reason, had hidden the truth all those years. Maybe Jen was right, she thought. She had so much hatred for Pauline that she couldn't recognize the good things she had done. Truth was, she had never really known her mother-in-law as a person. She had never sat down and talked to Pauline as a friend. She only saw her mother-in-law at family functions and, during those times, Pauline had always seemed distant and threatening. Maybe she should reassess her opinion.

They rode for almost an hour without speaking.

"Why aren't you talking?" Jen asked.

"No particular reason," Shirley Ann said. "I'm just thinking...."

They rode quietly. Finally, Shirley Ann spoke again.

"Did Pauline foot the bill for Scott's summer camp in high school?"

Jen nodded.

"And the reception hall for Pam's wedding?"

Jen nodded again. "Sounds like Glenn told you some more lies."

"I never knew about any of those things."

"Why didn't you ask?"

"I didn't have a reason to," Shirley Ann said. "I always felt Pauline was who she was and not me or anybody else on this earth could ever change her."

***

By late afternoon, they had crossed western Arizona and

were rapidly approaching the Colorado River and California.

"Let stay at Lazy Days on the River tonight," Jen said. "It's a beautiful campground. Then we'll get an early start in the morning. Surely we can get there by midnight tomorrow night."

Twenty minutes later, Jen pulled the station wagon and camper off the highway and onto the campground property. Once the fee was paid, Jen parked the rig on the far side of the campground overlooking the river. Then they settled in for the night. The next morning, after breakfast, they were ready to leave when Jen noticed the station wagon was sagging in the rear.

"Look at this!" she said. "We've got to fix a flat."

"How are we going to do that?"

"We got to disconnect the trailer, move Mother aside to get to the tools, then jack up the car and put on a good tire."

Shirley Ann shook her head in frustration.

Ten minutes later, Jen was at the rear of the vehicle and furiously cranking the jack while Shirley Ann was waiting for the flat tire to clear the ground. As Jen cranked, the station wagon body was lifted higher and higher.

"Tell me when it's high enough," she said.

"You got to go higher," Shirley Ann said.

Jen continued cranking.

"That should be enough," Shirley Ann said.

Jen stopped cranking, then started rolling the good tire around the side of the station wagon. Suddenly, they heard an ominous creaking sound and the station wagon started to lean on the jack. Then, as they watched in horror, the back end of the station wagon fell off the jack and started to slide in the soft gravel.

"Oh, no!" Jen said.

As they watched, the station wagon, back end first, continued sliding down the embankment toward the river. It started gaining speed, then suddenly slammed into a huge boulder and came to a stop. At the abrupt halt, the coffin slid out of the back of the station wagon, hit the rocks below, and tumbled over. The corpse was thrown out of the coffin and onto the rocks.

"Oh, my God!" Jen said.

"Come on," Shirley Ann said. "We've got to get her back in the coffin."

Jen peered at her, shock and surprise in her eyes.

Then, as Jen watched, Shirley Ann quickly scrambled over the rocks down the embankment. She looked at the corpse, then back at Jen.

"Come on," she called. "I'll need your help to lift her back in."

Instantly, Jen, heavier and slower, started down the embankment.

Shirley Ann peered at Pauline's body. It was cold and stiff to the touch. Her eyes were closed and she had a faint smile on her face. For the first time ever, Shirley Ann saw Pauline up close. She examined her face. The deep lines testified to a life of hardship. Her hands were wrinkled and drawn like someone who had worked hard throughout their life. In death, Pauline seemed to be much smaller and more vulnerable than Shirley Ann had remembered. There was a slight stoop to her shoulders and she had a long red scar on her right arm Shirley Ann had never seen before. Shirley Ann touched her face. Suddenly, after all those years, she realized that Pauline had been a human being, a living creature that wanted to breathe the air, take nourishment, and raise her offspring.

Moments later, Jen was at her side. For a moment, she stared at the body.

"Oh, Mother," she said. "I'm so sorry about this."

"Come on," Shirley Ann said. "Grab the arm on that side. I'll get the other and we'll lift her back into the coffin."

As instructed, Jen grabbed one arm and Shirley took the other. They were poised to return the body to the coffin.

"On three," Shirley Ann said. "One! Two! Three!"

At the count of three, they lifted the body and returned it to the coffin.

"Thank God!" Jen said, replacing the lid.

By now, a crowd of other campers had gathered along the riverbank to witness the scene.

An older man with two teenage boys called, "Can we help you?"

"Please!" Shirley Ann replied.

Moments later, the man and two boys were at the coffin. After some struggling, with the man on one end and the two boys on the other, they carried the coffin back up the embankment and returned it inside the station wagon.

"Me and these boys will fix that flat for you," he said. "You two have had enough problems for one day."

***

An hour later, the flat was fixed, Jen checked out of the campground, and the two old friends were back on I-10 headed to Palm Springs.

They rode quietly.

"Thanks for helping me back there," Jen said finally. "With all the hard feelings you have toward Mother, I know it had to be difficult."

"I was glad to help," Shirley Ann replied.

***

Over the next two hours, they crossed the desolate wilds of the Mojave Desert between Blythe and Indio. On the outskirts of Indio, they topped a rise in the highway and could see traffic backed up on I-10 as far as the eye could see. Several local policemen were stationed along the highway.

Jen slowed to speak to one of the officers.

"What happened, officer?"

"There's has been a sandstorm between Indio and Palm Springs and there is a forty-car pileup down around La Quinta."

"A sandstorm?"

"Yeah," he said. "It blew over four semis. They've got to get those moved, then bring in sweepers to get the sand off the highway."

"How long do you think it will be?"

"Five, maybe six hours," the officer said. "Where you going?"

"Palm Springs."

"You know, you can go out to Borrego Springs and take the back road over the top of the mountain. It'll put you in Palm Springs in about three hours. It's a two-lane road, but it's a good surface."

"I know that road," Jen said. "I used to go camping up there."

"It will be a lot quicker than waiting for all this traffic to be cleared," the officer said.

"Thanks!" Jen said.

Twenty minutes later, they were in Borrego Springs, climbing upward through the foothills of the Mount San Gorgonio Mountain.

"This is a good road," Jen said. "We'll be in Palm Springs in two hours."

They rode quietly for some thirty minutes, then suddenly, near the top of the mountain, the station wagon started coughing and sputtering.

"I was afraid of this," Jen said. "That damn gas gauge. I should have had it fixed."

"It says we've got half a tank," Shirley Ann said. "How do you know we are out of gas?"

"I know how a car acts when it runs out of gas."

"Pull off at the rest stop," Shirley Ann said, indicating a sign ahead. "We can't run out of gas in the middle of the road."

Moments later, the station wagon pulled into the rest stop. For a moment, the engine sputtered and coughed, then finally died. Jen spun the engine over several times, but to no avail.

"Come on! We've got to get some gas," she said.

They got out and surveyed the surroundings. In both directions, the road traced across the backbone of the mountain. On one side, the landscape was mountainous with small trees, desert chaparral, and volcanic rocks. The other side was an endless expanse of bare desert sand, which dissolved into the foothills beyond.

"Look," Jen said, peering toward the valley floor. "There's a road."

Her eyes followed the road further south and fell upon a lone gas station.

"And a service station," she said happily.

Shirley Ann peered into the distance.

"It's half a mile down there," she said. "It's going to be a hike going down there and getting back."

"We don't have a choice," Jen said.

"Do we have a gas can?" Shirley Ann asked.

"There's one in the trailer," Jen said.

Thirty minutes later, they were stumbling over the rocks and desert foliage to the valley floor. At the station, they bought an extra gas can, then, with each lugging a can, started the tortuous climb back up the mountainside. Twice, they stopped to rest. Finally, exhausted from the climb, they arrived back at the station wagon and emptied both cans into the tank.

As they started to get back into the station wagon, they heard a voice.

"Hello, American ladies!"

They turned. Before them stood a young, stocky Mexican man wearing several gold chains and a muscle shirt that revealed numerous gang tattoos. He was training an automatic pistol on them. Some ten to twelve feet behind him, they could see three more young Mexicans, all armed with automatic pistols.

"Oh my God!" Jen said.

"I hope you ladies aren't in a big hurry," the man said.

"What do you want?" Shirley Ann asked. "Why are you bothering us?"

The man glared angrily at her.

"Shut up!" he said. "I'm the one asking questions here! Hands up!"

Both held their hands up.

"I can blow you away with the snap of my fingers or I can let you live to breathe again tomorrow. Which do you want?"

"We want to breathe again tomorrow," Jen said.

"Then get on the ground," he ordered.

Instantly, Shirley Ann was sitting on the ground.

"You too!" he shouted at Jen. "On the ground!"

"Why do you want me on the ground?" asked Jen, trembling with fear.

Quickly, he threw a cartridge in the chamber and put the gun to the side of Jen's head.

"Would you like for me to blow your brains out?"

"No! No!" Jen said. "Please don't hurt me! I'm going! I'm going!"

Jen crumpled to the ground.

They lay on the ground several minutes as the Mexican man and his minions gathered around them.

"You ladies have nice watches," the leader said. "Give them to me!"

Both removed their watches and handed them over.

For a moment, he examined the watches, then smiled and shoved them into his pocket. Then, he turned to his minions.

"Traiga el trailer," he barked.

Instantly, the three others started to disconnect the trailer.

"They're taking the trailer," Jen said, her voice breaking with fear.

"Let 'em have it," Shirley Ann said. "They're drug dealers. Just hope they don't kill us."

"Oh, God!" Jen said. "I don't want to die."

In the afternoon twilight, they watched as the men disconnected the trailer from the station wagon. Once it was free, one of the men peered curiously inside the station wagon. For a moment, he hesitated, then ventured further.

"Jefe! Jefe!" he shouted. "Un cuerpo! Un cuerpo!"

Instantly, the leader turned at the sound, ran to the station wagon, and peered inside.

Then he opened the tailgate and peeked into the coffin.

"Dios mio!" he shouted, crossing himself and looking skyward. "Oh, Madre Maria!"

Absolute fear written in his face, he turned, placed his fingers to his lips, and let out a shrill whistle. Seconds later, a late model pickup truck appeared and backed up to the trailer. Quickly, it was connected to the pickup.

"Vamanos!" the leader shouted, then raced to the truck and jumped into the cab. Right behind him were his minions, who climbed into the pickup bed. The engine roared and the truck and trailer started out of the rest area. Suddenly, it lurched to stop.

"Oh, God!" Shirley Ann said. "They're coming back to kill us."

"Oh, God!" Jen replied. "I don't want to die."

Instantly, the leader burst out of the truck, produced the two watches, and threw them in the sand toward Shirley Ann and Jen. Then, in a flash, he jumped back inside, and the truck roared out of the rest area in a cloud of dust.

Jen watched as the pickup and the trailer disappeared down the highway, then collapsed on the ground, crying hysterically.

"Pauline saved us that time," Shirley Ann said, breathing a sigh of relief. "I really thought I was going to die. Never in my life have I been so scared."

She turned to Jen.

"I give up!" Jen cried, sitting in the desert sand and wringing her hands. "No matter how hard I try, nothing goes right! Oh God, what have I done to deserve all of this? I've always tried to be a good person and love and help my fellow man. Now I'm not sure if it has been worth anything. Oh God, where did I go wrong?"

Shirley Ann, calmer now, peered down impatiently at Jen, then turned, walked to the watches, and picked them up.

Jen was still crying hysterically.

To the west, Shirley Ann could see a tiny sliver of sun peeking over the horizon. For several more minutes, she waited for Jen to finish her sobbing. She had seen this before. Finally, when Jen was quiet, Shirley Ann went to her.

"You aren't doing anything to get us to the crematorium," she said.

Jen, wiping her tears, looked up. She was calmer now.

"You're right," she replied finally. "Give me just a minute."

"Here's your watch," Shirley Ann said.

"Thanks," Jen said, taking the watch.

Shirley Ann reached down her hand and pulled Jen to her feet.

"Come on!" she said. "Let's get this finished. I'm going to drive."

"That's fine," Jen said. "I'm too upset."

They both got into the station wagon. The mighty engine roared to life.

"I thank God we're still alive," Jen said. "Do you know where the crematorium's located?"

"I know exactly where it is."

***

An hour later, they were in downtown Palm Springs. Shirley Ann, racing to meet the deadline, was weaving in and out of traffic, going through yellow lights, and only slowing briefly for stop signs.

"Slow down!" Jen said. "You're going to get us killed."

"Sit tight and keep quiet," Shirley Ann said. "I'm going to get this over with."

Jen remained silent as Shirley Ann expertly maneuvered the station wagon through the night traffic.

"I think we're going to make it," Jen said. "Oh God, I think we're going to make it. It's only a few more blocks."

They were nearing the street where the crematorium was located.

"Slow down!" Jen said. "You've got to turn up here."

"No," Shirley Ann replied. "It's the next block."

"No!" Jen shouted. "Right here! Right here!! Turn! Turn!"

Realizing that Jen was right, Shirley Ann suddenly slammed on the brakes and, as the station wagon swerved around the corner on two wheels, the coffin slammed hard against the tailgate and jarred it open. The station wagon's inertia sent the coffin sliding across the street into the path of an oncoming gasoline truck. Instantly, the truck driver swerved to miss the sliding coffin and crashed into a power pole.

"Stop! Stop!" Jen said.

Shirley Ann pulled the station wagon to the curb and they got out.

"Oh my God!" Jen said upon witnessing the scene.

The sliding coffin had come to rest under the ruptured belly of the gasoline truck and gas was pouring out of the tanker and onto the coffin. When the truck crashed into the power pole, a small fire had started in the engine and was rapidly making its way to the storage tank.

"It's going to explode," Shirley Ann said.

Inside the truck, Shirley Ann and Jen could see the driver frantically trying to escape. Again and again, he desperately threw his weight against the door, but it was stuck. Moments later, seeing his efforts were futile, he rolled down the window, climbed out, and started running. Moments later, a deafening explosion shattered the desert night. A giant blaze of fuel-fed fire and black smoke mushroomed forty or fifty feet high into the night sky and pieces of flaming debris flew hither and yon. A crowd of spectators stopped to witness the scene as the truck and the coffin blazed brightly, illuminating several blocks of the street.

"Can you believe this?" Jen asked.

"Nothing surprises me anymore," Shirley Ann said.

Moments later, they heard the wail of a police car and fire engines arriving on the scene. Quickly, firemen with high-pressure hoses brought the conflagration under control. Once the fire was extinguished, the truck, the body, and the coffin had been reduced to a heap of smoldering ashes.

"You're both lucky to be alive," the police officer said.

"You don't know the half of it," Shirley Ann said.

After filling out the police report, the officer explained that he would have to write Shirley Ann a ticket for reckless driving since she was operating the motor vehicle at the time of the accident. Also, she was be at fault, so he advised her to contact her insurance company. Under California law, the officer said, any time a cadaver is accidentally destroyed, the deceased's next of kin must file a special addendum to the death certificate that fully explained the circumstances of the loss. Jen said she would do that if the officer could have the court mail the form to her Colorado address. The officer agreed. Once Jen showed adequate proof of insurance, the officer said now all that would be necessary would be for both to appear before the local judge and testify to the details of the accident. He said the court date was set for the following month. Both Jen and Shirley Ann agreed they would appear and signed the policeman's court summons.

***

It was 8:40 p.m. when they reached the Happy Home Crematorium. The night attendant, like the director at Winkenhoffer, had no time for small talk.

"You don't have the body?" he asked.

"No," Jen said.

"What was the final disposition?"

"It was burned in the accident," she said, producing the police report.

The attendant read the police document.

"So, in a manner of speaking, the deceased was cremated as originally proposed?"

"You could say that," Jen replied.

"Very well," he replied. "I'm sure you know that, in this case, there won't be any ashes."

"I understand," Jen said.

"These are the release papers," he said, producing a completed, official-looking form. "Sign here."

Back outside, Shirley Ann turned to Jen.

"Come on," she said. "Let's go to my house and rest for a day, then we'll go back to Colorado and go hiking."

"I'm ready," Jen said.

"Can you give me just a minute?" Shirley Ann said.

"Sure!" Jen said.

For a long moment, Shirley Ann peered thoughtfully at Jen, then turned her back and peered off into the pitch blackness of the desert night. Suddenly, she fell to her knees and started sobbing. They were huge, heart-rending sobs. Jen, shocked and surprised, stared at her old friend. She had never seen Shirley Ann sob like that. She had always been the strong one. Finally, Jen went to her.

"It's okay, baby," she said, kneeling beside Shirley Ann and putting
her arms lovingly around her. "It's over now. Everything is going to
be okay."

For several minutes, Jen held Shirley Ann as she sobbed uncontrollably. All the spiteful emotions Shirley Ann had held inside all those years came gushing forth. Her heart-rending wails became almost screams and echoed against the nearby mountains as she poured out her heart and soul into the desert night. It was a gigantic release.

Finally, Shirley Ann stopped sobbing and broke the embrace.

"Are you okay?" Jen asked.

"I'm fine now," Shirley Ann said, wiping her eyes and standing upright.

"Come on," she said. "Let's go!"

"Oh, Shirley Ann," Jen said. "Thank you so much for helping me. I knew I could count on you. You'll be my best friend until the day I die."

For a long moment, Shirley Ann peered at Jen, irritation in her eyes.

Then she turned back to the station wagon.

"Come on!" she said impatiently. "Let's go!"

***

Over the ensuing years, Shirley Ann would remember her former mother-in-law with a new kindness. In her heart, she made a conscious effort to recall Pauline's good deeds rather than memories of the abuse. She never totally forgot the abuse. The memories were buried too deeply to totally forget them, but she tempered them with thoughts of kindness and forgiveness. With some work on her part and the healing passage of time, the old animosities slowly faded away and she could talk about Pauline without becoming angry. Shirley Ann had learned a mighty lesson and it had brought a much-needed peace into her heart. It was a trip she would always remember!

****The End****

SERPENTUS SARAGOSSII

1

Little Wilton didn't have long for this earth. Only days after his eighth birthday, he had been diagnosed with a rare form of anemia, a debilitating disease that slowly but surely destroys the red blood cells in the body. From the first, doctors said the disease was incurable but noted that, if he took his medication and led a sedate lifestyle, he might live up to two, maybe three more years. Doctors said his frail body couldn't handle the stress of going to school, so he would have to remain quietly in the family home, take his medications, and try to live out his final days as peacefully and as comfortably as possible. At the time of the diagnosis, his parents had brought in as part-time nurse to attend to his medical needs and Wilton seemed be living quite comfortably. Now, two years after the original diagnosis, the frail youngster found himself living in pure hell after a tragic accident befell his parents.

While returning from a dinner party one night, both parents were killed in a head-on car crash and little Wilton was left an orphan. Shortly afterward, the court designated Miss Hilda Westbrook, his mother's oldest sister, as his new guardian. In his decision, the judge noted that the aunt had some nursing experience and could also attend to his medical needs while serving as his protector. Once she was installed in the home, however, Wilton's life became a daily struggle to maintain his sanity. It seemed that the aunt, a large, late-forties, never-married woman, only lived to make Wilton's final days on this earth as miserable as possible.

If the frail ten-year-old was in the kitchen making a sandwich, she would always come in and start shouting about the way he was proceeding. She never said anything softly and calmly.

"Look at you," she would yell angrily. "You're using too much mayonnaise! And you only need two slices of meat. Why are you using three?"

Little Wilton would look sadly at her, then, rather than argue, scoop off a portion of mayonnaise as per her specifications and put only two slices of meat on his sandwich.

If Wilton was feeling cold and wanted to lower the living room window to warm up the room, he was instant prey.

"Get away from that window!" she would shout. "It's warm enough in here already. Get away! Now!!"

Obediently, the child would turn from the window and retreat to his room.

His aunt knew that Wilton liked to sleep until 8:30, but promptly at 7 a.m. each morning, his tormentor would burst into his room, turn on the overhead light, and begin shouting.

"Get up! Get out of bed!" she would say. "You're sleeping your life away."

Poor Wilton, sleepy-eyed and fatigued, would sit up in bed.

"But, Aunt Hilda," he would plead, rubbing his eyes, "it's only seven a.m. Can't I sleep a little longer?"

"No!" she would shout. "Get up, go wash yourself, and have your breakfast."

Wilton would look pitifully at his tormenter, then, knowing it was useless to argue, he would throw his feet over the side of the bed and begin his day.

There seemed to be no end to the torment. Many times, he felt his aunt was doing everything in her power to hasten his death. After all, once he was gone, she would receive the handsome family trust his parents had left to him upon their deaths.

Worst of all was the constant loneliness. Since he was an only child and not in school, he had no playmates. There were two housekeepers, but he couldn't befriend them. All they knew how to say was: "How are you feeling today, Wilton? Can I get you anything? Isn't it a lovely day…" And he certainly couldn't befriend his Aunt Hilda. She never had a kind word for him. Wilton wanted someone or something to talk to, to relate to and share his life with.

The final blow came when his Aunt Hilda refused to let him have a pet. Once, he had caught a small white lizard, a *Lacertilia blanca*, and hid it in a clear glass jug under his bed. When his aunt was away, he would spend hours playing with the lizard and watching as the reptile skittered about the bedroom floor catching an occasional fly. Fearful that his prize might starve, Wilton dug up an ant bed in the back yard, then placed the ants and earth into another clear jug and hid it under his bed. At feeding time, he would place the lizard inside, then would watch happily as the hungry beast made a feast of the trapped ants.

Then disaster struck. One morning, one of the housekeepers and his Aunt Hilda barged into his room following a trail of ants from the kitchen. Once they had followed the trail of tiny insects to his treasure trove under the bed, his aunt exploded.

"You little brat!" she shouted. "Bringing ants into this house. Have you no brains? Now we have ants in the kitchen crawling among the food and silverware."

Quickly, she gathered up both of the glass jars, then went outside to the back yard. Through his bedroom window, Wilton watched as she dumped the contents of both jugs on the ground, then cruelly stomped the life out of the lizard when it tried to escape. His eyes filled with tears as he watched.

Task completed, she rushed back inside to give the child a lecture.

"But I don't have any friends," Wilton would protest. "Can't I just have a little creature of nature to talk to and share my life with?"

"No! You don't need any friends," she shouted. "You're sick and need to stay quiet for your health's sake. Look at me! I don't have any friends and I'm perfectly happy."

Then he would look away dejectedly. He wanted to say to her, *Who in the world could possibly want to be your friend? As mean and cruel as you are, who would ever want to be your friend?* But he didn't. He knew it would only bring on more hell.

"Now go to your room, take your bath, and go to bed!"

"Aunt Hilda, its only 6:30."

"Do as I say!" she would shout.

Then Wilton would turn away obediently and do as she ordered.

Now, for the past two weeks, Wilton had had a small turtle hidden in the old tool shed in the back yard. It was an eastern snapping turtle, a *Chelydra serpentine*, that Wilton had named Oscar. The child had captured the turtle and placed it in a small wooden box on a shelf near a window so it could receive sunlight. Once the box was in place, he moved several gardening tools in front to conceal it from prying eyes and, whenever his aunt was out of sight, Wilton would sneak into the shed and feed it lettuce and vegetables he had stolen from the kitchen. He loved to watch the tiny creature nip off pieces of lettuce in tiny mouthfuls and chew endlessly before it swallowed and was ready for another bite. All the while, he would marvel at its tiny claw-like feet, its oblong olive-green head, and the light brown and dark yellow ringed formations nature had placed on its protective shell.

2

An imaginative, highly intelligent child, the single joy Wilton had in his loneliness was the time he spent at the marshes near the family home studying reptiles. He loved anything and everything about reptiles. The family home in southeast Georgia abutted the backwaters of the famous Okefenokee swamps and, for Wilton, this broad expanse of black water that contained lush, verdant flora and a rich diversity of reptiles was a sheer paradise. Frogs, snakes, turtles, lizards and such held a special fascination for his curious eyes and he could spend endless hours observing and studying them.

The only days he had any peace in his life were Tuesday and Saturday mornings. Those were the times when his Aunt Hilda went into town with one of the housekeepers to buy groceries. Oh, how he treasured those times! On these days, as soon as his aunt was gone, he would shoulder his backpack with his books inside, then trek the 150 yards across an open field behind the family home to the marshy bog beyond. Then he would sit for hours watching the creatures of nature go about their daily lives. His favorites were the frogs and snakes. He loved the quietness and beauty of the bog. The mysterious black water, the verdant, filigreed ferns, the strangely shaped air plants that lived in the trees, and the tall, reedy bulrushes along its edges were pure visual delights for Wilton. Oftentimes, he would watch a water moccasin conceal itself in the thick foliage along the water's edge, then wait for its prey. Moments later, to his delight, he would watch a field mouse who lived in the thick broom sage in the nearby field scurry up the water's edge to have a drink. Suddenly, an unseen enemy would spring out of nowhere, clasp the unsuspecting mouse in its jaws, then wrap its muscular body around the helpless creature and squeeze its life away. Its giant jaws would unhinge and the viper would slowly ingest the tiny rodent. The beauty of nature, the unrelenting laws of the jungle, was what

Wilton loved the most.

On one particular Tuesday, some three weeks after he had hidden the turtle in the old tool shed, his Aunt Hilda announced that she was going into town to buy groceries. His heart leapt with joy at the words. Only moments after she was gone, Wilton shouldered his backpack with his herpetology books inside and started across the broom-sage-filled field to the marsh. Upon arrival, he swung down the load, then spread out an old towel and took up a vigil to observe his reptilian friends. After only a few moments, he spotted a southern red-legged frog, a *Rana aurora*, sitting quietly on a log, dining on insects. He would watch closely as the amphibian, body perfectly still but eyes forever vigilant, waited patiently, then, once an insect was within range, shoot out its narrow tongue, grasp the prey, then snatch the hapless insect back into its mouth. After he had been there only a few minutes, he heard someone call his name.

"Wilton!" the person called.

Wilton turned.

It was his friend Carlton, a lanky, long-faced young man in his early twenties who had a beard and always wore a baseball cap, Carlton worked for the pet shop in town, collecting reptiles. He was dressed in camouflage gear and, in one hand, he carried a burlap bag and, in the other, a snake-handler's tool. Wilton had encountered Carlton several times during his visits to the marsh. He knew Carlton loved reptiles as much as he did.

"Wilton! What you doing?" Carlton said in a deep southern drawl.

"Watching a red-legged frog have breakfast," Wilton replied. "What you got in that sack?"

"A velvet tail rattler and a couple garter snakes."

"Can I see the velvet tail?"

"Sure," Carlton replied.

Then, holding the bag open with one hand, he used the other to probe around inside the sack with the snake-handler's tool. After a few moments, he pulled out an earth-colored viper, which was twisting and turning under the pressure of the snake-handler's tool.

Wilton moved closer to inspect the creature.

"He's a beauty," Wilton said expertly. "He's less than two years old."

"How do you know that?" Carlton said.

"Look at the tip of the tail," Wilton said. "Just between the tail itself and the torso. Do you see how the color is a dark purple?"

"Yeah," Carlton said, looking closely at the snake's tail. "Never noticed that before."

"The tail won't turn a bright velvet color until the snake is at least two years old."

Carlton was impressed.

"Where did you learn that?" he asked.

Wilton reached down to the backpack on the ground and withdrew a large book.

"From my *Encyclopedia of Herpetology*," Wilton said, handing the book to Carlton.

Carlton laid aside the burlap bag and the snake-handling tool, then began thumbing through the book.

"My goodness!" he said. "Look at all this! I've never seen so much information about reptiles. It's got all of the subspecies of water moccasins, copperheads, rattlers, garters, and even some coral snakes."

He gazed intently at one of the pictures.

"Oh my Lord," he said. "I couldn't imagine seeing a coral snake as big as that one. Where did you get this book?"

"My mother bought it for me," Wilton replied.

"You want to sell it?"

"Oh, I couldn't do that," Wilton said. "It's a gift from my mother."

Carlton handed the book back to Wilton.

"Let me ask you something," Wilton said, replacing the book in his backpack. "Have you ever seen a *Serpentus saragossii* in these marshes?"

"Oh, yeah," Carlton replied. "I saw one last week sleeping on a log down at the east end of the marsh. They're rare, but I see one from time to time. If I see one, though, I don't mess with it because they're too dangerous."

"Yes, I know," Wilton said. "Their poison coagulates

human blood in less than four seconds. It's instant death."

Carlton laughed.

"Did you hear the story about the guy who was bitten by a saragossii?"

"No!"

"A man told his friend: 'I've been bitten by a saragossii. What do I do now?' The friend replied: 'Find a nice, quiet place to lie down and die.'"

Both had a big laugh.

"Are you interested in getting a saragossii?" Carlton asked.

"I would love to have one," Wilton said. "I understand they have the most beautiful coloration of any snake in nature."

"Oh yes," Carlton said. "They're a yellowish, mint-green color. When the sun shines on a saragossii, there is a beautiful golden-green luster to the scales. If you ever see a saragossii in bright sunlight, you will never forget it."

"Could I keep one at home?"

"Sure," Carlton said. "But you would need one of those store-bought poisonous reptile cages. The cage has a special door for food and water and a locked top so he can't get out."

"What would you feed it?"

"Frozen mice," he said. "We got plenty of them at the shop. How long you planning on keeping it?"

"Not sure," Wilton replied.

Carlton studied his friend for a moment.

"Tell you what," Carlton continued. "I'll make you a deal. I'll get you a saragossii and one of those poisonous snake cages. We've got some used ones at the shop. I'll even throw in three or four frozen mice."

"What do you want in return?" Wilton asked.

"That book on reptiles," Carlton said.

Wilton studied him for a moment.

"Let me think about it," Wilton said. "I'd love to have one. I've seen pictures of them in books but have never seen one in real life. I could spend hours and hours watching him."

"Well, I've got to get going," Carlton said. "The shop wants me to find a rainbow garter snake. Some guy came in last week and offered to pay $100 for one. I promised the owner I'd find one. I'll see you later."

Then he turned and started walking away.

"Bye, Carlton," Wilton said.

"If you decide you want a saragossii, let me know," he said.

"I will," Wilton replied. "Remember, I'm here on Tuesday and Saturday mornings."

Carlton waved good-bye, then disappeared behind a thick stand of bulrushes.

3

Thirty minutes later, Wilton was back at home. The family car was still gone, so he knew his Aunt Hilda was absent. The moment he stepped into the back yard, he knew he had to use the bathroom immediately, but he wanted to check on Oscar first. Quickly, he ducked inside the shed, removed the old clothes and gardening tools, then peered inside the cage at his friend. Oscar was sleeping soundly. Satisfied that his prize was safe, he exited the shed and started for the house. In his haste, he forgot to close the shed door. At the back porch steps, he wiped the mud off his feet on the mat, then dashed into the house to use the bathroom. Once he exited the bathroom, he went into the kitchen to make his favorite snack: heavily buttered toast and raspberry jam with a glass of cold milk.

The moment he took the buttered toast out of the oven, he heard the family car pull up in the front yard. Then, he heard a car door slam and he knew his Aunt Hilda and the housekeeper would be bringing groceries into the kitchen. Instinctively, he knew to prepare himself for an attack.

Moments later, Aunt Hilda, her arms laden with sacks of food, appeared in the kitchen.

"Good morning, Aunt Hilda," Wilton said.

She glanced absently at the child, then she and the domestic began putting the food items into the cupboards and the pantry. Moments later, they were finished and the aunt approached him at the table.

"Look at the mess you're making," she shouted. "Melted butter is dripping off the toast on to the linen tablecloth. You always put on too much butter. And you don't have to use all of the raspberry jam," she said, picking up the jar and noting that it was almost empty. "Go on!" she said. "Get out of my kitchen and go to your room to eat."

Dejectedly, the child got up from the table, then went to his room to finish his raspberry toast. Poor Wilton! There seemed to be no salvation for him.

Moments later, as he was finishing his toast, he heard Aunt Hilda at the back porch.

"Wilton!" she shouted. "Have you been in the shed?"

Through the bedroom window, he watched as she strode across the back yard, peered into the shed, then went inside. Instantly, his heart filled with fear that she would go looking for Oscar. Moments later, his worst fears were confirmed when he heard the loud thumps of boxes and other objects were being shifted in the shed. His heart sank.

Moments later, she came out of the tool shed carrying the old wooden box Oscar had been calling home.

Instantly, he dashed out of his room, down the hallway, and into the back yard.

"Wait! Wait!" the child pleaded. "Please!!! Please!! Please don't hurt Oscar!! Please don't kill my turtle."

Then, totally unmindful of the child's words, she reached her hand inside the box and withdrew the turtle. The frightened creature had curled up into a ball within its protective shell.

Then, in a single motion, she drew back and threw the balled-up turtle against the oak tree in the back yard. The sudden impact made a sickening thud as it bounced off the sturdy oak tree and came to rest in the brown mulch at its trunk.

"Now don't bring any more creatures near this house," she shouted. "Frogs and turtles are nasty, filthy creatures. They belong outside, not in the house!!"

Then, arms akimbo, she stood over a child like a slave master would a charge.

"Do you hear me?" she shouted.

"Yes, ma'am," he said sadly.

Finally, she turned, marched back up the back porch steps, and slammed the door behind her. Instantly, Wilton went to the oak tree and picked up the turtle. Its beautiful, multi-colored shell had been split open from the impact of hitting the oak tree. Blood was oozing out of the bottom of the shell and the poor creature's green head, its eyes closed in death, was hanging limply to one side. Wilton burst into tears.

4

The following Tuesday, once his aunt and the domestic had gone into town, he shouldered his backpack and headed across the broom sage field to the marshy bog beyond. As he approached the bog, he saw Carlton, his burlap bag and snake tool in hand, probing through the tall grasses some fifty yards away.

He called.

Carlton waved and started walking toward him.

After greetings, Carlton turned immediately to business.

"I got a saragossii," he said. "Caught him last week down on the south end of the marsh. He's a nice one. A full three feet long. You ready to make a deal?"

"I'm ready," Wilton said. "When do you want to bring him?"

"I can meet you here tomorrow," Carlton said.

"I can't come tomorrow," Wilton said. "Let's make it Saturday morning."

"Suit yourself," Carlton said. "I've got everything I promised. The snake, the cage, and some frozen rats."

"I'll be here," Wilton said.

"Don't forget to bring the book," Carlton said.

"I won't," Wilton replied.

***

Over the next five days, Wilton was a perfect child when he was around his Aunt Hilda. He went out of his way to not make a mess in the kitchen. He didn't protest when she rushed in each morning to rouse him out of bed. If he went outside, he checked his shoes closely before reentering the house. His table manners were impeccable and everything was "Yes, ma'am" and "No, ma'am" and "Can I help?" and "Would it be ok if I went outside." In each and every way, he tried to be a perfect gentleman. In fact, on the following Friday, Aunt Hilda even complimented him on his behavior.

"It looks like you're finally learning to take orders," she said. "It's about time."

***

The following morning, after Aunt Hilda and the housekeeper were gone, Wilton shouldered his backpack and headed back to the marsh. Carlton was waiting at the point where they had met previously. The moment Wilton spotted him, he started across the field toward him. On the ground in front of Carlton was a metal, finely meshed wire cage.

Wilton rushed up.

"I want to see the saragossii," he said excitedly.

Instantly, he unshouldered the backpack and was on the ground beside the cage, peering inside.

"My! My!" Wilton said with sheer wonder in his eyes. "What a beautiful creature!"

For several minutes, he peered delightedly inside the cage, admiring the reptile's brilliant yellowish mint-green color. The perfect oval shape of the snake's head and the fine-looking sculptured lines from its immediate neck to its torso was a thing of beauty to Wilton.

"Never have I seen a more beautiful reptile," he said.

"Now let me explain about the cage," Carlton said. "Always keep the top locked. If for some reason you have to put your hand in there, you'll need one of those special heavy leather gloves with the long sleeves. That's what we use at the shop."

Carlton indicated two doors on either end of the cage.

"This one," he said, indicating with his forefinger, "is where you drop in the frozen rats. This one over here," he said, indicating again, "is where you pour in water."

"I got it," Wilton said.

"And here are four frozen mice to feed it," Carlton said, holding up a plastic bag containing the carcasses of four dead mice. "They've thawed a little since this morning, but if you put them in the freezer, they'll be fresh when you're ready to feed him. Now I've already fed him one today, so there will be no need to feed him again for a week."

Wilton didn't answer right away. He was still admiring the beauty of the creature.

"You got all that?" Carlton asked.

"I got it," Wilton replied.

"So we got a deal?"

"Yep!" Wilton said happily. "We got a deal."

Instantly, he turned, unzipped the backpack, and handed Carlton the *Encyclopedia of Herpetology*.

Carlton smiled as he took the book.

"Thanks!" he said, admiring the volume. "I'm going to enjoy this."

Wasting no time, Wilton placed the package of dead mice inside his backpack and prepared to leave.

"Well, I've got to go now," he said. "Thanks, Carlton!"

"Thank you!" Carlton said.

Then, hurriedly, Wilton picked up his backpack and the cage with the snake inside, and dashed back across the field. Back at home, he went straight to the old shed. Once inside, he placed the metal cage on the same table where Oscar had been housed. Then, he went into the house and straight to his room, where he retrieved an old lock and key he had once used to lock his toy box. Back at the shed, he locked the cage door, then stacked two boxes atop the cage, then some old clothes on top of the boxes, and finally some old sheets atop the clothes. Finally, satisfied with himself, he turned and started for the house, leaving the shed door open. At the back porch, he wiped the mud off his shoes, then went to his room and placed the key in an old shoebox he kept on the top shelf of the closet. He waited.

5

Thirty minutes later, he heard the family car pulling up in the driveway. He could hear his aunt and the housekeeper chattering as they brought the groceries into the house. At the back porch steps, he could hear his Aunt Hilda voice her consternation at the sight of the mud.

"Look at that!" she said. "That little brat! He's been down at the bog again and brought some new creature into this house. Just wait till I get ahold of him."

Wilton waited. He knew she and the housekeeper would put away the groceries before she came to his room. For several moments, he could hear the opening and closing of cupboards and the refrigerator door. Finally, the sounds of putting away food ended, then he heard the marching step of her feet coming down the hallway to his room.

The door burst open.

"Good morning, Aunt Hilda," he said.

She snarled.

"Don't good morning me, you little brat!" she screamed. "You've been back in the swamps again, haven't you?"

"No," the child said.

"Don't you lie to me!" she screamed. "There is fresh marsh mud on the back porch steps."

Wilton looked up at her with pitiful eyes.

"I know that look," she said.

Wilton looked away dejectedly.

"Where it is?" she shouted angrily. "Tell me where it is or I'll search until I find it."

He didn't answer.

Instantly, she started tearing the room apart. First, she looked under the bed, then she started checking all of the drawers in the bureau. Next, she peeked in both drawers of the small table beside his bed, then she went to the closet and started pulling out clothes. Finally, after she had found nothing, she glared angrily at the child.

"Tell me!! Tell me where it is!" she demanded. "Tell me where you hid that creature."

Wilton didn't answer.

Suddenly, she stopped as if she had a realization.

"The shed!" she said suddenly. "You put it in the same place where you tried to hide the turtle, didn't you?"

Wilton looked away without speaking.

Quickly, she stepped to the window and glanced toward the shed. She could see the door was open.

"That's all I need to know," she said, turning to leave the room. "Your silence confirms your guilt."

With that, she stormed out of his room and slammed the door. Wilton could hear her footsteps passing through the hallway and the slam of the back door.

Through the open bedroom window, he watched as she entered the shed. For a long moment, there was silence, then a clamor of movement and several loud thuds as if large objects were being jostled about. Moments later, she exited the shed and marched back across the back yard and into the house.

"I found your little treasure trove," she said. "Now where's the key?"

The child shrugged his shoulders in ignorance.

"Don't you mess with me!" she shouted. "Where's the key?"

Wilton didn't answer.

Suddenly, she rushed toward him. Then, standing over him like a slave master, she reached down, grasped the front of his shirt, and started shaking him violently.

"Tell me, you little brat!!" she shouted. "Tell me where the key is!!"

Wilton's frail body withered quickly under the violent shaking.

"It's in the shoebox," he blurted out. "On the top shelf of the closet."

She stopped shaking him, then glared at him angrily again and released her grip.

Instantly, she went to the closet and pulled down the shoebox from the top shelf. Then, gleefully removing the top, she pulled out the key.

"Ah, ha!" she said with pure delight. "Look what I found!"

Then, thrusting the key into his face, she stood threateningly over the child.

"You can't fool me, you little brat!" she said. "I know all of your dirty little secrets!"

Once she exited the room, Wilton turned to watch through the bedroom window as she crossed the yard and went into the old tool shed again. He waited. He tried to time her actions in his mind. *Now she is unlocking the lock,* he told himself. *Now she is opening the hinged flap at the top of the cage.* He waited. Now she was feeling very proud of herself that she had discovered another one of Wilton's reptile friends. He knew she was thrusting her hand inside the darkened cage to grasp the creature and pull it out. For a long moment, he waited and watched the open door of the shed for some movement. Finally, seconds later, he saw a human hand and part of an arm thrust through the door opening, then, after a few seconds, fall to earth. For a long moment, the hand trembled slightly, then fell limp. He waited. Seconds later, he saw a yellowish-green creature slither over the motionless human hand, then make its way across the green grass of the back yard. As it curled and twisted its way across the grass, he marveled at how brilliantly its neon mint-green coloring stood out against the forest green of the lawn grass. He watched the creature slowly complete its journey across the grass to the dirty white sand beyond, then head for the open field and the marshy bog. Wilton smiled at the sight.

Instantly, he was in the kitchen. Carefully, he carved off two thick slices of fresh bread, then, after dabbing them with more than adequate butter, he popped them into the oven. Next, he went to the refrigerator and poured a tall glass of cold milk. Moments later, he removed the hot buttered toast, then placed it on a plate and the table. Once seated, he spread huge globs of raspberry jam across the bread's buttery surface. As he brought the delicacy to his mouth, huge globs of melted butter dripped off the toast and onto the white linen tablecloth. Moments later, without fear, he took a huge bite and luxuriated in its fruity, buttery flavor.

Suddenly, in the hallway, he heard one of the housekeepers strolling through the house, calling for his aunt.

"Miss Westbrook!!" she called. "Yoo-hoo! Miss Westbrook! Where are you?"

Wilton heard the back door slam, then watched as the young woman strode along the rock walkway to the old tool shed.

Suddenly, there was a horrific scream, then a loud clamor. Moments later, the housekeeper burst through the back door and announced to the other housekeeper:

"Miss Westbrook!! Miss Westbrook!!" she screamed. "Something terrible has happened to Miss Westbrook."

"What is it?" yelled the second housekeeper.

"In the shed. She's face down in the shed!" screamed the first housekeeper. "I think she's dead."

"Oh, my heavens," said the second housekeeper frantically. "What a terrible tragedy! Oh, such grief and sorrow!! Who is going to tell little Wilton?"

In the kitchen, Wilton listened quietly as he took another huge bite of heavily buttered raspberry toast, then washed it down with a swig of fresh milk.

****The End****

TEMBO MAKABURI

1

Serengeti plains, 1968

In the distance, through the shimmering African heat, a hunting party of three vehicles—a Land Rover and two open-air jeeps—lumbered slowly across the vast savannah of rolling grass lands. As it moved, giant clouds of red dust boiled in its wake, and intermittently, as the caravan drew near, grazing wildebeest jumped at their approach, then scampered off to a safe distance and watched the party pass. Nearby, scattered about under a stand of baobab trees, a pride of lions—their mouths bloodied by a fresh morning kill—lazed quietly in the late afternoon heat. In the far distance, the snow-capped rim of Mount Kilimanjaro loomed like a giant white halo in the cloudless sky.

Moments later, the caravan slowed as it approached a cluster of Masai huts, then the Land Rover, the lead vehicle, suddenly jerked to a stop. Instantly, the other two vehicles stopped behind it. Slowly, a cloud of red dust cleared away and the passenger door of the Land Rover opened. Walter "Big Bwana" Cravens, leader of the party, stepped out. Rifle in hand and decked out in safari garb, he strode some twenty yards ahead of the Land Rover, then stopped and gazed into the distance. At well over six feet with broad, muscular shoulders and a burly, rough and ready look, Cravens was a big, imposing man. Seconds later, he turned his attention to the earth in front of him. After taking several steps, he knelt on the ground and pulled back a clump of lemon grass to better view an elephant print. Satisfied, he pursed his lips thoughtfully, then stood up and, for a long minute, trained a pair of binoculars on the terrain ahead.

"Abasi!" he called, taking down the binoculars.

Seconds later, a smallish, early-thirties Masai native emerged from the Land Rover and was at his side.

"Yes, Bwana?" he said.

"He's two, maybe three hours ahead of us," said Cravens, indicating the trail leading into the tall grass. "He's moving fast, really fast for an old bull elephant."

The guide nodded, then knelt to examine the footprints.

"He knows where he's going," the guide said. "And he's clever. He is trying to stay in the deep grass so his trail will be harder to follow."

"He's headed for those black mountains," Cravens said, pointing to a range of lava-black promontories to the northeast. "What's in those mountains?"

"Don't know," Abasi replied. "I've been to them, but never inside."

"There's something in those mountains he's interested in," said Cravens. "Maybe a female."

"Maybe more than one," the guide replied.

"You mean like a harem?"

"Yes," Abasi said.

For a long moment, the hunter and his guide stood side by side, peering across the savannah toward the mountains. For almost ten years now, they had been hunting the savannah together. Nine years earlier, Abasi, in a fit of rage, had killed his wife's sister and was given a life sentence in the prison in Nairobi. Cravens, upon learning of his friend's fate, used his influence and paid a handsome bribe to local officials to win Abasi's release. Afterward, as was the local custom in such cases, the court named Cravens Abasi's "keeper." Since his release, Abasi had been essentially an indentured servant to Cravens.

Soon, Cravens turned and surveyed the cluster of Masai huts scattered among the tall grass behind them.

"Let's camp here for the night," he said, pointing to an open area. "I know this village. We'll pick up his trail again tomorrow."

***

Two hours later, darkness had fallen and the five porters—all Masai natives—had unloaded the vehicles and set up camp around a huge fire. There was the smell of coffee and sizzling elephant steaks in the air. High overhead, the moon was a glowering mound of yellow and, from the darkness beyond the camp, came the night sounds of the Serengeti: the constant screech of the ground cicada, the distant bark of a jackal, or the faint call of a spotted African owl.

While they waited to eat, Cravens and his guide sat at a small table examining a map by the light of an oil lantern.

"It's a matter of whether or not he goes across the open savannah to the mountains or to the Olanga River, then to the mountains," Cravens said. "He can move faster in the open savannah."

"He's too smart to cross the open savannah," Abasi said. "He can move faster, but there is no place to hide. There's only one watering hole if he crosses the open plain. He'll go to the river, where there is plenty of water and places to hide."

Cravens nodded, then began folding the map.

"You're probably right," he said. "He'll stay in the tall grass as much as possible."

"The tall grass continues from here to the river," Abasi continued. "That's probably the way he'll go…"

"We'll know tomorrow," Cravens replied.

Suddenly, the chief porter appeared and spoke to Abasi in Swahili.

Abasi turned to Cravens.

"Let's eat, Bwana," the guide said.

***

In a while, Cravens and his guide were seated at a small table in front of the fire. It was laden with an array of steaming hot food. There were elephant steaks, Zanzabari-flavored rice, yellow African beans, and peanut soup. As Cravens started to fill his plate, his eye caught the movement of several hyenas gathered at the edge of the campsite, their eyes glowing like tiny, illuminated orbs in the light of the campfire. They had been drawn to the camp by the smell of the elephant steaks.

"Bloody hyenas!" Cravens said.

Then, irritation in his eyes, he stopped serving his plate.

"Abasi, go chase off those hyenas," he said. "I can't eat when those devils are watching."

Immediately, Abasi got up from the table, took a stick, and made a threatening charge toward the hyenas. Instantly, the dog-like creatures retreated into the bush.

Satisfied they were gone, Abasi returned to the table. No sooner was he seated than they appeared again.

Immediately, Cravens noticed their return.

"Those bloody devils!" he said.

"Want me to chase them again?" Abasi asked.

"No," Cravens said. "I'll do it."

Quickly, he pushed back his chair, strode to a nearby hunting pack, and took his rifle. Wrapping the shoulder strap tightly around his forearm, he put a shell in the chamber, closed the breech, steadied his aim, and pulled the trigger. The sound of the shot exploded in the night air, and instantly, the hyena at the front of the pack collapsed dead on the ground. Quickly, the other hyenas darted back into the bush.

"I can't stand those damn things," he said, putting away the rifle and returning to the table. "Especially when I'm eating."

He reseated himself at the table.

"Hyenas are the lowest creatures on earth," he continued, serving his plate again. "The filthy, ravenous dogs only come out at night and they will eat anything, dead or alive. A lion or a tiger will have the decency to kill its prey before eating it. Not a hyena. If their prey is helpless and can't escape, they will eat it alive. No dignity, no grace, no mercy… The only thing they have any loyalty to is their mouths. I hate hyenas. I bloody hate 'em."

Now his plate was filled and he was ready to eat. Before he took the first bite, he glanced back toward the hyenas. They were dragging their dead comrade into the bush.

"Look at them," Cravens said, shaking his head in disgust. "They eat their own. Could you imagine being eaten alive by a pack of hyenas? Oh, sweet mother of Jesus, save me from such a fate."

***

Two hours later, the party had finished their evening meal, the tables had been cleared, and the members of the hunting party were in their tents fast asleep. In his tent, Cravens was dreaming about his childhood. One of six children, he had grown up in a small village in England's Lake District, and, as a young man, was expected to enter the family hardware business. At age 22, however, after finishing his military service, he told his father he had no interest in hardware and wanted to go to Africa and become a big game hunter. His father laughed. Two weeks later, Cravens was in London working as a clerk at an insurance company; then six months afterward, he shipped out from Liverpool for east Africa. Shortly after arrival in Nairobi, he took a driver's job with a safari company. Now twenty years later, at age 42, Cravens had become a hunting legend in East Africa and was known as a "master of animals." From Nairobi down to Johannesburg, everybody knew the name Walter "Big Bwana" Cravens. It would be another five years before Kenya would enact laws banning the ivory trade.

2

The following morning, the hunting party was up early, the porters had the vehicles loaded again, and Cravens, having eaten and shaved for the new day, was ready to continue the hunt. He looked around for Abasi, but he was nowhere to be seen.

"Abasi!" he called.

"Here, Bwana!"

Cravens turned and looked toward the sound of the voice. Then, some one hundred feet away along a dirt trail, he spotted Abasi in front of a Masai hut.

He strode over.

Abasi was standing in front of an old Masai woman who was squatted on the ground reading his fortune by throwing a handful of colored shells. Lean, leathery, and puffing on a pipe, a huge mass of gray hair was bundled on top of her head in a red cloth. Nearby, a pot of gruel boiled on a small fire. Cravens watched as the old woman shook the shells in both hands, then spilled them on the ground. For a long period of time, she studied the arrangement.

Finally, she spoke her conclusions in Swahili.

"What did she say?" Cravens asked.

"She says I should be very careful in three days," Abasi replied. "Lots of danger for me."

"What is that supposed to mean?"

Abasi, speaking in Swahili, asked the old woman to explain.

For a moment, she looked up at Abasi, then at Cravens. Finally, she spoke.

"She said the price will be paid," Abasi said.

"What price?" Cravens asked, obvious irritation in his eyes. "Price for what?"

The old woman glanced from one to the other again, then launched into a long tirade in Swahili. Finally, she was finished.

"What did she say?" Cravens said.

"She says, 'Before the white hunters came, her people lived in peace with the animals and took food from their cattle. Now the hunters are killing the animals for power and greed.' She said you have your vehicles and your guns and your big house in Nairobi only because you took the lives of sacred animals."

Cravens laughed and shook his head in contempt.

"I've heard all of that before," he said. "Tell her that people like me represent the new world. Tell her she's not ready for progress and the civilization I am bringing to this God-forsaken country."

Abasi delivered the message.

The old woman puffed on her pipe and didn't reply.

There was a long, uncomfortable silence.

"You ready to go, Bwana?" Abasi asked.

"No," Cravens replied. "Tell her I want her to read my fortune."

Abasi spoke to the old woman.

"She says it will cost a cigar."

Cravens put his rifle aside, then reached into an inside pocket of his hunting shirt, produced a cigar, and handed it to Abasi. The old woman took the cigar, then picked up the colored shells again. Vigorously, she shook them in both hands, then spilled them on the ground. For a long moment, she studied the arrangement, then spoke.

"She said, 'Your death awaits.'"

"My death awaits?" Cravens said. "What the hell does that mean? Death awaits all of us."

He studied the old woman. Then he laughed and turned to go.

"Come on!" he said. "Let's go."

Abasi stood up, moved to his master's side, and together they started walking away. Suddenly, Cravens stopped.

"Wait!!" he said, then he turned back to the old woman.

"Ask her if she can tell the truth."

Abasi posed the question.

The old woman, her face expressionless, glanced up at

Cravens, then she spoke.

"She says she always tells the truth."

"Ask her what's in those black mountains," he said, pointing into the distance.

Abasi relayed the question.

The old woman trembled slightly, then smiled.

A long silence.

The guide asked the question again.

"Tembo Makaburi," she said finally.

"What?" Cravens asked.

"She says there is an elephant graveyard in the mountains," Abasi replied.

"An elephant graveyard?" Cravens replied sarcastically. "Yeah! Sure! And I'm the man in the moon…"

The old woman spoke again.

"What did she say?" Cravens asked.

"She said you are a fool."

At the sound of the word, Cravens' anger started to rise.

"A fool? Huh?" he said, moving closer to the old woman. "She thinks I'm a fool?"

The old woman smiled and puffed on her pipe.

Suddenly, Cravens stepped forward with a threatening gesture.

"Do you see this?" he said, holding forth the rifle for her to see.

The old woman glanced briefly at the rifle, then into Cravens' eyes.

Suddenly, Cravens brought the rifle to his shoulder, loaded the breech, and trained it on the old woman's head.

"Now," Cravens said, livid with anger. "Am I still a fool?"

The old woman didn't flinch. She calmly looked at the barrel of the gun, then spoke.

"What did she say?" Cravens said.

"She said, 'Go ahead and shoot. All you'll do is kill an old woman.'"

Still training the gun on her, Cravens was at a loss at what to do next. He looked at the sad eyes, the sagging skin around her eyes and mouth, her two teeth, and the deep lines around her lips.

"She's not afraid," Abasi said.

"I can see that," Cravens replied. "Come on!!"

Then, without another word, the great white hunter lowered the gun, turned, and started back to the waiting caravan.

The old woman called after them.

"What did she say?" Cravens asked without breaking stride.

"She said the price will be paid."

Cravens laughed, then continued to the loaded vehicles. Soon, they arrived at the caravan.

"I'll drive, you track today," Cravens said.

Abasi nodded. Then, before he opened the passenger side door, Abasi looked back toward the old woman.

She was dancing a jig.

3

Once back on the savannah, the hunting party returned to the same point in the tall grass where they had seen the elephant tracks the previous day. Like a giant wheat field, the forest of lemon grass—some sixteen feet high and waving gently in the breeze—extended eastward as far as the eye could see. Along its outer western edge, where the vehicles were, an old safari road had been carved out years before and, two, maybe three miles away, they could see the tree line of the Olanga River. As Cravens eased the Land Rover slowly along the old safari road, Abasi, some thirty yards ahead, searched for signs where the old bull might have re-entered the grass.

For almost three hours, Abasi tried to pick up the trail. Again and again, he ducked in and out of the tall grass. Then he would come out and follow the safari road a short distance, then reenter the grass. Meanwhile, Cravens and the porters slowly eased the vehicles along the safari road behind him.

By noon, Abasi still had not picked up the trail and the midday heat was becoming unbearable. Finally, the guide returned to the vehicles for water and a brief rest.

"This elephant is so smart," Abasi said. "Somehow he stays just ahead of me at every turn."

"He's somewhere in that grass," Cravens said. "We're just going to have to keep looking. I want this elephant and I want him bad."

Abasi took a long drink of water, then wiped a stream of sweat from his forehead.

"We'll get him," the guide said. "It's just a matter of…"

Suddenly, he stopped and peered curiously at a small stand of turpentine trees at the edge of the grass. One of the tree's upper limbs had been recently broken and was dangling from its stem. Quickly, Abasi put aside the water container and strode to the turpentine trees. First, he inspected the ground for tracks, then checked the back side of the trees.

With a big smile, he glanced over at Cravens.

"Tree rub," he said. "I'm going back in. I can smell him now."

Abasi disappeared back into the forest of grass. Almost immediately, he reappeared.

"Fresh droppings," he said. "Maybe two hours old."

"Two hours?"

"Yes," Abasi said. "He's very close. He slept here last night. You and the porters drive ahead. Maybe half a mile and wait. I will follow him."

***

Over the next twenty minutes, Cravens, the porters, and the vehicles moved slowly along the old safari road toward the river. Finally, they stopped and waited for Abasi. They didn't have to wait long.

Suddenly, Cravens saw his guide running up the road toward him.

"He's about fifty, maybe sixty yards up ahead," Abasi said, pointing into the distance. "There is a clearing up ahead between the grass and the river. He has to cross the clearing to get to the river. You can probably get a shot there."

"How far is the clearing?" Cravens said.

"Maybe half a mile," Abasi said. "Go down there. You'll see it. He should be there in twenty, maybe thirty minutes."

"I'll be waiting," Cravens said.

***

Twenty minutes later, Cravens was positioned at the clearing. Rifle at the ready, his eyes were trained along the outer edges of the lemon grass. Behind him, the porters and the vehicles, their engines quiet, waited. Abasi, some one hundred yards away, darted out of the grass and frantically pointed ahead, waving his fist up and down, the signal that the prey was very near.

Cravens gazed across the clearing.

Suddenly, the big bull elephant, ears flared and tail flying high, lunged out of the tall grass about one hundred yards away. Then, as fast as his heavy legs would carry him, he raced out into the clearing.

Cravens was caught off guard by the suddenness of the animal's appearance. Quickly, he threw a shell in the chamber, then took aim.

Blam!!

At the sound of the shot, the elephant didn't break stride. By the time Cravens could throw another shell in the breech, the elephant had disappeared into a grove of yellow fever trees along the river.

Moments later, Abasi was at his side.

"Damn!!" Cravens said. "Missed him. He was moving too fast!!"

"He's at the river now," Abasi said. "We can go to him or we can wait for him to come to us."

"Let's go to the river and wait for him," Cravens said. "Can we get the vehicles along the river?"

"Not sure," Abasi replied. "Years ago, there was an old mining road along the river banks. The gold mining company built it so trucks could get in and out to haul away the gold. It ends at the mountains. I'm not sure how good it is."

***

That night, the party camped around a huge fire along the banks of the Olanga River. Twice, Cravens had chosen campsites for the night, but both times, Abasi said they were too near the crocodiles lazing along the massive sandbar at the water's edge. Finally, the porters set up the tents among a grove of buffalo thorn trees that had recently been thinned by fire. Abasi said they would be safe there. Once they had eaten, Cravens, sipping Irish whiskey and puffing on a cigar, sat in front of the fire with his guide.

"What do you know about this elephant graveyard?" he asked.

"Tembo Makaburi?" Abasi said. "According to stories, it's

the place where elephants go to die. Elephants are very private animals and they want to be alone, away from the group, when they die…"

Cravens didn't answer at first.

Nearby, they could hear the constant roar of the rushing water.

"Do you think it's true?" Cravens asked.

"No," Abasi said. "It's just an old tribal legend…"

"What if it was true?" Cravens ventured. "What if we got into those mountains and found an elephant graveyard?"

Abasi laughed.

"It's only a story," he said.

A long silence.

"Finding the elephant graveyard would be a dream come true for an ivory hunter," Cravens mused. "An absolute miracle."

Abasi laughed.

"It's just a story that ivory hunters like to tell one another when they're drinking," Abasi said. "There is no truth to it."

4

Early the following morning, the porters had everything packed and loaded and the party was ready to move again. As the porters waited, Cravens and Abasi were studying a map spread out across the hood of the Land Rover.

"If he's going to the black mountains," Cravens said, "he's got to come up this river. Let's wait for him here."

"This elephant is too smart for that," Abasi said, shaking his head. "He's not going to walk into a trap."

"As party leader, I say we wait here for him," Cravens said.

"You're the boss," Abasi replied.

For several minutes, Cravens studied the foliage along the water's edge. Some fifty yards to the north, he could see a cleared area, bounded on one side by the river and a dense stand of mangroves and pawpaw trees on the other.

"We'll hide the vehicles and ourselves in those mangroves," he said. "When he comes up the river banks and into the clearing, I'll kill him. I won't miss next time."

Thirty minutes later, the plan was in place. Over the next two hours, they waited. All that time, the only motion they saw in the clearing was a pair of leopards that emerged from the jungle, went to the river to drink, then melted into the jungle again.

"We're wasting time," Abasi said.

"So where did he go?" Cravens asked.

"I don't know," Abasi said. "We know he didn't go south. I also know he's not just waiting. He's too smart."

"So where did he go?" Cravens asked again.

Suddenly, Abasi had a realization.

"Maybe he went around us," the guide said. "Maybe he went around us during the night."

"He's not that smart," Cravens said.

"Let's check," Abasi said.

Moments later, the guide was trekking along the edge of

the dense jungle that paralleled the river. Cravens and the porters watched as he disappeared into the dense foliage, then seconds later reappeared and called.

"Here are his tracks," Abasi said, looking toward the black mountains. "He went around us while we were asleep."

"I don't believe it," Cravens said.

"Come look at the tracks," Abasi said.

Right away, Cravens was at his side.

"Damn!" Craven said, shaking his head in frustration. "He headed south to throw us off, then he slipped around us during the night."

"He won't get too far," Abasi said. "He'll hit that rock wall when he reaches the mountains and he can't go any further. The water is too swift for him to cross and the jungle is too dense for an animal his size to enter."

"How far are the black mountains?"

"About two miles."

"Think we can corner him there?"

"Probably," Abasi said.

"How good is the road?"

"I don't know," Abasi said. "We'll have to see."

For a moment, Cravens studied his guide, then shook his head in amazement.

"You're a good tracker," he said.

"I know the animals," the guide replied.

***

Over the next two hours, the party followed the elephant's trail along the winding river's edge. Twice, the Land Rover mired up to its axle in the soft river mud and the porters, after hacking away giant swaths of mangrove limbs, had to manually push and pull the vehicles out to solid ground again. The old mining road was better than Abasi had expected and, over the next hour, they moved rapidly northward and, as they did, the black mountains loomed larger and larger.

Finally, thirty minutes later, the vehicles jerked to a stop at a point where the old mining road dead-ended into the base of a majestic volcanic mountain. The party admired the awe-inspiring beauty of nature.

"Well, look at that!" Cravens said.

As they gazed upward, the black rock wall, like a giant fortress, loomed foreboding and impenetrable in the midday sun, reaching heights of over two hundred feet in places. They could see a thick forest of native trees—umbrella, pawpaw, and baobab—thriving on the flat top of the escarpment. At the base, the rushing river water crashed mightily into the rock wall, creating a roaring fountain of misty water that hung in the air, then continued its path eastward along the outer edge of the escarpment. To the west was deep, dark jungle, which traced as far as the eye could see.

Finally, Cravens turned to Abasi.

"Come on," he said. "Let's find that elephant."

***

Fifteen minutes later, Cravens and his guide were trekking along the edge of the jungle.

"There is only one way for him to go," Cravens said. "That's into the jungle."

Abasi nodded his agreement, then quickly moved ahead and started probing along the edge of the jungle looking for footprints or an opening. The black earth under his feet was moist from the misting water. Suddenly, he stopped and ducked his head into the foliage. Seeing no signs, he continued along the jungle's edge.

Suddenly, he stopped again.

"Bwana!" Abasi called.

Seconds later, Cravens was at his side.

Abasi pointed to the elephant track in the wet ground.

"That's him!" Cravens said.

Abasi shook his head in confusion.

"What's wrong?" Cravens asked

"I can't believe he would leave a clear track like that," Abasi said. "At times, I think we are tracking this elephant. Other times, I think we are being led."

Cravens laughed.

"No, he's not that smart," Cravens replied. "No animal is

smarter than a human being."

Abasi didn't reply. Quickly, he stepped ahead again and followed the tracks along the jungle's edge for another thirty to forty feet. Then he stopped again and peeked into the foliage. There he saw footprints and a trail.

"Here!" Abasi called. "He went into the jungle here."

Very quickly, Cravens was at the point Abasi had indicated. He poked his head into the jungle.

"It's a good trail," he said.

"So what do we do, Bwana?"

"Tell the porters to put together provisions for a day," he said. "We can't take the vehicles in there, so we're going to have to track him on foot."

"We don't know how deep this jungle is," Abasi said.

"That's true," said Cravens, "but we don't have any choice. I've chased this elephant for five days. I'm not going to let him get away now."

5

Back at the vehicles, the porters were putting together a day pack—enough food, water, and provisions for a single day.

"Tell them to be sure to pack the tusk saws," Cravens said, referring to the fine-toothed saws he used to harvest tusks. "If we kill him in that jungle, there's no need to have to come back for them."

"Yes, Bwana," Abasi replied.

"Also, tell them to pack a pint of that Irish whiskey."

An hour later, Cravens, his guide, and the five porters were deep inside the jungle on a wide, well-trodden trail. Both Cravens and Abasi could see that several elephants, big elephants, had recently used the trail. On either side, huge mahogany trees, their tall, moss-covered roots extending outwards from the trunk up to thirty feet in places, loomed massive and foreboding within the thick jungle foliage. There were giant tangles of cacao and rubber trees bound together by years upon years of thick, twisting columbine vines. At one point, Cravens stopped briefly and pointed to a giant green African python dangling from the limb of an oil palm. Above them, a thick jungle canopy blotted out the midday sun.

"Human beings have never been on this trail before," Abasi said. "We are the first."

"It's leading straight into the mountain," Cravens said.

Ten minutes later, the jungle canopy began to thin and patches of bright sunlight started to poke through and illuminate the trail. For another ten minutes, the party continued, then, after making a turn, Cravens saw a huge patch of sunlight at the point where the trail ended and the rock wall began. As he moved closer, his heart skipped a beat when he saw what appeared to be a passageway.

"Look!" Cravens said, pointing to the patch of light.

Abasi stepped up and looked where Cravens was pointing.

"Are you thinking what I'm thinking?" the hunter asked.

"What's that?"

"That this is the elephant graveyard and that old bull came here to die?"

Abasi looked at Cravens.

"If this is Tembo Makaburi," Abasi said, "We shouldn't be here. Such a place is only for animals."

Cravens didn't reply.

***

Moments later, Cravens and his guide were standing in front of the entrance to the passageway. The entrance—an opening about twenty feet high and fifteen feet wide—stood like an open door into the side of the mountain. Cravens hesitated, gazed into the darkness, and listened for a sound. Then, rifle at the ready, he took several steps inside, proceeding slowly and cautiously. After he had ventured some twenty feet into the darkness, he could see light at the other end of the passageway. Taking courage at the sight of the light, Cravens rushed forward through the tunnel to the light. Abasi was directly behind him.

Very soon, Cravens and his guide stood in front of a spectacle never before seen by human beings. They looked around in awe and sheer wonder. In front of them, for as far as the eye could see, lay an endless desolation of elephant skeletons.

"Oh, my God," Cravens said, his face filled with joyful wonder. "This is it! We've found the elephant graveyard. The old woman was telling the truth."

Suddenly, behind them, they heard screams.

Cravens and the guide turned.

The lead porter, the whites of his eyes as big as saucers, was shouting in Swahili and slowly backing away. Behind him, there were only two porters with their bundles.

"Ask him what's wrong," Cravens said.

Abasi spoke to the head porter.

"He says there is only death and evil here and they can't stay."

"It's nothing more than a bunch of dead elephants,"

Cravens said.

He looked behind the head porter.

"Where are the other three porters?" he said.

Abasi posed the question.

"He says they are afraid to come in and went back to the vehicles," Abasi said.

"What about their bundles?"

"They took the bundles with them," Abasi said.

"Tell him I hired them to stay with me."

The head porter laughed and answered.

"He said they didn't agree to disturb the gods."

There was a long silence, then the head porter spoke again.

"He said he and the others are leaving now," Abasi said.

"Tell him to stop," Cravens said.

The head porter, abject fear in his eyes, stopped.

"Tell him that if anything is missing from the vehicles, I know the police chief in Ngorongoro. He doesn't like thieves."

Abasi relayed the message, then the head porter replied.

"He says they want nothing that belongs to you," Abasi said.

Cravens nodded his understanding.

Then, the head porter and his two remaining minions, after dumping their bundles on the ground, quickly turned and fled back through the passageway.

"Now we are alone, Bwana," Abasi said.

"Let 'em go," Cravens said. "We don't need them. Look at all this. We're going to be rich. I mean rich! Rich! Rich! Rich!"

Abasi surveyed the expanse of weathered elephant bones.

"What happened to the old bull we were chasing?" he asked.

"Who cares?!" Cravens replied. "That's only two tusks. Here we've got hundreds, even thousands of tusks."

There was a long silence.

"I'm afraid," Abasi said.

"Afraid of what?" Cravens said. "As long as I've got this rifle, there is nothing to fear."

"Please, Bwana," Abasi said, falling to his knees and raising his folded hands to his master. "Let's go back. Please!

Please! There is only death here."

His pleading angered Cravens.

"Abasi, get up!!" he said.

The guide reluctantly rose to his feet.

"Are you crazy?" Cravens said. "Look at all this ivory; we're going to have more money than we can spend. We've struck the mother lode. We're going to have anything we ever wanted in this world. Beautiful women!! Good whiskey!! Good cigars!! Good food!! Anything we want."

Abasi didn't reply.

Cravens, with the excitement of a small child, laughed with pure joy.

"I can't believe we've found it," he said. "How in the world could we be so lucky?!!"

Finally, his excitement subsided. He turned to the guide.

"Come on," Cravens said. "Let's take a tour."

Cravens, with Abasi close behind him, strolled along a pathway that led through the heart of the escarpment. Now that he was inside, Cravens could see the fullness of the formation. At some point over the millennia, a massive volcanic eruption had formed a giant bathtub out of lava rock. The bathtub, which stretched south and north, was five, maybe six miles long and half a mile wide. Over the years, winds had deposited soil and seeds into the northern end to create a dense jungle. The southern end, where the elephants came to die, was almost totally black lava rock with an occasional stand of cacao and oil palm trees. The entrance was a tiny slit in the wall on the southern end. Apparently, the walls of the escarpment had been formed by one lava flow, then a much later, much hotter lava flow had burned the slit to create an entrance. It was a perfect place for an elephant graveyard, Cravens concluded.

Along either side of the pathway lay weathered elephant remains. Skulls, rib cages and backbones, hip and leg joints as well as neck bones lay scattered along either side of the path. As Cravens studied the knobby shape of the skulls, he could see there was very little bone in an elephant's face and trunk. It was mostly tissue and cartilage. Over the years, the ravages of the weather and sun had bleached the older skeletons a dirty, off-white color and the skeletal structure was beginning to fall apart. A skull from a backbone. Hip joints from a thighbone and a leg bone from the torso. Scattered about here and there were large sheets of what appeared to be old, well-worn pieces of brown leather, but these were actually the weathered remains of elephant hides. Despite this, all of the tusks were as shiny and new as if the creatures were still alive.

Finally, the hunter and guide arrived at a natural gorge that separated the north part of the giant bathtub from the south. It was a deep, narrow crevice, maybe six or seven feet across. A nimble jungle animal could jump across it, but a human being would need some sort of bridge to traverse it. Cravens strolled to the edge of the gorge and looked into the ravine below. Some one hundred feet down, he could see the skeletal remains of animals that had failed to complete the jump. On the opposite side of the gorge, he saw a dense jungle.

"Some sort of animal is living over there," Cravens said. "Probably the animals that eat the elephants after they die."

He studied the foliage on the other side of the gorge.

"What kind of animal do you think lives over there?"

"Probably tigers or leopards," Abasi said.

6

Twenty minutes later, they had returned to the escarpment entrance.

"Check and see what provisions we have," Cravens said. "If we have to, we'll go back to the vehicles."

Abasi opened the two bundles abandoned by the mutinous porters. As he sat on the ground, one by one, he pulled articles out of the bundles.

"We've got two bedrolls, a canvas ground cover, and tusk saws," he said.

Then he turned to the other pack.

"Food, an oil lantern, and bed covering."

"How much food?"

"Six pieces of elephant jerky, a box of vanilla cookies, four apples, and a small loaf of brown bread."

"That should last us until tomorrow," Cravens said. "I want to get this ivory out of here as soon as we can. What about that pint of whiskey?"

Abasi searched through the first bundle, then held up the bottle of dark yellow liquid.

Cravens smiled.

"Good!" Cravens replied. "Let's use that ground canvas to make a tent for me on that elevated space over there," he said, pointing to a flat area where the floor of the escarpment butted into the surrounding wall. "You can put your bedroll in front of my tent."

Ten minutes later, Abasi had set up Cravens' tent as instructed; stones for a small fire had been collected and placed and the food and water had been stored safely.

"Let's go back, Bwana," Abasi said.

The hunter could see the fear in his eyes.

"No," he replied. "Not until we've gathered all of the ivory we can carry back to Ngorongoro. Here is what we're going to do. This afternoon, we'll harvest enough tusks to fill two vehicles and stack them here at the entrance. No need to harvest more than that since there is only us two drivers. I figure there is only enough room in the vehicles for about two hundred tusks, so that's what we'll harvest. Tomorrow, we'll carry them back through the jungle, load up the vehicles, and head back to Ngorongoro."

Abasi nodded.

"Let's get started," he said.

***

All that afternoon, Cravens and Abasi harvested ivory tusks from the remains of the elephants. Tusk saw in hand, Cravens moved expertly from one skeleton to the next, cutting away the ivory tusks and tossing them onto the pathway. Then Abasi would gather the tusks and carry them back to the passageway. After Cravens had cut away two hundred tusks, he helped Abasi carry the remaining ivory. When darkness fell, two massive piles of ivory tusks were stacked near the escarpment entrance.

***

That night, they dined on elephant jerky, vanilla crackers, and an apple each. Afterward, they sat around a small fire and, while he sipped from the bottle of Irish whiskey, Cravens mused about how he was going to spend the money.

"After I cash in this ivory, I'm going back to England for a while," he said. "First, I'm going back to London and buy me some fancy clothes. Then I'm going to get all dressed up and go back to the pubs on Maddox Street and show all of those bloody snobs how rich I am. I'll buy drinks for everybody in the house all night. Then I'm going to get me a woman and I'm going to make up for all these lonely nights I've spent on the savannah…"

He stopped. All was quiet for a moment.

"Let's leave!!" Abasi said. "Let's leave tonight."

"We can't leave all of this ivory here for somebody else," Cravens said. "Let's get the ivory to the vehicles, then you'll feel safe."

Abasi didn't reply.

Cravens took another sip of whiskey and looked into the fire.

"After I leave London, I'm going to my family's village in the Lake District and I want all my friends to see me dressed up in my fine clothes. I might even buy a big sign and put it on the village's High Street…"

He smiled at the thought.

"'Walter Cravens is in town!' the sign will say. "Then I'll walk down High Street and people will look at me and say, 'My! My! Look at what Walter Cravens has made of himself.'"

He took another sip of whiskey.

"Then I'm going to my family's home and let them see me in all my finery. Most of all, I want my father to see me. He won't be laughing anymore…"

A long silence.

"I wonder if he's still alive," Cravens said. "I hope he is still living, just so he can see what a success I have made of myself…"

Shaking his head, Cravens came out of his reverie and glanced at his guide.

"Abasi," he asked. "Why are you so quiet? You should be happy! You're going to have more money than you know what to do with…"

His guide looked sullenly into the fire and didn't answer.

"Let's get some sleep," Cravens said finally. "We've got a big day ahead of us tomorrow."

Twenty minutes later, Cravens was inside the makeshift tent Abasi had constructed from the canvas ground covering. The ground beneath him was solid lava rock and the thin, cotton bedroll did little to alleviate the discomfort. Outside, Abasi was asleep on his bedroll, the light from the nearby oil lantern flickering intermittently. Finally, after tossing and turning for another ten minutes, Cravens drifted off to sleep.

7

The next morning, Cravens and his guide were up early. After washing themselves, they sat on boulders and ate the last of the rations, two pieces of elephant jerky, a handful of vanilla wafers, and some horse apples.

"That's all of the food," Abasi said.

"That's okay," Cravens said. "There's plenty more food in the vehicles. We'll eat when we get back with the first load of ivory."

Cravens stood up.

"Come on," he said. "Let's get this ivory to the vehicles."

Abasi stacked elephant tusks into Cravens' outstretched arms. Finally, once his arms were laden with tusks, Cravens waited for Abasi, who, his arms loaded with ivory, was directly behind him. Together, they started for the passageway.

Suddenly, they heard the clarion call of an elephant.

"Look," Abasi said, pointing to the top of the escarpment near the passageway. "It's the old bull we've been chasing."

Cravens, straining from the load of elephant tusks, gazed up at the elephant. Then, as they watched curiously, the old bull began to pound his head into the side of the earthworks along the outer edge of the rock escarpment.

"What's he doing?" Abasi asked.

"I don't know."

They watched as the animal slammed his head again and again into the earthworks, each blow mightier than the last.

"Shoot him!" Abasi said.

"The rifle is back at the tent," Cravens replied. "My arms are full of ivory."

Again and again, the mighty beast pounded his head against the earthworks. Suddenly, as a result of the powerful, continued blows, the earthworks started to slowly crumble. First, there was only the low rumbling sound of small rocks tumbling down a mountainside, then it grew louder and louder until it became the roaring sound of an avalanche. As they watched, thousands of tons of earth and stones and uprooted vegetation tumbled down outside the escarpment. Finally, the dust settled and all was quiet.

At that moment, Cravens realized what had happened. Quickly, he threw down the stack of ivory tusks and ran to the passageway. He went inside the darkness, then seconds later, reemerged. Abasi could see the horror in his face.

"Oh my God," he said. "The passageway is sealed off. He's locked us in here!"

"Oh, Bwana," Abasi said. "I was afraid of something like this. What are we going to do?"

"We're not dead yet," Cravens said. "First, let's find some food. We've got plenty of water, but nothing to eat."

He gazed toward the other end of the escarpment.

"Come on," he said, standing up and shouldering the rifle. "There has got to be something down there we can kill to eat."

Over the next four hours, they explored either side of the pathway looking for some sort of game. They sought out ground animals among the rocks and holes along the walls of the escarpment; they examined the trees for birds; they hunted snakes and lizards along the rock crevices and scoured the ledges and stone embankments for some living creature. During that entire time, they found nothing.

Finally, they arrived at the gorge that separated the north portion of the escarpment from the south and took a seat on a huge boulder. High overhead, the relentless African sun was beating down. Neither man spoke for a full ten minutes. They were studying their dilemma. Finally, Abasi spoke.

"What are we going to do?"

Cravens shook his head slowly.

"We've got to find some food," he said.

Absently, he glanced across the gorge at the deep jungle on the other side.

"What kind of animal do you think lives over there?" he asked.

"Probably tigers… or leopards."

Cravens carefully studied the surroundings. Suddenly, his eyes fell on a pool of water situated in a corner between the gorge and the edge of the escarpment wall.

"Look," he said. "There's a watering hole. Let's see what's over there."

In a few minutes, the two were looking down at their reflections in the watering hole. The mouth of the dimple-shaped hole was about twelve feet across. Cravens leaned over the edge and stared into the crystal clear water; he estimated the depth to be thirty, maybe forty feet. Over the millennia, winds had blown soil and birds had delivered seeds, which resulted in plants taking root around the edges of the watering hole. They could see the blooms of yellow hyacinth and African water lilies.

"Look!" Abasi said, pointing to a small ledge some three feet above the water's surface. "There are wild African yams growing down there. There must seven or eight of them. If we had those, we could eat. At least for a few days."

Cravens peered at the point where Abasi was pointing. Then, for a long moment, he studied the situation.

"Here!" he said finally. "Give me your hand. I'm going to swing down to that ledge and get those yams."

As instructed, Abasi positioned himself on the edge of the hole, braced himself, and offered his hand. Then Cravens, his rifle still on his shoulder, took Abasi's hand and swung himself from ground level down to the ledge. Safely on the ledge, he checked his footing; it seemed safe, then he squatted, leaned forward, and reached for the wild yams.

As he grasped the yams, he heard a cracking sound under his feet like a rock being split apart. Suddenly, the ledge gave way under the hunter's weight. In a single motion, Cravens fell headlong into the side of the hole, then his body made an enormous splash as it hit the water. Abasi watched helplessly as Cravens' head disappeared under the water.

The guide thought the hunter was gone.

"Bwana! Bwana!" Abasi called frantically. "Bwana! Bwana!!"

Cravens' head finally reappeared above the water's surface. Blood was streaming down the side of his face. Like a swimmer, he quickly threw his head sideways to dispel the water, then for a moment, grasping the edge of the broken ledge for support, he tried to regain his senses.

"Where is the rifle?" Abasi asked.

"I lost it," Cravens replied.

Their eyes met briefly. Both men knew there was nothing else to be said.

"Here!" Abasi said finally. "Let me help you out."

Lying on his stomach, Abasi reached over the edge of the lava embankment and grasped Cravens' hand. Finally, using all his strength and with Cravens helping by pulling himself up with his other hand, Abasi finally managed to pull Cravens to ground level, seating Cravens on the edge of the watering hole.

"Are you okay?" Abasi asked.

"I'm hurt," Cravens said finally. "I think my right ankle is broken. I'm not sure I can walk."

Blood was streaming down the side of his face.

"Let me look at your head," Abasi said.

Abasi removed his shirt and tore off two strips of cloth. Then he looked around. Nearby, he saw a small oil palm tree.

"Wait here!" he said.

Soon, he returned with several leaves. Then, making a bandage from the torn shirt sleeve and the leaves, Abasi applied it to Cravens' head wound. Using the remainder of the shirt sleeve, he wiped the blood from the side of Cravens' face.

"Now…" Abasi said. "The leaves will stop the bleeding."

"That's better," Cravens said. "Much better… Thanks!"

The two sat quietly for several minutes.

"What are we going to do, Bwana?"

"We can't stay here," Cravens said. "We've got to make it back to the day camp."

Abasi nodded.

"I can't walk on this ankle," he continued. "Can you make some sort of crutch?"

Abasi picked through the branches of a dead cacao tree. Finally, he selected a branch, broke it off, then broke it off a second time to fashion a crude crutch.

"Here," he said. "Try this."

Then Abasi helped Cravens rise to a standing position. While holding Cravens steady, he placed the crude crutch under Cravens' right arm.

"Now put weight on it," Abasi said.

"Yeah," Cravens said. "This will work."

Abasi then took Cravens' free arm and draped it across his shoulder.

"Let's go!" he said.

Moments later, slowly, but steadily, with Abasi's help, Cravens limped back down the pathway toward the day camp. As Abasi walked, he suddenly sensed that the calamity at the watering hole had alerted the animals who lived across the gorge to their presence. Briefly, he glanced into the deep foliage of the jungle on the other side of the gorge. In the late afternoon sun, hidden in the foliage, he could see the glowing eyes of the animals that lived there following their every move.

8

By the time the hunter and his guide had made it back to the day camp, darkness had fallen. Upon arrival, Abasi lowered Cravens to the ground at the entrance of the makeshift tent, then collapsed on his bedroll. Cravens crawled inside the tent and lay on his bedroll. An excruciating pain was shooting through his right ankle. He reached his hand to touch it. The ankle was swollen to the size of a large balloon. Outside the tent, Abasi lit the oil lantern and shafts of light illuminated the camp area. Fearfully, again and again, Abasi looked back into the darkness along the pathway to the gorge. He feared to mention to Cravens what he was thinking.

All was quiet.

"We die tonight, Bwana," Abasi said.

"Why do you say that?"

"I know the animals," the guide replied.

Inside the makeshift tent, Cravens, tired, hungry, and immobile, closed his eyes and tried to sleep. Now the great hunter knew his fate was near. There was no place to run. No place to hide. No rifle to defend himself. The great master of animals was now like a helpless, defenseless animal on the savannah, waiting to be eaten.

"This bloody beast led us to our deaths," Cravens said. "He knew what he was doing. We thought we were following him, but actually, he was leading us. The great master of animals was led to his death by an animal."

Abasi could hear the bitterness in Cravens' voice.

"Now he's roaming free out there in that jungle," Cravens continued, "while we are locked in this rock prison for all time…"

"Bwana! No more talking," Abasi said. "You must rest."

Cravens knew Abasi was right.

"Okay," Cravens said finally, "I'm going to sleep now."

Cravens tried to get comfortable on the thin bedroll. The

pain in his ankle was unbearable. Sharp, intense pain shot through the entire leg at the slightest movement. Maybe, he thought, if he could sleep, he could get some relief from the pain. He closed his eyes, then, several minutes later, he was fast asleep and dreaming.

In the dream, he was standing on the hood of the Land Rover, peering across the expanse of the savannah. All around him lay the bloody corpses of the animals—elephants, lions, tigers, leopards, water buffalo, and rhino—he had slain over the years. On either side of the vehicle, the dead carcasses stretched for as far as the eye could see. In particular, his eyes fell on the corpse of one huge bull he had wounded, then chased three miles before it collapsed. Cravens had to shoot the animal three more times before it finally died. He trembled at the sight of the dead elephant. Now, in the dream, he was walking along an elevated stage and, as he looked down at audience level, he saw thousands of baby elephants peering pitifully up at him, crying elephant tears because they no longer had a father. As he walked further, he saw hundreds of infant water buffalo, tiger and lion cubs, and baby rhinoceroses whom he had orphaned. As the innocent creatures raised their pitiful faces, Cravens trembled in fear. Suddenly, he awoke.

"Oh, God no!!" he screamed aloud. "No! No! No!"

Now, wide awake, he sat up, stark terror etched into his face.

"Bwana!" Abasi called from outside. "Are you okay?"

Cravens, mad with hunger and fear, wiped the sweat from his feverish brow.

"I'm okay," Cravens said.

A long silence.

"Do you see anything?"

"No, Bwana," Abasi replied. "You sleep. I watch."

Another long silence,

Then, hungry and in intense pain, Cravens closed his eyes and tried to sleep again. His body was at the breaking point and could no longer resist rest. Then, moments later, by some miracle, he fell asleep again. This time, he was dreaming about his boyhood days in the Lake District. He and his father, fishing poles, bait and tackle in hand, were going fishing at a small lake near their home. It was a beautiful day and Cravens, aged nine or ten, was walking beside his father along a path through an expansive green meadow in warm sunshine. Both sides of the path were dotted with clusters of yellow and red flowers. Overhead, bluebirds flitted happily about and called to them. His father was singing an old military song and Cravens' heart was wild with joy. There was nothing on this earth Cravens loved more as a child than going fishing with his father. Suddenly, the dream evaporated into nothingness when Cravens sprang wide awake at the sudden sound of Abasi's voice.

"Bwana! Bwana!!" the guide shouted.

Now Cravens could hear the low growls of angry animals.

"Bwana! Bwana!" Abasi shouted again, then his voice suddenly broke off with a hideous scream.

"Yaeiii! Yaeiii!" Abasi screamed.

"Abasi!!" Cravens shouted. "What is it?"

Now the animal growls grew louder and more furious. Through the thin canvas walls, Cravens could see the dark shadows of furry animals slowly circling the lantern and Abasi as if they were about to attack.

"Abasi! Abasi!" he yelled again. "What is it?"

Cravens watched in horror as the light of the lantern jerked suddenly one way, then another as Abasi jumped and dodged desperately to escape the animals.

"Yaeiii! Yaeiii!" Abasi screamed again and again in agonizing pain.

"What is it!!" Cravens shouted again at the top of his lungs. "Tell me!! What is it?"

There was another, blood-curdling cry of anguished pain, then Abasi screamed a single word into the night.

"Hyenas!"

****The End****

THE OLD MEN

I'll always remember the day in the late spring of 1956 when my father told me he had bought a grocery store. I had just gotten off the school bus, rushed into the house, and threw my books on the sofa when my daddy called me into the kitchen. I sat down at the kitchen table and he explained I would be helping him in the store on afternoons and weekends pumping gas, stocking shelves, and sacking groceries. His words were pure music to my thirteen-year-old ears. I loved doing things with my father and I couldn't wait to launch into this new adventure.

It was just a little country store, a place where the locals could buy gas, fresh meat, milk and bread, knick-knacks, and other basic food items. When my daddy bought the business, it had been in existence for more than twenty years under the proprietorship of Mr. E.B. White and his wife Dorothy. In fact, my father had traded with Mr. White in previous years, but, after a falling out over a set of car tires, my father had taken his business to Dillard's, Mr. White's primary competitor down the street. However, after my father learned the business was up for sale, old rivalries were forgotten and my father and Mr. White sealed the deal.

So, when school was out the following May, my great adventure during the summer of 1956 in my father's grocery store was underway. Over that summer, I learned every nook and cranny of the country store business. I pumped gas, helped customers to cars with their groceries, stocked shelves, learned to mark up items for a profit, checked the oil and water in cars, swept the floor, dusted the shelves, made milk shakes, sliced and wrapped meats as well as perform any other chore my father deemed necessary.

Also, I learned the politics of the business. If a male customer said he wanted my father to help him, I knew he wanted to buy condoms. My father cautioned me that certain better-dressed professional women had to be treated more politely than others. Also, he cautioned me to never enter the conversation when he was discussing a bill with a customer. Anytime a customer came in who had a past due balance, my father was always the one to help them. Anytime a customer made some off-color comment about sex or body parts, it was to be ignored. Most of all, my father's watchword was that the customer was always right.

It was a good business. During the school year, young kids by the droves would come in and buy drinks, candy, and school supplies in the morning. Mr. White had had a solid base of established customers, most of which my father inherited. Then there were the "once-in-a-while customers," as my father called them, who came in once or twice a week for emergency items like milk and bread. Overall, it was a good business and, with some work, my father felt it would get better and better.

My father had known about the old men at the store long before he bought the business. In fact, they had been a fixture – a tradition, so to speak – in the store during the years he had traded with Mr. White. They were mostly retirees in their sixties and seventies from the local neighborhood who would gather each day to while away the hours. They would sit on up-ended soda pop crates and spend the day gossiping, playing checkers and dominoes, talking about politics and religion, and recalling the past. The ring leader of the group was Mr. McAdams, a medium height, red-faced man in his late sixties who always wore overalls and chewed tobacco. He was the most vocal of the group and there was no filter on the subjects he discussed. The second most prominent member was Mr. Hill, a tall, sallow-faced man in his sixties who always wore a brown felt hat and overalls, had played some AAA baseball, and liked to brag about forcing other men to do his bidding. Then there were Mr. Gibbs, Mr. Whisenant, Mr. Waddell, and others, but mostly they didn't offer many comments and would sit around and listen while Mr. McAdams and Mr. Hill did most of the talking.

My daddy had reasons to justify their presence in the store.

First, all of their families had been trading at the store for years. Mr. McAdams, who was a widower, always bought a few items before he left for the day. His son delivered fresh milk to the store two days a week and was a regular customer. Mr. Hill's wife Sally always stopped by the store in the afternoon for milk and bread and his son Billy was a regular gas and oil customer. Also, during their loitering hours, the old men would spend some money on snacks and soft drinks and occasionally a piece of fruit to nibble on during their sessions. My father had economic reasons for allowing them to stay.

On the other hand, they presented problems. Two spittoons were required for the snuff dippers and tobacco chewers. Some smoked and there were always ash droppings on the floor where they had been sitting. Sometimes, they would get into bitter arguments about the checkers and dominoes and one or another would angrily stomp off in a huff. Sometimes their raucous laughter would be disruptive for customers, but, worst of all, the subjects of their conversations were not always fit for womanly and decent-minded people's ears. Somehow, from the start, I sensed the vulgarity was going to present the greatest problem. My father was not a prude. In fact, he was a tolerant man in many ways, but he had the utmost respect for women and he felt the F-word had no place in public conversations. In my heart, I knew there was going to a confrontation between the old men and my father at some point.

****

Miss Lois Kirkland, a smallish, gray-haired, never-married woman in her fifties who was the principal at the local elementary school, was a frequent customer at the store. At the beginning of each school year, she would come in and buy paper, pencils, crayons, art paper, and other supplies for the students who could not afford them. Of course, my father would order extra school supplies ahead of time for Miss Kirkland's annual visit. Every year, he sold more school supplies to her during one visit than he sold during the remainder of the year. Thus, he wanted to make the meeting and sale as pleasant as possible. Considering her position in the community and her personal bearing, my father considered her a "proper" lady.

The first incident occurred on a Saturday in early September when Miss Kirkland came in to buy school supplies. On that particular day, Miss Kirkland was reading from a list and, as she called each item, my father would gather it and place it on the counter. As my father worked with Miss Kirkland, Mr. McAdams was launching into a story about Lucille, a loose woman who lived in Hokes Bluff. I had heard him tell the story many times about how he and his friends would pick her up, take her to the woods, and have their way with her. As always, he had no filter on the words he used.

After some fifteen minutes, a huge pile of school supplies had been placed on the counter and Miss Kirkland was finishing up her list. Meanwhile, Mr. McAdams was telling his story.

"Well, we got her in the truck and started to the woods," he was saying. "That's when I told her, 'You're going to f**k tonight.'"

At the sound of the F-word, Miss Kirkland looked up from her list and turned and glared at Mr. McAdams with eyes that could kill. Then, with fury in her eyes, she turned to my father as if she wanted him to do something. Immediately, my father moved toward the old men.

"Fred," my father said. "Watch the words you are using over there. There is a lady in my store."

Mr. McAdams looked at my father, then at Miss Kirkland, then lowered his voice and continued with the story.

Miss Kirkland, calmer now, paid for her items, and my father helped her to her car with her purchases. When my father came back in, he approached the old men.

"Now I don't mind you fellows gathering around here," he said, "because you're my friends and customers, but when women are in the store, you've got to watch your language."

"What are you going to do?" Mr. Hill asked.

"I'll put an end to it," my father said. "This is my store and I make the rules."

"It ain't a word she's never heard before," Mr. Hill said.

"Maybe not," my father said. "But I'm not going to allow that word when women are in the store. That's my rule!"

"Rules!! Rules!" Mr. Hill said.

"You heard what I said," my father said. "If I hear that word again when there is a woman in the store, I'm going to ask the person who said it to leave."

Mr. Hill laughed.

"If anybody don't believe me," my father said, "just try me."

Mr. Hill laughed again.

Mr. McAdams touched Mr. Hill's knee to indicate that he should calm down.

"We understand," Mr. McAdams said. "I know you're running a business here. I apologize for using the word. It won't happen again."

Tempers cooled. The old men returned to talking and my father started to help another customer. It was a moment to remember. Peace had been made for the moment, but swords had been crossed.

****

In the fall of 1956, the presidential election between Eisenhower and Stevenson was the primary topic of conversation among the old men. Eisenhower was the Republican incumbent, although his health had been an issue. He had ended the Korean War and had a strong economic record, but Stevenson promised less taxes and more jobs. Mr. McAdams and Mr. Hill, both Stevenson supporters, made their opinions known not only among the assembled group but to anyone who came into the store. If anyone stated an opinion to the contrary, both Mr. McAdams and Mr. Hill would turn on them at a moment's notice.

Mr. Chandler was the store's bread deliveryman. A gentle, dignified middle-aged man, he would appear every Monday and Saturday morning to deliver loaves of bread, sweet cakes, and fruit pies from the local bakery. I liked Mr. Chandler. His wife had been my third grade teacher and he had a pleasant, non-assuming demeanor about him. Usually, after he had made his delivery, he would take time to have a soft drink and chat with the old men.

In late October, some two weeks before the election, Mr. Chandler made his delivery and, once my father had paid him, joined in the conversation.

"Eisenhower is going to win," he said. "He has had a good record over the past four years and he's a war hero."

"What's he done?" Mr. McAdams shot back. "Play golf, raise taxes, and give our money away to all these foreign countries…"

"And he's going to put niggers in school with our kids," Mr. Hill added. "We can't have somebody like that in the White House."

"You're going to be surprised come election day," Mr. Chandler said. "He's going to go in with a landslide."

"You want to bet on it?" Mr. Hill said.

"Well, I'm not a betting man," Mr. Chandler said with a big smile, "But I'm confident Eisenhower will get reelected."

"No! No! No!" Mr. McAdams said. "It's going to be Stevenson all the way."

"Wall Street has put up lots of money to get Eisenhower elected," Mr. Chandler said. "He's going to get California and New York."

"I don't believe that," Mr. Hill said.

"We'll wait and see," Mr. Chandler said.

"Come on!" Mr. Hill replied. "Put your money where your mouth is…"

Mr. Chandler smiled and hesitated for a moment.

"OK," he said finally. "I'll bet you a Coca-Cola that Eisenhower wins."

"That's a bet!" Mr. Hill replied. "I can tell you now you're going to lose…"

"We'll see," Mr. Chandler replied.

So the bets were placed and the participants awaited the outcome.

The election was held on Tuesday, November 6, 1956, and Eisenhower handily won reelection and Mr. Chandler won the bet. I anxiously waited to see how it would be settled. I sensed

Mr. Hill wasn't going to take the loss lightly.

The following Saturday, Mr. Chandler came in at the regular time and made his delivery. Once all the bread and cakes and pies were neatly stacked in their racks, my father paid Mr. Chandler and he approached the group.

"Looks like you owe me a Coca-Cola," he said, looking straight at Mr. Hill.

"Yeah, guess I do," Mr. Hill said with a scowl.

Mr. Hill stood up, went to the counter, and placed down a dime to pay for the soft drink, then motioned for Mr. Chandler to get his prize. Instantly, Mr. Chandler pulled a cold soft drink out of the cooler, popped the cap, and took a long swig.

"Tastes good!" he said.

I could see that didn't set well with Mr. Hill.

"You don't have to rub it in," Mr. Hill said. I could see his anger rising.

"I'm not rubbing it in," Mr. Chandler said. "It's politics. The election was fair and square."

"Eisenhower won because the Wall Street bankers put their money up and got him all the votes in New York and California," Mr. Hill replied angrily.

"I told you that," Mr. Chandler said.

Mr. Hill stood up, walked over, and faced Mr. Chandler.

"Drink your God-damn Coca-Cola and shut up!" he said angrily.

Mr. Chandler was taken aback at the aggression.

"Now I don't want any trouble," he said, backing away from Mr. Hill.

Mr. Hill stepped forward and got into Mr. Chandler's face.

"If you'll go out there in that road," Mr. Hill said, "you can show me what kind of man you are."

"I don't want any trouble," Mr. Chandler said, backing away.

My father, who was behind the counter, quickly came out and stepped between them.

"Hold on!" my father said, facing Mr. Hill. "There's not going to be any trouble in my store."

Mr. Hill, his face livid with anger, looked at my father, then back at Mr. Chandler.

"Do you understand?" my father said to Mr. Hill again.

The aggressor wasn't finished. He turned to Mr. Chandler, wagging his finger.

"You're going to learn to keep your mouth shut or somebody is going to clean your plough," he said.

"That's enough!" my father said. "You either respect me and my store or get out of here."

Sullenly, Mr. Hill looked at my father, then turned and went back to his seat among the group.

Mr. Chandler said nothing more and left the store.

At the dinner table that night, my father said he wasn't sure what he was going to do about the old men, but he felt his business would be better if they were gone. That same night, he also predicted that someone someday was going to kill Mr. Hill.

****

On a Saturday in late April in 1957, it all came to a head. The day had turned off cold, but by midmorning, temperatures warmed, and by midafternoon, all of the regulars among the old men were present. It had been a busy day for me and my father. I had spent the morning pumping gas and stocking shelves. Early that morning, there had been a major delivery from the grocery wholesaler and there were forty, maybe fifty boxes of goods that needed to be opened, marked with prices, and shelved. Meanwhile, Thomas Meat Wholesalers had delivered a calf for the meat case, and my father, when he wasn't helping customers, was busy in the meat room butchering the calf.

Around 1:30 that afternoon, Mrs. Charles Hamilton, a quiet, well-respected nurse in the community, came into the store. When she came in, her eyes swept over to the counter where my father usually was, then up to the shelves where the sanitary napkins were housed. She peered up at a full-stocked shelf. An hour earlier, I had unpacked and stacked a box of twenty-four packages into the small space on the top shelf and I had packed them tightly. She wasn't tall enough to reach the top shelf, so she turned to see who could help her. The only people in her line of sight were me and the old men who were watching her. Presumably too embarrassed to ask a man for help with such a personal item, she decided she would serve herself. Undaunted, she took the long hickory stick with a nail on the end that my father used to tip items from the top shelves. With much uncertainty, she maneuvered the stick until the nail was on one of the top boxes, then made a sudden downward motion. As she hooked the top box of sanitary napkins and pulled down, the top box came tumbling down, but as it did, so did the entire shelf. As the boxes came tumbling down, she raised her arms to block their fall, but it was too late. With the shock and the sudden onslaught of boxes, she fell to the floor and screamed in fright. As she did, Mr. Hill and Mr. McAdams were beside themselves with raucous laughter.

At the sound of the scream, my father emerged from the meat room, still wearing his butcher's apron.

"What's going on?" he said.

The moment he saw Mrs. Hamilton on the floor surrounded by sanitary napkins and the old men giggling with delight, he quickly surmised the situation. His first instinct was to save the customer.

"Mrs. Hamilton!! Mrs. Hamilton!!" he called, rushing across the floor to the front of the store.

By the time he reached her, she was in tears and immediately jumped up and rushed out the door. My father was right behind her.

"Mrs. Hamilton!! Mrs. Hamilton!! I'm sorry!" my father said again and again as he followed her to her car.

But it was too late. Mrs. Hamilton, distraught and crying, wasted no time getting into her car and roaring out of the parking lot.

My father came back into the store, still wearing his butcher's apron with blood on the front. He was livid with anger as he approached the group.

"That's all!" he said. "I want all of y'all out of my store. Right now!!"

"We was just having a little fun," Mr. Hill said.

"Not at my customer's expense," my father shouted. "Get

out!! All of you!!"

Mr. McAdams glared at my father and didn't move. My father grabbed his arm and pulled him to his feet.

"Get out of my store," my father shouted.

Mr. McAdams scowled and slowly started toward the door. Mr. Hill begrudgingly followed. Mr. Whisenant and Mr. Gibbs, seeing that my father meant business, quickly grabbed their hats and went outside. The only members of the group now were Mr. McAdams and Mr. Hill.

"You ungrateful son of a bitch," Mr. McAdams said. "We was coming in here long before you ever got here."

"Well, I'm here now," my father said. "Get the hell out of my store!"

"You low-down son-of-a-bitch."

Then Mr. McAdams turned and stalked out of the door.

Quickly, my father turned to face Mr. Hill.

"Go on! Get out!!"

Mr. Hill backed off a little, then glared at my daddy.

"Tell you what, you little son-of-a-bitch," he said. "You meet me out there in that road and I'll whoop yo ass."

My father didn't flinch. Mr. Hill had used the wrong word when he referred to my father as "little." At age fifty-three, my father was short, maybe five foot six, but he was strong and stocky. I knew he didn't take kindly to being called "little."

My father smiled confidently.

"I'll be right out," he said.

"I'll be waiting," Mr. Hill replied.

With that, he turned and went out the door.

I had never thought of my father as a violent man. I had heard my uncle say once that my father had pistol-whipped a man in a café in town over a woman. I had heard my daddy talking about fighting with other boys when he was young, but I couldn't imagine my father in a fight with another man, but here it was.

Before he started out, my father untied his butcher's apron, folded it neatly, and placed it under the counter. As he turned to go, he grabbed the .38 special he kept wrapped in a wool cloth under the cash register.

Outside, Mr. Hill was waiting for my father in the dusty

dirt road. Mr. McAdams, Mr. Gibbs, and Mr. Whisenant were waiting to watch.

"Come on! Come on!" Mr. Hill said, putting up his fists. He was a full head taller than my father.

My father put up his fists and the two men circled one another. Mr. Hill threw a haymaker, but my father ducked, took the pistol from his hip pocket, and swung upward with a mighty blow at Mr. Hill.

Instantly, Mr. Hill went down into the dust and gravel. The barrel of the pistol had caught him on the bridge of the nose and the blow was sufficient to shake his brain within his skull and send him to the ground. For a long moment, he sat on the ground, dazed and confused, as if he didn't know what had happened. Then he put his hand to his face and felt the warm blood coming out of his nose. For another ten to fifteen seconds, he sat in the gravel of the dusty road, trying to regain his senses. Finally, having re-gathered his faculties, he peered at my father standing over him and, from the look in his eyes, you could see that he had no more fight in him. My father waited for him to get up. For a moment, Mr. Hill stood up, then staggered slightly as if he was trying to regain his balance. He peered at my father and started to walk haltingly through the dust and gravel to his home some one hundred yards away.

"Don't ever come back to my store!!" my father shouted after him.

Mr. Hill didn't look back.

Then my father turned to McAdams.

"Go on!! Get off my property," he shouted. "Don't ever come back to my store!"

Mr. McAdams gave my father the middle finger, then turned and started walking to his home.

Next, my father turned to Mr. Gibbs and Mr. Whisenant. He was calmer now.

"I'm sorry about all this," he said. "I got no fight with you two. If you want to continue to trade with me, I'd be obliged, but there is not going to be any more congregating at my store."

Mr. Gibbs smiled.

"Wife and I will be back," Mr. Gibbs said.

"Same here," said Mr. Whisenant said.

My father turned and went back into the store. He lost no time removing the trappings of the old men. He gathered the wooden soda pop crates and took them to the store room. The dominoes, checkerboard and checkers, as well as the spittoons, he took out to the side of the store and burned them in the trash. Now there was no reason for the old men to return.

And they didn't. Mr. Hill and Mr. McAdams never returned to the store, although Mr. Hill's oldest son Raymond, a good friend of my father, did continue trading after the incident. Mr. McAdams' son Robert, who delivered milk to the store, never returned, and my father started stocking milk from his cross-town competitor. Meanwhile, Mr. Gibbs and Mr. Whisenant and their wives continued shopping at my father's store as if the incident had never happened. It was the end of an era.

Over the ensuing years, the business grew. Once the old men were gone, women and young children seemed to feel more comfortable in the store and, slowly but surely, the business started to draw a higher class of customers. In 1959, my father added an extra room where he stocked a variety of gardening tools and supplies. It was safe to say the business improved dramatically after the old men were gone.

****

In the spring of 1969, after having owned the store for thirteen years, my father sold the business for $13,000. That was quite a bit of money in those days and, after handing over the keys to the new owner, he returned to farming. He said farming and being close to the land was his first love. He said he had always felt closer to the land than he did people, so he went back to growing corn, sweet potatoes, cotton, and vegetables. He was a past master at growing vegetables, and every year, his proudest accomplishment was the vegetables he produced in his beloved vegetable garden.

In the spring of 1978, my father was in the vegetable garden, weeding okra. The morning had turned off cool, but by ten a.m., the sun was blazing hot. My mother was at the kitchen sink washing dishes and watching him through the window. Suddenly, she saw him grab his chest, fall to his knees, then slump to the ground. Frantic, my mother dashed to the garden and, upon examination, saw that he was unconscious. She called an ambulance, and he was rushed to the local hospital. Upon arrival, he was pronounced dead of a heart attack. He was seventy-five.

Three days later at his funeral, my heart was breaking with grief as my mother and I stood over his grave. As the belt on the gold-plated lowering platform slowly delivered my father's coffin into its final resting place, my mind suddenly flashed back to that cold day in April of 1957 when he had dispatched the old men from his grocery store. In my mind's eye, I could still see my father, his face flushed with anger, and the .38 special in his hand, standing over a dazed Mr. Hill and daring him to get up out of the dust and gravel. The loss of my father had a profound effect on me.

* * *

During the early fall of 1961, five years after my father had dispatched the old men from his store, a cousin of mine told me that Mr. Hill was stopped at a red light in Hokes Bluff when another driver slammed into the rear of his car. Furious, Mr. Hill got out of his vehicle, confronted the other motorist, and threatened to beat him to death. When the other motorist didn't respond in kind, Mr. Hill reached through the open car window and grabbed the man by the throat. Immediately, the other motorist produced a pistol and shot Mr. Hill through the heart. He died instantly.

The End

GRANDFATHERS
From a Barlow® to a Pentium®

Everybody in the McKinney family knew that William Vernon Johnson, the first-born of the McKinney's oldest daughter Virginia, was grandfather McKinney's favorite grandchild. When he was born in early April of 1941, the child's grandfather had made a special trip to the hospital to see the day-old infant. Although there was another grandson, that was the one and only time the grandfather had made such a trip. And while the parents of the other grandson were aware that their offspring was playing second fiddle to Little Billy, as the grandfather called him, they never mentioned it. They just looked the other way and accepted it. So, in late July of 1946, while grandmother McKinney was in south Alabama visiting a sick sister, no one was surprised when the grandfather asked that Little Billy, who was five years old, come spend a few days with him at the McKinney homestead.

On a warm Saturday morning, oldest daughter Virginia Johnson delivered the child, along with a bagful of toys, clothes, and coloring books to the McKinney's non-electric home deep in the backwoods of North Alabama. Once the daughter's car had stopped, the five year old jumped out and ran up to the front porch to greet his grandfather.

"How's Little Billy doing?" the grandfather asked.

"Oh, he's doing fine, Granddaddy," the child's mother said. "He can count to a hundred, he knows all of his ABCs, and he is a big fan of Roy Rogers and the Lone Ranger."

"And Tonto," the child said, correcting his mother.

"Oh, yes," the child's mother said. "I forgot about Tonto."

Virginia smiled at her father and then turned to the child again.

"I'll be back Monday morning," the mother said. "Now, you be a good boy and mind your Granddaddy."

"I will, Mommy," the child promised. Billy kissed his mother goodbye. The grandfather and grandson watched as she returned to the family car and drove back down the dirt road that led to the main highway. Once the car was out of sight, the grandfather turned to his grandson.

"Let's go, Little Billy," the grandfather said. "We got things to do."

Some ten minutes later, the two were in a small greenhouse behind the barn where the grandfather grew tomato seedlings for later transplanting into the garden.

"First, we've got to cut some strings," the grandfather said.

"What are strings, Granddaddy?"

The grandfather took down a roll of cotton twine from a shelf and held it before the child.

"We get strings from this," the grandfather said. "First, we pull off a little bit at a time, then we cut it."

The grandfather showed the child how to pull a length of string off the roll and hold it steady while he clipped it with a pocket knife. After working for some 20 minutes, the two had cut more than 20 lengths of string, which would be used to hang earth-filled Styrofoam cups from the greenhouse ceiling.

"What are those?" the child asked, curiously examining the small round objects the grandfather had shaken out of a small envelope.

"Those are tomato seeds," the grandfather explained. "When we put these in the dirt in the cups, a little tomato plant will grow. Just like those," he said, pointing to several cups already hanging from the ceiling. The grandfather lowered one of the cups so the five year old could examine it. Inside the cup, several small tomato plants had sprouted.

"All life begins with little seeds," the grandfather explained. "All living things—plants, animals, insects, humans—everything begins life with a little seed."

The grandfather proceeded to show the child how to push the tiny seeds into the fertile soil in the cups. Once the seeds were planted, he gave the child a small container of water and showed him how to water each and every plant. Finally, as the grandson watched, the grandfather tied the strings around each of the cups and hung them from the greenhouse ceiling.

"Now," the grandfather said, "after a few days, the seeds will sprout into young tomato plants and each and every one will have a new life all its own."

"Yeah," the grandson agreed thoughtfully, still holding the small empty water container.

Once the seedlings were planted, the grandson and grandfather returned to the backyard of the farmhouse where the grandfather took a seat in a rocking chair, withdrew his pocket knife again, and began whittling. Nearby, the grandson, on his knees in front of a chair, began coloring pictures in a Roy Rogers coloring book.

"What was it like when you were a little boy, Granddaddy?" the child asked, using a black crayon to color the bridle of Roy Rogers' horse, Trigger.

"Well, that was a long, long time ago," the grandfather said, "and the world back then wasn't like it is today. When I was growing up there was thirteen of us kids, and we all lived on a big farm and everybody had to work. We had to pick cotton and milk the cows and bale the hay and tend the crops. There was always lots of work to do on the farm."

"What kind of car did your daddy have?" the child asked, coloring Trigger's long mane with a white crayon.

"Oh, we didn't have a car," the grandfather answered, "but we had a good rubber tire buggy."

The grandson looked up from the coloring book.

"What's a buggy?" the child asked.

"A buggy is like a wagon," the grandfather continued. "A horse pulls it and you can ride in it."

The child was still coloring Trigger's mane.

"Would the horse doo-doo on the street when it pulled the buggy?" the child asked seriously.

"Sometimes," the grandfather laughed.

"I saw a zebra doo-doo one time when I was at the zoo," the grandson noted thoughtfully. "All the zebras were running and running and running. Then, one stopped and started doo-dooing right in front of everybody at the zoo."

The grandfather chuckled to himself.

"That's the way those zebras are," the grandfather noted.

Some ten minutes later, the child grew bored with the coloring book and went to the rocking chair to inspect his grandfather's activity. For several minutes, the child watched as his grandfather, in sure even strokes, sliced small, curled strips of wood shavings from a small wooden block. The grandson knew that his grandfather's prize possession was his pocket knife.

"That's my Barlow," the grandfather said, looking longingly at the pocket knife. "A Barlow is the best friend a man ever had. You can cut a limb with it, clean your fingernails, skin an animal, turn a screw—even kill a man with it if you had to."

The child looked curiously at his grandfather.

"Have you ever killed anybody, Granddaddy?"

"Oh, no," he said.

The child continued to watch his grandfather's whittling.

"I got my first Barlow when I was sixteen years old," the grandfather continued. "It was a knife my father had given to Paul, my oldest brother. I had to give Paul two dollars and a pair of good work boots for that knife. You wouldn't believe how happy I was when I put it in my pocket the first time."

"Can I touch the blade?" the child asked.

"Okay, but be careful, the grandfather cautioned. "It's sharp. Give me your hand."

The large older hand grasped the young smaller hand and moved it toward the sharp blade. The child knew exactly what to do and expertly ran his index finger across the sharp edge of the knife blade.

"It's sharp, isn't it," the grandfather commented.

"Yeah, real sharp," the child said.

"When you're twelve years old, I'll buy you a Barlow," the grandfather said. Then, almost as an afterthought, he added, "No, when you're ten, I'll buy you a Barlow."

Later that evening, after the child had followed his grandfather around the farm to feed the cattle, the pigs, and the chickens, they returned to the farmhouse for supper. Once seated at the table, the grandfather had prepared two bowls of shredded wheat with fresh milk and peach slices. They ate quietly by the flickering light of a kerosene lamp.

"Look, Granddaddy," the child said, eating the last few bites of shredded wheat and looking at the box. "It's the Lone Ranger and Tonto."

The grandfather glanced at the cereal box and saw three cartoon drawings of the famous cowboy hero and his faithful Indian companion on the back of the box.

"Let's make us a little comic book," the grandfather suggested.

"Oh, boy!" the child said anxiously.

The grandfather removed the remaining shredded wheat biscuits from the box and placed the waxed paper foil packet in the cupboard. Next, he ripped apart the cereal box with strong hands and placed the cartoon panels flat on the table. Using his trusty Barlow again, he carefully cut the cartoon panels out of the cardboard. Once removed, the grandfather folded the panels and set up them up on their edges to display them.

"What does this one say, Granddaddy," the child asked, anxiously peering at the first panel.

"In this one," the grandfather noted, "the bad guys are stealing the rancher's cattle."

The young child peered at the indicated panel and examined an evil-looking man in a dark hat who was ordering his minions to drive the cattle away off the ranch.

"And in this one," the grandfather said, moving to the second panel, "the Lone Ranger and Tonto are chasing the bad guys and trying to get the cattle back."

The child, with infinite interest, peered at the second panel and wondered if his heroes would get the bad guys.

"And here," the grandfather said, indicating the third panel, "the Lone Ranger and Tonto have captured the bad guys and turned them in to the sheriff."

"Hooray!" said the child, examining the third panel. "We don't like people that steal and hurt other people, do we, Granddaddy?"

"Oh, no," the grandfather said. "We like people that are honest and good, and do the right thing."

"People like the Lone Ranger and Tonto," the child said. "They're our friends, aren't they."

"That's right," the grandfather said.

"And Roy Rogers and Gene Autry?"

"Oh, they're our friends, too," the grandfather added.

The child smiled at the thought that good, honest people would always win out over bad, dishonest people.

"Did you have the Lone Ranger and Tonto when you were a little boy?"

"No," the grandfather answered thoughtfully. "At least not on cereal boxes. We had dime novels about Jesse James and Wild Bill Hickok, but we didn't have pictures on cereal boxes."

Some 20 minutes later, the grandfather, using a kerosene lamp for light, led the child up the stairs to his bedroom and helped him into bed.

"Goodnight," the grandson said.

"Goodnight," the grandfather answered, getting up to leave the room.

"Granddaddy," the child called.

"Yes," the grandfather answered, turning back to the child, the kerosene lamp illuminating his weathered face.

"When we put water on the tomato plants today, you said we did it so they would have a good life."

"That's right," the grandfather said.

"What is life?" the child asked.

The grandfather, still holding the kerosene lamp, took a seat on the side of the bed.

"Well," the grandfather said thoughtfully, "life is like a big wheel. It's always turning and turning and turning. When anything is born, a big wheel starts going round and round."

The child looked at his grandfather.

"When the tomatoes are born, does a wheel start turning?"

"That's right," the grandfather said.

The child, still thoughtful, peered at the adult.

"Is there a wheel in me, Granddaddy?"

"Of course," the grandfather answered. "There is a big wheel in every life, but your wheel has just started to turn. In my life, the wheel has been turning for a long, long time."

The child pondered the thought.

"And when somebody dies, does the wheel stop turning?"

the child asked.

"That's right," the grandfather said.

The five year old looked away from his grandfather. His questions had been answered, and he was lost in thought.

"I'll see you tomorrow," the grandfather said, the kerosene lamp still illuminating his face.

"Goodnight, Granddaddy" the child answered. Alone in the darkness, he listened as his grandfather's footsteps echoed back down the stairs. Five minutes later, Billy Johnson was sound asleep.

Early the following morning, the grandfather was back at the child's bedside at the break of day.

"You ready?" the grandfather asked.

The five year old sat up in bed and rubbed his eyes. "I'm ready, Granddaddy."

The grandfather helped the child get dressed and fed him another bowl of shredded wheat and fresh peaches. Then he packed warm, buttered biscuits in a wooden bucket and led the child to a motor scooter that was parked at the side of the house.

Next to his Barlow knife, the grandson knew that his grandfather's prize possession was his Cushman motor scooter. After he had retired, the grandfather said he was finished with cars and he had bought the scooter because it was cheaper on gas.

"Can I push it, Granddaddy?" the child asked.

The grandfather knew that nothing delighted the child more than pushing down the motor scooter's kick starter to start the engine.

"Let me get it ready," the grandfather said. After adjusting the throttle and lifting the crank, he picked up the child and sat him on the motor scooter.

"Now," the grandfather instructed, putting the child's foot on the crank. "Push!"

The child pushed downward with his foot. The engine turned over, but failed to start.

Again, the grandfather checked the throttle and lifted the crank.

"Okay," he said, "now push real hard!"

Again, the child pushed down on the crank, but again, the engine failed to start. The grandfather manually used the crank to turn the engine over so that the next slightest movement would start the engine.

"Okay," the grandfather said, holding the child's body so he could grasp the seat for support and use his full body weight in the effort. "We're going to do it this time."

The child pushed down on the crank a third time. Instantly, the small two-cycle engine roared to life.

"I did it! I did it!" the five year old screamed delightedly, beaming with personal pride at his accomplishment. "I did it! I did it!"

"You sure did," the grandfather said. "Come on."

The grandfather placed the wooden bucket between his legs on the floorboard of the motor scooter. Then he swung the child up behind him and instructed him to put his arms around him.

"Now hold on tight," the grandfather instructed. "Real tight!"

The grandfather turned the throttle, and the motor scooter with the grandfather, the grandson, and the wooden bucket safely in tow, chugged across the farm's front yard to the driveway and down a small hill to the main road.

Over the next hour, the grandfather guided the motor scooter over several miles of bumpy, unpaved country roads deep into the North Alabama backwoods. Finally, the motor scooter turned off on a narrow, muddy side road and, after some ten minutes, came to a stop under the shade of several oak trees.

"Come on," the grandfather said.

The grandfather, carrying the wooden bucket, led the child across a small field and into a patch of shady undergrowth thick with pines, oaks, and water reeds.

"Listen," the grandfather said.

The grandson listened with all his might. Somewhere nearby, he could hear a high buzzing sound. He looked at his grandfather.

"I hear it, Granddaddy."

The grandfather peered through the undergrowth into a

stand of black oaks some 50 feet away. Finally, his eyes stopped, and he motioned to the child to come closer. As the child stepped up, the grandfather parted the leaves and lifted up his grandson so he could see.

"Look!" the grandfather said, indicating a black oak tree that was growing out of a large mound of earth. "See the bee hive?"

The child peered into the dense undergrowth. In the forks of the black oak, not more than 6–7 feet off the ground, the child could see thousands upon thousands of wild black bees swarming around a hive.

"I see it," the child said.

The bees had built the hive into a huge gaping hole in the forks of the black oak. The hive hadn't been disturbed in several years and there was so much honey that parts of the combs had spilled out of the hive into the forks of the tree.

"The bees are quiet now," the grandfather said expertly, studying the hive. "Bees are like people. They can be quiet for a while, but any kind of excitement will cause them to jump up and run off."

For several minutes, the grandfather studied the beehive. Then, when he was ready to make his move, the grandfather took a pair of gloves, a long woman's woolen stocking, and a small toy bell out of his pocket. Next, he removed his hat, placed the stocking over his head, and tied it to his shirt collar to protect against the bee stings. Then he slipped on the gloves and, toy bell in hand, turned to the child.

"Now you wait right here," the grandfather instructed. "I'll be back in few minutes."

The child watched as his grandfather skirted the beehive through the undergrowth of oaks and pines and took up a position in a small clearing some 30 feet from the bee tree.

Then very faintly, the child could hear the gentle tinkling of the toy bell. At the sound, the mood of the bees changed instantly. The swarm became instantly agitated, and the buzzing grew louder as most of the bees left the hive and began flying around the hive in an ever-widening circle.

Then the bell rang again. Suddenly, more bees left the hive and began circling. Then, when the bell rang again—this time a long, almost singing sound—the vast majority of the bees flew away from the hive toward the sound of the bell. The child watched as his grandfather moved even farther away from the hive and rang the toy bell a fourth time. Suddenly, a full 95 percent of the bees gathered in a huge swarm and flew toward the direction of the bell.

Now that the hive was basically unguarded, the child watched as his grandfather darted back through the undergrowth to the bee tree. Standing on a small log under the tree, the grandfather, using his trusty Barlow and protected by the woolen stocking and the gloves, reached into the interior of the bee hive and began slicing off huge chunks of fresh honeycombs and placing them in the wooden bucket. As he worked furiously, the remaining bees lunged at him angrily to protect their life's work.

Then, almost as quickly as he had appeared at the hive, the grandfather disappeared. An expert, he had needed only a few minutes to fill the wooden bucket with fresh honey. Mission accomplished, the grandfather darted back out of the wooded area and into the undergrowth. Then, together the grandfather and grandson made their way out of the undergrowth.

Back at the motor scooter, the two took a seat under the oak trees and examined their prize. The grandson peered into the wooden bucket and saw the dark brown and black natural combs of honey. As he looked at the honey, Billy Johnson was extremely proud of his grandfather for having outsmarted the bees and taking their life's work so easily. The grandfather said he had been stung only once.

"When you rob a wild bee tree," he instructed, "you have to work fast and have lots of protection. Always remember that."

The grandfather unpacked the container of buttered biscuits and spread a cloth on the ground. Then, again, using his trusty Barlow, he cut a large piece of honeycomb filled with fresh honey and placed it on a buttered biscuit.

"Taste this," the grandfather said, handing the honeyed biscuit to the child.

The child examined the morsel and took a bite. As he

began to chew, he looked at his grandfather and smiled delightedly.

"It's so sweet, Granddaddy."

"It's supposed to be. It's honey."

In almost no time, the child, who was feeling very grown-up, had wolfed down the honeyed biscuit and was ready for another.

"Damn! That's good," the child said, using a word he had heard his father use when he wanted to emphasize something.

The grandfather looked sternly at his grandson.

"What did you say?"

"I said it was damn good honey," the child said again, thinking that, after he and his grandfather had gallantly joined forces to steal the honey, the use of that word would be acceptable.

Saying nothing, the grandfather rapped the child in the middle of the forehead with the blunt handle of the pocket knife.

"Don't talk like that around me," he said sternly. "Little boys aren't supposed to talk like that."

Although the rap on the child's forehead didn't hurt all that much, it had done enormous damage to the child's pride. While his grandfather had opened his heart and his life to the child by taking him to the secret bee tree, the child didn't understand why the word had been so offensive. After all, his grandfather had been treating him like an adult all day then suddenly he started treating him like a child. The child was confused. Inside, a secret part of him wanted to cry, but he knew he couldn't and he mustn't. Although tears formed in his eyes, he knew he must not cry. If his mother had been present, he could not have stopped himself from crying, but under these circumstances, the very facts of the situation prevented him from crying. Quietly and strongly, the five year old gallantly held back the tears, said nothing, and continued eating the fresh honey.

Finally, after the two had eaten their fill of buttered biscuits and honey, the grandfather covered the wooden bucket with a cloth, tied the top, and placed it securely in the floorboard of the motor scooter.

"Are we ready?" the grandfather asked.

"Yeah," the child answered, feeling much better now.

The grandfather hesitated.

"Let's go over here first," the grandfather said.

The child followed his grandfather who had stopped under an oak tree. When he saw his grandfather unzipping his pants, he knew he was going to urinate at the base of the oak tree. The child, who had tried to bond with his grandfather in every other way, wasted no time unzipping his pants and joining in this exclusively male ritual.

The adult and the child looked down at the respective streams of urine forming the puddle. The child's hormone-less urine was a stream of light-brown liquid, the same color of day-old tea. The adult's urine was a pale yellowish color and caused huge bubbles to form on top of the puddle.

"Look," the child said, peering at the puddle of urine. "Your pee has got white bubbles in it."

The grandfather looked, and then he turned to the child.

"When you get big like me," the grandfather explained, "your pee will have white bubbles like that."

The child looked at his grandfather, but said nothing. Both had finished urinating. His grandfather buttoned his fly. The five year old did the same.

Back at the motor scooter, the grandfather swung the child up behind him on the seat.

"Now hold on tight," the grandfather said.

With his short arms, Billy Johnson reached around his grandfather's waist and clasped one hand inside the other and held tight. The grandfather started the motor scooter engine and, minutes later, the two were chugging back along the narrow, muddy path back to the main road.

Three years later, the big wheel in Billy Johnson's grandfather's life ceased to turn.

On a Thursday afternoon in early May, the County sheriff, a long-time friend of Billy's grandfather, came by the homestead and asked him if he could go into town the following day to serve on a jury. He said the judge had had the trial scheduled for over a week, but they could only find eleven jurors. The sheriff said he would see that Billy's grandfather was paid 50 cents a day for as long as the trial lasted, and he would get a free, hot lunch every day in the courthouse cafeteria. The old man hadn't been into town for a while, so he accepted the invitation.

The following morning, after he had put on his brogans and dressed in his khaki pants and shirt with the top button fastened, he went outside and started the motor scooter. His wife came out on the back porch to say goodbye.

"I'll be back about dark," he said.

"Alright," she said.

He revved the engine and the motor scooter started off.

"John!" the wife called.

He slammed on the brakes and the motor scooter jerked to a sudden halt.

"What?"

"Now don't you go around Ross," she said, shaking her finger and referring to his younger brother who worked for the Alabama Power Company down the street from the County Courthouse. The wife knew that Ross was trouble. Big trouble. Ross had always managed to get her husband in trouble each and every time they got together. Ross liked to drink whiskey.

"Okay," he said, "I won't."

The wife waved goodbye and then watched as the motor scooter disappeared up the dirt road in a cloud of red dust.

Well, as fate would have it, John Davis McKinney did go into town and did serve on the jury on Friday. That night, however, he did meet his younger brother Ross and they drank a pint of whiskey each. Billy's grandfather didn't get home until about 9:30 that night.

The next morning, John Davis McKinney woke up and threw his legs over the side of the bed. Suddenly, his body lurched forward. Instinctively, he grabbed his chest and grimaced in pain as the heart muscles inside his chest cavity failed to perform. After several seconds of clutching his chest, his body went limp, and he fell back dead on the bed.

At the funeral, eight-year-old Billy Johnson cried his heart out. After the services, he watched as the workmen lowered the casket containing his grandfather's body onto a bed of crushed rock in the bottom of the grave. Then, he watched as they placed two-inch pine strips over the casket until there was a little wooden floor built over the top of the casket. Billy knew his grandfather would like that. He always felt comfortable around wood. As the workmen began filling the grave, Billy Johnson cried and cried and cried.

For all the years afterward, he would remember the sharp rap on the forehead his grandfather had given him with the butt handle of the Barlow. When he was 12 or 13 years old and young boys would test their "dirty" words on one another, he would invariably hesitate before he used the word "damn." Even after he was a grown man, he found himself using words like "durn" and "dang" and "darn" as substitutes for the word "damn." The rap on his forehead had made a lasting impression.

***

By the early summer of 1996, the big wheel was still turning in William Vernon Johnson's life. At age 55, he had been married twice, had a grown daughter and a five year old grandson of his own. Although he loved the grandson dearly, it seemed that he could never find time to go to Alabama and visit with the child. His Atlanta publishing company—which now printed four magazines—had become very successful and his job required 10–16 hours six days a week in the office. Recently, his wife Elaine had said that now was the time Billy should be doing things with Christopher. In another four to five years, she explained, the child would be in his own world and would have his own individual set of interests.

So, in mid-July of that year, during the summer lull, Billy decided to take some time off work, drive over to Birmingham, and spend a few days with his grandson. Billy had a close friend who had a weekend cabin in the mountains north of Birmingham and it would be a perfect place for the grandfather and the child to spend some time together. For the trip, Billy had packed a small computer, several children's books, and some nature videos.

Upon arrival at his daughter's house in Birmingham, the

grandson was the first to greet him at the door.

"Granddaddy!" the child yelped happily as he leaped into his grandfather's arms.

"Mistopher Christopher!" the grandfather said, hugging his grandson. "How are you?"

Billy greeted his daughter Barbara.

"So how's this little boy doing?" the grandfather asked.

"Oh, he's doing fine," the daughter said. "He can count to a hundred, he knows all of his ABCs, and he is a big fan of the Teenage Mutant Ninja Turtles® and the Power Rangers®."

"And Biker Mice from Mars," the child added firmly.

The child's mother smiled knowingly at her father.

"Now I've packed toys, clothes, and coloring books in here," the mother continued, referring to a canvas bag she was holding. "Also, there is an extra pair of tennis shoes and clean pajamas in the side pocket."

The mother turned to her son.

"Now, you mind Granddaddy," the child's mother instructed. "And have a good time."

"We will, Mommy," the child promised as the grandfather hefted the canvas bag over his shoulder and started out the door.

"And be sure to call me when you and Granddaddy get ready to leave the mountain house."

"I will, Mommy," the child promised again.

Some ten minutes later, the grandfather and grandson were headed north on I-59 out of Birmingham.

"I want to go to Toys 'R Us," the grandson said.

"You don't have enough toys?" the grandfather asked. "I've got Pac-Man and Duke Nukem on the computer."

"Yeah, I know," the child said, "but I want to get a set of Super Blocks to make a fire truck and a fire station," referring to a popular child's toy that consisted of numerous pieces of molded plastic used for building.

Some 20 minutes later, the grandfather and grandson were walking hand-in-hand down the aisles of a Toys 'R Us® store in North Birmingham.

"There it is," the child said, pointing to a big red box.

The grandfather took down the box and examined it. The

box said the enclosed kit—a complete fire station with two fully equipped trucks—represented the company's biggest project. There were 1,154 pieces, and a total of 6 hours was required for complete assembly.

"You'll never finish this in two days," the grandfather said.

"Yes, I will."

"To finish it you'll have to spend at least three hours each day."

"I can do it!"

"Yeah, but WILL you do it?"

"Yeah."

"Promise?"

"Promise."

The grandfather looked at the grandson.

"I'm going to hold you to it," the adult said.

"Okay."

The grandfather and grandson took a place in the check-out line to pay for the toy. As they approached the cash register, the grandfather looked up at a display rack with a big sign that read, "Name Bracelets! Make your own name bracelets with our kit!" Billy Johnson peered at one of the packages. Inside, he could see several pieces of stiff cotton string and an assortment of 500 colored beads that bore inscriptions of the ABCs and numbers 1 to 100. The child watched as his grandfather removed one of the packages from the display and placed it beside the Super Blocks.

"What is that, Granddaddy?" he asked curiously.

"It's a surprise."

"I want to see."

"No. If you see it, it won't be a surprise," the grandfather explained. "Like I told you, I'll show it to you later."

"But I want to see it now."

"I told you it's a surprise," the grandfather said. "I'll show it to you when we get to the mountain house."

An hour later, the two were cruising along I-59, high in the mountains of North Alabama. As the grandfather pulled the car off the expressway into a gas station, a brisk wind was whipping through the mountains, bending the trees, and picking up giant swirls of loose debris.

"Now stay in the car," the grandfather said as he opened the door. "It's very windy out here."

Billy Johnson gave instructions to the attendant and then went inside the service station. Moments later, when he started back to the car, he had to shield his face from the powerful wind that was whipping about stronger than ever. Quickly, he opened the car door and got inside.

"Look, Granddaddy! Look!" the child shouted suddenly.

In the gas stall in front of the car, the strong wind was about to blow over a motorcycle. As the two watched, the motorcycle leaned slowly with the force of the wind and then suddenly toppled over on its side with a loud crash.

"Damn!" the child said anxiously, standing up in the seat as high as possible and pressing his nose against the windshield to peer over at the fallen motorcycle. At the sound of the word, the electronic grandfather immediately looked at the child but said nothing.

"The man that owns that motorcycle is going to be mad. Really mad," the grandson continued, still pressing his nose against the windshield.

Five minutes later, back on the expressway again, the grandfather withdrew a bag of candy he had bought at the service station. As the grandson watched, the grandfather unwrapped one of the candies.

"Taste this," the grandfather said.

"What is it?" the child asked.

"Just taste it."

The child examined the object and then plopped it into his mouth. For a moment he chewed, and then he looked at his grandfather and smiled happily.

"It's so sweet, Granddaddy."

"It's supposed to be," the grandfather said. "It's a chocolate-covered cherry."

For the next ten minutes the child and the adult rode quietly, sharing the bag of chocolate-covered cherries.

"Where did you hear that word you said back there," the grandfather asked.

"Which word?" the child asked innocently.

"The word you used when the motorcycle fell over."

The child looked at the electronic grandfather, trying to read the adult's intentions. He could sense no anger or sternness in the face.

"I heard it from Tyler," the child said.

"Oh," the grandfather said, remembering that Tyler was a member of his grandson's kindergarten class.

"He's older, and he knows about grown-up things."

"How old is Tyler?"

"Oh, he's seven," the child said, with a certain air of respect.

Around 3:30 in the afternoon, Billy Johnson turned his car off the expressway, onto a two-lane, farm-to-market road that led deep into the mountains. Finally, after guiding the car through several miles of winding, mountain roads, Billy maneuvered the vehicle up a steep hill and brought the car to a stop.

"We're here!" the grandfather said.

Once the car had been unloaded, the grandfather and grandson worked together connecting appliances, putting food away, and unpacking toys, books, and clothes. Finally, after their arduous journey, the grandfather and grandson plopped down on the couch with two fruit punch soft drinks.

"Now I want to see my surprise," the child said. "You promised."

"Okay," the grandfather said. He withdrew the name bracelet kit and opened it.

"Now we're going to make some little strings," Billy said, as he withdrew several pieces of stiff cotton string from the package.

"What are strings, Granddaddy?"

"Strings are the building blocks of information," the grandfather explained. "A word is a string of letters. A sentence is a string of words. A paragraph is a string of sentences."

The child listened, pretending to understand.

"Okay," the grandfather said, "first, let's make a string that spells your name."

Billy Johnson gave the child a piece of string and then

handed him each of the letters in his name in sequence. Next, he watched as the child carefully placed each bead on the string.

"Now," the grandfather said, "what does that say?"

"C-H-R-I-S-T-O-P-H-E-R," the child said, spelling out the letters. "That's my name."

"It's a little string of letters," the grandfather said.

"That's neat, Granddaddy," the child said happily, examining the string. "Let's do another one."

"Okay," Billy said, "Let's do Mommy's telephone number."

Billy handed the child another piece of string and withdrew each of the individual digits for 1-205-369-1187, his daughter's Birmingham telephone number, and handed them to the child. The child quickly threaded the beads on the string.

"What does that say?"

"1-205-369-1187."

"Now, as long as you have that," the grandfather explained, "you'll always know Mommy's telephone number."

The child studied the stringed beads.

"Now, if this is a string of letters," the grandfather said, indicating the beads with the child's name, "what is this a string of?" the grandfather asked, indicating the telephone number.

"A string of numbers," the child said.

"Very good!" the grandfather said. "And how many numbers are in the string?"

The child counted.

"Eleven," the child said. "The same as the number of letters in my name."

"Very, very good," the grandfather said.

That night, after a dinner of frozen pepperoni pizzas and soft drinks, the grandfather and grandson began the Super Blocks project. Once the package was opened and spread on the floor, there were a total of 1,154 pieces. After working together for more than two hours, the two had completed one fire truck and assembled a small portion of the fire station.

Finally, around 10:30, the child turned to his grandfather.

"I'm tired, Granddaddy," the child said.

"I know. It's late," Billy said. "We've had a big day. We'll stop now."

The grandson crawled up into his grandfather's arms. Five minutes later, the child was sound asleep.

Early the following morning, the grandfather was up at the break of day, setting up the computer. Once the child was out of bed and dressed, the grandfather fed him scrambled eggs, canned biscuits, and orange juice. As the child gulped down his last sip of juice, he saw that the computer had been set up.

"Come on, Granddaddy," he said. "Let's play on the computer."

The grandfather took a seat in front of the computer, and the grandson plopped into his lap.

"This is my new Pentium®," the grandfather said proudly, flipping the switch to boot the computer.

Instantly, the image of a cartoon-like, mischievous-looking black cat wearing an oversized red bow-tie and a red hat with white circles around the crown, flashed on the computer screen.

"What does that say?" the grandfather asked, indicating the caption.

"The Cat in the Hat®," the child answered eagerly.

"How many words is that?"

"Five," the child said.

"What are the two words that are the same?"

The child studied for a moment and then pointed to both instances of the word "The."

"Very good," the grandfather said.

"And which two words are similar, but not exactly the same?"

Again the child studied for another moment. Then he pointed to the words "Cat" and "Hat."

"And what's the one word that's different from all the others?"

The child pointed to the word "in."

"Very good," the grandfather said.

"A word is a little string of letters," the grandfather explained.

"Like Christopher," the child commented.

"That's right," the grandfather added, "and a sentence is a string of—?"

"Words," the child answered.

The grandfather studied for a moment, trying to come up with a new and different question.

"Very good. Now can you give me an example of a sentence?"

The child pondered for a moment and then looked at his grandfather.

The child shrugged.

"What?" he asked.

"The Cat in the Hat," the grandfather said finally. "There are five separate words, but when they are all strung together, they form a sentence: The Cat in the Hat."

"The Cat in the Hat," the child said out loud. "The Cat in the Hat," he said again.

Then he turned to his grandfather.

"It's fun learning on the computer."

"A computer is the best friend a man can have in the world today," the grandfather said. "There is no end to the ways that computers can handle information."

"What's information, Granddaddy?"

"Information is little pieces of new knowledge that everybody needs to make their lives better."

The child was listening.

"I got my first computer in 1984," the grandfather explained. "It was a little Apple IIE. I saved for over a month to buy it. You won't believe how proud I was when I set it up for the first time."

"Someday I'll have my own computer," the child said.

"I'll buy you a computer when you're twelve," the grandfather said. "No, ten," Billy added. "I'll buy you a computer when you're ten."

"I want to color," the child said, jumping down from his grandfather's lap and going to the canvas bag filled with toys.

"You don't want to play Pac-Man®?" the grandfather

asked.

"No," the child said, withdrawing a box of crayons and a Teenage Mutant Ninja Turtle® coloring book from the bag and plopping down on the floor.

Billy Johnson watched as the child occupied himself with the coloring book, while he played Pac-Man on the computer. For some ten minutes, the two entertained themselves independently.

"Granddaddy, did you read *The Cat in the Hat*® on a computer when you were a little boy?" the child asked as he colored Leonardo's mask a dark green color.

"No," Billy said. "The first words I learned were 'See Dick run! See Jane run!' I learned to read from a book, not a computer."

The grandfather, bored with the Pac-Man game, got up from the computer and turned on the television. As he flipped through the channels, there was a news show, a golf match, a rock and roll show, and two talk tabloid shows. Absently, the child looked up from the coloring book at the precise moment the grandfather flipped the channel to the opening credits of the Mighty Morphin Power Rangers show.

"Right there! Right there!" the child said frantically, upon seeing the images of his masked heroes. "I want to see the Power Rangers."

Instantly, Billy Johnson changed the channel back, and the child wasted no time abandoning the coloring book and plopping down in front of the television. On the screen, the show's title read, "Power Rangers Vs. Rebel Aliens from Zor."

The grandfather and grandson took a seat in front of the television and watched as the Mighty Morphin Power Rangers, regular high school students in real life, donned their ranger suits and did battle with the evil renegade rebels from the planet Zor. Once the Power Rangers get wind of the renegade's evil plans to take over earth, they use a combination of expert karate moves and some gymnastic expertise to drive the Zorians from earth and save all mankind.

"Hooray!" Christopher said happily as he watched the rebels' spaceship escape the earth's atmosphere en route back to its own planet. “The Power Rangers won again!”

The grandfather turned to the child.

“Don’t you think it’s time we finished the fire station and fire trucks?” the grandfather asked.

“No, I want to watch TV,” the child said.

“Come on, let’s finish the fire station and the trucks.”

“Granddaddy, I’m tired,” the child pleaded.

“Remember the promise.”

“I know,” the child said.

“Then let’s go,” the grandfather said, getting up and going to the corner where the Super Blocks project was laid out on the floor. Billy sat down and started connecting the plastic pieces. After working for some five minutes as the grandson watched, Billy turned back to the child.

“Come on now. We said we would do it.”

The child looked away from the grandfather.

“Let’s do 200 more pieces and then we’ll go to see *The Lion King*. Okay?”

“Oh, boy!” the child said. Instantly, he was in the corner to help with the Super Blocks.

Just after sundown that evening, Billy Johnson and his grandson drove into the nearby town of Blue Ridge, Alabama. After a stop at McDonald’s®, they drove to a small movie house that was featuring *The Lion King*. It was an animated movie about a young lion cub named Simba, who, after his father was deposed as king of the lions by his wicked uncle, spent his days being happy-go-lucky in the jungle with his devil-may-care friends. After a childhood friend discovers Simba leading a free and irresponsible life, she convinces the young lion prince that he must go back to the pride and take his rightful place as Lion King from the wicked uncle. Finally, Simba accomplishes that feat. The title song to the movie was a catchy little tune called “The Circle of Life.” Throughout the trip from town back to the mountain house, the child was singing “The Circle of Life.”

Finally, once back at the mountain house, the child made a beeline for the Teenage Mutant Ninja Turtle coloring book.

“I’m going to color,” the child said.

“We still haven’t finished the fire station and the fire

trucks."

The child frowned.

"I don't want to play with the building blocks," the child said, looking away from the adult and back at the coloring book.

"You remember the promise?" the grandfather said. "You said we'd finish it before we went back home. We're leaving in the morning."

"I know, Granddaddy," the child said, "but I don't feel like it."

The child continued coloring. The grandfather could see he was getting nowhere.

"Okay," the grandfather said finally. "Somebody's got to do it."

He got up, took a seat on the floor and began assembling the plastic pieces. For several minutes, the two worked independently.

"Now, let's see here," the grandfather said, speaking to himself. "I need to find the right headlight for this fire truck."

He started sorting through the plastic pieces. Suddenly, the child looked over at the grandfather.

"I can find it, Granddaddy," the child said.

Instantly, the child was on to the floor beside the grandfather. An hour later, the project—including both of the fire trucks and the fire station complete with a flag on top—was near completion. As the child snapped the last few pieces into place, he knew he had lived up to his commitment.

"All done," the child said happily. "I did it just like I said."

"You sure did," the grandfather said proudly. "You did what you said you would do. That's very important."

"I'm glad we finished it, Granddaddy," the child said happily.

"So am I," the adult said. "Now we've got to call Mommy and tell her when we'll be home."

"Can I dial?" the child asked.

"Do you have the number?"

"Right here," the child said, indicating the string of beads attached to his wrist.

"And what's that called?"

"A string," the child answered. "A string of numbers."

"Very good, little boy," the grandfather said. "Very good! Now let's go call Mommy."

The child, and the grandfather sat down at the table in the living room where the house's only phone was located. Then, as the grandfather watched, the child, using the string of numbers as a guide, started to dial.

"1-2-0-5-3-6-8…," the child said, stopping to look back at the number.

"No," the grandfather said. "Not an eight, a nine comes after the three."

"Darn," the child said. "I'll have to start all over."

The child tried again.

"1-2-0-5-3-6-9-1-1-8-8," the child said, saying each number as he dialed it.

Although the grandfather saw that the child had dialed the last digit wrong, he said nothing.

The child and the grandfather listened. Then they both heard an operator saying, "If you'd like to make a call…"

"I can't do it, Granddaddy," the child said, frustration in his voice.

"Oh, yes you can," the grandfather said. "Let me call out the numbers and you dial. Okay?"

"Okay," the child said, calmer now.

The child dialed each of the numbers as the grandfather called them out. Then they waited. Moments later, the child's eyes lighted up when he heard his mother's voice on the answering machine.

"Mommy, this is Christopher," the child said. "Granddaddy and I will be back at home about three o'clock tomorrow. Okay—I love you. Bye."

The child hung up the phone.

"I did it! I did it!" the child yelled joyfully. "I knew I could do it! I did it! I did it!"

"You sure did," the grandfather said with a big smile. "Now don't you think it's about time for bed?"

"Yeah, I am pretty tired," the child said.

The grandfather led the child into the kitchen where he

fed him warm milk and fresh chocolate drop cookies. Then, once the child had a bath and was dressed in his night clothes, the grandfather tucked him into bed.

"Goodnight," the grandfather said, turning off the electric light.

"Granddaddy?" the child called out in the darkness.

The grandfather flipped the switch, and the room was instantly filled with electric light again.

"What is it?" he asked.

"When you were a little boy, did you have the Teenage Mutant Ninja Turtles® and the Power Rangers®?"

"No," Billy said thoughtfully. "But we had Roy Rogers and the Lone Ranger and Tonto."

"Did they save the world from the bad guys?"

"Oh, of course," the grandfather answered. "That's the reason we liked them so much."

"I'm glad," the child said.

The grandfather started to reach for the light switch again.

"Granddaddy," the child called again.

"Yes."

"At *The Lion King* tonight, the main song was about the circle of life. What's the circle of life?"

The grandfather returned inside the room and took a seat on the side of the bed.

"Well," the grandfather said thoughtfully, "life is a like a big wheel. It's always turning and turning and turning. When anything is born, a big wheel starts going round and round. That wheel is the circle of life."

The child, still thoughtful, peered at the adult.

"Is there a wheel in me, Granddaddy."

"Of course," the grandfather answered. "There is a big wheel in all lives, but your wheel has just started to turn. In my life, the wheel has been turning for a long, long time."

The child paused for a moment so that the enormity of the thought could register.

"And when something dies," the child asked finally, "the wheel stops turning?"

"That's right," the grandfather answered.

The child looked away from his grandfather. He was lost

in thought.

"Goodnight, Granddaddy," the child said, plumping his pillow.

"Goodnight, Christopher," the grandfather said as he flipped off the electric light.

The following morning, the grandson was out of bed at 8:00 a.m. While his grandfather was still asleep, Christopher was busy playing with the name bracelet kit. Finally, around 8:30, the child went into his sleeping grandfather's room.

"Granddaddy!" the child called.

Billy was sound asleep.

"Granddaddy!" the child called again.

Billy Johnson rolled over, raised himself on one elbow, and rubbed his eyes.

"Good morning, little boy."

"I have a surprise," the child said playfully, holding his right hand behind his back.

"What is it?"

"I can't show it to you now," the child said playfully. "If I do, it won't be a surprise."

"Then when can I see it?" Billy asked, playing along.

"When you get up," the child said.

The grandfather sat up, stretched his arms, and threw his feet over the side of the bed.

"Now," he said, "what's my surprise?"

"Okay," the child relented, not wanting to delay the suspense any longer.

"Look!" the child said, suddenly holding up his latest name bracelet creation.

The grandfather looked at the string. It read, "The Cat in the Hat."

The grandfather beamed at his grandson.

"And what's that called?" the grandfather asked delightedly.

"A string of words," the child answered. "A sentence."

Billy Johnson's innermost heart glowed with delight. Instantly, he fell on his knees and took the child into his arms.

"You're the finest little grandson I could ever have asked for," Billy said, hugging the child. "I love you so much."

"I love you, too, Granddaddy," the child said.

The grandfather dressed and once again prepared canned biscuits, scrambled eggs, and orange juice for himself and the child. After eating, the two started making preparations to leave the mountain house. Together, they cleaned the kitchen, packed up the computer, the toys, the videotapes and recorder, their clothes, and the books, and then loaded everything into the car.

Some 30 minutes later, as they cruised back south along I-59 toward Birmingham, the child fell asleep in the front seat. Finally, over an hour later, the child awoke, sat up in the seat, and rubbed his eyes.

"Granddaddy," he said, "I've got to use the bathroom."

"Can you wait until we get to a service station?"

"I've got to go now," the child said.

The grandfather pulled off the expressway on to a narrow, farm-to-market road and drove a short ways, pulling into a small turnout. Some ten minutes later, the two were out of the car and the grandfather was leading the child up a muddy, weed-choked path into an area thick with scrub pine and oak trees.

"Okay," the grandfather said, realizing now that he had to urinate himself.

The adult and the child began urinating into the same puddle at the base of an old oak tree.

"Look, Granddaddy," the child said curiously, staring into the puddle of urine forming at their feet. "Your pee has got white bubbles in it."

"Someday, when you're big like me," the grandfather said, "your pee will have white bubbles like that."

The child looked at his grandfather, but said nothing. He finished urinating then tried to zip his pants closed again.

"Granddaddy, will you help me?"

The grandfather could see that the zipper was stuck.

"Hold still," the grandfather said, bending down to inspect the problem. With a quick jerk, the grandfather untangled the zipper from the material and zipped up the child's pants.

"There," the grandfather said.

The five year old looked at the fixed zipper and then at his grandfather. He smiled.

"Thanks, Granddaddy."

Fifty-five-year-old William Vernon Johnson took his grandson's hand, and together they started walking back down the muddy, weed-choked path to the car.

Later that afternoon, they arrived back in Birmingham at Billy's daughter's house. Billy unloaded the child's belongings and reported the events of the past two days to his mother. Finally, it was time for Billy drive back to Atlanta.

"Okay, Billy's daughter said. "Say goodbye to your grandfather."

The child smiled and perfunctorily went to his grandfather and gave him a hug. The child released his grandparent then went back to his mother.

"Bye, Granddaddy," the child said, slightly waving his hand.

"Bye, little boy," the grandfather replied.

Billy turned and started to walk to the car.

"Granddaddy!!" the child called suddenly.

Billy turned back to the child.

"I like talking to you, Granddaddy," the child said.

"I like talking to you, too, little boy," the grandfather said.

Suddenly, the child burst into tears and ran to his grandparent.

"Oh, Granddaddy," the child sobbed, leaping into his grandfather's arms. "I love you! I love you!"

For a full ten seconds, the child clung to the grandfather's neck with all his might, shedding huge tears.

As the grandfather and grandson held one another in a tight embrace, it was if the future was trying to hold on to the past. In his heart, the child knew that someday the big wheel would stop turning in his grandfather's life. The grandfather also knew that. He knew this child would someday stand over his grave and weep for him as he had for his own grandfather. That was what made it so terribly sad. Both knew instinctively that nothing could stop the eternal transition from the old to the new. The forward movement of the big wheel was an undeniable certainty. Nothing, absolutely nothing, could stop its forward progress.

Finally, the grandfather broke the embrace.

"I've got to go now, little boy," Billy Johnson said.

The child, huge tears still streaming down his face, slowly released the grip on his grandfather's neck. Then, without looking at the grandparent, he ran to his mother's side.

"Bye, Granddaddy," the child said, turning to look back at his grandfather.

"Bye, little boy," Billy Johnson replied.

The mother and child watched as Billy strode to the car, got inside, and slowly backed out of the driveway. Before starting the car forward, Billy looked back and waved one last time to his grandson. The child waved and blew his grandfather a kiss. Billy blew back the kiss and then gunned the car's engine as he pulled out on the main highway.

As Billy drove back to Atlanta, he felt an overwhelming sense of completeness within himself. Over the past three days, he had shared himself with his grandson as honestly and as completely as he knew how. Like his own grandfather 50 years earlier, Billy Johnson had tried to prepare his grandson for the future that he foresaw. The time they had spent together making word strings, going to the movies, and playing on the computer had been little more than an updated version of the time he had spent with his own grandfather in the spring of 1946. In their own special way, Billy Johnson and his grandson had planted tomato seedlings, examined the blade of a pocket knife, cut out cereal box cartoon panels, and robbed a wild bee tree. Human technology had moved from the Barlow® to the Pentium®. What an incredible leap in 50 short years! From a hard-bitten, agricultural-yeoman society to a kinder, gentler, electronic culture in which information was king. In the process, something had been gained, but something had been lost.

For William Vernon Johnson, the big wheel was still turning.

The End

THE ANGEL YEARS

1

Now we Johnsons were just simple country folks. Like most of the other families in Hawkins Valley, Georgia, we farmed the land, went to church and school, and tried to present ourselves as God-fearing, respectable members of the community. In all, there were five of us: Mama and Daddy and us three girls. My sister Audrey was the oldest at age 19; then there was me, Cornelia, in the middle at 15, and finally, Betty Jean, the youngest at 13. Since we lived on a farm, we always had plenty to eat and decent clothes to wear, but not any of the so-called "luxuries." Daddy worked in the fields minding the cotton and corn crops, Mama cooked and kept house, and me and the other two girls helped any way we could with the vegetable garden, the chickens, milking the cows, and feeding the hogs. Although it was 1954, we didn't have a television, but we did have a telephone and indoor plumbing. We never went on vacation and we never dreamed of owning a fancy car, so we all rode around in Daddy's old Chevy pickup truck with bald tires and floppy fenders. Like I said, we were just simple country folks. We didn't have a lot of material things, but we had our pride.

***

It all started one sunny Saturday morning in late March when my youngest sister Betty Jean blurted out these four words while we were in the backyard washing clothes.

"I think I'm pregnant."

She didn't look at me when she said it; she just kind of stared straight down at the washboard where she was grating

Mama's old blue print dress up and down across the ridges. I heard her words, but, since she was always funning, I wasn't sure I had heard correctly.

"What?"

She didn't answer again right away.

"I think I'm pregnant."

"Why do you say that?"

"I haven't had a period in two months."

I started shaking my head in disbelief.

"Mama is going to have a raving fit."

"Daddy's the one I'm scared of."

"Oh, he'll rave and rant and threaten, but Mama will have the final say-so. Who's the daddy?"

Betty Jean looked up from the washboard. She hesitated, then finally spoke.

"Shadrack Griffin."

"The one that drives the school bus?"

"That's him."

My heart sank as I fished another pair of Daddy's denim overalls out of the wash pot and dipped them into the rinse tub to cool.

"Have you told him?"

"Yes. Yesterday, before I got off the school bus."

"And what did he say?"

"He was mad. Cussing and fuming and carrying on. He said the baby was all mine. He said he wasn't going to have nothing to do with it."

"That's all?"

Betty Jean nodded.

"That low-down dog! I should have known. I saw you and him talking at the church picnic. How'd it happen?"

Again, she hesitated before she spoke.

"Well, you know he drives the school bus and our house is the last stop on the route. Me and him stopped down at the creek a few times and started messing around. You know… one thing led to another…"

"You make it sound like it was no big deal."

"It wasn't… at the time."

I could feel the anger growing in my guts, refusing to

believe my closest sister had been so careless. Finally, I blurted it out.

"Now you're pregnant!"

She turned angrily to me.

"Not so loud! We've got to keep it a secret. You ain't going to tell Mama, are you?"

I stared at her in disbelief.

"Are you crazy? We've got to tell her. You can't hide something like this from Mama. In a few months, you're going to be bigger than a barrel. How are you going to hide something like that?"

Betty Jean's face screwed up in a frown.

"Yeah, I guess you're right. Mama's going to know sooner or later."

She stopped and looked at me.

"Will you tell her?"

"Yeah. I'll tell her. Maybe she won't be as hard on you if I tell her."

"Thanks! You ever know anybody that's been to one of those homes for unwed mothers?"

"No."

"When are you going to tell Mama?"

"Tomorrow…. after church."

***

The following day, like most Sunday mornings, we put on our church clothes and attended services at the Old Harmony Baptist Church over at Morgan's Crossroads. On Sundays, Mama would always start the afternoon meal in the morning before we left for church. That way, by the time the sermon finished at noon and we got home, she could finish quickly so we could all eat by about 1 p.m. During those times, my mother, a smallish, leathery woman in her early forties, was a blur of constant motion in the kitchen. One moment, she would be stirring the green beans; seconds later, she would be turning the frying chicken, then putting more wood in the cook stove, then checking the biscuits, then throwing the tea bags into the boiling water. While she was darting about, I went into the kitchen and took a seat at the table.

"Mama!"

She was stirring the green beans when she glanced up at me.

"Yes, Cornpone."

Mama always called me "Cornpone." Somehow, she got that out of Cornelia. Cornpone is corn bread made without milk or eggs and is usually baked or fried. I loved to eat it, but I didn't particularly like it as a nickname. It sounded so plain and homely, but I never said anything. After all, she was my mama.

"I have something to tell you."

"It better be important. I'm busy."

She stopped briefly, then reached both hands behind her head and, for a moment, fidgeted with the bun of salt and pepper hair at the nape of her neck. Then, almost absently, she returned her attention to me.

"What do you want to tell me?"

"I hope you won't be too mad…"

"Are you in trouble at school?"

"No!"

"Then say what you got to say! I'm busy."

I waited still another moment, then blurted it out.

"Betty Jean is going to have a baby."

As I said it, she was reaching into the oven to remove a pan of hot biscuits. Seconds later, as she placed the pan on top of the stove, the thought registered and she instantly froze in place.

For a long moment, she peered at me.

"What did you say?"

"Betty Jean is going to have a baby."

"Lord God! Where did you hear that?"

"She told me. She hasn't had a period in over two months."

Mama continued to stare at me as if she were collecting her thoughts. Finally, she spoke.

"Well, I'm just going to have to talk to her. Have you told anybody else?"

"No."

"Well, don't mention it to anybody else in the family until I can talk to her."

***

Now my mama was not the kind of person that would fly off the handle. That was Daddy's department. Mama would study something over and over before she would do anything. I knew she would talk to Betty Jean before she mentioned anything to Daddy, so I waited. That afternoon, after we had eaten and she had cleaned up the kitchen, Mama came to my and Betty Jean's room. Betty Jean and I had had our own room for as long as I could remember. Early on, Mama recognized how close we were, so she put us in the same room together. When Mama came into our room that day, she said she wanted to talk to Betty Jean in private and asked me to leave and close the door. I did as she instructed and waited outside while they talked. They were in there for over an hour. I could hear Betty Jean crying and Mama talking very sternly to her. Finally, Mama came out. Her face was red with anger and I could see she had been crying. Only moments after Mama left, I ducked back inside the bedroom.

"What did Mama say?"

"She said we needed to be sure I was pregnant first. She said she didn't want to go off half-cocked. She said she would do a test."

"A test? What kind of test?"

"Mama said she knew how to do a pregnancy test."

"How's she going to do that?"

"Not sure."

"Come on, let's go ask her."

Moments later, we were in the kitchen, where we found Mama washing the big iron skillet she used for frying chicken.

"Mama," I started. "Betty Jean said you were going to do a test to see if she was pregnant."

"I sure am," Mama said. "You girls want to watch? You might have to use it yourself one of these days."

"Does it work?"

"It worked for all three of you girls."

"When are you going to do it?"

"Soon as I finish these dishes."

She stopped.

"Do you think we should wait for Audrey?" I asked.

"She won't be here until dinner time," Mama said. Audrey had gone home from church with the Thompsons and promised to be home by dark. "I don't want to wait that long. I want to get it over and done with."

"Have you told her?" Betty Jean asked.

"No," Mama said. "She'll hear about it tonight."

***

Fifteen minutes later, Betty Jean, Mama, and I were in the old wood shed behind the house where Mama would grow tomato seedlings. On the work bench in front of her, she had a small jar containing a little bit of Betty Jean's pee, a box of baking soda, and a bowl of sugar.

"When a woman gets pregnant, nature puts a whole new set of chemicals in her body," Mama said. "If those new chemicals are in Betty Jean's body, this test will tell us."

Betty Jean and I were all eyes as we watched Mama take two level tablespoonfuls of sugar and dump them into the jar of urine. Then she opened the box of baking soda and took a pinch.

"Now if the sugar doesn't dissolve when I drop in this little bit of soda, it means she's pregnant. If it dissolves, then she's not. Y'all got that?"

"Yes, Mama," we said in unison.

"Okay. Here goes!"

Both of us watched closely as Mama sprinkled the baking soda into the jar of urine. Slowly, the grains of sugar floated aimlessly down through the yellow liquid and, grain by grain, settled on the bottom of the container.

"The sugar is not dissolving," Mama said conclusively.

She turned to Betty jean.

"You're with child. That's for sure. When was the last day of your last period?"

Betty Jean reflected for a moment.

"January 18th or 19th," Betty Jean said.

Mama took a pencil out of her apron pocket and started doing calculations on the back of an empty seed packet.

"You're going to have that baby on September 8," Mama said.

***

That night, when we gathered around the table for the evening meal, Daddy hadn't come in yet. All that afternoon, he had been in the river bottoms repairing a fence. When he finally came in, he said he wanted to wash up before he ate and asked us to wait for him. Once seated, he had on a clean shirt and pants. My daddy was a big bear of a man who wore glasses and always had a stubble of beard except on Sundays. His face was sun-burned and, when he took off his hat, you could see the tan line across the middle of his white forehead.

"All right, Ila," he said. "You say the blessing."

With that, Mama blessed the food and we began to eat. Over the next thirty to forty minutes, we chowed down on Mama's roast ham, green beans, and mashed potatoes and biscuits and finished up with a slab of peach cobbler. Once she was finished, Audrey got up to leave the table.

"Keep your seat, Audrey!" Mama said. "As soon as everybody is finished, we're going to have a family meeting."

"What's the meeting about?" Daddy asked.

"Go ahead and finish your meal," Mama said. "You'll find out soon enough."

Thirty minutes later, everybody had finished eating and Mama had cleared off the table. Then she took the floor.

"Now the five of us have always been a family and done everything together and it's going to stay that way. We're having this meeting because we have to decide what to do about Betty Jean's condition."

"Condition?" Daddy said. "What condition?"

"Betty Jean has got herself pregnant," Mama said.

For a moment, you could have heard a pin drop as we all waited for the thought to register with Daddy.

Slowly, Daddy turned and peered across the table at Betty

Jean.

"Betty Jean?" he said. "Is that right?"

"Yes, Daddy."

"Who's the daddy?"

"Shadrack Griffin."

"That brown-haired kid that drives the school bus?"

Betty Jean nodded.

"Are y'all going to get married?"

"No, Daddy."

Daddy inhaled and looked away.

"Have you told him?"

"Yeah. I told him last Friday when I got off the school bus."

"And what did he say?"

"He said he didn't have time to raise a child."

Daddy's face screwed up in anger. For a long moment, he didn't speak.

"That low-down rascal," he said finally. "He's going to do right by you. I'm going to see to that. Tomorrow I'm going to get my shotgun and go down and have a talk with him."

Mama could see that Daddy was becoming agitated.

"Horace!!! Calm down!!" Mama said. "That's why I didn't tell you. You're always so cock-sure about these things."

"This is our daughter we're talking about here," Daddy said, pointing to Betty Jean. "I'm not going to let some no-count do this to my daughter."

"Can you be reasonable for once in your life?" Mama said.

"So what do you want to do?"

"We're both going to talk to him tomorrow and see if he'll do the right thing."

"Talk! Talk! Talk! In these situations, you can't talk people into doing something. You have to make them do it. Tomorrow I'm going to get my shotgun and go make him do the right thing by my daughter."

"No!" Mama said again. "You ain't going to do no such thing. We're both going to talk to him. If we can't convince him, there's not going to be any violence."

Daddy glowered at Mama for a long moment.

"Now listen here, Ila…"

Mama turned to face him.

"No! You listen, Horace! You always feel like you can make other people do what you want. You think all you got to do is show somebody a gun and they'll do what you say. That's the way it used to be. It ain't like that anymore."

"I can scare hell out of him."

"All you'll do is make him mad."

"No, I'm going to tell him if he can't do the right thing by my girl, I'm going to kill him."

"Then where will that leave us?" Mama said. "You'll be in prison and me and these girls will be without a father and a husband. No, tomorrow we'll go talk to him together."

"I'm taking my shotgun!"

"No!" Mama said. "You ain't taking no shotgun."

***

Late that afternoon, as usual, Audrey, Betty Jean, and I headed to the barn to milk the cows. We had two cows, Topsy and Flossie; I would milk one and Audrey would milk the other. With each cow, me and Audrey milked the two big front teats for the table and saved the smaller back teats for the calves. Betty Jean's job was to tussle the two calves in and out of the stalls to the cows so they could suckle, then get them back into the stall when they were finished.

As we walked, Audrey kept glancing over at Betty Jean. I knew she was going to start trouble. Since she was the oldest, she thought it was her job to boss me and Betty Jean around. At age 19, she was the biggest of us three girls. Tall for her age, Audrey had a pleasant face, long brown hair, and wore thick glasses. When Audrey was born, doctors said she would have to wear glasses until she got a special eye operation. The operation cost way more money than Mama and Daddy had, so Audrey had been wearing glasses all of her life.

Finally, Betty Jean looked back at her.

That was all the opening Audrey needed.

"Don't you have a lick of sense?" Audrey started. "What you doing letting that no-good Shadrack Griffin go playing with yo' tomato. You're not even fourteen years old. Now your life is going to be ruined."

Betty Jean didn't reply. She glanced over at me for help.

Audrey stopped.

"Did you hear me?" she shouted at Betty Jean. "I'm talking to you."

"You shut up!" Betty Jean shot back. "You don't run my life!!"

"No, you shut up!" Audrey said. "Somebody's going to have to knock some sense into that thick head of yours."

Then, in a sudden flash of anger, Audrey turned, grabbed Betty Jean by the shoulders, and started shaking her. Betty Jean tried to fend of the attack as best she could, but Audrey was much stronger and bigger.

"Stop!! Stop!" Betty Jean screamed, slapping frantically at Audrey with both hands. As Betty Jean tried to pull away, Audrey grabbed her hair so she couldn't escape.

"Turn her loose," I shouted.

As if she had not heard, Audrey angrily jerked Betty Jean's hair harder as the younger sister yelled in pain. I stepped forward and slapped Audrey hard across the face. The pain of the blow startled her and she released Betty Jean's hair. Then she came at me, fists first. Although I was four years younger, I was almost as big and strong as she was. When she grabbed me in a bear hug, I wrestled her to the ground and we rolled over and over in the grass. Suddenly, Audrey's glasses fell off and she stopped fighting.

"Wait! Wait!" she shouted. "I've lost my glasses."

I stood up and looked down at her.

"My glasses!! My glasses! Where are my glasses?"

Helplessly, she floundered about the ground, feeling in the grass for her glasses. She was blind without them. I walked over and retrieved her glasses.

"I've got your glasses," I said.

"Give 'em to me!!" she said. "I can't see without them."

"Only if you'll promise to leave Betty Jean alone."

"Give me my glasses!" Audrey shouted.

"No!" I said again. "I'll give you the glasses only if you'll promise…"

I waited.

"Okay!" Audrey said finally. "I promise."

I handed her the glasses. She put them on.

For a moment, still sitting on the ground, she looked up at me, then to Betty Jean. She was still angry, but the fight was gone. Finally, her eyes stopped on Betty Jean.

"I can't believe you would do something like this to yourself," she said. "You better be glad you're not a daughter of mine. I'd whip your butt all the way from here to Albany."

"That's enough!" I said. "Come on!! Let's get these cows milked."

***

The following morning, which was Monday, there was a new driver on the school bus, a fat, round-faced woman named Tina Mae. I knew that didn't look good for Betty Jean, but I didn't say anything. All that day at school, I wondered what happened when Mama and Daddy went to talk to Shadrack. Finally, that afternoon when me and Betty Jean got home, we rushed into the house and went straight to Mama. She was sewing up the shoulder on one of Daddy's old denim shirts.

"Did you and Daddy talk to Shadrack?" Betty Jean asked.

"There wasn't no talking to it," Mama said, piercing the garment with the needle and pulling the long thread through to make a stitch. "He flew the coop. First, we went to the saw mill. The straw boss said Shadrack told him on Saturday morning he was quitting the job and wouldn't be coming back. Then we went to his grandmother's house."

"And what did she say?" Betty jean said.

"She said he had left Saturday afternoon to go back to Kentucky. You might as well forget about him."

"I figured something like that," Betty Jean said finally. "There was a new driver on the school bus today."

Another long pause.

"It's going to be all right," Mama said, using a pair of a scissors to cut the thread. "We're going to have to deal with this baby on our own. We'll figure it out."

"What are we going to do?"

"We're going to have another family meeting tonight," Mama said, holding up the shirt to inspect her work. "We'll make a decision."

2

That night, after all of the supper dishes were washed and the table was cleared off, Mama took the floor. After she explained that Shadrack had disappeared, Mama said we were going to have to make a decision about Betty Jean's "condition."

"Looks like we're back to square one," Mama said. "Now I'm not going to have my daughter shamed like that Anderson girl over at the Crossroads. When she had a child out of wedlock, they kicked her out of church. She was the daughter of a deacon and everybody in this valley knew about it and talked about it. I know the way people are. People will see Betty Jean with that baby and they'll whisper, 'Horace Johnson's daughter has been fornicating.' I'm not going to let that happen to my daughter."

Mama looked at Daddy.

"What do you think we should do, Horace?"

"I say we send her to the doctor down in Valdosta."

"You mean you want Betty Jean to have an abortion?"

"Yeah, that's what I'm saying. We don't need to be taking on another mouth to feed. At the rate we're going, we're never going to pay off this farm."

Mama looked at Audrey.

"What do you say, Audrey?"

"I agree," she said. "If Betty Jean already has the baby, it's going to ruin her chances of ever being married. No man wants to marry a woman with another man's child."

"Cornelia?"

"It's not right to kill an innocent little baby that's never been born," I said. "There are not enough reasons in all the world that makes it right."

"Let's be practical," Daddy said. "We don't need another mouth to feed."

For a moment, Mama looked thoughtfully at Daddy, then

she turned to Betty Jean.

"What do you want to do?"

Betty Jean didn't answer at first.

"I would feel like a murderer if I killed this baby," she said finally. "I want to keep it."

"Do you realize how much time and effort and money goes into raising a child?" Daddy said.

"No amount of money or time or effort is more valuable than a human life," I said.

Another long silence.

"I'm ashamed of you," Daddy said finally, looking at Betty Jean. "We never had nothing like this in my family."

"Now don't be too hasty," Mama said. "Remember your sister Maisy…"

Daddy's head dropped.

"What happened, Mama?" I asked.

"Several years ago, your Aunt Maisy got pregnant with a no-count and they sent her to the doctor in Valdosta for an abortion. After the operation, she started flooding and almost bled to death. Your grandmother and Maisy's oldest sister kept her packed for three days. She was lucky to come out alive."

"That was a long time ago," Daddy said.

"Maybe it was," Mama said. "But something like that could happen to Betty Jean."

Another long silence.

"We're going to put it to a vote," Mama said. "The vote will decide what we're going to do. What do you say, Horace?"

"I say send her to the doctor in Valdosta. We don't need another mouth to feed."

"Audrey?"

"I agree with Daddy. No thirteen-year-old girl needs a baby that doesn't have a father."

"Cornelia?"

"I couldn't bear to take responsibility for killing an innocent little baby. If there is a God in heaven, he wouldn't agree to killing a baby. It's just not right."

Mama looked at Betty Jean.

"Betty Jean?"

"I want to have this baby," she said.

"No man will ever want you," Audrey said. "You'll spend your whole life alone with that child."

"Let me be the one to worry about that. It's my baby."

"You're too young to know what you're getting into," Audrey said.

A long silence.

"How do you vote, Mama?" I asked finally.

Mama inhaled, then spoke.

"We're not going to throw this baby away like an old shoe. Betty Jean is going to have this baby and we're going to keep it a secret from the outside world."

"How we going to do that?" Audrey asked.

"I'll think of something," Mama said.

"Mama, you get some crazy ideas," Audrey said, "but this one takes the cake. You don't realize what you're doing by letting Betty Jean keep this baby."

"You shut up!!" Mama said. "We took a vote and we're going to stick by it."

"You stupid old woman!" Audrey said. "You're going to ruin Betty Jean's life."

Audrey got up to leave the table. As she stood up, Mama grabbed her arm and pushed her down into the chair.

"You keep your seat, young lady," Mama said. "I'm running this meeting. Not you!"

Audrey's face turned red with anger.

Mama glared at her.

"One of these days, I'm going to knock some sense into that thick head of yours."

Hot, angry tears welled in Audrey's eyes.

"Y'all can stop now," Daddy said. "That's enough!"

Suddenly, everybody grew quiet. Then Mama continued.

"All right. We've made our decision. Betty Jean is going to have this child and we're going to hide this pregnancy from the outside world. When she starts getting really big, I'm going to take her to the unwed mothers home in Milledgeville. If we all work together, we can do this."

She looked around the table.

"Are we agreed?"

Daddy nodded. Betty Jean and I indicated our agreement.

"Audrey?"

"You're making a big mistake by saddling Betty Jean with this baby. You'll regret it someday."

"The decision has been made," Mama said. "If you don't like the decision, you can get your things and leave this house. Do you understand?"

Audrey dropped her head in angry silence. She knew better than to argue when Mama had that tone.

"We're all going to pitch in and help Betty Jean through this. We're a family here and everybody is going to do their part. We know what we've got to do and we can do it if we all work together. All we got to do is just do it!!"

She stopped and looked around the table.

"Now remember, there is nobody going to know about this except the five of us. Y'all can't tell nobody… Your friends, your uncles, your teachers… Nobody! This is our family secret."

***

So, in late March of 1954, we began our great adventure into hiding Betty Jean's pregnancy. Over the first few weeks, she didn't need much help. She showed no visible signs of pregnancy; she helped us with the chores and continued as an eighth grader at Hawkins Valley High. By late April, however, she was four months gone and we could see signs. There was a noticeable bump on her belly and she started getting really picky about what she ate. She started throwing up in the mornings and she seemed to be tired all the time. In her face, I could see the discomfort in everything she did. Then, one day when we were feeding the cows, Mama noticed that it took all the strength Betty Jean had to lift the five-gallon bucket of feed up to the trough. She called me and Audrey aside.

"Now you girls are going to give Betty Jean some relief from her chores. She's in her fifth month and she's slowing down."

And we did. When the three of us went to milk the cows,

Audrey and I would tell her to just rest on the extra milking stool and we would tussle with calves. She agreed and welcomed our help.

***

The following week, Betty Jean got sick at school and called Mama and Daddy to come get her. I always hated when my parents came to the school. Mama had enough pride to dress up a little, but Daddy wore the same clothes: overalls, khaki shirt, heavy shoes, and his old brown jumper that he wore in the fields. I knew the other kids were looking at him and had him pegged as just another local farmer with calloused hands and faded overalls. I was so ashamed of my father during those times. Anyway, when Mama and Daddy arrived, the principal got me out of history class for a meeting. The principal was a small, unsmiling, gray-haired woman named Miss Strickland.

"Why was Betty Jean throwing up in the girls' room?"

"The doctor said she has got a 'nervous stomach' condition," Mama lied. "If she eats the wrong thing, it comes right back up. I'm going to have to take her out of school for a while."

"We can have the school nurse examine her."

"Oh, no!" Mama said. "That won't be necessary. Her problem has already been diagnosed. I've got medicine. I know what to do for her."

"As you wish," Miss Strickland said. "You're her mother. What about her homework assignments?"

"Can Cornelia get her assignments and bring them home so Betty Jean can do them? Once they're finished, Cornelia will return them to the teachers."

Miss Strickland looked at me.

"Is that all right with you, Cornelia?"

"Yes, ma'am. That's fine."

Miss Strickland peered at Mama thoughtfully.

"That should work," she said finally. "There are only two more weeks left in the term. We can do that, but I expect the assignments to be handed in in a timely fashion."

"I promise you that the assignments will be on time."

"That will be acceptable."

***

So Betty Jean was removed from public view at the school. A month later, on a Sunday in late June, Mama made another decision. While Betty Jean was getting ready for church, Mama came to our room. When Mama walked in and saw her trying to dress herself, Mama started shaking her head.

"You're too big to go to church. If those old women get a look at you, they're going to know for sure you're with child and their tongues will be wagging. I want you to stay at home today."

So Betty Jean stayed home that Sunday and the rest of us went to Sunday services. As we started to Daddy's pickup, Mama made another announcement.

"After today, we going to quit going to church until Betty Jean has this baby."

"Why?" Daddy asked.

"There are too many nosy old women. I don't want them to start gossiping and shaming my daughter."

"If we do that," Audrey replied, "I won't get to see May Nell."

May Nell Thompson was her long-time friend from high school who she frequently visited after church.

"May Nell will have to wait," Mama said. "Betty Jean comes first."

***

As usual, when the sermon was over that Sunday, the pastor, Rev. Mize, was at the church steps saying good-bye to members. As always, Mama was up front when our family left the church.

"Mrs. Johnson!" Rev. Mize said. "I'm so happy you and your family could be with us today."

"Well, we ain't coming back until you get rid of that smell."

The reverend was taken aback at Mama's comment.

"Smell? What smell?"

"Something has gone in this church house and died. A rat, a snake, or something…. And it's stinking to high heaven. Me and my family won't be back until you get rid of that smell."

"Mrs. Johnson, nobody else has smelled it."

"Well, I can!" Mama said "And we ain't coming back until you get rid of it."

"I'm very sorry," he said, "but…"

"That's all I got to say," Mama said.

Then she quickly turned and stalked down the church house steps. Without looking at the preacher, the rest of us strode down the steps behind her. Then, as the reverend watched helplessly, we headed across the churchyard to Daddy's old pickup.

***

That afternoon, like I did most Sunday afternoons, I ventured down to the catfish pond to paint pictures of birds. About fifty yards behind the barn, Daddy had a pond, maybe two acres in area, where he raised catfish. If Mama wanted a mess of fish for the table, he would wade into the pond with a net, scoop up several pounds of fresh catfish, and deliver them to Mama. Two sides of the pond were surrounded by trees and the third side by cow pasture, but a huge forest of bulrushes lived on the fourth side. I liked to sit in a grassy spot in front of the bulrushes, so I would paint the birds as they flitted about the dark green reedy plants in search of insects. Usually, when I was painting, I would spread an old quilt in front of the bulrushes and set up my easel.

That same afternoon, as usual, I saw Betty Jean, her motorcycle magazines in hand, coming down the path behind the barn to join me. At the pond, she could get away from Mama to read her "dirty magazines," as Mama called them, and smoke cigarettes. She knew Mama would have a fit if she caught her doing either one, so she would sneak around behind Mama's back. She knew I wouldn't say anything.

When she arrived, Betty Jean peered at the hummingbird I

was painting.

"Oh, Cornelia," she said, taking a seat on the old quilt. "I love that. It looks so real!!"

"Thanks!"

For several minutes, she watched as I painted in a flourish of red on the hummingbird's throat. Finally, she spoke.

"Why do you spend so much time painting birds?"

"I love birds," I replied. "When you look at birds, you are looking at God's little miracles."

She studied me for a moment.

"You don't get any money for it," she said. "Why waste the time?"

"That's all right. Maybe I will get some money for them someday. If I don't, then I've had lots of fun admiring God's little creations."

Betty Jean shook her head doubtfully and opened one of the magazines. The cover read "Motorcycle Mamas."

We were quiet for several minutes while I painted and Betty Jean read her magazine. Finally, she looked up at me.

"How much do you think a motorcycle would cost?"

"I don't know. I never priced one."

"If you were guessing, how much do you think one would cost?"

"I have no idea."

She returned to the magazine for a long moment then turned back to me.

"What about a tattoo? How much you think a tattoo would cost?"

I stopped painting and peered at her.

"You thinking about getting a tattoo?"

"Maybe. What's wrong with that?"

"Daddy would have a raving fit if he saw you with a tattoo."

She didn't answer at first.

"I'm not sure I care…" she said finally.

Another long silence as she buried her head in the motorcycle magazine again.

I knew Betty Jean had some wild ideas, but I thought I always felt like I knew what she was capable of doing. When she said things like that, I wasn't so sure.

"Can you imagine spending your life riding through the world on a motorcycle?" she said almost wistfully. "Just cruising along in bright sunshine, the wind in your hair, the sound of the engine below you and not a worry in the world? I don't know why people feel like they have to settle down and do the same things over and over day after day after day. The world is too big to stay cooped up all your life."

"What kind of life are you looking for?"

"I want to be free. Free from worry and work and responsibility. When I wake up every morning, the only thing I want to do is exactly what my little heart desires."

"What about money? You're going to have to work to get money to pay your bills."

"Nah! I'd find some way to make money. Do you see how Daddy worries about money all the time? I never want to be like that."

She was quiet for a moment.

"I'll never spend my life on a farm," she continued. "One of these days, I'm leaving here and never coming back."

"What about that baby you're carrying?"

She looked at me.

"I don't know. I guess I could just carry it with me."

"A child needs a place to call home. You can't expect a little baby to sleep on the side of the road every night."

She inhaled.

"Yeah, I guess you're right. I never thought of that."

***

Over the next few weeks, Betty Jean started getting big, really big. Her belly was pooched out like a knot on a log. Since she was so short and tiny anyway, the bulge at her belly stood out more than ever. As she got bigger and bigger, Mama would let out her clothes, especially her pants. Mama got the idea to sew some elastic into the waist of her pants so they would stretch and, as Mama put it: "It will make it easier on the baby."

One Saturday morning in early July, all of us went to

Albany so Audrey could go to the eye doctor. Mama and Daddy were in the front seat of Daddy's pickup and we three girls were in the back. Once we arrived at the eye doctor's office, there were no parking spaces left, so Daddy parked at the Magic Burger next door. Once parked, Audrey got out and went inside while we waited in the parking lot. The Magic Burger was a drive-in that served hamburgers, fries, shakes, and such. On Saturdays, there was always a bunch of boys from Hawkins Valley High hanging out in the parking lot talking about cars, girls, and football.

Once Daddy's truck was parked, several of the boys glanced over at us. Mama had given Betty Jean one of her old long raincoats to cover her belly. There were several older boys in the crowd that Betty Jean and I knew from school. They included Ron Holloway, Wendell Jenkins, and Tommy McCartney.

Ron peered at Betty Jean.

"Oh, Betty Jean Johnson," he said. "You're such a pretty little thing. What you doing wearing that big coat? It's May."

Betty Jean looked at me.

"You hush up, Ron," I said. "Go mind your own business."

"Now, Cornelia," he replied. "You don't have to get upset. I was just bragging on your sister. We all know how pretty she is."

"Ain't that the truth," Wendell Jenkins said. "You ought to be showing off what she's got rather than hiding it."

The boys had a big laugh.

"I told y'all to shut up and leave Betty Jean alone," I said.

Another round of giggles.

Mama was sitting in the passenger seat in the front and could hear every word.

"You didn't tell us why you're wearing that coat," Tommy McCartney said. "You ain't getting fat, are you?"

"No! You blabbermouth!" I said. "She's not getting fat!"

"You ain't pregnant, are you?" said Tommy.

This brought an even bigger laugh.

I knew that would bring Mama into the conversation.

"Now you boys quit aggravating Betty Jean," she said.

"Y'all leave her alone or I'll call the county on you."

The three boys drew back at Mama's words. They were quiet for a moment.

"We was just having some fun," Ron said. "We didn't mean no harm."

"Betty Jean is not laughing," Mama said.

Ron turned to the other boys.

"Come on, let's go get a hamburger!"

Instantly, they turned and headed for the order window. Thirty minutes later, Audrey had finished with the eye doctor.

On the return trip, Mama was quiet for a long time. Finally, she turned to Daddy.

"Did you hear what that McCartney boy said?"

"About her being pregnant?"

Mama nodded.

"I heard what he said, but it don't mean nothing. He was just funning like boys do. He don't have a clue that Betty Jean is really pregnant."

"You don't think he suspects anything?"

"No. Nothing at all."

3

That night, after supper, Mama made a new announcement.

"It's time to send Betty Jean to Milledgeville," she said. "She's getting so big now that it's really hard to hide it. We've had good luck so far keeping this a secret and I don't want to push our luck. I'm going to take her to Milledgeville tomorrow."

"Can you give me just a little more time at home?" Betty Jean said. "I don't know those people at the home. It's going to be lonesome."

"No, I think it's time," Mama said. "That baby that's growing inside you is going to need some things we can't give it. They've got doctors and nurses and tests and such at the home. Professional medical people that can attend to yours and the baby's needs."

***

Late that night, I got out of bed and went into the kitchen to get a glass of milk. Mama and Daddy, dressed in their nightclothes, were seated at the table.

"We're going to need $85 to get Betty Jean registered at the home," Mama said.

Daddy inhaled.

"I can take some money out of savings," he said. "I hope Betty Jean's baby don't send us to the poorhouse."

"You quit talking like that," Mama said. "This is something we have to do and money hasn't got nothing to do with it. This child is going to be your flesh and blood as much as it is mine."

Daddy didn't reply.

"At the rate we're going, we're never going to pay off this farm."

"Just keep quiet and get the money."

***

The next morning, me, Audrey, Betty Jean, and Mama walked from the house to the highway so Mama and Betty Jean could catch the Greyhound bus that would take her to Milledgeville. Mama was all decked out in the dark blue dress she wore for funerals and her grey pillbox hat with the two red roses on top. Betty Jean was pretty as a picture in her pregnancy. Mama had done up her blonde hair in braids and she was wearing a pair of special light blue pants Mama had made with elastic in the waist. I hugged and kissed both of them as they boarded the bus. Audrey waved good-bye as the bus pulled away. Late that night, Mama arrived back at home. She said Betty Jean had been registered; everybody was nice to her and she was happy that Betty Jean had professional doctors now. She said the director promised that all information about Betty Jean's pregnancy would remain strictly confidential.

***

Over the next few months, we got three letters from Betty Jean. Mama asked her to write because phone calls were so expensive.

July 21, 1954
Dear Family,

I'm so glad Mama made me come early. The doctors did several tests and found that there was blockage in my right breast. They fixed it and said if they hadn't discovered it, the baby would not have gotten any milk from my right breast.

Other than that, they say I'm going to have a healthy pregnancy and should deliver on September 9. That's one day later than Mama said. You got to give Mama credit, she does pretty good without all of the scientific stuff.

They're all very nice here. My room is clean and the food is good. I'm meeting girls who are in the same situation as myself. After talking to them, I don't feel as bad about what happened.

I'll just be glad when it's over.

Betty Jean

***

August 13, 1954

Dear Family,

Oh, Lord, I'll be so glad when this is over. Every move I make, every breath I take has got some connection with this baby. My back and shoulders ache from carrying this baby. My legs go weak for no reason and I spend a lot of time sitting down.

Carrying this baby is like having a little sack of cow feed tied to my middle. Anything I do, I have to consider the sack of cow feed. I have to sleep on my back night every night and it really is tiresome. When I go to sleep, I'm looking at the ceiling, and when I wake up, I'm still looking at the ceiling.

Mama was right when she said a first pregnancy changes everything about a woman. Now I can feel every part of me going through changes. I guess all I can do is let nature take its course.

I'll be so glad when this is over.

Betty Jean

***

September 6, 1954.

Dear Family,

Doctors say I will deliver any day now. All I am now is just a big blob of flesh with a little human growing inside me. I can't stand to look at myself anymore. I asked one of the girls here who just delivered if it hurts to have a baby.

She told me I have never felt the kind of pain that's involved in having a child. She said they can give you shots, but it still hurts. I guess I won't know till it happens.

It just a matter of waiting now. Lord, I'll be so glad when it's over.

Betty Jean

***

On the evening of September 8, 1954, the administrator at the Margaret Baker Home for Unwed Mothers called Mama and announced that Betty Jean had delivered a healthy eight-pound, nine-ounce baby girl and was ready to go home. Mama told the administrator she would be there the afternoon of the following day.

I will always remember the day Mama and Betty Jean came home with the baby. Daddy, Audrey, and I were all waiting at the highway to see them get off the bus. When Mama pulled back the blanket and I saw the baby's face, I was instantly in love. She was a beautiful child with a big patch of blonde hair, blue eyes, and a sort of sly half-smile. The very first time I reached down to touch her hand, she grabbed my finger and held on for dear life. At that very moment, I knew she was a special child. A very special child.

Even Daddy was happy to see the new baby. When Mama pulled back the blanket, he broke into a big smile and said: "Got eyes like her mama." Audrey, when she saw the baby, hardly broke a smile. I knew she didn't approve. She didn't approve of anything. As we walked back to the house, Audrey lagged behind, sulking like an old dog that had just been whipped. I didn't understand why anyone couldn't find joy and love in their heart for a new baby.

Once we got to the house, I knew Mama would be ready for a family meeting, so we all gathered around the table. Once everybody was seated, Mama, holding Betty Jean's baby in her arms, took the floor.

"What I'm holding here is the newest member of the Johnson family. As far as the outside world is concerned, me and your daddy are going to be this child's parents and you girls are going to have another sister."

"What are we going to call her?" I asked.

"Her name will be Shirley Temple Johnson and we're going to call her Shirley."

"Where did that come from?" Daddy asked.

Mama inhaled and looked around the table.

"If anybody wants to know where we got her, we adopted her from a Catholic Mission in California. We're going to tell the world that her natural mother, who put the baby up for adoption, was a first cousin of Shirley Temple. You know, the little girl in the movies."

"We know, Mama," Audrey said impatiently.

"That's why we're going to call her Shirley. I had some papers put together to make it look official."

She produced a newly-printed document and showed it to us.

At the top of the paper was a picture of Jesus in front of a cross lovingly holding out his arms to a small child. The name at the top read:

Sacred Heart of Jesus Catholic Ministry, 1206 Mission Street, Los Angeles, Ca. Underneath, the text read: "On this day, Mr. and Mrs. Horace Johnson are hereby awarded the sole and final parental custody of Shirley Temple Johnson."

Also, there was another paper that read "State of California Certificate of Birth" at the top and listed the mother's name as Charlotte Ann Brown of Culver City, California and the father as "unknown." It contained all of the details of the birth.

Each of us looked at the papers.

"Mama!" Audrey said finally. "Where did you get these?"

"Never mind where they came from," Mama said. "They look official and that's all that matters. If anybody wants to see proof of our story, we have it here."

Daddy took the birth certificate and looked at it.

"Looks real," he said, handing it back to Mama. "Your mother has been talking to her sister over in Valdosta."

"Yeah, but we're not going to talk about that right now," Mama said.

Daddy was referring to Aunt Edna, Mama's sister that ran a printing company in Valdosta.

A long silence.

"Mama," Audrey said finally. "That's the biggest lie I ever heard in my life."

Mama turned to Audrey.

"Maybe it is," Mama said. "But it's what we're going to tell the world about where this baby came from. This family has worked hard to give Betty Jean and this baby a clean start in life and we're going to keep it that way."

"What if I told…" Audrey said.

I knew that would set Mama off. Instantly, she walked around the table and handed off the baby to Betty Jean, then she went back to face Audrey. I could see the fires of hell in her eyes.

First, she got into Audrey's face and glared at her. Then, suddenly, with both hands, she grabbed the front of Audrey's dress.

"Now you hear me and you hear me good," Mama said, pulling Audrey's face to hers. "If you ever tell this, I'll hunt you down and beat the holy stuffing out of you."

Then, still grasping two fists full of Audrey's shirt, Mama waited for a reply. There was none. Audrey's face was white as a sheet. Finally, Mama released her grip. Calmer now, she turned to the other family members.

"Now, this child is going to be loved. There's not going to be any talk about how she came into this world. Nobody can change the way they were born and that's the way it's going to be with Shirley."

A pause. Then she turned back to Audrey.

"And if you don't like it, you can get up and leave this house."

Audrey didn't reply.

"Did you hear me?"

Audrey dropped her head.

"I heard."

***

Now it's safe to say that Audrey was not Mama's favorite child. In fact, it seemed that the two of them were constantly at one another's throats. Ever since I can remember, they had been fighting.

"Audrey takes after your daddy's side of the family," Mama would say when we were alone. "She's a lot like your daddy's mother… a mean, contrary woman who couldn't get along with the devil himself. What's more, having to wear glasses has done something to her head. She's thinks no man will ever love her as long as she wears glasses."

And Mama was right. Audrey would soon be twenty, but she never did anything to primp herself. She never wore lipstick or perfume or makeup and she never dressed up like she was trying to get a man. Sometimes, I would go to the door of her room and watch as she sat at the dresser looking at herself in the mirror, first with her glasses, then without them. Once, as I was watching her, she smiled when she looked at herself without glasses; then, when she returned to her glasses, she peered at herself for a long moment. Then, suddenly, she put her head on the dresser and started sobbing.

***

Over the next few weeks, everything returned to normal. Betty Jean went back to school. We started going back to church again; Betty Jean started helping with chores again and we girls had a new baby sister. It was funny how the different family members took to Shirley over the next few months. Of course, Mama and I were always there to help Betty Jean and the baby any way we could. We loved to change her diapers and powder her bottom and give her a bottle and burp her. I imagined that being a mother had to be the most wonderful experience in all the world. Daddy and Audrey, on the other hand, kept their distance. I'm thinking Audrey was that way because first, she didn't approve of the birth, and second, because she was just plain contrary.

4

My, oh, my, but Shirley was such a special child. Always smiling, good-natured, and as pretty as the day is long, she could charm the horns right off a billy goat. Her smile was pure sunshine and she quickly became the light of our lives. As an infant, she seldom cried and, if she did, you could bet your bottom dollar something was really wrong. Her diaper needed changing, her bottle was empty, or a pin was sticking her. By the time she was walking, she was into anything and everything. She wanted to help Mama cook, she wanted me to draw pictures for her, she wanted Betty Jean to play patty-cake and sing with her; there was no end to her interests. When she was two, Mama bought a coloring book filled with pictures of jungle animals, lions, tigers, giraffes, elephants, and such. The moment she got the coloring book, rather than coloring in the pictures, she started drawing the animals. I was amazed at how good she was. By the time she was three, we could see how smart she was. When she heard a children's song like "Twinkle, Twinkle Little Star" or "Itsy Bitsy Spider," she knew all the words upon hearing the song a single time.

I will always remember the day Mama sat down with Shirley at age four to teach her to read. By then, Shirley could already say her ABCs forwards and backwards. She had been reading and writing simple words and sentences for almost a year and sometimes she would ask me how to spell certain words or explain what that meant. So when Mama sat down with her that Sunday afternoon and opened a book of nursery rhymes, I was not surprised at what happened.

"Now we're going to start reading right here," Mama said, pointing to the opening lines in the book as Shirley sat in her lap.

Mama, trying to prime the pump, started to read.

"Now Old King Cole was a merry old soul…"

Then Shirley started to read.

"Now Old King Cole was a merry old soul and a merry old soul was he, he called for his pipe and he called for his bowl, and he called for his fiddlers three."

Not a single stumble or hesitation.

Then she continued.

"Every fiddler he had a fiddle, and a very fine fiddle had he; Oh there's none so rare, as can compare, with King Cole and his fiddlers three."

She stopped.

"Do you want me to read some more, Mama?" she asked, a look of pure innocence on her face.

Mama turned from the book and looked up at me. First, there was a look of bewilderment, then suddenly, she burst out laughing.

"My! My!" Mama said. "Now aren't you something?"

***

And Mama was right. Shirley knew things that kids her age were not supposed to know. For her fifth Christmas, Mama bought a toy tea set of white plastic cups, saucers, and sugar bowls, and Shirley loved to play hostess for me, Betty Jean, and Mama as guests. One by one, she would go around the table and pour water into our cups as we politely waited. Then she would go around the table asking if we wanted one lump of sugar or two. Once everyone's cup was prepared, she would seat herself.

"Now we will have our tea," she would say.

If anyone failed to bring their cup to their mouth without a "free pinkie," Shirley was quick to correct them. Once, when Mama didn't toe the line, Shirley instructed her: "Mama, please show a free pinkie."

Suddenly, Mama began giggling with delight at the ridiculousness of a five-year-old telling her how to drink tea. Moments later, Mama was quiet again and took another sip of tea, this time with a waving pinkie.

"Much better," Shirley said.

Where this child learned these things, none of us ever knew. We didn't have television and she wasn't old enough to read books about such things. I'll tell you, Shirley was something else.

***

As a small child, one of Shirley's favorite pastimes was playing with Truman. We had a family dog, a beagle with short legs, floppy ears, and sad eyes named Truman. Daddy named the dog Truman because he was born on the same day Truman officially beat Dewey in the 1948 presidential election. On the day of the election, several newspapers incorrectly announced Dewey had won, but, after all of the votes were counted, Truman was named the official winner. It was on that day that an old mongrel dog Mama had been feeding had three little pups in a hayrack at the barn. Once Daddy saw the puppies, he decided to keep the strongest and healthiest for a family dog and gave the others away. The one he kept he named Truman.

For hours on end, Shirley would play fetch in the front yard with Truman. She would laugh out loud as she watched him race across the yard to retrieve the stick she had thrown, then return it to her. In the summertime, when we went swimming in the river, Shirley would throw an old yellow rubber ball into the water, then watch delightedly as Truman swam into the river, took the ball in his mouth, and returned it to her. She loved Truman.

***

Then there was the day Daddy tried to teach Shirley, at age five, to shuck corn. Every night, after Daddy came in from the fields, he would unharness the mules and bring them into the barn. He would put them in their stalls and feed each of them two forkfuls of hay and six ears of corn. On that particular day, Audrey and I were milking the cows in an adjacent stall while Shirley sat on the extra milking stool watching us.

After Daddy put up the mules, he stopped in front of the stall where we were milking.

"Audrey," he said. "Will you shuck the corn and feed the

mules after the milking?"

"Why do I have to do it?" Audrey said. "When is Shirley going to learn to help around here?"

Daddy looked at Shirley.

"That's a good idea."

"Come on!" Daddy said, motioning for Shirley to follow him. "It's time you learned to shuck corn."

Shirley got up from the milking stool and followed Daddy to the corncrib at the end of the barn hallway. At the crib, Daddy opened the door and took out several ears of corn. Meanwhile, Mama was in the backyard hanging out clothes and was within earshot.

"Watch me!" Daddy said.

Shirley watched as Daddy took an ear of corn, expertly pulled back the husk, then broke off the stem and threw it into a waiting bucket.

"Now you do it," he said, handing an ear to Shirley.

Before taking it, she looked at it curiously, then back at Daddy. Finally, she took the ear of corn. Then, as she pulled back the husk, she saw a black wiggle worm and immediately threw the ear of corn on the ground in fright.

"It's a bug!" Shirley said. "I'm afraid of bugs."

Daddy picked up the ear of corn.

"It's just a wiggle worm," Daddy said, picking up the ear of corn. "He's not going to hurt you."

Daddy brushed away the black worm, then finished pulling back the husk.

"Now," he said, handing the ear of corn back to Shirley, "break off the stem!"

"No!" Shirley said. "I don't want to. I'm afraid."

"Now you listen to me, young lady," Daddy said. "It's time you learned to help around here. Finish shucking this!"

"No!" Shirley said, pulling her hands to her chest. "I don't want to! I'm afraid!"

For a moment, Daddy peered angrily at her. Then, suddenly, he grabbed her arm, pulled her to him, and started spanking her. Right away, Shirley started bawling.

That very moment, Mama, who was still hanging out clothes, heard Shirley wailing. She came running.

"Shirley!! Shirley!!" she called as she ran toward the barn.

Once she was in the barn hallway, she saw Daddy in front of the corn crib spanking Shirley.

"Stop!! Stop!!" Mama shouted.

She rushed forward and grabbed Daddy's spanking hand.

Daddy, still holding Shirley's arm, turned to her.

"This child is going to have to learn to work."

"No!" Mama said, still holding Daddy's hand. "Turn her loose."

When Daddy didn't immediately release Shirley's arm, Mama pulled Shirley's arm out of Daddy's grasp. Shirley, still wailing at the top of her lungs, rushed into Mama's arms.

"Baby, are you okay?" Mama said, holding her close and stroking her back. "Hush up now. Mama's here. Everything is going to be okay."

Shirley stopped crying.

Daddy peered helplessly at Mama.

"Look at you! All you're doing is raising a spoiled brat. She can learn to work like the rest of us."

"Not this one. This one is different." Mama glared angrily at him. "Don't you ever touch this baby again!"

"You just going to let her sit on her butt and look pretty all her life?"

"God has sent us a very special child," Mama said. "This child is going to be somebody in this family one of these days. I aim to keep her that way."

Daddy didn't reply. Quiet settled upon the barn again.

"She's the little princess," Audrey said. "She thinks she's better than the rest of us…"

"You hush up too!!" Mama said.

Then, with Shirley clinging to her neck, Mama headed to the house.

***

Betty Jean was the first daughter to leave home. I always knew it was coming; I just didn't know when. In late May of 1959, she graduated Hawkins Valley High and got a job as a clerk at Brannon's Hardware over at the Crossroads. It was there she met Clyde Brannon, the younger brother of the owner, who was a mechanic in Tifton. He owned a motorcycle shop and, from the very first time I saw them together, I knew they were two of a kind.

I was sitting in the front porch swing one Saturday morning when I heard a motorcycle come roaring down the driveway toward our house. As it pulled up in the yard, I could see Clyde behind the handlebars, and Betty Jean, a package in her hand, perched comfortably behind him.

"Hi, Clyde," I said as he shut down the engine.

I knew Clyde. He had been in my history class in high school. He was decked out in black leather and heavy boots with silver buckles.

"Cornelia Johnson!" he said. "How you doing?"

"I'm doing fine, Clyde. How 'bout you?"

"Fine. Just dropping off your sister."

Betty Jean got off the motorcycle and turned to Clyde.

"I'll call you tomorrow."

We watched as Clyde fired up the motorcycle again and roared off down the driveway to the main highway.

"What you got in that package?"

"Come on!" Betty Jean said. "And I'll show you."

Moments later, we were in our room and Betty Jean started opening the package. Once open, she didn't reveal the contents immediately.

"Are you ready for this?"

"I'm ready."

Then she pulled a black leather jacket with an eagle on the back out of the package. She proudly held it up for me to see.

"Someday I'm going to wear this in public," she said. "I'm going to show the world who I am. The time is not right yet, but it will be."

Then she refolded the jacket and replaced it in the box.

"I'm going to hide this at the bottom of the closet. You won't say anything to Mama, will you?"

"No!"

"Thanks, Cornelia!" she said, hugging me. "I can always count on you."

***

I knew Mama and Daddy, once they learned about it, would never approve of the path Betty Jean was on, but I also knew that, for Betty Jean, there was no turning back. Clyde was making a motorcycle girl out of her. One night, a few months later, she came to the family table with a small tattoo of a broken red heart on her arm.

Once everybody was seated and Mama said the blessing, Audrey wasted no time causing trouble.

"Daddy, look at the trash that Betty Jean has got on her arm."

Daddy leaned over and squinted through his glasses to see Betty Jean's arm.

"What you doing putting something like that on your arm? Ain't you got no sense?"

Even Mama took Daddy's side on this one.

"The good Lord gave us skin to cover and nourish our body. Not to be used to draw pictures."

"Oh, Mama!" Betty Jean said. "It's no big deal."

"You get that off your arm," Daddy said.

"I can't get it off," Betty Jean said. "It will be there for the rest of my life."

"You heard what I said," Daddy replied. "Get that trash off your arm or don't come back to this table."

Daddy peered angrily at her.

Instantly, Betty Jean got up from the table.

"Come back here!!" Daddy said.

As if she hadn't heard, Betty Jean left the house, slamming the door behind her. She disappeared for almost a month. Then one Saturday morning, she and Clyde roared into the front yard again. Daddy and Audrey were in town and me and Mama were sitting on the front porch peeling apples. Shirley was inside the house asleep.

"I've come to say good-bye, Mama," Betty Jean said. "Me and Clyde are leaving Hawkins Valley."

"Where you going?"

"Everywhere," she said. "I've come to get my things."

"Well, go on in there and get them. Your daddy's not here,

so you'll be fine."

Moments later, Betty Jean and I were in our room.

"You leaving for good?"

She nodded as she started throwing clothes and personal items into a suitcase. Once the suitcase was filled, she pulled out the black leather jacket she had hidden in the closet two months earlier. Quickly, she put on the jacket then turned to look at herself in the mirror.

"I told you this day would come."

I nodded.

"I guess this is goodbye," she said. "Not sure if I'll ever see you again. Take care!"

"Will you write?"

"Maybe."

Then she hugged me and, suitcase in hand, headed for the door.

"Good luck," I said. "I love you."

"I love you too."

Outside again, Betty Jean went straight to Mama.

"I'm sorry, Mama. I have to do what makes me happy."

"I understand. I hope you know what you're doing. Good luck! I love you!!"

"I love you too, Mama."

Then, decked out in her black jacket and holding the suitcase, she mounted the motorcycle. The engine roared to life and, in a cloud of dust, it sped off down the driveway.

Tears welled in Mama's eyes as she watched the motorcycle disappear into the distance.

"I always knew she was wild as a jack rabbit," Mama said to no one in particular, "but I didn't know what to do about it."

It was the last time we would ever see Betty Jean.

5

In the springtime, Shirley liked to go with me and Mama and Audrey and Truman to the river bottoms to pick blackberries. At the bend in the river, there was a big stand of wild blackberries that stretched for thirty, maybe forty yards along the river's edge and, by late April, the thorny bushes would be sagging with oodles and oodles of ripe, juicy fruit. When we went picking blackberries, we would get up early and trudge the half mile across the pasture to the river bottoms. Then Mama, Audrey, and I would get down on our knees, negotiate the stickers, and easily pick two or three gallons of fresh berries in a couple hours. Shirley complained that the thorns hurt her fingers, so Mama always gave her the easiest task, holding the bucket while we picked.

One day in the spring of 1959, some six months before Shirley started school, we were just finishing up our blackberry picking, when Mama said we had to stop because a big rain was coming. In the east, the sky was dark with heavy thunderclouds.

"Come on!" Mama said. "We better run for the house. If we don't, we're going to get soaking wet."

Mama grabbed one bucketful of blackberries and I grabbed the other and we started running. By the time we reached the house, rain was coming down in buckets. When I mounted the front porch steps, I saw Daddy had already come in and was sitting in the porch swing. Moments later, the entire family was sitting on the front porch, quietly watching the rain come down in buckets. From time to time, bright flashes of lightning streaked across the sky and huge claps of thunder rattled the tin roof above our heads.

"Have you ever noticed that you always hear thunder, then see the lightning," Audrey said. "The thunder causes the lightning."

"No," Shirley said. "It's just the opposite. When lightning

shoots through the air, it warms up the air around it and causes it to explode. Thunder is what you hear as the air around the lightning explodes. Lightning comes first."

Everybody was quiet.

"The electrostatic particles collide together to create the sound of thunder," Shirley continued. "The thunder we hear is the collision of those electrostatic particles."

Everybody in the family looked from one to the other.

"What kind of particles?" Daddy said.

"Electrostatic particles," Shirley said. "Tiny little new particles of energy that have electronic charges."

"Oh Lord, Honey," Mama said. "I don't know what you talking about."

Finally, Daddy looked over at Shirley.

"Where did you learn that?"

"I don't know," Shirley said. "I just know it."

"I been telling y'all this child is special," Mama said.

For a long moment, everyone was quiet again.

"The little princess thinks she knows everything," Audrey said. "If you got any questions, just ask her."

Suddenly, Audrey stood up, glared at Shirley, then went into the house, slamming the screen door behind her.

"Mama," Shirley said. "Can I have some more ice cream and peach cobbler?"

"Yeah, but you need to get those wet clothes off first."

Mama stood up and took the two buckets of blackberries in hand. Then, with her head, she motioned for me to open the screen door.

"You're spoiling that child rotten," Daddy said as I held the door.

Mama peered at him.

"I told you! This is my child and I'm going to raise her the way I want to."

Then she turned to Shirley.

"Come on, baby, let's go inside."

***

As Shirley got older, she wouldn't do farm work, but she

liked to tag along with me and Mama while we were doing ours. Lots of times, she would go with us to the barn to milk the cows. While we were milking, she liked to play on the old tire swing at the end of the "cow lane." Years before, Daddy had built an old tire swing under an oak tree at the end of what we called the cow lane. The cow lane was a fenced stretch of about 50 yards from the barn to the main pasture and the cows had to pass down this narrow passageway to come to the barn.

Late one afternoon, when Shirley was seven, me and Mama were milking the cows and Shirley was swinging when she suddenly started screaming at the top of her lungs.

"Mama! Mama!"

I jumped up from my milking and peered down the cow lane. I could see Shirley, frightened out of her wits, tearing down the lane.

When she saw me, she rushed into my arms.

"Shirley! What's wrong?"

"A ghost jumped out at me!"

"A ghost?" Mama said. "What ghost?"

"Look!" Shirley said, pointing into the darkness. "It's still chasing me!! Look!"

Moments later, I saw a white, human-looking form coming down the lane toward us. Once it drew closer, I could see it was Audrey. She had an old sheet wrapped around her head and body and was laughing her head off.

"What you doing scaring this baby like that?" Mama said.

Audrey threw the sheet over her head and rushed at Shirley again.

"Boo!! I'm a ghost! Boo!! Boo!"

"No! No!" Shirley said, clinging tighter. "Tell her to go away."

I shoved Audrey away.

"Now you leave her alone," Mama said. "And I mean now!!!"

Audrey removed the sheet from her head.

"Oh, Mama, I was just having some fun," Audrey said. "The little princess is scared of her own shadow."

***

In September of 1960, when Mama took Shirley to be registered for school, the health department nurse said she had to see a birth certificate before she could give her the vaccinations. Mama explained that Shirley was adopted and presented the falsified birth certificate she had received with the falsified adoption papers. The nurse took down all of the information, then handed it back to Mama without question.

Once Shirley started the first grade, she was just as special to the teachers as she was to us. In the second grade, she got a "Best Reader" commendation from her teacher and a certificate for having grades of 100 on all of her spelling tests. She was the most popular member of her class, and her fellow students voted her president of the second grade. When the school sponsored a finger-painting contest, Shirley's entry of a setting sun was the winner in the grammar school division. This meant Shirley, as a second grader, had won out over lots of fifth and sixth graders.

***

When Mama took Shirley to school to begin the third grade, the principal called Mama into her office.

"This child's mind is far ahead of the other students in the third grade," she said. "I suggest she begin the fourth grade this year."

"I know how smart she is," Mama said, "but I want her to grow up around children her own age, so let's go ahead and put her in the third grade. It will be better in the long run…"

"As you wish," the principal replied.

***

On Sunday afternoons, Shirley liked to tag along with me when I went down to the catfish pond to paint birds. Most of the time, she seemed like a normal child, but other times, it was like she was from another world. On one particular Sunday in late September of 1962, I was putting the final touches on a blue jay when I saw her coming down the path to the pond. When she arrived, she walked right up to my painting and studied it for a several moments without saying a word.

"There is such a glory and beauty in nature," she said finally. "Everything in the world works so perfectly with everything else. Photosynthesis and plant life. The cycle of rain. The rhythm of the tides. The movement of the planets around the sun. How could anyone say there is no God?"

I stopped painting and peered at her.

"Where did you ever hear a word like that?"

"Like what?"

"Like photosynthesis."

"I just know it…"

I returned to my painting and didn't pursue the subject further.

Shirley took a seat on the quilt at my feet and gazed quietly across the pond for several minutes.

"I can understand why you love painting nature so much," she said finally. "It's a celebration of nature's beauty. Once, when I was nineteen years old, I knew a woman who spent endless hours at the ocean painting shore birds. She could get all of these different shades of blue in her work."

"Shirley, you've never been nineteen years old."

"Yes I have."

"When?"

"Many years ago."

"Honey, you're only eight years old now. How could you ever have been nineteen?"

She smiled.

"Someday I'll tell you."

We were quiet for a moment.

"Someday I'll be famous," she continued. "I'll have lots of money and I'll get awards and they will have parades in my honor."

I couldn't believe what she was saying.

"You seem so sure about it."

"Oh, it will happen."

"How do you know things like that?"

"I just know."

I tried to pursue the subject, but she refused to talk further of it.

***

One night in the fall of 1965, Shirley, at age 11, announced at the dinner table that her teacher told the class there was a woman over in Albany who taught singing and acting classes.

"Her name is Mrs. Benefield and she teaches the lessons every Saturday afternoon for three hours. I want you to start taking me over there for lessons."

"How much are the lessons?" Mama asked.

"Ten dollars."

"Ten dollars?" Daddy said. "We can't afford that."

"Did the teacher say the woman had experience as an actress?" Mama asked.

"The teacher said Mrs. Benefield had been an actress and singer on Broadway for several years."

"We'll go over next Saturday and talk to her."

"Now, Ila, we can't be throwing away our money for acting lessons," Daddy said. "That money could be better put to work for other things."

"Like what?"

"I need barbed wire and fence posts for the lower pasture."

"I'll get the money for the lessons."

"How?"

"I'll figure out something."

Daddy shook his head helplessly.

"This child is going to drive us into the poorhouse."

Mama turned to Shirley.

"Don't worry," she said. "On Saturday, we're going over to Albany and talk to this woman."

***

So Shirley started her acting and singing lessons. Every Saturday afternoon, Mama would take her over to Albany to meet with Mrs. Benefield. Once the lessons started, Shirley had me and Mama acting out scenes from famous plays. In particular, I remember Mama, with a wig on her head, trying to play the role of Wendy in *Peter Pan* while Shirley pranced around as Peter. When Daddy came in and saw us, he burst out laughing.

"Y'all have gone plumb crazy."

Audrey, as usual, not only wanted no part of it, but mocked Shirley every chance she got. When Shirley would show up at the dinner table each night, Audrey would get in her licks.

"Oh, look who's here!" Audrey would say. "The famous movie star has arrived to show us how wonderful she is. Let's all applaud her royal highness!"

"Now you leave Shirley alone," Mama said. "All this has got nothing to do with you."

For two years, Mama took Shirley over to Albany every Saturday morning for her acting and singing lessons with Mrs. Benefield. At night, while Mama and Daddy were in the living room listening to the radio, we would hear Shirley in her room singing "Goodnight Ladies," "Old Black Joe," or "Alexander's Ragtime Band." Night after night, her singing would drone on and on. After a while, the other members of the family knew the words to "Goodnight Ladies" as well as Shirley. I even found myself singing it during idle moments. On Saturday nights, when Daddy tried to listen to the news and the Grand Ole Opry on the radio, he would turn up the volume to drown out Shirley's singing.

***

One afternoon in the late summer of 1966, Shirley said something in idle conversation I would always remember. By late August of that year, the purple hull peas were hanging in thick bunches on the vines and were ripe for picking. During these times, me, Mama, Audrey, and Shirley would get up early in the morning and, together with Truman, go to the fields, and pick peas until about midday. Once we had several bushel baskets filled, we would lug them back home, sit on the back porch, and shell peas for the rest of the day. Me, Mama and Audrey would sit in a circle around the unshelled peas, take handfuls into our laps to shell, then, once they were shelled, throw the husks into a separate empty basket. When you shell purple hull peas, you get a dark purplish stain on the palm of your hand that lasts for several days. After Shirley told Mama that she didn't want to get the purple stain on her hands, Mama gave her the job of emptying the basket of husks once it had been filled. Now, shelling peas is a really boring task and, to pass the time, Mama always like to reminisce about her younger years.

"When I was a young girl growing up in Tifton," Mama said, "I had my dreams. I wanted to be a public speaker and have people come and listen to me talk. I wanted people to know me and know who I was. Not all over the world, but I did want people in Hawkins Valley to know me and to know my name."

She stopped, took another handful of peas into her lap, then began shelling again.

"Then, when I met your daddy," she continued, "everything changed. We got married, set up a home, and then you kids started coming. My dream ended when I married your daddy. Marriage really changes your life."

We were quiet for several minutes.

"Audrey," I said. "Think you'll ever get married?"

She didn't answer at first.

"You know the old saying," she said finally. "Boys don't make passes at girls who wear glasses."

"That's not true," Mama said. "Women that wear glasses get married all the time."

"No," Audrey said. "I won't get married until I have my eye operation and don't have to wear glasses."

"Someday you'll get your eye operation," I said.

"Where is the money going to come from?" Audrey replied.

"I'll get the money," Shirley said. "Someday I'll give you the money to get your operation."

Audrey laughed out loud.

"Ha-ha!" she said. "The little princess is going to give me the money for my eye operation? That'll be the day."

We were quiet again.

Audrey, her lap full of unshelled peas, turned to me.

"What about you? When are you going to get married? You're 27 and still single."

"I don't know. The right man just hasn't come along."

"Why didn't you like Nathan McCartney?" Audrey said. "You went out with him several times."

"Nathan? Oh, I could never marry a mechanic. I want to marry a man with some education. Some refinement."

"Wendell Campbell was sweet on you in high school," Audrey continued. "He's a teacher at the college over in Tifton now. He would have been a good catch."

I didn't answer at first.

"I don't think I would make a good wife," I said finally. "I just don't think I could take a man bossing me around all the time. I don't think there's a man alive I could love more than my paintings."

A long silence as we shelled peas.

"Has it got anything to do with Lawrence Calloway?" Mama asked.

"Who is Lawrence Calloway," Shirley asked.

"Cornelia fell in love with Lawrence Calloway during high school," Mama said. "they dated for almost two years and planned to be married then, when he went off to college…"

"Mama!" I said suddenly. "Do we have to talk about this?"

"Shirley needs to know about Lawrence…." Mama said.

"I don't want to talk about it" I said.

Audrey, of course, had to get in her two cents worth.

"Cornelia and Lawrence fell in love in high school, then when he went up to north Georgia to go to college, he met somebody else and left Cornelia holding the bag."

"You've got a big mouth!" I said.

"Maybe so, but the truth is the truth and it should be told."

We were quiet again.

The bushel basket that held the pea husks was full now and Shirley picked it up, emptied the husks into a nearby trash bin, and replaced it for us to use again.

"You'll be married someday, Cornelia," Shirley said as she replaced the now empty bushel basket in its original position. "And you'll have to learn to cook Italian food. Especially ravioli."

All of us stopped shelling peas, startled at Shirley's comment.

Audrey burst out laughing.

"The little princess has lost her marbles."

She turned to me.

"Hey, Sister Cornelia, didn't you know you got to learn to cook Italian food? Don't you think it's time you learned to cook ravioli?"

Once Audrey's mocking laughter ended, I turned to Shirley.

"Ravioli? You mean those little squares of pasta with meat inside?"

"That's right."

"Now why in the world would I ever want to learn to cook ravioli?"

"It will happen."

I laughed at the thought.

"Shirley, I love you, but sometimes you just don't make any sense," I said.

"You'll see."

***

That night, as I lay awake in bed, my mind wandered back to that conversation. The real reason I wasn't married was because I was afraid of love. My experience with Lawrence had left too many scars on my heart and I wasn't sure if I wanted to ever go through it again. Yes, I wanted to be married and have children someday, but, after what happened between me and Lawrence, my heart always raised warning flags every time the opportunity for love approached. It needed lots of healing after Lawrence. As I drifted off to sleep that night, I laughed out loud at Shirley's comment about me learning to cook ravioli.

***

Somehow, way down deep, I had always suspected that Shirley was sent to us from another world, but my suspicions were not confirmed until the winter of 1966 when Truman, the family dog, took sick. One night, at the dinner table, Daddy announced that he had taken Truman to the veterinarian.

"You paid good money to a veterinarian to look at that old dog?"

"Not exactly," Daddy said. "He did the examination for free. He owed me some money for some field work I did for him last spring."

"What did he say about Truman?" Mama asked.

"He's got a cancer in his stomach and he's not going to live more than a few days."

"Oh, no!" Shirley, who was twelve, replied. "We can't let Truman die."

"There's nothing we can do," Daddy said. "He's eighteen years old. That's a good long life for a dog."

"No!" Shirley said. "I want to see him. I want to make him healthy."

"You can't make him healthy. The vet said he would be dead in three days."

"Where is he?"

"He's in the barn."

Instantly, Shirley pushed her chair back from the table.

"Finish your meal first," Mama said.

"No. I want to see Truman. Now!"

She turned to me.

"Cornelia, will you go to the barn with me?"

"Sure."

So we took a flashlight and started out the back door to the barn.

Truman was lying on an old blanket that had been thrown across a pile of hay. Food was in his bowl, but had not been touched. When he saw us, he was too weak to raise his head, so he just looked up at us with those sad, weary eyes.

"Poor Truman," Shirley said as she bent down to examine him. "He's sick. Very sick, but I'm going to make him well."

"What are you going to do?"

"You must never reveal what I'm about to do. Promise?"

"Promise."

Shirley stood in front of the dog and held both hands over her head with index fingers fully extended. Then she brought her hands down together in a sudden thrusting motion. As her hands swept downward, bolts of fiery light emanated from her fingertips and, instantly, Truman's entire body was enveloped by a luminous white light as if a giant electrical charge was being passed through it. For several seconds, the dog's body trembled in this state of electrified illumination, then Shirley threw her hands up again and the glowing aura disappeared.

For a moment, the dog looked around as if he was confused or in a daze. Then he stood up, went to the bowl, and started eating. We watched as he finished the food in his bowl.

"Come on," Shirley said. "Let's go to the house."

Instantly, the dog, frisky as ever, fell in lockstep behind us and followed us to the house.

"Truman is just fine!" Shirley announced when we walked back inside where the family was still eating.

Daddy gazed at her in disbelief.

"Fine? Where is he now?"

"He's on the back porch."

Daddy's face turned into a scowl, then unable contain himself, he got up from the table and went to the back porch. When he opened the back door, Truman ran to him and began rubbing his body against his leg to be petted.

Daddy shook his head in disbelief.

"What is God's name did you do to that dog? I've never in my life seen anything like that. I thought he was a goner. I guess miracles just happen sometimes."

6

In the fall of 1967, at age 13, Shirley entered the seventh grade at Hawkins Valley High. During the second week, fellow students voted her president of the class. At the dinner table that night, she told Mama she wanted to start wearing store-bought dresses to school.

"Why do you need store-bought dresses?"

"I can't be class president in a flour sack dress, Mama. It just doesn't look right."

"Let me see what I can do," Mama said.

"Ila, we can't afford it."

"I don't care," Mama said. "This child is going to get what she needs to make it in this world."

"Where are you going to get the money?"

"I don't know."

***

Two days later, on a Saturday morning, me and Mama went into Albany to the pawn shop. Mama had a brooch with a red ruby inside that her mother had given her when she died. Mother asked the man to give her one hundred dollars for the brooch, but he wouldn't go higher than seventy-five dollars. Finally, Mama took it. Then we went to Holcomb's Clothing Store and Mama spent forty-eight dollars for five new dresses and two pairs of new shoes for Shirley.

That night, while Shirley was trying on the new dresses in her bedroom, Audrey came in and had a raving fit.

"It's not fair!" she shouted. "Me and Cornelia had to wear flour sack dresses all the way through high school. Now the little princess gets store-bought dresses and shoes in junior high."

Mama didn't say a word. She turned, went to Audrey, put her in a headlock, and started leading her out of the bedroom.

"Mama!" Audrey screamed. "You're hurting my neck."

"I'm going to hurt something else if you don't get out of here."

At the bedroom door, Mama released her, then shoved her through the open doorway. Defiantly, Audrey stood in the doorway, glaring at Mama.

"Now don't you come back until I'm finished."

Then she slammed the door in Audrey's face.

Throughout the rest of her junior and senior high school days at Hawkins Valley High, Shirley wore store-bought dresses.

***

That same year, Shirley wrote a little play titled *The Gallant Knight* about a handsome prince who won the hand of the beautiful princess after slaying the mighty dragon. When she showed it to Miss Elizabeth Poe, her seventh-grade teacher, the teacher was very impressed and decided to have the class perform it. After the class acted out the play, with Shirley in the role of the princess, Miss Poe sent a note home to Mama that read "Shirley is a truly gifted child."

In the fall of 1969, Shirley turned fifteen and started high school. By then, Miss Poe, the seventh-grade teacher who had staged her play two years earlier, was the drama coach at Hawkins Valley High. Every year, the school put on a production and, that year, they were staging *Joan of Arc*, the story of the teenage girl who led French Troops against the English at the Battle of Orleans. Despite numerous try-outs, Miss Poe was unable to find a suitable actress for the lead. Then remembering Shirley's play, she asked her former student to try out. The very instant she saw Shirley outfitted and reciting lines, she was sold, and Shirley was cast in the lead.

***

The dress rehearsal for the Hawkins Valley High production of *Joan of Arc* was held on the night on March 22,

1970 in the high school auditorium. Mama and I accompanied Shirley to the event. After it was finished, me, Mama, and Shirley were leaving, when Miss Poe pulled Shirley aside.

"I wanted to tell you that my brother Thomas, a theatrical producer in Atlanta, will be in the audience tomorrow night to see your performance. I've been telling him about your many talents and I wanted him to see you on stage with his own eyes. He is just one more reason you should give tomorrow night's performance your very best effort."

"Oh, I will," Shirley said. "I'll give it my best."

***

When *Joan of Arc* was staged the following night, it was a big hit. Mother and I attended and, as they say, Shirley "brought down the house." She got three curtain calls and, afterward, a huge mob of students rushed backstage to congratulate her. Finally, once the celebrations were finished, we started to leave. Outside, in front of the school, we saw Miss Poe.

"Was your brother here?" Shirley asked.

"Oh yes. He was here, but I didn't get a chance to talk to him after the performance. I'll talk to him next week."

***

During school the following week, Miss Poe called Shirley out of class to come to her office. She said she had finally had a chance to talk to her brother and he had greatly admired her performance. After explaining that her brother and another producer were planning to bring *Joan of Arc* to the big screen, Miss Poe said he had asked her to have Mama give him a call. He wanted to talk to her about Shirley coming to Atlanta for some screen tests.

The following morning, Mama called Mr. Thomas Poe and they made arrangements for Shirley to go to Atlanta. That night at the dinner table, Mama relayed the details of the call.

"Horace, do you want to go to Atlanta with me and Shirley for her movie tests?"

"Ila, you know I don't know nothing about all that. All this acting and singing business has been you and Shirley's doings from the first."

Mama looked at Audrey.

"I'm not interested," Audrey said. "Why would I want to go watch the little princess preen herself like a peacock?"

Mama turned to me.

"Cornpone?"

"I'd love to go."

***

Me, Mama, and Shirley were in Atlanta for four days. The movie company put us up in a fancy hotel with king-size beds and chandeliers in the lobby. We ate food I'd never heard of. Potatoes au gratin, beef Stroganoff, filet mignon, and some other dishes I couldn't pronounce their names. That night, from the hotel window, I could see all the bright lights and tall buildings in Atlanta.

The next morning, we went to Shamrock Productions, a movie studio in downtown Atlanta where they were going to do the screen tests. During the tests, Shirley would spend hours getting her face and hair done, then they would dress her up in different costumes and she would sit in front of the camera for hours while the director tried this or that shot or some new angle. It was all very interesting. At night, Mama would go through the script with Shirley, practicing and memorizing her lines.

Finally, at the end of the third day, Mr. Poe, a tall, unsmiling man with dark hair, sad eyes, and a mustache, told Mama he wanted to sign Shirley up to play the lead in the movie version of *Joan of Arc*.

"I want to start shooting in Northern California in two weeks," he said. "Who is her agent?"

Mama stopped at the word.

"Agent? She doesn't have an agent."

"She's got to have an agent to draw up and oversee her contract," he said. "And probably a chaperone. You realize that, as a professional actress, she will be constantly traveling and will need personal and professional supervision."

"Supervision?"

"Yes, she's not of age," he said. "She'll need someone to care for her personal needs and schooling while she is travelling."

"Lordy mercy, I don't know nothing about movie contracts. I'll going to call my cousin Troy and get some advice."

Mama had a first cousin named Troy Franklin she had grown up with in Tifton. The oldest son of her sister Marjorie, Troy was in his late fifties, was a graduate of the University of Georgia law school, and had a successful practice in Atlanta. That afternoon, Mama gave him a call.

***

When we went into Troy's office that afternoon, he looked a little pudgier and a little grayer than I remembered him at Grandma's funeral seventeen years earlier. At age 58, he had a round face and a quick smile. Every time I saw him, he reminded me of a used car salesman. He liked to shake hands, had a toothy smile, and loved to slap people on the back.

"My! My! Cornelia!" he said when he saw me. "You're all grown up now. And you're so pretty."

Then Mama introduced Shirley.

"And this is my pride and joy. She's the reason we're here for this meeting."

Over the next few minutes, Mama explained that Shirley had an offer to star in a film production of *Joan of Arc.* She relayed all of the details of what Mr. Poe had said and finished by saying the production was due to start shooting in northern California in two weeks.

"I can be her agent," Troy said, "but we're going to have to work fast. How old is Shirley?"

"She'll be sixteen in September."

"Are you going to travel with her and be a stage mother?"

"Me? Travel with her?"

"She's not of age. She's going to have to have an adult to attend to her personal needs, take care of her appointments, schedule her school sessions, and serve as her publicist. Are you going to do all that?"

"Heavens no! I couldn't leave the farm."

"What about Cornelia?"

"Oh, she couldn't leave the farm either."

"Then you're going to need a child entertainer coordinator."

Mama peered at him for a moment, not knowing what to say next.

"Where could I find someone like that?"

"I think I know just the person," Troy said. "I'm going to give her a call and we'll have dinner with her tonight."

"What's her name?"

"Sophia. Sophia LaFollette. She's French-Canadian."

***

Sophia LaFollette was a small, boyish-looking woman in her early thirties with hay-colored hair and alert blues eyes. She was wearing one of those little round beret hats that you see French painters in magazines wearing when standing in front of an easel. Immediately, I could sense the worldliness, the city manners, and the quiet confidence in her bearing. Even before she started speaking with a slight French accent, I could see she would be perfect for Shirley.

Over dinner, Shirley asked her questions. Sophia said, in her last job, she had been the personal assistant to Clarice Sinclair, the famous Canadian opera singer, for three years. Together, they had travelled across Canada several times with an opera company.

"What did you do before that?" Shirley said.

"I was personal assistant to Baby Jane Campbell, the child actress who starred in *Salad Days* and *One More Take*."

"Oh, yes," Shirley said. "I've heard of her. She's in Europe now on the London stage. How old is she now?"

"She's thirteen now. I was her personal assistant for five years."

"From ages eight to thirteen?"

"That's correct."

From that point on, I could see the deal was done. Over the

next hour, Shirley and Sophia were chatting, laughing, and sharing life experiences as if they had been life-long friends. When we parted that night, each of us hugged Sophia and Troy said he would call her the following morning with Shirley's decision.

"So what do you think?" Troy asked Shirley as we rode in the taxi back to the hotel.

"She will be perfect," Shirley said. "I couldn't be happier."

Mama turned to her.

"Remember, you're going to be with her all the time now. It won't be me and Cornpone with you every day. All you'll have is this little French woman."

"She'll be fine, Mama."

We were quiet for a moment.

"Then I'm going to meet with Shamrock executives tomorrow," Troy said. "I'll draw up the contracts and Shirley and Sophia will leave for California in two weeks."

"Everything sure is moving fast," Mama said.

"That's the way these things are," Troy replied.

The following morning, we checked out of the hotel and said good-bye to Troy. Before we got into a taxi to go to the bus station, Troy had some parting words for Mama.

"Ila, you know this could be big. Really big!"

"I hope so."

7

So Shirley's movie career was on its way. Over the first year, while she was working on the *Joan of Arc* movie, I talked to her four, maybe five times. Mama talked to her every week or two, so, between us, we kept a close watch on Shirley's pursuit of Hollywood stardom. When Shirley called, Mama would hold the receiver between us so we could both listen and talk at the same time. We loved to hear her talk about making movies. It all sounded so glamourous and exciting. Also, early on, we learned to not talk about Shirley's career in front of Daddy or Audrey. Neither had an interest in her success. In fact, Audrey, if Mama and I started to discuss Shirley in her presence, would get up and leave.

In April, the first time I talked to her, she was in northern California shooting village scenes, which focused on Joan of Arc's childhood days in the French countryside.

"Making movies is not everything it appears to the outside world," she said. "Some days I'll be in makeup for two or three hours to shoot a scene, which will only be a couple minutes of film."

"At least you're getting to see the world. Are you happy?"

"Oh yes, very happy. I'm doing what I love."

When the conversation ended, I told Mama we were going to have to start a scrapbook of Shirley's career. She agreed.

When we talked to her again the following September, she was in "the flatlands of Eastern Canada" shooting scenes that recreated the famous battle at Orleans, France, where Joan, at age 14, had led the French Army against the English.

"Three of the last four days I have spent on a horse. I don't like horses. They have an unpleasant smell and I'm afraid of them."

At Thanksgiving, she said they were filming the final scenes of the episode, where Joan is tried, convicted of heresy, and burned at the stake.

"Oh, how terrible," I said.

"It's a very sad ending. The director says we will be finished in the next two weeks and the studio wants to release it on Christmas Day. Once it goes into theaters, we'll see the reviews and box office returns. Then we'll know where my career is going."

"Have you been doing interviews with the Hollywood magazines?" I asked.

"Oh, yes. Loads and loads. Sophia and I did four just last week."

***

In early January of the new year, I couldn't wait to get to Snellgrove's to see what articles the movie magazines had about Shirley. I went through every page of all five magazines and I saw only one little story and a small photo of Shirley buried deep inside. The photo, which was taken from a battle scene in the movie, didn't even look like Shirley. Her hair was cut short like a boy's and, with all of the makeup around her eyes, she looked like everybody but my baby sister. In spite of the poor picture, the article praised her performance. I bought a copy and read it to Mama at the dinner table that night.

"Shirley Temple Johnson is the newest rising star on the Hollywood horizon," the article said. "Her performance as Joan of Arc in the new Christmas release is a jewel of a performance. She brings an energy and a passion to the role, which stands head and shoulders above Joan of Arcs of the past. An Oscar nomination could well be in store for this newcomer."

When I finished reading the article, Mama applauded. Daddy didn't blink an eyelash. He just kept eating his meat loaf and green beans. When I started reading, Audrey had gotten up and left the table without finishing her meal. There was no end to the jealousy in that girl.

In late February, me and Mama went to Valdosta to see the *Joan of Arc* movie. Mama had been saving her butter and egg money for a month so we could go. As I sat there chewing popcorn and watching the movie, I was so happy. I couldn't believe that was my baby sister Shirley up there on the big screen. It was like a dream come true. Mama cried like a little baby during the scene where Joan was burned at the stake.

It would be another two months before we talked to her again. One Sunday afternoon in late April, me and Mama were washing clothes when we heard the phone ring.

"Good news," Shirley began. "After the studio saw the *Joan of Arc* box office receipts for January, February, and March, Mr. Leonard Cohen, the president of Shamrock, called Troy. Tomorrow, we're going to his office to sign a contract for a four-picture deal."

"Four pictures?" I said. "That's great!"

"Looks like I'm on my way."

"I couldn't be happier for you," Mama replied. "Are you coming to visit?"

"No time for that. I'm going to Idaho next week to start filming a western movie."

"What's the title?" I asked

"*The Man from Cheyenne*. It's the story of a sheriff, who, after being accused of murder, goes on the run with a school teacher."

***

In late June of 1971, Shirley was in Montana finishing up *The Man From Cheyenne*.

"I had forgotten how much I hated horses," she began. "During one scene, the horse I was riding threw me and I sprained my ankle. Oh, it was so painful. Over the next two weeks, we had to shoot scenes where I was sitting down while my ankle healed. I'm fine now. I hate horses."

"How do you like making a western?"

"Too many guns and violence. Too much blood. This movie has four gunfight scenes. There's already enough killing and violence in this world. I'll be glad when it's over."

When *The Man From Cheyenne* was released the following November, I went through all of the December issues of the movie magazines at Snellgrove's. Not a single mention of my baby sister. When the movie came to Valdosta, Mama and I didn't go see it. We didn't have the money. What's more, neither one of us liked westerns.

***

In the early spring of 1972, Shirley began work on the third movie. The title was *Executioner's Song*, a courtroom drama about a holdout on a jury that was considering the fate of a man who, from all the evidence, appeared to be guilty.

"I didn't like this film from the start," she said. "I let Troy talk me into it because he said the studio really wanted me in the role of the only female juror. Courtroom stories are so dry and have no heart-felt feelings. I have no interest in trials and lawyers and objections. Such things bore me to death."

She stopped.

"But there is one silver living."

"What's that?"

"I'm working with Rock Hamilton. He is playing one of the jurors."

"Rock Hamilton?" I screamed into the phone. "The most handsome man in all of Hollywood?"

"That's the one."

I could feel myself swoon.

"Oh, Shirley! I would just like to look into his eyes."

"One more thing."

"What's that?"

"We're dating."

That took the cake. My sister Shirley was not only a rising Hollywood star, but she was dating the most handsome actor in Hollywood. Talk about hitting the jackpot!

"Oh, Shirley," I said. "I'm so happy for you."

I was jumping with joy when I hung up the phone. I knew Shirley was having a romance with Rock Hamilton before the

Hollywood magazines.

***

At Christmas of 1973, there was more news of Shirley and Rock.

"Oh, Cornelia," she began. "Now don't faint when I tell you this."

"I won't. What is it?"

"The next movie I'm making is a romantic comedy. I have the female lead and guess who is playing the male lead."

"Rock Hamilton!"

"You got it. We start shooting in two weeks in Los Angeles."

"You mean you'll get to kiss him?"

"I'm already kissing him for real. We're dating. Remember?"

"Oh yeah. I forgot."

"What's the name of the new movie?"

"*A Kiss in the Dark*. It's the story of a secretary in New York who falls in love with her boss, but they can't get married because her ex-husband won't give her a divorce. I read the script. It's going to be lots of fun. No guns. No killing. No horses. Only laughter and good clean fun."

I had stars in my eyes when I hung up the phone. Here I was a grown woman, over thirty-four years old, acting like a teenager as I watched my baby sister's rise to Hollywood stardom.

***

When *Kiss in the Dark* was released in May, 1974, it was a huge hit. With the release, Shamrock announced that not only were the leads two of the brightest stars in Hollywood, but they had fallen in love during production of the movie. When I saw the story announcing the release, I wanted to write the editors and tell them they had it wrong. Shirley and Rock had fallen in love during the making of *Executioner's Song*, not *Kiss in the Dark*, but I didn't.

In October, when the Motion Picture Association announced that year's winners, Shirley won the award for best actress. This meant that the November issues of the movie magazines were going to have lots of stories about her.

***

On November 1, 1974, me and Mama went to Albany and straight to Snellgrove's. At the magazine section, I could see that the new issues were still bundled up and had not been placed on the rack. At the front of the store, I saw Mr. Snellgrove, a thin, middle-aged man with balding hair and glasses, making change at the cash register.

"Mr. Snellgrove," I said, "can you open the new movie magazines so me and Mama can see them?"

"Why are you in such a rush?"

"I want to read all about my baby sister."

"Who is your sister?"

"Shirley Temple Johnson."

He peered at me for a long moment.

"Why, I remember her," he said. "Didn't she used to come in here with you? As I recall, she was a little blonde girl, very pretty, always smiling and happy."

"That's Shirley. She won a big award for best actress."

"I'm going to have to talk to the mayor about this."

Then he returned to the task at hand.

"Come on. I'll open these bundles and put the copies in the rack."

Shirley was on the front cover of all five movie magazines. Mama bought three and I bought two. It was for our scrapbook.

Two months later, when *Kiss in the Dark* came to the theater in Valdosta, me and Mama pooled our money and went to see it. It was a comedy, but me and Mama were so proud to see Shirley on the big screen that we cried all the way through it. We were so happy.

***

By the spring of 1975, Shirley was famous all over the

world. On Saturdays, when me and Mama went to Albany, we couldn't wait to get to Snellgrove's. Some Saturdays, we would see ten to fifteen different photos and stories about her. She would be at a premiere, a charity event, signing autographs, posing for photos, or vacationing with Rock Hamilton in places like Monaco or Bermuda. One Saturday, I almost fell over when I saw a photo of myself in *Movie Day* magazine. It had a story about Shirley's childhood and there was an Easter photo that Mama had made of Shirley and me at church. Shirley, who was seven or eight, was all dressed up in her Easter outfit and sitting in my lap. As I stared at the photo, I was so proud. Now, because of Shirley, I was becoming a celebrity myself. On the street, people I didn't know would come up to me and say: "Aren't you Shirley Temple Johnson's sister?" When I answered, they would reply: "Oh, I just love her movies." Old high school friends would see me and ask, "When was the last time you saw Shirley?" or "I'll bet you're proud of your sister…" Oh yes, I was proud beyond words.

***

In May, there was a front-page picture of Shirley and a story in the *Albany Herald.* The headline read: 'Local girl makes good in Hollywood.' It talked all about Shirley's achievements, her childhood, and her days at Hawkins Valley High. In the article, Miss Elizabeth Poe, who was still the drama teacher, went on and on about how she always knew Shirley was destined for great things. Mama cut the article out of the paper, placed it in a picture frame, and put it on the mantel over the fireplace in the living room.

***

One afternoon in late June, two weeks after the newspaper article appeared, a strange car pulled into our front yard. It was a big black sedan and a smallish man in his early fifties, clean-shaven and well-dressed with a noticeable paunch, got out and strode across the yard. He stopped at the bottom of the porch steps when he saw Mama standing in the doorway.

"Mrs. Horace Johnson?"

"Yes, sir! That's me."

"I'm Thomas Booker, the Mayor of Albany. Can I speak with you?"

"Sure. Come on up and have a seat on the porch. I'll fix you a glass of iced tea."

Once he was comfortably situated on the porch, he and Mama talked. The Mayor of Albany had never been to our house before. I stood at the screen door and listened.

"The county commission and the city council have decided we want to honor your daughter Shirley," he began. "She has bought new recognition to both the town of Albany and Hawkins Valley, and we want to honor her for her contribution to the community."

"How are you going to do that?"

"We want to have a Shirley Temple Johnson Day celebration. We'll have a big parade, a public ceremony in the town square, and a banquet with speeches and flowers and such."

"Has all of this already been set up?"

"No. We didn't want to plan anything until we were sure your daughter could be present for the celebration. If we can get a commitment from your daughter for a given day, then we'll proceed."

"What day did you have in mind?"

"This upcoming August 30. That's five weeks away."

"Shirley is in Montana right now making a movie. I can call her and see if that date fits her schedule."

"That will be fine," he said. "I'll wait to hear from you."

***

On Sunday, Mama called Shirley and explained what the mayor had said.

"The director says this film will be finished sometime in July. After that, I'll have some free time. What day did you say?"

"August 30. It's a Saturday."

"Let me check the calendar."

A pause.

"I can do that. I'll have a month of free time and I can be there for the big celebration. And I'll be able to spend some time with my family."

Mama let out a whoop of joy.

"We can't wait to see you."

"And I can't wait to see my family."

"I love you, baby," Mama said.

"I love you too, Mama."

"Hallelujah!" Mama said as she hung up the phone. "Our baby is coming home!"

8

When Shirley's new sedan rolled into our yard that afternoon on July 28, 1975, it was a day to remember. When she got out, she hugged Mama first, then me, and then Daddy. Audrey didn't hug her; she greeted Shirley with a cold "Hello."

Now, five years later, Shirley looked different. There was more maturity to her face, a little more sadness in her eyes, her hair and dress were more stylish, and she had put on a little weight, but, when she smiled, the sparkle in those deep blue eyes was just as bright as ever. The beautiful flower living inside her had not been touched by age.

"Oh, I'm so glad to be home again," she said. "Mama, can I sleep in Cornelia's room?"

"I knew that's what you would want. I've already made a bed in there for you."

***

For dinner that night, Mama cooked a meal of baked ham, green beans, mashed potatoes, and cornbread with blackberry cobbler. While we were eating, Shirley said she had some announcements to make after dinner. Once we were finished, however, Daddy and Audrey got up from the table and went into the living room. Daddy wanted to read the newspaper and Audrey wanted to listen to the Grand Ole Opry on the radio. After clearing off the table, Mama saw that Daddy and Audrey were absent, so she went into the living room to get them.

"What are y'all doing in here? Y'all come on back to the kitchen table. Shirley has got some things she wants to say."

"What do you want me for?" Daddy said. "I've told you a hundred times I don't know nothing about Hollywood stuff."

"What's the little princess going to do?" Audrey said. "Show us the little gold statue she won in Hollywood?"

"Y'all are part of this family and you need to hear what Shirley has to say."

Daddy looked up from the newspaper.

"Oh, all right," he said finally. "I guess it can't hurt nothing."

Daddy got up and started to the kitchen table.

Audrey had her ear glued to the radio.

"Audrey, come on in here and listen to what Shirley has to say."

"I don't want to miss the Grand Ole Opry."

Anger flashed across Mama's face.

She walked across the room and turned off the radio.

"What did you do that for?"

"Because you're going to go to the kitchen table for this family meeting," she said, grabbing Audrey's arm and pulling her to her feet.

"All right! All right! Let go my arm!"

Once everyone was seated around the table, Shirley took the floor.

"First of all, I wanted to say I've missed y'all. Over the past five years, I've had great success in my career and now I want to do some things for my family."

Daddy's face formed a scowl. He and Audrey looked at one another with suspicion.

"What you going to do?" Daddy said.

"First of all, I'm going to pay off the farm and get you a new pickup."

An expression of pure shock flashed across Daddy's face. He pushed his glasses up on his nose so he could see Shirley better.

"I don't think I heard right. You said you're going to pay off the farm and buy me a new pickup?"

"That's right!"

"Not really?"

"Yes. Really."

Daddy was still in shock.

"You mean, after all these years, I'm going to be free of the mortgage on this farm?"

"That's right. Troy talked to the bank last week about the

pay-off and the check has been sent. Troy said for you to go to the Ford dealership in Valdosta, pick out the truck you want, and call him. He'll send them a check."

"Well, hallelujah. My day has finally come. Thank you, Shirley. You have taken a big load off my mind."

Then he got up, went around the table, and hugged Shirley.

"Thank you!" he said again.

"You're welcome, Daddy."

"The little princess got rich in Hollywood and now she's showing off," Audrey said.

Shirley looked at Audrey but didn't reply

"What else you going to do, baby?" Mama said.

"Next I want to do something for Audrey."

Audrey's face screwed up in a scowl.

"What you going to do?"

"I'm going to pay for your operation. I told you years ago I would do it and now the day has come."

For a moment, Audrey looked at Shirley, then she looked at Daddy.

"You really going to pay for my operation?"

"Yes. I've contacted the hospital in Minnesota. Sophia will call you tomorrow and arrange to buy you a train ticket. You're going to be gone a week. Troy will send a check as soon as you check in to the hospital."

I could see the confusion in Audrey's eyes. Suddenly, she bowed her head on the table and started crying. Then, head down. she quickly got up from the table and rushed out of the room.

"She has made fun of and mocked you for so long," Mama said. "She doesn't know how to accept your kindness."

"That's all right, Mama."

Then Shirley reached down to the purse beside her chair and withdrew an envelope.

"Cornelia told me about the time you pawned your mother's brooch so I could have nice clothes and shoes to wear in junior high. Now I want to pay you back."

Mama's eyes widened with interest as Shirley opened the envelope.

"Here is five hundred dollars cash. I want you to go to

Valdosta and buy ten new dresses for yourself and spend the rest of the money to buy anything you like."

Mama looked at the five hundred-dollar bills.

"Why would I want to buy ten dresses? I don't need ten dresses."

"Then spend the money however you like. I've been making lots of money and I want to spend it on the people I love."

***

On Monday of the following week, Audrey left for Minnesota to get her operation. On Tuesday, Daddy went into Albany and got the pay-off papers from the bank and, the following afternoon, he drove his new Ford pickup into the front yard.

"Ila!" he called when he got out of the truck.

Mama came to the door.

"Come out here and look at my new truck."

"Looks like a nice one."

"It's about time I started enjoying life a little."

Over the next few weeks, I had never seen Daddy so happy. Somehow, Shirley's gifts gave him a whole new outlook on life. Suddenly, he started taking more pride in the farm. He had the barn roof painted. He hauled away two old broken-down pieces of sawmill machinery that had been rusting in the pasture for God knows how many years. He cleaned out the barn like he had been promising for years. He planted five fruit trees, two apple and three peach, along one side of the vegetable garden. He even talked about selling the mules and buying a tractor. I can honestly say that I had never seen my daddy so happy.

***

Audrey was gone eight days and, when she got back, it was really strange to see her without glasses. Now, at age 40 and without glasses, she became a totally new person. Everything about her, I mean absolutely everything, changed once she had the operation. Most of all, she now had confidence in herself; she wanted to be around other people, she laughed a lot more and, most of all, she started wearing lipstick and makeup. Only a week after she had the operation, she met Hollis Abernathy at a church social. Hollis wasn't much to look at, but he was good-natured, hard-working, and owned a trucking company over in Tifton. Anyway, over the next two weeks, Audrey and Hollis started dating. At the end of the second week, she was spending nights with him.

On Monday of the following week, Audrey returned to the family home.

Me, Mama, and Shirley were in the sitting room looking at old family photos. When Audrey came in the door, Mama glared at her.

"Where you been the last three nights?"

"I've been with Hollis."

"If you and him want to spend nights together, why don't y'all get married? It don't look good for you to go spending the night with a man, then coming back home when you get hungry."

Audrey turned angrily to Mama.

"I'm sick and tired of taking orders from you."

"If you come to this house and put your feet under my table, you'll take orders from me. This is my house."

"You go to hell!" Audrey said.

"You don't talk to me like that!"

The mother and daughter squared off as if they were about to fight.

"Wait!" Shirley shouted.

Quickly, she stepped between them.

"Please! Please! Let's have some peace. I've only got another two weeks to spend with y'all and I want to enjoy your company and not listen to arguing and fighting."

Audrey looked at her mother then angrily stormed out of the room.

***

August 30, 1975, the day the Mayor of Albany designated

for Shirley Temple Johnson day, was probably the happiest day of Mama's life. She got up early that morning, cooked breakfast, then took a bath and put on one of her new dresses. She checked herself several times in the mirror before we left. She had prepared a speech for the ceremony in the town square and she had Shirley read it and approve it. When Mama asked Audrey if she wanted to be in the parade, she said no. She and Hollis were going to Valdosta to look at wedding rings. Mama knew better than to ask Daddy to be in the parade. He had no time for social events.

So, on the morning of the big day, Shirley, Mama, and me loaded up in a big, black open-air car and, along with the Albany mayor and the Hawkins Valley county commissioner, we went riding down Main Street waving to the cheering crowds. There were marching bands, the local boy scouts, floats from the PTA, the Kiwanis Club, the National Guard, the Chamber of Commerce, and a whole bunch of other civic organizations I never heard of. At the ceremony, Mama gave her speech about being the mother of a celebrity. She was a little nervous at first, but once she got started, she calmed down and, once finished, received a rousing round of applause from the crowd. Next there were speeches by local politicians, well-wishes from old friends and, at the conclusion, the mayor presented Shirley with a key to the city. After the ceremony, Shirley spent over an hour signing autographs and greeting old friends and classmates. The following night, which was a Sunday, Mama delivered a speech to the Friends of the Hawkins Valley Library. This time, she looked like a professional speaker up there on the podium. A reporter with the *Albany Herald* and a TV crew from Atlanta were also in attendance and interviewed Mama. I took my camera and I snapped lots of pictures.

***

On Monday morning, I went to the Crossroads to get all of the photos I had made on Shirley Temple Johnson day. There were photos of the parade, a group photo of Mama, me, and Shirley, various shots of the Shirley signing autographs, and a picture of Mama speaking at the ceremony.

Shirley and I sat at the kitchen table and watched Mama open the package of photos and thumb through them. When she got to the photo of herself on the podium, all decked out in her new store-bought dress and speaking to the crowd, she lingered for a long moment, beaming from ear to ear with pride. Then she suddenly broke down in heart-rending sobs.

"Mama! Mama!!" I said. "What's wrong? I thought you would be happy to see the pictures."

"Oh, Cornpone," she said, using her apron to wipe away the tears. "I am so very, very happy. When I was a little girl growing up, I wanted to be somebody. I didn't want to be known all over Georgia, but I did want people in Hawkins Valley to know who I was. Now, thanks to Shirley, my dream has come true."

I went to comfort her.

"I guess I'm just getting old," she said as I hugged her. "As you get older, you see the fullness of your life. You know the ending is closer than the beginning."

Mama turned to Shirley and took her in her arms.

"Oh, baby," Mama said. "You've made me so happy. I love you."

"I love you too, Mama."

***

The following afternoon, I was so happy to be back at the pond painting birds and being alone with Shirley. I set up my easel in front of the old log and, while I sketched out and started painting a red cardinal, she lazed quietly on the old quilt reading a book about Alexander the Great. The only sounds were the twittering of the birds and the occasional splash of a catfish. Finally, she looked up from the book. She was in reflective mood.

"You know, in some ways, my life is like Alexander the Great's."

"How do you mean?"

"Like him, I don't have any more worlds to conquer. I am famous around the globe; I am rich and can buy anything I like; I have found the great love of my life in Rock… All of my dreams have come true."

"You sound like you're sad about your accomplishments."

"No. Not sad… just tired with the world."

"You've got to go on living," I said as I painted in the jet-black color in the cardinal's beak.

"Not necessarily. The bird of time has not far to fly. Death can be a beautiful thing."

I turned from my painting to look at her.

"Do you know what you're saying?"

"I know exactly what I'm saying."

"Aren't you afraid to die?"

"Death is a beginning, not an end."

My eyes filled with tears at the thought of losing her.

"Can I tell you a secret?"

"You can tell me anything."

"I've lived many lives. This life here with you and Mama is just one more. Just a different time. A different place. A different world."

"How do you know that?"

"I just know it!!"

"So what are your plans?"

"I'll be back in New York on Monday and meet Rock. We'll spend the night at the Rockefeller Plaza, then me and Troy will meet with the producer and sign the contracts for the war film the studio wants to make in Italy."

"What's the title of the war movie?"

"*Road to Glory*. It's the story of an American bomber pilot who falls in love with a member of the Italian resistance after they join forces to destroy a German ammunition depot near Palermo, Italy."

I looked up from my painting.

"Oh, I envy you so. I would love to see Italy. Florence. Venice. The Sistine chapel."

"I don't get a chance to do much sight-seeing."

"Yes, but just being there must be an incredible experience."

We were quiet for a moment.

"What are your plans after you finish the war movie?"

"Rock and I will go to Greece, probably Santorini, get married, and buy a white house with a blue roof overlooking the Aegean."

"Then what?"

"We'll live happily ever after."

A long silence.

Suddenly, Shirley burst out laughing.

"Why are you laughing?"

"Happily ever after… What a concept!"

We were quiet for several minutes, then Shirley got up from the quilt to examine my painting of the cardinal.

"Oh, Cornelia, it's such a beautiful painting. I just love the scarlet red in the wings and the way the wing feathers graduate down to the lighter colors. You are so talented!"

"Thanks!"

"You know you could make money with your paintings, but you've got to get them into the hands of the right people."

"You mean people would pay me for my paintings?"

"Sure! You're good! Magazine and book publishers are always looking for talented artists."

"I never dreamed I could get paid for my painting. I always did it just for fun."

"When I leave, I want to take some of your work and show it to a friend of Troy's in Atlanta. Can you get me your five best paintings?"

***

An hour later, I had finished my painting. I folded up the easel and Shirley and I started back up the path to the house. When we reached the barn hallway, we could hear the loud voices of Mama and Audrey arguing at the clothesline.

"Don't hand me a clothespin until I'm ready," Mama was saying.

"You have to tell me when you're ready. I'm not a mind reader."

A pause.

"Are you ready now?" Audrey asked.

"No!" Mama shouted. "Can't you see that I'm not ready?

Don't you have eyes in your head?"

We listened for a moment, then Shirley turned to me.

"There's one more thing I need to do before I leave."

"What's that?"

"I'm going to stop this constant bickering between Mama and Audrey."

I peered at her.

"How in the world are you going to do that? That would take a miracle."

"Come on!"

As Shirley and I approached Mama and Shirley, two lines of hanging clothes in front of them shielded us from their view. Neither of them knew we were nearby. Then I watched as Shirley carefully slipped behind the nearest line of clothes. For a moment, she waited, then, just like she did with Truman, she raised her hands over her head with index fingers fully extended. She waited another moment, then suddenly, she stepped from behind the line of clothes and directed her index fingers toward Mama and Audrey. Instantly, lines of bright light emanated from her fingertips and enveloped the bodies of both Mama and Audrey. Instantly, both were frozen in space like statues in a public park. Audrey was posed handing a clothespin to Mama and Mama was reaching out her hand to take it.

I stared at the frozen forms of Mama and Audrey.

"Oh, my God!"

Shirley looked at me with an impish grin.

"Maybe I should leave them like this."

"Oh, you wouldn't do that?"

"No. I wouldn't."

Then, as if she knew exactly what she was doing, she held out her right hand and blew her breath on the palm. Suddenly, a small pile of glowing dust formed in the palm of the right hand. Then, using her left hand, she took a pinch and went to the motionless form of Audrey. Starting at the top of Audrey's head, she began sprinkling the dust in a downward spiral from the top of her head to her feet. Once finished with Audrey, she took another pinch of the dust and performed the same action on Mama. Now their motionless bodies were glowing from top to bottom with an indescribable brightness. I held my hand over my face to shield my eyes from the blinding light.

For a moment, Shirley stood back from her creation. Then, suddenly, she spoke.

"Never ever again will these two have another cross word with one another!"

The bodies of Mama and Audrey, glowing with a blindingly bright light, remained frozen in time and space.

"That should do it."

Then she stepped back and snapped her fingers.

Instantly, the bright illumination around their bodies disappeared and Mama and Audrey were back in motion.

"Mother, dear," Audrey said. "I have a clothespin for you."

Mama took the clothespin.

"Thank you, Audrey. I'll tell you when I'm ready for another."

Shirley and I burst out laughing like a couple of school girls.

Mama looked at us.

"Shirley, why are you and Cornpone laughing?" Mama said as she secured one of Daddy's old work shirts on the clothesline.

"Oh, it's nothing, Mama."

Mama accepted that, then turned back to Audrey.

"Audrey, dear, can you please hand me another clothespin?"

***

That night, Mama prepared a dinner of baked ham, turnip greens, mashed potatoes, and cornbread. Once we were all seated, Mama asked Daddy to bless the food. Once the prayer was said, the family was ready to eat.

"Audrey, dear," Mama said. "Can you please pass me the cornbread?"

"Sure," Audrey replied, reaching for the plate of cornbread.

Mama took the plate.

"Would you also like some butter for your cornbread?"

Audrey asked.

"Yes, please!"

Audrey reached for the butter dish and passed it to Mama.

"Thank you," Mama said.

"You're welcome," Audrey replied.

Daddy stopped serving his plate and peered first at Mama, then at Audrey.

"Why are you two being so all-fired nice to each other all of a sudden?"

"What are you talking about?" Mama said.

"You two are always fussing and jawing. I've never seen y'all be nice to one another. Did something happen?"

"No, nothing at all," Mama said.

"Nothing I know of," Audrey replied.

Shirley, sitting at the end of the table, winked at me.

I winked back.

***

The following afternoon, we all gathered in the front yard of the family home to say good-bye to Shirley. I watched as she placed my paintings, along with her suitcases, in the back seat of the car.

She closed the rear door and turned to me.

"I'll show these to Troy's friend when I get back to Atlanta."

Finally, each of us waited our turn to say goodbye. There was Mama, then Daddy, and finally me. Then Shirley looked to Audrey.

Suddenly, Audrey ran to Shirley and hugged her.

"Bye, Shirley! Thanks again for paying for my operation. Me and Hollis are getting married next month. I owe it all to you."

"You're welcome."

Inside my heart, I smiled. After all those years, my oldest sister had finally found the kindness in her heart.

Shirley started to get into the car.

"One last thing…" Mama said.

"What's that, Mama?"

"You've done something special for everybody in the family except Cornelia. Horace has a new pickup and the farm is paid off. Audrey got her operation and found Hollis, and I got the recognition I always wanted. What you going to do for Cornelia?"

I was embarrassed.

"Mama!" I said. "Shirley doesn't have to do anything for me. I love her whether she does anything for me or not."

Shirley smiled and looked at me.

"Her time will come."

The car engine started and we waved good-bye one last time, then watched as the big black sedan pulled out of the driveway and disappeared down the highway.

9

The early morning of October 5, 1975 is a day I will always remember. I was in bed at the family home sound asleep, when I heard the phone ring. I woke up and looked at the clock. It was 3:30. I wondered who in the world could be calling at this hour. In the living room, I saw a light come on and could hear Mama answering the phone. Moments later, I had my clothes on and was in the living room.

Mama was already crying when I reached her. I knew something was wrong. Bad wrong.

"Mama! Who is it?"

She didn't hear me at first; she was hanging on to every word the caller was saying.

"Mama, who is it?"

Then, seeing my persistence, she wiped tears on the shoulder of her nightgown and removed the receiver.

"It's Troy."

"What is it?"

For a long moment, she looked at me, then burst into sobs.

"Mama! Tell me what's wrong!"

"Cornpone…"

Then she stopped.

"Mama!" I shouted. "Tell me what's wrong!"

Then she blurted out the words.

"Shirley is dead!"

Suddenly, I felt my heart go into my mouth.

"Oh, no!" I said. "Not Shirley! Not our beloved Shirley!"

Then I ran back to my bedroom and collapsed on the bed in tears.

That afternoon, I got the details.

Earlier that night, Troy had received a phone call from the producer of the war film Shirley and Rock were making in Italy. While shooting an action sequence, the helicopter they were riding in crashed into a radio tower and all those aboard, including Shirley and Rock, were killed instantly. She was 21.

***

Four days later, Shirley's body was returned to Hawkins Valley. Our little community had never seen a funeral like that. The church house at Old Harmony wasn't big enough to hold all of the people and, during the services, there must have been two or three thousand people standing around outside. There were political bigwigs and television cameras and newspaper reporters from New York, Los Angeles, and London. It was the biggest funeral ever held in Hawkins Valley. We all just cried and cried.

***

A month after the funeral, Mama was still grieving. She said it was as if the good Lord had sent a miracle to our family to spread happiness and joy among us.

"God just let us borrow her for just a little while. He never meant for us to keep her very long…"

Then she bowed her head and began weeping softly into a handkerchief. Then I remembered what Shirley had said about living other lives. Somehow, in my heart, I knew she had just gone on to the next life. After that, somehow, I didn't feel as bad. During the entire time I had known her, she never once made mention of or asked who her real mother was. As far as she was concerned, Mama was her one and only mother. On the other hand, she had such a deep spiritual connection with the universe that I suspect she may have known, but she never mentioned it. She was too gracious to mention it.

Later that year, Mama and Daddy put up a headstone on her grave down at Old Harmony. It read:

Shirley Temple Johnson

1954 -1975

"Heaven Couldn't Wait!"

***

So, just like that, the innocent little child who had changed all of our lives was gone. As it turned out, I didn't learn what Shirley did for me until the following spring. In March, some six months after the funeral, I got a call from a woman who was an assistant director at the Georgia Department of Wildlife in Atlanta. Her name was Francesca Romano. She said she loved the paintings Shirley had shown her the previous fall and asked if I would be interested in doing a book of illustrations for the department. The books would go into libraries, state museums, and bookstores, and be an official record of the state's birdlife. I told her I would be delighted.

Once the book was published, it was a big hit. It sold oodles and oodles of copies. Thanks to Shirley, the door to success had been opened, and not only was I making money with my paintings, but I was making more money than I could ever have imagined. Shirley had gotten me my big break.

But that's not all.

After the book had been out for about six months, I was having lunch in the cafeteria at the state capital with Francesca when she introduced me to her brother Vincent. He was forty-three, an electrical engineer, and had recently moved from New York to Atlanta to work for Georgia Power Company. He said Francesca had told him about me, he liked my book and, before we parted, he asked for a dinner date. That was the very last thing I had expected, but, when he asked, a little voice inside me told me to accept. And I did. Over the next two months, we dated, became close friends, and eventually were married. I was 37. Once we set up housekeeping in East Atlanta, Vincent said he wanted me to learn to cook Italian like his mother used to make when he was a child growing up in Brooklyn. His favorite dish was ravioli he said, an Italian delicacy made with tiny pieces of fresh meat inside squares of chewy pasta. The first time I set about preparing ravioli for my new husband, I remembered what Shirley had said ten years earlier while we were shelling purple hull peas.

***

So ends the story of this special little person that God or fate or destiny or something sent into our lives. For whatever reason, she appeared out of the blue and, over the span of some twenty years, changed all of our lives for the better. It was something none of us could ever have expected, much less predicted. Now, many years later, when I think back on it, it all seems so far, far away and so incredibly unreal. The whole thing was like an absolute miracle. Finally, for me, the most amazing part of the entire episode was this simple fact: if it hadn't been for Mama's single deciding vote, none of it would ever have happened.

The End

Dear Reader:

Thanks for taking the time to read *Thirteen Stories by John Isaac Jones.*
If you enjoyed it, please consider telling your friends or posting a short review.
Reviews make a difference.
It only takes a few words and it can help enormously.
Without your reviews and favorable mentions, my hard work might go unnoticed.
Thanks a million for your support.

John I. Jones

A * JIJ * Book

Manufactured in the United States of America
First edition/First printing

Formatting by BZHercules.com
Cover design by patricia@betaimages.com.

www.ingramcontent.com/pod-product-compliance
Lightning Source LLC
Chambersburg PA
CBHW050857130726
47900CB00013B/71

* 9 7 8 1 7 3 3 3 5 0 0 3 7 *